Penguin Modern Psychology U PS 12

The Nature of Emotion

Penguin Modern Psychology Readings

General Editor
B. M. Foss

The Nature of Emotion

Selected Readings

Edited by Magda B. Arnold

Penguin Books

Penguin Books Ltd, Harmondsworth,
Middlesex, England
Penguin Books Inc, 7110 Ambassador Road
Baltimore, Md 21207, U.S.A.
Penguin Books Australia Ltd, Ringwood
Victoria, Australia

First published 1968

Printed in the United States of America
Set in Monotype Times

Contents

Contents

Introduction

Emotion is one of the topics that have immediate appeal and human relevance but yield only reluctantly to scientific research and explanation. An emotional experience is a peculiarly private experience. What arouses strong emotion in one person may leave another cold. While a sensory experience can be verified by others, given the same object or situation, an emotional experience is essentially unique even though the emotion can be recognized by others. For this reason, the fortunes of emotion as a scientific category have fluctuated sharply. Whenever subjective experience was frowned upon and repeatable experience or observable behaviour was emphasized, emotion fell into disrepute.

There are a few questions that have always agitated those who have reflected on emotion. First of all, what is emotion? How is it aroused? Is it a purely psychological experience? If it is, what is the connexion with the physiological changes so noticeable in emotion? We have all experienced the blush of embarrassment, the nausea of disgust, the tremor of fear, the excitement of anger. Are these sensations the result of emotions or their cause? Do emotions have a dynamic quality? If not, what accounts for the urge to flee in fear, to fight in anger? How do we recognize emotions? What do we know about brain function in emotion? About the associated physiological changes?

These Readings are intended to show how some of these questions have been answered. Since this is a psychological series, it seemed best to include the most important psychological contributions even though that meant that the writings of philosophers had to be excluded. Also, it seemed preferable to concentrate on articles that offer some original theory or research, or a creative integration of data, rather than a mere review. And finally, the articles selected deal with emotion as such rather than feelings, unless the author discusses the relation of feelings to emotions in a larger framework. These writings emphasize emotion in general rather than particular emotions such as love or anxiety. The literature on anxiety alone is so extensive that the most rigorous selection would fill a book.

Of all the questions that can be asked, the question 'What is emotion?' is central. Parts One to Seven give a selection of some of the answers that have been given by psychologists. I believe they are representative selections, though that, of course, is a matter of personal opinion. In the nature of the case, the emphasis is on emotion as experience rather than on emotional behaviour. Whether we like it or not, emotion is a 'mentalistic' phenomenon. If its experience character is excluded, there is not much that remains to be discussed.[1]

As far as possible, I have tried to include selections from French and German sources, though the bulk of the writings is by English-speaking authors. Some of the differences of opinion and emphasis between writers of these three nationalities can be traced to differences in the meaning carried by the words for emotion. The German word *Gefühl* means both feelings and emotions and has usually a positive significance; for instance, a *Gefühlsmensch* is a man of heart. The word for acute emotional episodes, *Gefühlsaufwallung*, can be either positive or negative. In contrast, the French *émotion* has the force of a rather negative emotional upset, with *passion* as its positive counterpart; and *sentiment* is the term for feelings in the broad sense. In English, emotion is taken by most contemporary psychologists as the basic affective process, while 'feelings' are usually restricted to pleasantness and unpleasantness, at least in professional writings; in some cases, 'affect' is used as a generic term, including both feelings and emotions. Perhaps it will help to remember that the term 'feeling' is used in a much broader sense in literary and colloquial English; the German *Gefühl* and the French *sentiment* are close to this broader usage.

The question as to the nature of emotion has been answered in different ways, depending on the point of view dominant at each period of history. Philosophers from Aristotle to Descartes and Spinoza have discussed the nature of emotions and have classified

1. There are several recent collections that have different principles of selection and should be consulted if a different point of view is preferred. (See Candland, 1962; Knapp, 1963; West and Greenblatt, 1960. Full references are given in the Further Reading list, p. 366.)

them. Biologists have tried to identify their evolutionary roots, and psychologists, their observable expression. Despite this venerable history, scientists have often ignored the centuries of philosophical analysis of emotional experience in favour of its more tangible behavioural and physiological expression. This development was hastened by the attempt of the first experimental psychologists, Wundt (1920) and Titchener (1908), to analyse emotions into their constituent elements, in imitation of the procedure of the physical sciences. For Wundt, feelings were elements into which emotion could be analysed; for Titchener, they were elements from which emotion could be reconstituted.

This preoccupation with elements of experience gradually led to the conviction that all experience can be reduced to sensation. From there it was only a step to the suggestion of James and Lange, that emotion is simply the sensory experience of physiological changes. This reduction of emotion to organic sensation was generally accepted until acute critics, like Lehmann in Germany and Cannon in the U.S. demolished it (Part One).

When emotion is considered the experience of organic sensation, it has no more impulsion than have other sensations. But Darwin (1873) had declared that emotional expression is the remnant of once serviceable habits – which implied a direct evolutionary connexion between instinctive action and emotion, and provided an obvious dynamic aspect. This connexion of emotion and instinct was supported by Shand and McDougall in the first quarter of this century. Plutchik, quite recently, was led to the same conclusion by the consideration that useful behavioural dispositions must be evolutionary constants which can be observed as emotional behaviour in higher mammals and man (Part Two).

Psychoanalysis also links emotion with instinct. For Freud, emotions are the consciously experienced affect charges of the twin instincts of love and aggression. For Jung, emotion is the conscious accompaniment of unconscious archetypal forces. In both cases, the emotion is the representative of unconscious instinct (Part Three).

For psychoanalysis as for Gestalt psychology, emotion remains a significant experience, This is true also for two exponents of the Gestalt point of view included in this selection, Krueger and

Klages. For Krueger, all experience develops out of feeling; and for Klages, feelings provide the connexion between the self and its functions. Dumas also emphasized the experience character of emotion, but at the price of depriving it of any kind of dynamism (Part Four).

All these psychologists, with the exception of Plutchik, think of emotion as an experience of some kind, no matter what the definition they offer. But the behaviouristic trend of the twenties soon led to discussions of emotional behaviour rather than emotional experience, and eventually produced the notion that emotion is either a chapter heading best done away with because it can be better explained as intense activation (Duffy); or a hypothetical construct used to explain emotional behaviour (Hebb). (See Part Five.)

Thus far, the authors of our selections have mainly discussed the nature of emotion, though some attention has usually been paid to the way in which it is aroused. But there was also an attempt to explain emotion on the basis of its arousal. This notion started with the philosopher John Dewey (1894) who accepted Darwin's idea of emotions as 'once serviceable habits' but added that emotions interfere with adaptive behaviour. This suggestion, that emotions are a sign of conflict or aroused by conflict, soon gained acceptance, perhaps because the term 'instinct' began to fall into disrepute and psychologists felt no longer free to use it in explaining the dynamic aspect of emotion. Emotion as the result of disturbance, or the clash of action tendencies, seemed an acceptable substitute. Claparede is one of the more distinguished partisans of this view, held with but minor variations by most academic psychologists in the thirties and forties, until Leeper published his spirited critique. A more sophisticated version of emotion as a disorganized response was published in the fifties by Pradines who makes, however, a careful distinction between regulative feelings and disorganizing emotions (Part Six).

It was not until the late fifties that the view of emotion as organized response came to the fore. Arnold and Gasson defined it as a 'felt tendency' leading to action, while Lazarus saw it as an example of coping behaviour, and Leeper insisted that it is a perceptual–motivational process. In all these theories, emotions not only have experience character but an impulsion of their own instead of borrowing it from instinct or arrested dispositions to action (Part Seven).

Whatever the explanation of emotion, the phenomenon itself has always posed a problem, for both the experimentalist and the clinician. The experimentalist has had difficulty in arousing emotions in the laboratory and has found his subjects' recognition of posed emotions extremely doubtful. However, emotions have sometimes been identified in experiments not intended to investigate emotion, as reported in Michotte's interesting study. Clinical observation has also yielded interesting and often unexpected results, particularly the clinical observation of infants, as reported by Spitz (Part Eight).

The psychology of emotion is difficult enough for the researcher and theorist. But the investigation of the neural mediation of emotion and the physiological changes that go with it has strained the ingenuity of everyone working in this field. Since Cannon's thalamic theory of emotion and Papez' suggestion of an 'emotional circuit' in the brain, an avalanche of research studies has often obscured rather than illuminated the search for valid explanations. As a result, there is a remarkable dearth of theories of brain function in emotion. It is a thankless task to suggest brain structures and circuits that could mediate emotion when research findings may at any moment call such a theory in question. Two alternatives are available for those who want to try regardless: either to speak of cells and cell assemblies in general, as Hebb does, and so to avoid any reference to particular neural structures; or to sketch tentative circuits on the basis of actual research findings published in recent years, as Arnold does, and hope that enough research has been included to make sure that at least the general outline will be correct.

Because research is so prolific and results are so confusing, most psychologists working in this field either content themselves with an uncritical review of findings related to emotions, or restrict themselves to their own work and a short review of the findings of others in a very limited area (e.g. stimulations and lesions of the septal area, the amygdala, the cingulate gyrus, etc.) without any attempt to relate these results to a connected theory of emotion. Arnold's theory based on an interpretation of neurophysiological research findings, is included as one attempt at an integrated theory.

There is highly original work going on that is relevant to emotion even though emotion may never be mentioned. Olds, for instance, has found what he calls a 'reward system' in the brain which, in terms closer to human experience, seems to mediate liking and dislike. Unfortunately, it was not possible to obtain permission to reproduce the article which describes the bulk of these studies. Instead, an article by Delgado is reproduced which gives a good review of the author's own work and describes the effect of brain stimulation and lesions on emotion in monkeys (Part Nine).

The physiological changes in emotion have been discussed by James and by Cannon (Part One). Cannon's 'emergency theory' of emotion, according to which the secretion of adrenaline in emotion facilitates fight and flight, is discussed in depth by Arnold who tries to show the significance of physiological changes in an integrated psychophysical theory of emotion. Readers interested in this area should also consult Gellhorn (1963) and West and Greenblatt (1960) (see Further Reading, page 366).

References
DARWIN, C. (1873), *The Expression of the Emotions in Man and Animals*, Appleton.
DEWEY, J. (1894), 'The theory of emotion. I. Emotional attitudes', *Psych. Rev.*, vol. 1, pp. 553–69.
TITCHENER, E. B. (1908), *Lectures on the Elementary Psychology of Feeling and Attention*, Macmillan.
WUNDT, W. (1920), *Grundriss der Psychologie*, 2nd edn, Stuttgart, W. Engelmann.

Part One Emotion as Organic Sensation

Often, when scientists examine a phenomenon they find it different from what common sense had assumed it to be. Pre-scientific theories had assumed that emotion is a felt experience that produces bodily changes. But in the James–Lange theory, the first contribution of the young science of psychology to emotion, it was affirmed that a stimulus situation produces bodily changes (circulatory, for Lange; visceral, for James) and that these changes are then experienced as emotion.

Lange worked out an excellent description of the various physiological and expressive changes in different emotions but his statement of the theory is laboured and unconvincing, while James's article, included here, is highly readable.

For many years, the James–Lange theory dominated psychological thinking because it could be used by theorists of different persuasions: if emotion is the sensory experience of physiological changes, the sensory psychologist can describe it as organic sensation, while the behaviourist can use it to support his notion that the behavioural changes *are* the emotion. But gradually, more and more voices were raised against it, by psychologists (Lehmann) and physiologists (Cannon) alike. The controversy was carried on for a time (Newman *et al.*, 1930; Cannon, 1931) but it can hardly be doubted that Cannon had the last word.

References

CANNON, W. B. (1931), 'Again the James–Lange and the thalamic theories of emotions', *Psych. Rev.*, vol. 38, pp. 281–95.

NEWMAN, E. B., PERKINS, F. T., and WHEELER, R. H. (1930), 'Cannon's theory of emotion: a critique', *Psych. Rev.*, vol. 37, pp. 305–26.

1 W. James

What is an Emotion?

W. James, 'What is an emotion?', *Mind*, vol. 9 (1884), pp. 188–205.

The physiologists who, during the past few years, have been so industriously exploring the functions of the brain, have limited their attempts at explanation to its cognitive and volitional performances. Dividing the brain into sensorial and motor centers, they have found their division to be exactly paralleled by the analysis made by empirical psychology, of the perceptive and volitional parts of the mind into their simplest elements. But the *aesthetic* sphere of the mind, its longings, its pleasures and pains, and its emotions, have been so ignored in all these researches that one is tempted to suppose that if either Dr Ferrier or Dr Munk were asked for a theory in brain-terms of the latter mental facts they might both reply either that they had as yet bestowed no thought upon the subject, or that they had found it so difficult to make distinct hypotheses that the matter lay for them among the problems of the future, only to be taken up after the simpler ones of the present should have been definitely solved.

And yet it is even now certain that of two things concerning the emotions one must be true. Either separate and special centers affected to them alone are their brain-seat, or else they correspond to processes occurring in the motor and sensory centers, already assigned, or in others like them, not yet mapped out. If the former be the case we must deny the current view, and hold the cortex to be something more than the surface of 'projection' for every sensitive spot and every muscle in the body. If the latter be the case, we must ask whether the emotional 'process' in the sensory or motor center be an altogether peculiar one, or whether it resembles the ordinary perceptive processes of which those centers are already recognized to be the seat. The purpose of the following pages is to show that the last alternative comes nearest to the truth, and that the emotional brain-processes not only resemble the ordinary sensorial brain-processes, but in very truth *are* nothing but such processes variously combined. The main result of this will be to simplify our notions of the possible complications of brain-physiology, and to make us see that we have already a brain-scheme in our hands whose applications are much wider than its authors dreamed. But although this seems to be the chief result of the arguments I am to urge, I should say that they were not originally framed for the sake of any such result. They grew out of fragmentary introspective observations, and it was only when these had already combined into a theory that the thought of the simplification the theory might bring to cerebral physiology occurred to me, and made it seem more important than before.

I should say first of all that the only emotions I propose expressly to consider here are those that have a distinct bodily expression. That there are feelings of pleasure and displeasure, of interest and excitement, bound up with mental operations, but having no obvious bodily expression for their consequence, would, I suppose, be held true by most readers. Certain arrangements of sounds, of lines, of colours, are agreeable, and others the reverse, without the degree of the feeling being sufficient to quicken the pulse or breathing, or to prompt to movements of either the body or the face. Certain sequences of ideas charm us as much as others tire us. It is a real intellectual delight to get a problem solved, and a real intellectual torment to have to leave it unfinished. The first set of examples, the sounds, lines, and colours, are either bodily sensations, or the images of such. The second set seem to depend on processes in the ideational centers exclusively. Taken together, they appear to prove that there are pleasures and pains inherent in certain forms of nerve-action as such, wherever that action occurs. The case of these feelings we will at present leave entirely aside, and confine our attention to the more complicated cases in which a wave of bodily disturbance of some kind accompanies the perception of the interesting sights or sounds, or the passage of the exciting train of ideas. Surprise, curiosity, rapture, fear, anger, lust, greed, and the like become then the names of the mental states with which the person is possessed. The bodily disturbances are said to be the 'manifestation' of these several emotions, their 'expression' or 'natural language'; and these emotions themselves, being so strongly characterized both from within and without, may be called the *standard* emotions.

Our natural way of thinking about these standard emotions is that the mental perception of some fact excites the mental affection called the emotion, and that this latter state of mind gives rise to the bodily expression. My thesis on the contrary is that *the bodily changes follow directly the* PERCEPTION *of the exciting fact, and that our feeling of the same changes as they occur* IS *the emotion.* Common sense says, we lose our fortune, are sorry and weep; we meet a bear, are frightened and run; we are insulted by a rival, are angry and strike. The hypothesis here to be defended says that this order of sequence is incorrect, that the one mental state is not immediately induced by the other, that the bodily manifestations must first be interposed between, and that the more rational statement is that we feel sorry because we cry, angry because we strike, afraid because we tremble, and not that we cry, strike, or tremble, because we are sorry, angry, or fearful as the case may be. Without the bodily states following on the perception, the latter would be purely cognitive in form, pale, colourless, destitute of emotional warmth. We might then see the bear, and judge it best to run, receive the insult and deem it right to strike, but we could not actually *feel* afraid or angry.

Stated in this crude way, the hypothesis is pretty sure to meet with immediate disbelief. And yet neither many nor far-fetched considerations are required to mitigate its paradoxical character, and possibly to produce conviction of its truth.

To begin with, readers of the Journal do not need to be reminded that the nervous system of every living thing is but a bundle of predispositions to react in particular ways upon the contact of particular features of the environment. As surely as the hermit crab's abdomen presupposes the existence of empty whelk-shells somewhere to be found, so surely do the hound's olfactories imply the existence, on the one hand, of deer's or foxes' feet, and on the other, the tendency to follow up their tracks. The neural machinery is but a hyphen between determinate arrangements of matter outside the body and determinate impulses to inhibition or discharge within its organs. When the hen sees a white oval object on the ground she cannot leave it; she must keep upon it and return to it, until at last its transformation into a little mass of moving, chirping down elicits from her machinery an entirely new set of performances. The love of man for woman, or of the human mother for her babe, our wrath at snakes and our fear of precipices, may all be described similarly, as instances of the way in which peculiarly conformed pieces of the world's furniture will fatally call forth most particular mental and bodily reactions, in advance of, and often in direct opposition to, the verdict of our deliberate reason concerning them. The labours of Darwin and his successors are only just beginning to reveal the universal parasitism of each special creature upon other special things, and the way in which each creature brings the signature of its special relations stamped on its nervous system with it upon the scene.

Every living creature is in fact a sort of lock, whose wards and springs presuppose special forms of keys, which keys however are not born attached to the locks, but are sure to be found in the world near by as life goes on. And the locks are indifferent to any but their own keys. The egg fails to fascinate the hound, the bird does not fear the precipice, the snake waxes not wroth at his kind, the deer cares nothing for the woman or the human babe. Those who wish for a full development of this point of view, should read Schneider's *Der thierische Wille* – no other book shows how accurately anticipatory are the actions of animals, of the specific features of the environment in which they are to live.

Now among these nervous anticipations are of course to be reckoned the emotions, so far as these may be called forth directly by the perception of certain facts. In advance of all experience of elephants no child can but be frightened if he suddenly finds one trumpeting and charging upon him. No woman can see a handsome little naked baby without delight, no man in the wilderness see a human form in the distance without excitement and curiosity. I said I should consider these emotions only so far as they have bodily movements of some sort for their accompaniments. But my first point is to show that their bodily accompaniments are much more far-reaching and complicated than we ordinarily suppose.

In the earlier books on expression, written mostly from the artistic point of view, the signs of emotion visible from without were the only ones taken account of. Sir Charles Bell's celebrated *Anatomy of Expression* noticed the respiratory changes; and Bain's and Darwin's treatises went more thoroughly still into the study of the visceral factors involved – changes in the functioning of glands and muscles, and in that of the circulatory apparatus. But not even a Darwin has exhaustively enumerated *all* the bodily affections characteristic of any one of the standard emotions. More and more, as physiology advances, we begin to discern how almost infinitely numerous and subtle they must be. The researches of Mosso with the plethysmograph have shown that not only the heart, but the entire circulatory system, forms a sort of sounding-board, which every change of our consciousness, however slight, may make reverberate. Hardly a sensation comes to us without sending waves of alternate constriction and dilatation down the arteries of our arms. The blood-vessels of the abdomen act reciprocally with those of the more outward parts. The bladder and bowels, the glands of the mouth, throat, and skin, and the liver, are known to be affected gravely in certain severe emotions, and are unquestionably affected transiently when the emotions are of a lighter sort. That the heart-beats and the rhythm of breathing play a leading part in all emotions whatsoever is a matter too notorious for proof. And what is really equally prominent, but less likely to be admitted until special attention is drawn to the fact, is the continuous co-operation of the voluntary muscles in our emotional states. Even when no change of outward attitude is produced, their inward tension alters to suit each varying mood, and is felt as a difference of tone or of strain. In depression the flexors tend to prevail; in elation or belligerent excitement the extensors take the lead. And the various permutations and combinations of which these organic activities are susceptible make it abstractly possible that no shade of emotion, however slight, should be without a bodily reverberation as unique, when taken in its totality, as is the mental mood itself.

The immense number of parts modified in each emotion is what makes it so difficult for us to reproduce in cold blood the total and integral expression of any one of them. We may catch the trick with the voluntary muscles, but fail with the skin, glands, heart, and other viscera. Just as an artificially imitated sneeze lacks something of the reality, so the attempt to imitate an emotion in the absence of its normal instigating cause is apt to be rather 'hollow'.

The next thing to be noticed is this, that every one of the bodily changes, whatsoever it be, is *felt*, acutely or obscurely, the moment it occurs. If the reader has never paid attention to this matter, he will be both interested and astonished to learn how many different local bodily feelings he can detect in himself as characteristic of his various emotional moods. It would be perhaps too much to expect him to arrest the tide of any strong gust of passion for the sake of any such curious analysis as this; but he can observe more tranquil states, and that may be assumed here to be true of the greater which is shown to be true of the less. Our whole cubic capacity is sensibly alive; and each morsel of it contributes its pulsations of feeling, dim or sharp, pleasant, painful, or dubious, to that sense of personality that everyone of us unfailingly carries with him. It is surprising what little items give accent to these complexes of sensibility. When worried by any slight trouble, one may find that the focus of one's bodily consciousness is the contraction, often quite inconsiderable, of the eyes and brows. When momentarily embarrassed, it is something in the pharynx that compels either a swallow, a clearing of the throat, or a slight cough; and so on for as many more instances as might be named. Our concern here being with the general view rather than with the details, I will not linger to discuss these, but, assuming the point admitted that every change that occurs must be felt, I will pass on.[1]

I now proceed to urge the vital point of my whole theory, which is this. If we fancy some strong emotion, and then try to abstract from our consciousness of it all the feelings of its characteristic

1. Of course the physiological question arises, *how* are the changes felt? – *after* they are produced, by the sensory nerves of the organs bringing back to the brain a report of the modifications that have occurred? or *before* they are produced, by our being conscious of the outgoing nerve-currents starting on their way downward towards the parts they are to excite? I believe all the evidence we have to be in favour of the former alternative. The question is too minute for discussion here, but I have said something about it in a paper entitled 'The Feeling of Effort', in the *Anniversary Memoirs of the Boston Natural History Society*, 1880 (translated in *La Critique Philosophique* for that year, and summarized in *Mind*, vol. 20, p. 582). See also G. E. Müller's *Grundlegung der Psychophysik*, para. 110.

bodily symptoms, we find we have nothing left behind, no 'mind-stuff' out of which the emotion can be constituted, and that a cold and neutral state of intellectual perception is all that remains. It is true that although most people, when asked, say that their introspection verifies this statement, some persist in saying theirs does not. Many cannot be made to understand the question. When you beg them to imagine away every feeling of laughter and of tendency to laugh from their consciousness of the ludicrousness of an object, and then to tell you what the feeling of its ludicrousness would be like, whether it be anything more than the perception that the object belongs to the class 'funny', they persist in replying that the thing proposed is a physical impossibility, and that they always *must* laugh, if they see a funny object. Of course the task proposed is not the practical one of seeing a ludicrous object and annihilating one's tendency to laugh. It is the purely speculative one of subtracting certain elements of feeling from an emotional state supposed to exist in its fulness, and saying what the residual elements are. I cannot help thinking that all who rightly apprehend this problem will agree with the proposition above laid down. What kind of an emotion of fear would be left, if the feelings neither of quickened heart-beats nor of shallow breathing, neither of trembling lips nor of weakened limbs, neither of goose-flesh nor of visceral stirrings, were present, it is quite impossible to think. Can one fancy the state of rage and picture no ebullition of it in the chest, no flushing of the face, no dilatation of the nostrils, no clenching of the teeth, no impulse to vigorous action, but in their stead limp muscles, calm breathing, and a placid face? The present writer, for one, certainly cannot. The rage is as completely evaporated as the sensation of its so-called manifestations, and the only thing that can possibly be supposed to take its place is some cold-blooded and dispassionate judicial sentence, confined entirely to the intellectual realm, to the effect that a certain person or persons merit chastisement for their sins. In like manner of grief: what would it be without its tears, its sobs, its suffocation of the heart, its pang in the breast-bone? A feelingless cognition that certain circumstances are deplorable, and nothing more. Every passion in turn tells the same story. A purely disembodied human emotion is a nonentity. I do not say that it is a contradiction in the nature of things, or that pure spirits are necessarily condemned to cold intellectual lives; but I say that for *us*, emotion dissociated from all bodily feeling is inconceivable. The more closely I scrutinize my states, the more persuaded I become that whatever moods, affections, and passions I have are in very truth constituted by, and made up of, those bodily changes we ordinarily call their expression or consequence; and the more it seems to me that if I were to become corporeally anaesthetic, I should be excluded from the life of the affections, harsh and tender alike, and drag out an existence of merely cognitive or intellectual form. Such an existence, although it seems to have been the ideal of ancient sages, is too apathetic to be keenly sought after by those born after the revival of the worship of sensibility, a few generations ago.

But if the emotion is nothing but the feeling of the reflex bodily effects of what we call its 'object', effects due to the connate adaptation of the nervous system to that object, we seem immediately faced by this objection: most of the objects of civilized man's emotions are things to which it would be preposterous to suppose their nervous systems connately adapted. Most occasions of shame and many insults are purely conventional, and vary with the social environment. The same is true of many matters of dread and of desire, and of many occasions of melancholy and regret. In these cases, at least, it would seem that the ideas of shame, desire, regret, etc., must first have been attached by education and association to these conventional objects before the bodily changes follow the ideas, instead of giving rise to them, why not then in all cases?

To discuss thoroughly this objection would carry us deep into the study of purely intellectual aesthetics. A few words must here suffice. We will say nothing of the argument's failure to distinguish between the idea of an emotion and the emotion itself. We will only recall the well-known evolutionary principle that when a certain power has once been fixed in an animal by virtue of its utility in presence of certain features of the environment, it may turn out to be useful in presence of other features of the environment that had originally nothing to do with either producing or preserving it. A nervous tendency to discharge being once there, all sorts of unforeseen things may pull the trigger and let loose the effects. That among these things should be conventionalities of man's contriving is a matter of no psychological consequence whatever. The most important part of my environment is my fellow-man. The consciousness of his attitude towards me is the perception that normally unlocks most of my shames and indignations and fears. The extraordinary sensitiveness of this consciousness is shown by the bodily modifications wrought in us by the awareness that our fellow-man is noticing us *at all*. No one can walk across the platform at a public meeting with just the same muscular innervation he uses to walk across his room at home. No one can give a message to such a meeting without organic excitement. 'Stage-fright' is only the extreme degree of that wholly irrational personal self-consciousness which everyone gets in some measure, as soon as he feels the eyes of a number of strangers fixed upon him, even though he be inwardly convinced that their feeling towards him is of no practical account.[2] This being so, it is not surprising that the additional persuasion that my fellow-man's attitude means either well or ill for me should awaken stronger emotions still. In primitive societies 'well' may mean handing me a piece of beef, and 'ill' may mean aiming a blow at my skull. In our 'cultured age', 'ill' may mean cutting me in the street, and 'well', giving me an honorary degree. What the action itself may be is quite insignificant, so long as I can perceive in it intent or *animus*. *That* is the emotion-arousing perception; and may give rise to as strong bodily convulsions in me, a civilized man experiencing the treatment of an artificial society, as in any savage prisoner of war, learning whether his captors are about to eat him or to make him a member of their tribe.

But now, this objection disposed of, there arises a more general doubt. Is there any evidence, it may be asked, for the assumption that particular perceptions *do* produce widespread bodily effects by a sort of immediate physical influence, antecedent to the arousal of an emotion or emotional idea?

The only possible reply is, that there is most assuredly such evidence. In listening to poetry, drama, or heroic narrative, we are often surprised at the cutaneous shiver which like a sudden

2. Let it be noted in passing that this personal self-consciousness seems an altogether bodily affair, largely a consciousness of our attitude, and that, like other emotions, it reacts on its physical condition, and leads to modifications of the attitude – to a certain rigidity in most men, but in children to a regular twisting and squirming fit, and in women to various gracefully shy poses.

wave flows over us, and at the heart-swelling and the lachrymal effusion that unexpectedly catch us at intervals. In listening to music, the same is even more strikingly true. If we abruptly see a dark moving form in the woods, our heart stops beating, and we catch our breath instantly and before any articulate idea of danger can arise. If our friend goes near to the edge of a precipice, we get the well-known feeling of 'all-overishness', and we shrink back, although we positively *know* him to be safe, and have no distinct imagination of his fall. The writer well remembers his astonishment, when a boy of seven or eight, at fainting when he saw a horse bled. The blood was in a bucket, with a stick in it, and, if memory does not deceive him, he stirred it round and saw it drip from the stick with no feeling save that of childish curiosity. Suddenly the world grew black before his eyes, his ears began to buzz, and he knew no more. He had never heard of the sight of blood producing faintness or sickness, and he had so little repugnance to it, and so little apprehension of any other sort of danger from it, that even at that tender age, as he well remembers, he could not help wondering how the mere physical presence of a pailful of crimson fluid could occasion in him such formidable bodily effects.

Imagine two steel knife-blades with their keen edges crossing each other at right angles, and moving to and fro. Our whole nervous organization is 'on edge' at the thought; and yet what emotion can be there except the unpleasant nervous feeling itself, or the dread that more of it may come? The entire fund and capital of the emotion here is the senseless bodily effect the blades immediately arouse. This case is typical of a class: where an ideal emotion seems to precede the bodily symptoms, it is often nothing but a representation of the symptoms themselves. One who has already fainted at the sight of blood may witness the preparations for a surgical operation with uncontrollable heart-sinking and anxiety. He anticipates certain feelings, and the anticipation precipitates their arrival. I am told of a case of morbid terror, of which the subject confessed that what possessed her seemed, more than anything, to be the fear of fear itself. In the various forms, of what Professor Bain calls 'tender emotion', although the appropriate object must usually be directly contemplated before the emotion can be aroused, yet sometimes thinking of the symptoms of the emotion itself may have the same effect. In sentimental natures, the thought of 'yearning' will produce real 'yearning'. And, not to speak of coarser examples, a mother's imagination of the caresses she bestows on her child may arouse a spasm of parental longing.

In such cases as these, we see plainly how the emotion both begins and ends with what we call its effects or manifestations. It has no mental *status* except as either the presented feeling, or the idea, of the manifestations; which latter thus constitute its entire material, its sum and substance, and its stock-in-trade. And these cases ought to make us see how in all cases the feeling of the manifestations may play a much deeper part in the constitution of the emotion than we are wont to suppose.

If our theory be true, a necessary corollary of it ought to be that any voluntary arousal of the so-called manifestations of a special emotion ought to give us the emotion itself. Of course in the majority of emotions, this test is inapplicable; for many of the manifestations are in organs over which we have no volitional control. Still, within the limits in which it can be verified, experience fully corroborates this test. Everyone knows how panic is increased by flight, and how the giving way to the symptoms of grief or anger increases those passions themselves. Each fit of sobbing makes the sorrow more acute, and calls forth another fit stronger still, until at last repose only ensues with lassitude and with the apparent exhaustion of the machinery. In rage, it is notorious how we 'work ourselves up' to a climax by repeated outbreaks of expression. Refuse to express a passion, and it dies. Count ten before venting your anger, and its occasion seems ridiculous. Whistling to keep up courage is no mere figure of speech. On the other hand, sit all day in a moping posture, sigh, and reply to everything with a dismal voice, and your melancholy lingers. There is no more valuable precept in moral education than this, as all who have experience know: if we wish to conquer undesirable emotional tendencies in ourselves, we must assiduously, and in the first instance cold-bloodedly, go through the *outward motions* of those contrary dispositions we prefer to cultivate. The reward of persistency will infallibly come, in the fading out of the sullenness or depression, and the advent of real cheerfulness and kindliness in their stead. Smooth the brow, brighten the eye, contract the dorsal rather than the ventral aspect of the frame, and speak in a major key, pass the genial compliment, and your heart must be frigid indeed if it does not gradually thaw!

The only exceptions to this are apparent, not real. The great emotional expressiveness and mobility of certain persons often lead us to say, 'They would feel more if they talked less.' And in another class of persons, the explosive energy with which passion manifests itself on critical occasions seems correlated with the way in which they bottle it up during the intervals. But these are only eccentric types of character, and within each type the law of the last paragraph prevails. The sentimentalist is so constructed that 'gushing' is his or her normal mode of expression. Putting a stopper on the 'gush' will only to a limited extent cause more 'real' activities to take its place; in the main it will simply produce listlessness. On the other hand the ponderous and bilious 'slumbering volcano', let him repress the expression of his passions as he will, will find them expire if they get no vent at all; whilst if the rare occasions multiply which he deems worthy of their outbreak, he will find them grow in intensity as life proceeds.

I feel persuaded there is no real exception to the law. The formidable effects of suppressed tears might be mentioned, and the calming results of speaking out your mind when angry and having done with it. But these are also but specious wanderings from the rule. Every perception must lead to *some* nervous result. If this be the normal emotional expression, it soon expends itself, and in the natural course of things a calm succeeds. But if the normal issue be blocked from any cause, the currents may under certain circumstances invade other tracts, and there work different and worse effects. Thus vengeful brooding may replace a burst of indignation; a dry heat may consume the frame of one who fain would weep, or he may, as Dante says, turn to stone within; and then tears or a storming-fit may bring a grateful relief. When we teach children to repress their emotions, it is not that they may *feel* more; quite the reverse. It is that they may *think* more; for to a certain extent whatever nerve-currents are diverted from the regions below must swell the activity of the thought-tracts of the brain.[3]

3. This is the opposite of what happens in injuries to the brain, whether from outward violence, inward rupture or tumor, or mere starvation from

The last great argument in favour of the priority of the bodily symptoms to the felt emotion is the ease with which we formulate by its means pathological cases and normal cases under a common scheme. In every asylum we find examples of absolutely un-motived fear, anger, melancholy, or conceit; and others of an equally unmotived apathy which persists in spite of the best of outward reasons why it should give way. In the former cases we must suppose the nervous machinery to be so 'labile' in some one emotional direction that almost every stimulus, however inap-propriate, will cause it to be upset in that way, and as a consequence to engender the particular complex of feelings of which the psychic body of the emotion consists. Thus, to take one special instance, if inability to draw deep breath, fluttering of the heart, and that peculiar epigastric change felt as 'precordial anxiety', with an irresistible tendency to take a somewhat crouching attitude and to sit still, and with perhaps other visceral processes not now known, all spontaneously occur together in a certain person; his feeling of their combination *is* the emotion of dread, and he is the victim of what is known as morbid fear. A friend who has had occasional attacks of this most distressing of all maladies tells me that in his case the whole drama seems to centre about the region of the heart and respiratory apparatus, that his main effort during the attacks is to get control of his inspirations and to slow his heart, and that the moment he attains to breathing deeply and to holding himself erect, the dread, *ipso facto*, seems to depart.[4]

---

disease. The cortical permeability seems reduced, so that excitement, instead of propagating itself laterally through the ideational channels as before, tends to take the downward track into the organs of the body. The consequence is that we have tears, laughter, and temper-fits, on the most insignificant provocation, accompanying a proportional feebleness in logical thought and the power of volitional attention and decision.

4. It must be confessed that there are cases of morbid fear in which ob-jectively the heart is not much perturbed. These however fail to prove any-thing against our theory, for it is of course possible that the cortical centres normally percipient of dread as a complex of cardiac and other organic sensations due to real bodily change, should become *primarily* excited in brain-disease, and give rise to an hallucination of the changes being there – an hallucination of dread, consequently, coexistent with a comparatively calm pulse, etc. I say it is possible, for I am ignorant of observations which

The account given to Brachet by one of his own patients of her opposite condition, that of emotional insensibility, has been often quoted, and deserves to be quoted again:

I still continue [she says] to suffer constantly; I have not a moment of comfort, and no human sensations. Surrounded by all that can render life happy and agreeable, still to me the faculty of enjoyment and of feeling is wanting – both have become physical impossibilities. In everything, even in the most tender caresses of my children, I find only bitterness. I cover them with kisses, but there is something between their lips and mine; and this horrid something is between me and all the enjoyments of life. My existence is incomplete. The functions and acts of ordinary life, it is true, still remain to me; but in every one of them there is something wanting – to wit, the feeling which is proper to them, and the pleasure which follows them. . . . *Each of my senses, each part of my proper self, is as if it were separated from me and can no longer afford me any feeling; this impossibility seems to depend upon a void which I feel in the front of my head, and to be due to the diminution of the sensibility over the whole surface of my body, for it seems to me that I never actually reach the objects which I touch.* . . . *I feel well enough the changes of temperature on my skin* but *I no longer experience the internal feeling of the air when I breathe*. . . . All this would be a small matter enough, but for its frightful result, which is that of the impossibility of any other kind of feeling and of any sort of enjoyment, although I experience a need and desire of them that render my life an incomprehensible torture. Every function, every action of my life remains, but deprived of the feeling that belongs to it, of the enjoyment that should follow it. My feet are cold; I warm them, but gain no pleasure from the warmth. I recognize the taste of all I eat, without getting any pleasure from it. . . . My children are growing handsome and healthy, everyone tells me so, I see it myself, but the delight, the inward comfort I ought to feel, I fail to get. Music has lost all charm for me, I used to love it dearly. My daughter plays very well, but for me it is mere noise. That lively interest which a year ago made me hear a

---

might test the fact. Trance, ecstasy, etc. offer analogous examples – not to speak of ordinary dreaming. Under all these conditions one may have the liveliest subjective feelings, either of eye or ear, or of the more visceral and emotional sort, as a result of pure nerve-central activity, with complete peripheral repose. Whether the subjective strength of the feeling be due in these cases to the actual energy of the central disturbance, or merely to the narrowing of the field of consciousness, need not concern us. In the asylum cases of melancholy, there is usually a narrowing of the field.

delicious concert in the smallest air their fingers played – that thrill, that general vibration which made me shed such tender tears – all that exists no more.[5]

Other victims describe themselves as closed in walls of ice or covered with an india-rubber integument, through which no impression penetrates to the sealed-up sensibility.

If our hypothesis be true, it makes us realize more deeply than ever how much our mental life is knit up with our corporeal frame, in the strictest sense of the term. Rapture, love, ambition, indignation, and pride, considered as feelings, are fruits of the same soil with the grossest bodily sensations of pleasure and of pain. But it was said at the outset that this would be affirmed only of what we then agreed to call the 'standard' emotions; and that those inward sensibilities that appeared devoid at first sight of bodily results should be left out of our account. We had better, before closing, say a word or two about these latter feelings.

They are, the reader will remember, the moral, intellectual, and aesthetic feelings. Concords of sounds, of colours, of lines, logical consistencies, teleological fitnesses, affect us with a pleasure that seems ingrained in the very form of the representation itself, and to borrow nothing from any reverberation surging up from the parts below the brain. The Herbartian psychologists have tried to distinguish feelings due to the *form* in which ideas may be arranged. A geometrical demonstration may be as 'pretty' and an act of justice as 'neat' as a drawing or a tune, although the prettiness and neatness seem here to be a pure matter of sensation, and there to have nothing to do with sensation. We have, then, or some of us seem to have, genuinely *cerebral* forms of pleasure and displeasure, apparently not agreeing in their mode of production with the so-called 'standard' emotions we have been analysing. And it is certain that readers whom our reasons have hitherto failed to convince will now start up at this admission, and consider that by it we give up our whole case. Since musical perceptions, since logical ideas, can immediately arouse a form of emotional feeling, they will say: Is it not more natural to suppose that in the case of the so-called 'standard' emotions, prompted by the presence of objects or the experience of events, the

5. Quoted by Semal, *De la Sensibilité générale dans les Affections mélancoliques*, Paris, 1876, pp. 130–5.

emotional feeling is equally immediate, and the bodily expression something that comes later and is added on?

But a sober scrutiny of the cases of pure cerebral emotion gives little force to this assimilation. Unless in them there actually be coupled with the intellectual feeling a bodily reverberation of some kind, unless we actually laugh at the neatness of the mechanical device, thrill at the justice of the act, or tingle at the perfection of the musical form, our mental condition is more allied to a judgement of *right* than to anything else. And such a judgement is rather to be classed among awarenesses of truth: it is a *cognitive* act. But as a matter of fact the intellectual feeling hardly ever does exist thus unaccompanied. The bodily sounding-board is at work, as careful introspection will show, far more than we usually suppose. Still, where long familiarity with a certain class of effects has blunted emotional sensibility thereto as much as it has sharpened the taste and judgement, we do get the intellectual emotion, if such it can be called, pure and undefiled. And the dryness of it, the paleness, the absence of all glow, as it may exist in a thoroughly expert critic's mind, not only shows us what an altogether different thing it is from the 'standard' emotions we considered first, but makes us suspect that almost the entire difference lies in the fact that the bodily sounding-board, vibrating in the one case, is in the other mute. 'Not so very bad' is, in a person of consummate taste, apt to be the highest limit of approving expression. '*Rien ne me choque*' is said to have been Chopin's superlative of praise of new music. A sentimental layman would feel, and ought to feel, horrified, on being admitted into such a critic's mind, to see how cold, how thin, how void of human significance, are the motives for favour or disfavour that there prevail. The capacity to make a nice spot on the wall will outweigh a picture's whole content; a foolish trick of words will preserve a poem; an utterly meaningless fitness of sequence in one musical composition set at naught any amount of 'expressiveness' in another.

I remember seeing an English couple sit for more than an hour on a piercing February day in the Academy at Venice before the celebrated *Assumption* by Titian; and when I, after being chased from room to room by the cold, concluded to get into the sunshine as fast as possible and let the pictures go, but before leaving drew reverently near to them to learn with what superior forms of susceptibility they might be endowed, all I overheard was the woman's voice murmuring: 'What a *deprecatory* expression her face wears! What self-abne*gation*! How *unworthy* she feels of the honour she is receiving!' Their honest hearts had been kept warm all the time by a glow of spurious sentiment that would have fairly made old Titian sick. Mr Ruskin somewhere makes the (for him) terrible admission that religious people as a rule care little for pictures, and that when they do care for them they generally prefer the worst ones to the best. Yes! in every art, in every science, there is the keen perception of certain relations being *right* or not, and there is the emotional flush and thrill consequent thereupon. And these are two things, not one. In the former of them it is that experts and masters are at home. The latter accompaniments are bodily commotions that they may hardly feel, but that may be experienced in their fulness by *crétins* and Philistines in whom the critical judgement is at its lowest ebb. The 'marvels' of science, about which so much edifying popular literature is written, are apt to be 'caviare' to the men in the laboratories. Cognition and emotion are parted even in this last retreat – who shall say that their antagonism may not just be one phase of the world-old struggle known as that between the spirit and the flesh? – a struggle in which it seems pretty certain that neither party will definitively drive the other off the field.

To return now to our starting-point, the physiology of the brain. If we suppose its cortex to contain centres for the perception of changes in each special sense-organ, in each portion of the skin, in each muscle, each joint, and each viscus, and to contain absolutely nothing else, we still have a scheme perfectly capable of representing the process of the emotions. An object falls on a sense-organ and is apperceived by the appropriate cortical centre; or else the latter, excited in some other way, gives rise to an idea of the same object. Quick as a flash, the reflex currents pass down through their preordained channels, alter the condition of muscle, skin and viscus; and these alterations, apperceived like the original object, in as many specific portions of the cortex, combine with it in consciousness and transform it from an object-simply-apprehended into an object-emotionally-felt. No new principles have to be invoked, nothing is postulated beyond the ordinary reflex circuit, and the topical centres admitted in one shape or another by all to exist.

It must be confessed that a crucial test of the truth of the hypothesis is quite as hard to obtain as its decisive refutation. A case of complete internal and external corporeal anaesthesia, without motor alteration or alteration of intelligence except emotional apathy, would afford, if not a crucial test, at least a strong presumption, in favour of the truth of the view we have set forth; whilst the persistence of strong emotional feeling in such a case would completely overthrow our case. Hysterical anaesthesias seem never to be complete enough to cover the ground. Complete anaesthesias from organic disease, on the other hand, are excessively rare. In the famous case of Remigius Leims, no mention is made by the reporters of his emotional condition, a circumstance which by itself affords no presumption that it was normal, since as a rule nothing ever *is* noticed without a pre-existing question in the mind. Dr Georg Winter has recently described a case somewhat similar,[6] and in reply to a question, kindly writes to me as follows:

The case has been for a year and a half entirely removed from my observation. But so far as I am able to state, the man was characterized by a certain mental inertia and indolence. He was tranquil, and had on the whole the temperament of a phlegmatic. He was not irritable, not quarrelsome, went quietly about his farm-work, and left the care of his business and house-keeping to other people. In short, he gave one the impression of a placid countryman, who has no interests beyond his work.

Dr Winter adds that in studying the case he paid no particular attention to the man's psychic condition, as this seemed *nebensächlich* to his main purpose. I should add that the form of my question to Dr Winter could give him no clue as to the kind of answer I expected.

Of course, this case proves nothing, but it is to be hoped that asylum physicians and nervous specialists may begin methodically to study the relation between anaesthesia and emotional apathy. If the hypothesis here suggested is ever to be definitively confirmed

6. 'Ein Fall von allgemeiner Anaesthesie', *Inaugural-Dissertation*, Heidelberg, winter, 1882.

or disproved it seems as if it must be by them, for they alone have the data in their hands.

P.S. By an unpardonable forgetfulness at the time of despatching my MS. to the Editor, I ignored the existence of the extraordinary case of total anaesthesia published by Professor Strümpell in *Ziemssen's Deutsches Archiv für klinische Medicin*, vol. 22, p. 321, of which I had nevertheless read reports at the time of its publication. (See the first report of the case in *Mind*, vol. 10, p. 263, translated from *Pflüger's Archiv*. – Ed.) I believe that it constitutes the only remaining case of the sort in medical literature, so that with it our survey is complete. On referring to the original, which is important in many connexions, I found that the patient, a shoemaker's apprentice of fifteen, entirely anaesthetic, inside and out, with the exception of one eye and one ear, had shown *shame* on the occasion of soiling his bed, and *grief*, when a formerly favourite dish was set before him, at the thought that he could no longer taste its flavour. As Dr Strümpell seemed however to have paid no special attention to his psychic states, so far as these are matter for our theory, I wrote to him in a few words what the essence of the theory was, and asked him to say whether he felt sure the grief and shame mentioned were real feelings in the boy's mind, or only the reflex manifestations provoked by certain perceptions, manifestations that an outside observer might note, but to which the boy himself might be insensible.

Dr Strümpell has sent me a very obliging reply, of which I translate the most important passage.

'I must indeed confess that I naturally failed to institute with my *Anaesthetiker* observations as special as the sense of your theory would require. Nevertheless I think I can decidedly make the statement, that he was by no means completely lacking in emotional affections. In addition to the feelings of *grief* and *shame* mentioned in my paper, I recall distinctly that he showed, e.g., *anger*, and frequently quarrelled with the hospital attendants. He also manifested *fear* lest I should punish him. In short, I do not think that my case speaks exactly in favour of your theory. On the other hand, I will not affirm that it positively refutes your theory. For my case was certainly one of a very centrally conditioned anaesthesia (perception-anaesthesia, like that of hysterics) and therefore the conduction of outward impressions may in him have been undisturbed.'

I confess that I do not see the relevancy of the last consideration, and this makes me suspect that my own letter was too briefly or obscurely expressed to put my correspondent fully in possession of my own thought. For his reply still makes no explicit reference to anything but the outward manifestations of emotion in the boy. Is it not at least conceivable that, just as a stranger, brought into the boy's presence for the first time, and seeing him eat and drink and satisfy other natural necessities, would suppose him to have the feelings of hunger, thirst, etc., until informed by the boy himself that he did all these things with no feeling at all but that of sight and sound – is it not, I say, at least possible, that Dr Strümpell, addressing no direct introspective questions to his patient, and the patient not being of a class from which one could expect voluntary revelations of that sort, should have similarly omitted to discriminate between a feeling and its habitual motor accompaniment, and erroneously taken the latter as proof that the former was there? Such a mistake is of course possible, and I must therefore repeat Dr Strümpell's own words, that his case does not yet refute my theory. Should a similar case recur, it ought to be interrogated as to the inward emotional state that co-existed with the outward expressions of shame, anger, etc. And if it then turned out that the patient recognized explicitly the same mood of feeling known under those names in his former normal state, my theory would of course fall. It is, however, to me incredible that the patient should have an *identical* feeling, for the dropping out of the organic sounding-board would necessarily diminish its volume in some way. The teacher of Dr Strümpell's patient found a mental deficiency in him during his anaesthesia, that may possibly have been due to the consequences resulting to his general intellectual vivacity from the subtraction of so important a mass of feelings, even though they were not the whole of his emotional life. Whoever wishes to extract from the next case of total anaesthesia the maximum of knowledge about the emotions, will have to interrogate the patient with some such notion as that of my article in his mind. We can define the pure psychic emotions far better by starting from such an hypothesis and modifying it in the way of restriction and subtraction, than by having no definite hypothesis at all. Thus will the publication of my article have been justified, even though the theory it advocates, rigorously taken, be erroneous. The best thing I can say for it is, that in writing it, I have almost persuaded *myself* it may be true.

2 A. Lehmann

Theory of Affectivity

Excerpt from A. Lehmann, *Die Hauptgesetze des menschlichen Gefühlslebens*, 2nd edn, Reisland, Leipzig, 1914, pp. 414–21. Newly translated by M. B. Arnold.

Until about thirty years ago, both common sense and scientific psychology considered it as proved that emotional expression really is expression, i.e. the consequence of emotion. Then James and Lange insisted that the situation is reversed. However, there is no doubt that the intense work that has since then been devoted to discover, first, the physiological accompaniment of various psychological states and, secondly, the causal relations between peripheral and central occurrences, has proved the lack of validity of the James–Lange theory in its usual formulation. First of all, the theory is inapplicable, and Lange himself has implicitly admitted as much; secondly, it does not agree with the facts; and thirdly, the phenomena which apparently support the theory can be explained much better according to the traditional view.

If an external stimulus has reflexly produced vegetative changes, it is easy to understand that the changed organic sensations should initiate a completely different state of mind. Consequently, there is no difficulty in explaining the origin of emotion from physiological changes. But if organic changes are produced reflexly, i.e. apart from the momentary state of mind, one wonders why a given stimulus does not always result in the same consequences in different individuals, and also, why one stimulus triggers the organic reflex while another similar one leaves us indifferent. A newspaper notice of the death of Mr N will arouse emotion only in his friends. This fact admits of no doubt, yet is completely inexplicable if the organic changes really occur reflexly and are independent of the content of consciousness produced by the stimulus. For instance, if a young man is told, 'Your fiancée has just died', he will certainly suffer an intense emotion. But the sentence: 'Two by two is four', which also consists of five words, will hardly have a similar effect. Why not? Can the subcortical centres really decide in every case whether there is a suitable occasion for a vasomotor reflex? If they make a mistake, bad news might leave us cold and a routine communication arouse the most profound affect. Lange countered this objection by a lengthy explanation which amounts to the assumption that a sensation or perception arouses an affect only when it produces unpleasant images which excite the vasomotor centres (1). This really means that the theory is abandoned and that the emotion as a central state must already exist, at least in part, before the physical changes can occur. The death of a loved bride would trigger the physical reaction only when the meaning, the implications of this loss have been grasped; and the multiplication table does not arouse emotion because it does not arouse such images. However, when very unpleasant memories are connected with it, even the seemingly most indifferent sentence can produce an emotion.

If the theory were valid, this affect, the psychological state, would have to occur as soon as the stimulus had tripped the organic changes. But in most cases we find that the emotion keeps on developing even though the external stimulus has disappeared, as can be shown by continuing changes in the circulation. These reactions occur even during completely indifferent psychological activity and are simply designed to maintain the efficiency of the brain – and nothing would indicate that the situation is different in emotion. If the affect were present as soon as the stimulus had produced organic changes, there would be no reason for these continuing vasomotor changes. But they become understandable if the bodily reactions depend on the state of the central organ.

In support of his theory, Lange mentions the fact that various drugs (alcohol, hashish, muscarin, ipecac) produce affect. Such drugs do not arouse images but profoundly affect the vasomotor system. If it could be proved that these drugs influence only vasomotor nerves, we could be sure that a particular bodily state is sufficient to arouse an emotion. But these drugs probably influence higher brain centres as well. Since this brings about a perceptible alteration of the self, the affect occurs as a result of the central disturbances. Drug effects prove nothing unless this direct central effect can be excluded.

The experiments with hysterical patients must be judged in a similar way. During hypnosis, it is possible to suggest insensitivity of skin and abdominal organs. If the experimenter now tries to arouse an emotion in the subject, the attempt remains unsuccessful; since the subject has no organic sensations, this apparently proves the peripheral origin of affect. Sollier, who conducted these experiments, emphasized, however, that hypnosis itself brings about profound changes of the central state which abolish the empirical self so that the subject hardly notices his own existence. The normal cause of emotions does not produce them now because the empirical self (which does not exist at this point) also cannot become aware of changes produced through the stimulus so that the organic reactions do not even occur. They are nothing but the consequences of central changes (2, p. 187).

Central theories. The peripheral and the central theories differ in the interpretation of central events. For the peripheral theory, central events occurring before the physiological changes are merely a condition of affect; for the central theory, however, they are essential constituents determining the character of the emotion. According to Lange, the chief factor in the arousal of emotion is always the excitation of the vasomotor centre. Essentially, Sergi and d'Alonnes agree with this view, except that Sergi suggests that all sensations produced by vegetative functions constitute the emotion, while d'Alonnes emphasizes visceral sensations (3, p. 17). D'Alonnes draws support for his view from the fact that his patient Alexandrine knew on numerous occasions that she should have felt fear, anger, shame, anxiety and that she would have done so in her normal state [i.e. before her skin and internal organs became anaesthetic – *Translator's note*], but now nothing could move her. Even though she showed facial reflex movements corresponding to the various emotions, she felt like a puppet. However, this view is refuted by Sherrington's physiological experiments with animals (4, p. 260). He transected the spinal cord of a dog, as well as the vagal and sympathetic strands, so that only lungs and diaphragm were still connected with the brain via centripetal nerves; the vasomotor apparatus was completely disconnected and so were all skeletal muscles from the shoulders down. Nevertheless, such a dog expressed joy, anger, disgust and fear just like a normal animal.

Particularly convincing seems the following experiment. Almost all normal dogs intensely dislike meat originating from dogs, and do not eat it, even when they are very hungry. The lesioned dog had intentionally never been tested as to his feelings towards such dogmeat, while he was still intact. He was fed daily with beef or horsemeat which had been cut into small pieces and given in a bowl of milk. After the operation, dogmeat was substituted for his usual meat, given as usual in a bowl of milk. The hungry dog immediately approached it, but had hardly dipped into the milk when he stopped and turned away. Despite the experimenter's encouragement, the dog could not be induced to eat. But after the bowl was cleaned and filled with milk and horsemeat, the animal ate voraciously. Sherrington added that it might well be possible that emotional expression could occur reflexly in animals even though the corresponding psychological state was not present. However, since the animal acted in a way that had meaning only on the assumption that it felt an emotion, it is not open to doubt that this psychological state was actually present. There could be no question of habit in this particular case because the animal was only nine weeks old at the time of the operation and never had tasted dogmeat. Moreover, since the operation had excluded any influx of visceral sensations, such organic sensations seem to be irrelevant for the arousal of an emotion.

The results of animal experiments and pathological observations seem to be directly opposed, if Sherrington's dog had felt real emotions. However, this seems to me exceedingly doubtful. Just as we see instinctive movements in infants which look like emotions but do not correspond to the essential meaning of affect, just so are the affects of animals instincts rather than emotions because of the relatively meagre conscious content. What Sherrington saw in his dog and interpreted as anger, fear and disgust are merely the expressions of the fight, flight and repulsion instincts. There is no need for real emotions. Most animals have, no doubt, an inherited 'disgust' of things that are not beneficial to them, and express it by instinctive avoidance; and this is what happened in the above example.

Piéron, however, draws different conclusions from Sherrington's experiments. According to his view, the animal must feel disgust when it does not want to eat the meat. Since the visceral sensations are excluded in the lesioned dog, the organic changes cannot be relevant for the emotion. However, Pagano reported that fear can be produced by injecting a solution of curare into the posterior part of the caudate nucleus of dogs; and anger occurs when the anterior part of this nucleus is injected. According to Piéron, this means that the caudate nucleus is the real centre of emotion; these psychological states are independent of the excitation of the cortex but gain their essential character from their extracortical origin (5, p. 441). Two objections can be raised against this interpretation. In the first place, ... certain images are decisive for the arousal and the particular character of the different emotions, at least in man. Since images, as far as we know, originate solely in the cortex, the caudate nucleus alone can hardly be the centre of emotions. Secondly, Pagano's experiments do not at all prove that the caudate is the real centre. They merely show that the circuits from the cortex to the periphery transverse the basal nuclei. Finally, it is unnecessary to insist on a special affect centre if the 'actions' of the lesioned animals are simply considered as instinctual movements which presuppose only an unpleasant olfactory sensation.[1]

Consequently, we cannot see the significance of animal experiments for this question. In contrast, pathological observations (the case of Alexandrine and others) show that emotions can occur without organic changes – Alexandrine undoubtedly shows symptoms of sadness as well as of joy – but do not 'grip' or move the subject. Such a state we have called an 'imaginal' affect; only through *l'émotion-choc*, as d'Alonnes calls the visceral changes, does it become a moving presence, an emotion. Thus our conclusion: The emotion is a complex phenomenon which starts with a central state aroused by an outer or inner cause; it is present to awareness as a change of the self, and under normal conditions trips facial reflex movements and organic changes of various kinds. In general, as the bodily symptoms increase in intensity, the affect becomes more moving, more gripping; if they are missing, the emotion remains an 'imagined' affect.

Many research workers who ordinarily oppose the peripheral theory consider it relatively valid for an explanation of moods. At

1. But the 'unpleasantness' of the sensation is affective in nature. Without this affect, the meat would not be refused. – *Editor's note*

first glance, this notion seems correct because experiments show that the bodily accompaniments of emotion continue beyond the emotional episode proper. The abnormal physiological state can be observed as long as the subject is aware of his mood (6). Since no definite images can be found in awareness which are causally related to such moods, it is possible to consider the changed organic sensations as the content of mood. This view, however, does not seem altogether satisfying. The results of my experiments show that any indifferent or deliberate activity, whether carried on for a long or short time, can cancel out the expression of mood; as soon as this activity is finished, the original mood appears again with all its physiological symptoms. It is not easy to see how heart, blood vessels and respiration can bring about this reversal. Only a central cause which has not been abolished by the intervening activity can reproduce the earlier bodily state. Consequently, we are forced to assume that *mood, like emotion, depends on a central process, a change of the self, which reflexly arouses an adequate reaction, the physiological accompaniment*. The organic sensations thus changed do represent an essential factor of mood. But other changes of the self usually contribute, for the self is not exclusively a bodily self. Accordingly, *affect and mood are distinguished only by the fact that the cause of the emotional state, i.e. the feeling from which the phenomenon develops, remains during affect, but has disappeared from awareness in mood. Hence, the participation of the empirical self is the necessary presupposition for all complicated affective states.*

References
1. LANGE, C. G., *Über Gemütsbewegungen*, Leipzig, 1887.
2. SOLLIER, P. *Le mécanisme des Émotions*, Alcan, Paris, 1905.
3. D'ALLONNES, G. R. 'L'éxplication physiologique de l'émotion', *Journal de Psychologie*, vol. 3 (1906), pp. 14–25.
4. SHERRINGTON, C. S., *The Integrative Action of the Nervous System*, London, 1910.
5. PIÉRON, 'La théorie de l'émotion et les données actuelles de la physiologie', *Journal de Psychologie*, vol. 4 (1907), pp. 438–51.
6. LEHMANN, A., *Die körperlichen Äusserungen psychischer Zustände*, O. R. Reisland, Leipzig, 1899.

3 W. B. Cannon

The James–Lange Theory of Emotion: A Critical Examination and an Alternative Theory

Excerpt from W. B. Cannon, 'The James–Lange theory of emotion: a critical examination and an alternative theory', *Am. J. Psychol.*, vol. 39 (1927), pp. 106–24.

In his introduction to the reprinting of the classic papers by James and Lange, Dunlap (1) declares that their theory of emotions as organic processes 'has not only become so strongly entrenched in scientific thought that it is practically assumed today as the basis for the study of the emotional life, but has also led to the development of the hypothesis of reaction or response as the basis of all mental life'. And Perry (2, p. 295) has written, 'This famous doctrine is so strongly fortified by proof and so repeatedly confirmed by experience that it cannot be denied substantial truth. In spite of elaborate refutation it shows no signs of obsolescence.' With some trepidation, therefore, one ventures to criticize a view of the nature of emotions which has proved so satisfactory as a means of interpreting affective experience and which has commended itself so generally to psychologists. There are now at hand, however, pertinent physiological facts which were not available when James and Lange developed their ideas and which should be brought to bear on those ideas, and there are alternative explanations of affective experience which should be considered, before the James–Lange theory is granted basal claims in this realm of psychology.

James first presented his view in 1884; Lange's monograph appeared in Danish in 1885. The cardinal points in their respective ideas of the nature of emotions are so well known that for purposes of comment only brief references need be made to them. James's theory may be summarized, in nearly his own terms, as follows. An object stimulates one or more sense organs; afferent impulses pass to the cortex and the object is perceived; thereupon currents run down to muscles and viscera and alter them in complex ways; afferent impulses from these disturbed organs course back to the cortex and when there perceived transform the 'object-simply-apprehended' to the 'object-emotionally-felt'. In other words, 'the feeling of the bodily changes as they occur is the emotion – the common sensational, associational and motor elements explain all' (1, p. 123). The main evidence cited for the theory is that we are aware of the tensions, throbs, flushes, pangs, suffocations – we feel them, indeed, the moment they occur – and that if we should take away from the picture of a fancied emotion these bodily symptoms, nothing would be left.

According to Lange (1, p. 73) stimulation of the vasomotor center is 'the root of the causes of the affections, however else they may be constituted'. 'We owe all the emotional side of our mental life,' he wrote, 'our joys and sorrows, our happy and unhappy hours, to our vasomotor system. If the impressions which fall upon our senses did not possess the power of stimulating it, we would wander through life unsympathetic and passionless, all impressions of the outer world would only enrich our experience, increase our knowledge, but would arouse neither joy nor anger, would give us neither care nor fear.' Since we are unable to differentiate subjectively between feelings of a central and peripheral origin, subjective evidence is unreliable. But because wine, certain mushrooms, hashish, opium, a cold shower, and other agencies cause physiological effects which are accompanied by altered states of feeling, and because abstraction of the bodily manifestations from a frightened individual leaves nothing of his fear, the emotion is only a perception of changes in the body. It is clear that Lange had the same conception as James, but elaborated it on a much narrower basis – on changes in the circulatory system alone.

A consideration of the visceral factors

The backflow of impulses from the periphery, on which James relied to account for the richness and variety of emotional feeling, was assumed to arise from all parts of the organism, from the muscles and skin as well as the viscera. To the latter, however, he inclined to attribute the major role – on 'the visceral and organic part of the expression,' he wrote, 'it is probable that the chief part of the felt emotion depends' (1, p. 116). We may distinguish, therefore, his two sources of the afferent stream. We shall first consider critically the visceral source. In connexion therewith we shall comment on

44

Lange's idea that the vasomotor center holds the explanation of emotional experience.

1. *Total separation of the viscera from the central nervous system does not alter emotional behavior.* Sherrington (3) transected the spinal cord and the vagus nerves of dogs so as to destroy any connexion of the brain with the heart, the lungs, the stomach and the bowels, the spleen, the liver and other abdominal organs – indeed, to isolate all the structures in which formerly feelings were supposed to reside. Recently Cannon, Lewis and Britton (4) have succeeded in keeping cats in a healthy state for many months after removal of the entire sympathetic division of the autonomic system, the division which operates in great excitement. Thus all vascular reactions controlled by the vasomotor center were abolished; secretion from the adrenal medulla could no longer be evoked; the action of the stomach and intestines could not be inhibited, the hairs could not be erected, and the liver could not be called upon to liberate sugar into the blood stream. These extensively disturbing operations had little if any effect on the emotional responses of the animals. In one of Sherrington's dogs, having a 'markedly emotional temperament', the surgical reduction of the sensory field caused no obvious change in her emotional behavior; 'her anger, her joy, her disgust, and when provocation arose, her fear, remained as evident as ever.' And in the sympathectomized cats all superficial signs of rage were manifested in the presence of a barking dog – hissing, growling, retraction of the ears, showing of the teeth, lifting of the paw to strike – *except* erection of the hairs. Both sets of animals behaved with full emotional expression in all the organs still connected with the brain; the only failure was in organs disconnected. The absence of reverberation from the viscera did not alter in any respect the appropriate emotional display; its only abbreviation was surgical.

As Sherrington has remarked, with reference to his head-and-shoulder dogs, it is difficult to think that the perception initiating the wrathful expression should bring in sequel angry conduct and yet have been impotent to produce 'angry feeling'.

At this point interpretations differ. Angell (5, p. 259) has argued that Sherrington's experiments afford no evidence that visceral sensation plays no part in the emotional psychosis, and further that they do not prove that the psychic state, 'emotion', precedes its 'expression'. And Perry (2, p. 298) has declared that whether in the absence of sensations from the organs surgically isolated the emotion is *felt* remains quite undecided.

It must be admitted, of course, that we have no real basis for either affirming or denying the presence of 'felt emotion' in these reduced animals. We have a basis, however, for judging their relation to the James–Lange theory. James attributed the chief part of the felt emotion to sensations from the viscera, Lange attributed it wholly to sensations from the circulatory system. Both affirmed that if these organic sensations are removed *imaginatively* from an emotional experience nothing is left. Sherrington and Cannon and collaborators varied this procedure by removing the sensations *surgically*. In their animals all visceral disturbances through sympathetic channels – the channels for nervous discharge in great excitement – were abolished. The possibility of return impulses by these channels, and in Sherrington's animals by vagus channels as well, were likewise abolished. According to James's statement of the theory the felt emotion should have very largely disappeared, and according to Lange's statement it should have wholly disappeared (without stimulation of our vasomotor system, it will be recalled, impressions of the outer world 'would arouse neither joy nor anger, would give us neither care nor fear'). The animals *acted*, however, in so far as nervous connexions permitted, with no lessening of the intensity of emotional display. In other words, operations which, in terms of the theory, largely or completely destroy emotional feeling, nevertheless leave the animals behaving as angrily, as joyfully, as fearfully as ever.

2. *The same visceral changes occur in very different emotional states and in non-emotional states*. – The preganglionic fibres of the sympathetic division of the autonomic system are so related to the outlying neurones that the resulting innervation of smooth muscles and glands throughout the body is not particular but diffuse (6, p. 26). At the same time with the diffuse emission of sympathetic impulses adrenin is poured into the blood. Since it is thereby generally distributed to all parts and has the same effects as the sympathetic impulses wherever it acts, the humoral and the neural agents cooperate in producing diffuse effects. In consequence of these arrangements the sympathetic system goes into action as a unit – there may be minor variations as, for example, the presence

or absence of sweating, but in the main features integration is characteristic.

The visceral changes wrought by sympathetic stimulation may be listed as follows: acceleration of the heart, contraction of arterioles, dilatation of bronchioles, increase of blood sugar, inhibition of activity of the digestive glands, inhibition of gastro-intestinal peristalsis, sweating, discharge of adrenin, widening of the pupils and erection of hairs. These changes are seen in great excitement under any circumstances. They occur in such readily distinguishable emotional states as fear and rage (6, p. 277). Fever (7) and also exposure to cold (8) are known to induce most of the changes – certainly a faster heart rate, vasoconstriction, increased blood sugar, discharge of adrenin and erection of the hairs. Asphyxia at the stimulating stage evokes all the changes enumerated above, with the possible exception of sweating. A too great reduction of blood sugar by insulin provokes the 'hypoglycemic reaction' – characterized by pallor, rapid heart, dilated pupils, discharge of adrenin, increase of blood sugar and profuse sweating (9).

In this group of conditions which bring about in the viscera changes which are typical of sympathetic discharge are such intense and distinct emotions as fear and rage, such relatively mild affective states as those attending chilliness, hypoglycemia and difficult respiration, and such a markedly different experience as that attending the onset of fever. As pointed out earlier by Cannon (6, p. 280) the responses in the viscera seem too uniform to offer a satisfactory means of distinguishing emotions which are very different in subjective quality. Furthermore, if the emotions were due to afferent impulses from the viscera, we should expect not only that fear and rage would feel alike but that chilliness, hypoglycemia, asphyxia, and fever should feel like them. Such is not the case.

In commenting on this criticism of the James–Lange theory Angell (5, p. 260) admits that there may be a considerable matrix of substantially identical visceral excitement for some emotions, but urges that the differential features may be found in the extra-visceral disturbances, particularly in the differences of tone in skeletal muscles. Perry (2, p. 300) likewise falls back on the conformation of the proprioceptive patterns, on the 'motor set' of the expression, to provide the distinctive elements of the various affective states. The possible contribution of skeletal muscles to the genesis of the felt emotion will be considered later. At present the fact may be emphasized that Lange derived no part of the emotional psychosis from that source; and James attributed to it a minor role – the chief part of the felt emotion depended on the visceral and organic part of the expression.

3. *The viscera are relatively insensitive structures.* – There is a common belief that the more deeply the body is penetrated the more sensitive does it become. Such is not the fact. Whereas in a spinal nerve trunk the sensory nerve fibers are probably always more numerous than the motor, in the nerves distributed to the viscera the afferent (sensory) fibers may be only one-tenth as numerous as the efferent (10). We are unaware of the contractions and relaxations of the stomach and intestines during digestion, of the rubbing of the stomach against the diaphragm, of the squeezing motions of the spleen, of the processes in the liver – only after long search have we learned what is occurring in these organs. Surgeons have found that the alimentary tract can be cut, torn, crushed or burned in operations on the unanesthetized human subject without evoking any feeling of discomfort. We can feel the thumping of the heart because it presses against the chest wall, we can also feel the throbbing of blood vessels because they pass through tissues well supplied with sensory nerves, and we may have abdominal pains but apparently because there are pulls on the parietal peritoneum (11). Normally the visceral processes are extraordinarily undemonstrative. And even when the most marked changes are induced in them, as when adrenalin acts, the results, as we shall see, are sensations mainly attributable to effects on the cardiovascular system.

4. *Visceral changes are too slow to be a source of emotional feeling.* – The viscera are composed of smooth muscle and glands – except the heart, which is modified striate muscle. The motions of the body with which we are familiar result from quick-acting striate muscle, having a true latent period of less than $0 \cdot 001$ sec. Notions of the speed of bodily processes acquired by observing the action of skeletal muscle we should not apply to other structures. Smooth muscle and glands respond with relative sluggishness. Although Stewart (12) found that the latent period of smooth

muscle of the cat was about 0·25 sec., Sertoli (13) observed that it lasted for 0·85 sec. in the dog and 0·8 sec. in the horse. Langley (14) reported a latent period of 2 to 4 secs. on stimulating the *chorda tympani* nerve supply to the submaxillary salivary gland; and Pavlov (15) a latent period of about 6 *minutes* on stimulating the vagus, the secretory nerve of the gastric glands. Again, Wells and Forbes (16) noted that the latent period of the psychogalvanic reflex (in man), which appears to be a glandular phenomenon, was about 3 secs.

In contrast to these long delays before peripheral action in visceral structures barely starts are the observations of Wells (17); he found that the latent period of affective reactions to pictures of men and women ended not uncommonly within 0·8 sec. More recent studies with odours as stimuli have yielded a similar figure (personal communication). According to the James–Lange theory, however, these affective reactions result from reverberations from the viscera. But how is that possible? To the long latent periods of smooth muscles and glands, cited above, there must be added the time required for the nerve impulses to pass from the brain to the periphery and thence back to the brain again. It is clear that the organic changes could not occur soon enough to be the occasion for the appearance of affective states, certainly not the affective states studied by Wells.

— 5. *Artificial induction of the visceral changes typical of strong emotions does not produce them.* – That adrenin, or the commercial extract of the adrenal glands, 'adrenalin' acts in the body so as to mimic the action of sympathetic nerve impulses has already been mentioned. When injected directly into the blood stream or under the skin it induces dilatation of the bronchioles, constriction of blood vessels, liberation of sugar from the liver, stoppage of gastro-intestinal functions, and other changes such as are characteristic of intense emotions. If the emotions are the consequence of the visceral changes we should reasonably expect them, in accordance with the postulates of the James–Lange theory, to follow these changes in all cases. Incidental observations on students who received injections of adrenalin sufficiently large to produce general bodily effects have brought out the fact that no specific emotion was experienced by them – a few who had been in athletic competitions testified to feeling 'on edge', 'keyed up', just as before a race (18). In a careful study of the effects of adrenalin on a large number of normal and abnormal persons Marañon (19) has reported that the subjective experiences included sensations of precordial or epigastric palpitation, of diffuse arterial throbbing, of oppression in the chest and tightness in the throat, of trembling, of chilliness, of dryness of the mouth, of nervousness, malaise, and weakness. Associated with these sensations there was *in certain cases* an indefinite affective state coldly appreciated, and without real emotion. The subjects remarked, 'I feel as if afraid', 'as if awaiting a great joy', 'as if moved', 'as if I were going to weep without knowing why', 'as if I had a great fright yet am calm', 'as if they are about to do something to me'. In other words, as Marañon remarks, a clear distinction is drawn 'between the perception of the peripheral phenomena of vegetative emotion (i.e. the bodily changes) and the psychical emotion proper, which does not exist and which permits the subjects to report on the vegetative syndrome with serenity, without true feeling'. In a smaller number of the affected cases a real emotion developed, usually that of sorrow, with tears, sobs and sighings. This occurs, however, 'only when the emotional predisposition of the patient is very marked', notably in hyperthyroid cases. In some instances Marañon found that this state supervened only when the adrenalin was injected after a talk with the patients concerning their sick children or their dead parents. In short, only when an emotional mood already exists does adrenalin have a supporting effect.

From the evidence adduced by Marañon we may conclude that adrenalin induces in human beings typical bodily changes which are reported as sensations, that in some cases these sensations are reminiscent of previous emotional experiences but do not renew or revive those experiences, that in exceptional cases of preparatory emotional sensitization the bodily changes may tip the scales towards a true affective disturbance. These last cases are exceptional, however, and are not the usual phenomena as James and Lange supposed. In normal conditions the bodily changes, though well marked, do not provoke emotion.

The numerous events occurring in the viscera in consequence of great excitement, as detailed by Cannon (6, p. 184) have been interpreted as supporting the James–Lange theory (20, p. 211). From the evidence presented under the five headings above it should be clear that that interpretation is unwarranted. Since visceral processes are fortunately not a considerable source of sensation, since even extreme disturbances in them yield no noteworthy emotional experience, we can further understand now why these disturbances cannot serve as a means for discriminating between such pronounced emotions as fear and rage, why chilliness, asphyxia, hyperglycemia and fever, though attended by these disturbances, are not attended by emotion, and also why total exclusion of visceral factors from emotional expression makes no difference in emotional behavior. It is because the returns from the thoracic and abdominal 'sounding-board', to use James's word, are very faint indeed, that they play such a minor role in the affective complex. The processes going on in the thoracic and abdominal organs are truly remarkable and various; their value to the organism, however, is not to add richness and flavor to experience, but rather to adapt the internal economy so that in spite of shifts of outer circumstance the even tenor of the inner life will not be profoundly disturbed.

[. . .]

References

1. JAMES, W., and LANGE, C. G., *The Emotions*, 1922.
2. PERRY, R. B., *General Theory of Value*, 1926.
3. SHERRINGTON, C. S., 'Experiments on the value of vascular and visceral factors for the genesis of emotion', *Proc. Roy. Soc.*, vol. 66 (1900), p. 397.
4. CANNON, W. B., LEWIS, J. T., and BRITTON, S. W., 'The dispensability of the sympathetic division of the autonomic system', *Boston Med. and Surg. J.*, vol. 197 (1927), p. 514.
5. ANGELL, J. R., 'A reconsideration of James's theory of emotion in the light of recent criticisms', *Psychol. Rev.*, vol. 23 (1916).
6. CANNON, W. B., *Bodily changes in Pain, Hunger, Fear and Rage*, 1915.
7. CANNON, W. B., and PEREIRA, J. B., 'Increase of adrenal secretion in fever', *Proc. Nat. Acad. Sci.*, vol. 10 (1924), p. 247.
8. CANNON, W. B., QUERIDO, A., BRITTON, S. W., and BRIGHT, E. M., 'The rôle of adrenal secretion in the chemical control of body temperature', *Amer. J. Physiol.*, vol. 79 (1927), p. 466.
9. CANNON, W. B., MCIVER, M. A., and BLISS, S. W., 'A sympathetic and adrenal mechanism for mobilizing sugar in hypoglycemia', *Amer. J. Physiol.*, vol. 69 (1924), p. 46.
10. LANGLEY, J. N., and ANDERSON, H. K., 'The constituents of the hypogastric nerves', *J. Physiol.*, vol. 17 (1894), p. 185.

References—cont.

11. LENNANDER, K. G., *et al.*, 'Abdominal pains, especially in ileus', *J. Amer. Med. Assoc.*, vol. 49 (1907), p. 836 (see also p. 1015).

12. STEWART, C. C., 'Mammalian smooth muscle – the cat's bladder', *Amer. J. Physiol.*, vol. 4 (1900), p. 192.

13. SERTOLI, E., 'Contribution à la physiologie générale des muscles lisses', *Arch. Ital. de Biol.*, vol. 3 (1883), p. 86.

14. LANGLEY, J. N., 'On the physiology of the salivary secretion', *J. Physiol.*, vol. 10 (1889), p. 300.

15. PAVLOV, J. P., and SCHUMOVA-SIMANOVSKAJA, E. O., 'Die Innervation der Magendrüsen beim Hunde', *Arch. f. Physiol.*, 1895, p. 66.

16. WELLS, F. L., and FORBES, A., 'On certain electrical processes in the human body and their relations to emotional reactions', *Arch. Psychol.*, vol. 2 (1911), no. 16, p. 8.

17. WELLS, F. L., 'Reactions to visual stimuli in affective settings', *J. Exper. Psychol.*, vol. 8 (1925), p. 64.

18. PEABODY, F. W., STURGIS, C. C., TOMPKINS, E. M., and WEARN, J. T., 'Epinephrin hypersensitiveness and its relation to hyperthyroidism', *Amer. J. Med. Sci.*, vol. 161 (1921), p. 508. (Also personal communication from J. T. Wearn.)

19. MARAÑÓN, G., 'Contribution à l'étude de l'action émotive de l'adrénaline', *Rev. franç. d'endocrinol.*, vol. 2 (1924), p. 301.

20. HUMPHREY, G., *The Story of Man's Mind*, 1923.

Part Two **Emotion Rooted in Instinct**

The attempt to define emotion as organic sensation led to the notion that emotional experience must be a simple receptive process, as is all other sensory experience. As a result, the urge to action experienced in such emotions as fear and anger had to be explained as the result of special forces, instincts or drives.

For Shand, this drive is the contribution of the body, while emotion is the contribution of the mind; for McDougall, emotion is the affective, and instinct the conative, aspect of human activity. In more recent times, Plutchik makes a similar distinction, but for different reasons. Since instinct is no more acceptable than emotion in his behaviouristic scheme, he links emotional behaviour to its evolutionary counterpart by postulating basic inherited behaviour patterns – the old instincts in brand new guise.

Shand does not convince us that instincts are bodily systems; and McDougall labours under the necessity of finding a suitable emotion for every instinct, and vice versa. Some of his 'instincts' are not credible as dynamic forces (e.g. laughter), and some emotions are not recognizable as such: for instance, what recognizable emotion do we experience when instinct urges us to build shelter? Plutchik has the same difficulty, and his solution is no happier.

4 A. F. Shand

The Nature of Emotional Systems

Excerpts from A. F. Shand, *The Foundations of Character*, Macmillan, 1914, pp. 27–33.

[. . .] Now as there are in the body certain greater systems and certain lesser systems, so there are such also in the character. And as in the body the greater systems include certain subsidiary organs or systems – as the nutritive system, its various organs, and the nervous systems, other systems, as the sympathetic, the peripheral, and the central nervous system – so in the character also there are certain principal systems which organize others subsidiary to them. Now among these lesser systems that are, or may be, organized in greater, are the primary emotions with their connected instincts. And here we may refer to the fact, which is well recognized, that the systems of the mind, as mental systems, cannot be separated from certain bodily systems. Every system of the mind is incomplete, and has part of its system in the body, and every system of the body, which is not merely reflex, is also incomplete, and has part of its system in the mind. Whatever stimulus may be given to an instinctive system by an emotion of the mind, the executive part of it is in the body, and there also is another or receptive part which arouses the emotion. Thus the instincts of flight and concealment, involving so many co-ordinated movements for the fulfilment of their ends, are a part, and at first the largest and principal part, of the emotional system of fear, as imposing the end at which the system aims. And that part of the system which is in the mind includes not only the feeling and impulse of fear, but all the thoughts that subserve escape from danger. As we advance in life these acquired constituents, which modify the inherited structure of fear, become ever more numerous and important in correspondence with the growth of our experience.

The same is also true of anger and disgust, two emotions whose systems also include instincts. But while disgust is included among the recognized emotions – although in origin and in respect of its most prominent side, it is the negative instinct which leads to the rejection by the organism of substances that are unsuitable or dangerous – yet the positive and complementary instinct is not held to belong to an emotion. The feeling and impulse which accompanies and controls the search for and absorption of food is known as the appetite, not as the emotion of hunger. An appetite is aroused by internal rather than by external stimulation, has a greater regularity of recurrence than an emotion, and becomes more urgent the longer it remains unsatisfied; but in other respects the psychological difference between them is unimportant. Both are psycho-physical systems, both include instincts and emotional impulses. [. . .]

We must place therefore in these lesser mental systems not only certain emotions, but also the appetites of hunger and sex. There are other systems which we call neither emotions nor appetites, but loosely refer to as impulses, needs, or wants. Among them are the impulses connected with exercise and repose. Whether these include instincts may be more open to question. But the mode in which an animal takes the exercise characteristic of its species is recognized to be an instinct – as the flight of birds, the swimming of ducks, or the sinuous movement of snakes. And this instinct is connected with the impulse for exercise, and co-operates sometimes with hunger, sometimes with anger or fear, sometimes with the play-impulse.

The impulse for repose or sleep seems also to include an instinct. Different groups of animals have different ways of pursuing rest and sleep. Some make lairs, some perch on boughs, and bury their heads under their wings; some, like snakes, coil up. And the impulse is no mere impulse, but includes its own feeling. The longing for rest when we are forced to work, and the body feels tired, the longing for exercise when it feels fresh, and we are pent up in the house reaches a high degree of emotional intensity. It was, we may surmise, for this reason that the old writers included Desire among the primary emotions[1]; a custom which the moderns have

1. 'Passions' as they were called. See Descartes, *Les Passions de l'Âme*, 2, art. 69; also Locke, *Essay on the Human Understanding*, 2, ch. 20, para. 6.

reversed, under the influence, perhaps, of the abstract psychologizing that was inclined to discern in an emotion only feeling, in an impulse only conation, and in other states only cognition.

The appetites and primary impulses, some of which we have noticed, we shall provisionally class with the primary emotions. Their feelings have not often the individual distinctness of fear and anger; and there are other differences which the course of our inquiry will elicit; but they belong to those lesser systems of the mind with which we are here concerned. They contain instincts, or, at least, innate tendencies. They are primary, or underived from any other existing impulse or emotion. They, therefore, belong to those fundamental forces of character, without a knowledge of which it were in vain to attempt to understand its later and more complex developments.

Of the primary emotions we have as yet noticed only fear, anger, and disgust; we must now briefly refer to those which remain; premising only that the attempt to furnish an exhaustive list must be provisional, and that we may come to conclude in the end many impulses or emotions that we overlooked in the beginning. Among those which we have been able to recognize, Curiosity is one of the most important. It presents more the character of an impulse than of an emotion as generally understood; but it is none the less a primary system, and the basis of the intellectual life. It appears to include a well-formed instinct, and to be susceptible of some degree of emotional excitement. This instinct induces animals to make such movements as are necessary for a fuller acquaintance with an object, as to approach it closely, to sniff at it, to regard it with attentive scrutiny.[2]

The next two systems, Joy and Sorrow, in contrast with Curiosity, present rather the character of emotions than that of impulses or wants. They have been commonly regarded as primary, and it is improbable that any one will succeed in deriving them from other existing emotions. They are manifested very early in child-life. They include, if not instincts, at least innate tendencies. The general innate tendency of all joy is directed to maintain some process already existing. We attend to some stimulus perhaps accidentally,

2. Dr McDougall has well described the behaviour of this instinct. See his *Social Psychology*, ch. 3.

or because of its unusual intensity, but if it gives us joy or delight, we continue to attend to it. One of the earliest joys common to both men and the higher animals is that of satisfying hunger, as one of the earliest sorrows is that caused by the lack of food. Through hunger the young animal seeks the teat, and sucks at it when found: that is the instinct of its hunger. The enjoyment which it feels leads it to suck as long as the enjoyment is felt; that is the innate tendency of the emotion. And this enjoyment sometimes outlasts the satisfaction of appetite, and some men continue eating through gluttonous enjoyment.

The impulse of joy is thus often consequent on some other impulse, and accompanies its satisfaction, and continues as long as the enjoyment is felt. But after this enjoyment there frequently succeeds to it an opposite impulse. For soon monotony or satiety provokes aversion. Thus we withdraw from many things that at first give us a lively enjoyment, to return to them after an interval, but generally with diminished enjoyment. This withdrawal is due to Repugnance or Aversion, like Joy a primary system, but having an impulse and end opposite to that emotion. For when things are repugnant to us we behave in an opposite way to that in which we behave when we have joy in them, namely by withdrawing attention from them, and the accommodation of the organs, and often the body itself from their neighbourhood.

There are other kinds of joy and repugnance which, in distinction from those we have examined, do not seem to be consequent on the activity of any impulse that we feel. Thus there are some things which are an enjoyment to look at from the first, and others which are as immediately repugnant to us. The eyes, we suppose, are as much exercised by the examination of an ugly as of a beautiful object; but in the former case we feel repugnance, in the latter, joy; in that, an impulse to withdraw the attention, in this, to maintain it.

Thus the child continues gazing at the light because he enjoys it, and cries to get back to it when he is turned away, because the gloom in front of him is distasteful; the cat who has lain curled up on the rug after a little time climbs up on a piece of furniture to look out of the window, where, if not warmth, is compensating cheerfulness. And we too avoid 'gloomy' people and 'gloomy' parties where the guests sit lost in their own reflections, and we use the term 'gloomy' to describe these things because they are immediately repugnant to us.

But often our repugnance is obstructed. We have to stay in places repugnant to us, or to live with people repugnant to us, or to do work repugnant to us. The little child cries to get back to the light, but he cannot turn his body round. This obstruction of an innate impulse tends to arouse in him either anger or sorrow, according to circumstances. For as the stimuli of curiosity and fear often differ only in degree – a slighter degree of strangeness arousing the former, and a greater, the latter – so the obstruction of an impulse may arouse either anger or sorrow according to the degree of its strength. When we make no headway against opposition, when it does not yield to our efforts, but remains immovably fixed, the anger which, perhaps, it first awakened, tends to be replaced by sorrow. We feel ourselves engaging in a hopeless contest against an invincible opponent. This the child cannot understand; but he feels its effects, and it is the cause of his earliest sorrows. Thus Descartes observes: 'Quelque fois . . . il est arrivé que le corps a eu faute de nourriture, et c'est ce qui doit faire à l'âme sa première tristesse.'[3] The sorrow of children appears to be connected with a peculiar cry, different from that of fear or anger, and one which mothers can distinguish – the dumb expression of weakness and failure, and of the appeal for help. This appeal is the essential impulse of sorrow.

There are two other impulses of great importance which Professor Ribot[4] and Dr McDougall have the merit of distinguishing as among the primary forces of character. The one is the impulse of self-display, the other the impulse of self-abasement. They have been excellently described by Dr McDougall[5]. The former 'is manifested by many of the higher social or gregarious animals, especially, perhaps, though not only, at the time of mating. Perhaps among mammals the horse displays it most clearly. The muscles of all parts are strongly innervated, the creature holds himself erect, his neck is arched, his tail lifted, his motions become superfluously vigorous and extensive, he lifts his hoofs high in the air as he parades before the eyes of his fellows. Many animals, especially

3. 'Les Passions de l'Âme', 2, art. 110.
4. *Psychology of the Emotions*, part 2, ch. 5, i.
5. All quotations are from *Social Psychology*, ch. 3.

the birds, but also some of the monkeys are provided with organs of display that are specially disposed on these occasions. Such are the tail of the peacock and the beautiful breast of the pigeon. The instinct is essentially a social one, and is only brought into play by the presence of spectators.' Of the impulse of self-abasement, Dr McDougall writes that it 'expresses itself in a slinking crest-fallen behaviour, a general diminution of muscular tone, slow restricted movements, a hanging down of the head, and sidelong glances. In the dog the picture is completed by the sinking of the tail between the legs.' At the approach of a larger, older dog, a younger dog under the influence of this impulse, 'crouches or crawls with legs so bent that his belly scrapes the ground, his back hollowed, his tail tucked away, his head sunk and turned a little on one side, and so approaches the imposing stranger with every mark of submission.'

We have called these primary systems impulses rather than emotions. They are at least primary impulses; but they are probably not the emotions with which they are apt to be identified. The impulse of display cannot be at once both of the emotions of pride and vanity; nor can the impulse of self-abasement be both of the emotions of humiliation and shame. They seem to belong to an earlier and more undifferentiated stage from which one or other of these later and more definite emotions developed. In respect of this later stage we notice that vanity only, not pride, can possess the instinct of self-display. And with respect to the impulse of self-abasement, do we find it present in either humiliation or shame? Humiliation is painful. A sullen anger accompanies the degrading situation; but it has no impulse of self-abasement. Other of our later emotions have this impulse in some cases, notably awe, admiration, and reverence; and we notice that in all three the emotion is pleasant. But pride and humiliation resist subjection to the last. And if shame feels abasement, being derived from fear, it possesses an instinct of concealment, and has not the impulse shown by the young dog to make the subject of it approach superiors and express submission.

5 W. McDougall

Emotion and Feeling Distinguished

W. McDougall, 'Emotion and feeling distinguished', in M. L.
Reymert (ed.), *Feelings and Emotions*, Clark University Press, 1928,
pp. 200–204.

There is still much uncertainty and confusion in the use of the
terms 'emotion' and 'feeling', corresponding to the uncertain-
ties and diversities of views as to the status, conditions, and functions of the processes to which these terms are applied. After many
years of gradual advance toward clarity of my own thinking on
these problems I feel able to offer a scheme which seems to me
comprehensive, coherent, and fundamentally correct, however
much in need of correction and elaboration in details.

The scheme I offer is founded on evolutionary and comparative
or genetic considerations and moulded in conformity with the
facts of human experience and behavior. It implies a voluntaristic
or hormic psychology, that is to say, a psychology which regards
as the most fundamental feature of all animal life the capacity
actively to seek goals by means of plastic behavior, of striving
expressed in bodily movements adjusted from moment to moment
to the details of each developing situation in the manner called
by common consent, intelligent.

As I have argued elsewhere, the capacity to strive towards an
end or ends, to seek goals, to sustain and renew activity adopted
to secure consequences beneficial to the organism or the species
must be accepted as a fundamental category of psychology (1).
Whether in the course of evolution such capacity has 'emerged'
from modes of being lacking all germ of it; whether it can be
explained in terms of physics and chemistry, as the psychologists
of the Gestalt School seek to show – these are questions for the
future. Psychology is not called upon to await affirmative answers
to these questions before recognizing purposive striving as a
mode of activity that pervades and characterizes all animal life.
Nor need we determine whether plant life exhibits in some lowly

degree the same essential functions, or whether some cognition, however lowly, is always and everywhere a cooperating function.

It is reasonable to assume that the primary forms of animal striving were the seeking of food and the turning away from the noxious, primitive appetition and aversion; and that from these two primitive forms all other modes of appetition and aversion have been differentiated and evolved.

Setting out from these assumptions, my thesis is, first, that all the modes of experience we call feeling and emotion are incidental to the striving activities, the conations of the organism, evoked either by impressions from the environment or by metabolic processes taking place within it or, more commonly, in both ways; secondly, that we may broadly and consistently distinguish feelings on the one hand and emotions on the other by their functional relations to the conative activities which they accompany and qualify, these relations being very different in the two cases.

There are two primary and fundamental modes of feeling, pleasure and pain, or satisfaction and dissatisfaction, which color and qualify in some degree, however slight, all strivings. Pleasure is the consequence of, and sign of, success whether partial or complete; pain, the consequence and sign of failure and frustration. It seems probable that primitive pleasure and pain were alternatives, perhaps not mutually exclusive in any absolute sense but practically so. But with the development of the cognitive powers came the simultaneous apprehension of diverse aspects of objects and situations and, further, the pleasures and pains of anticipation and recollection. The former brought the possibility of the simultaneous excitation of diverse impulses conflicting or cooperating with reciprocal modifications. The latter rendered possible the conjunction of present success with anticipation of failure, and of present frustration with anticipation of success. With these came corresponding complications of the modes of feeling.

The organism that has attained such a level of cognitive development no longer oscillates between simple pleasure and simple pain; beside and between these simple primitive extremes, it attains a range of feelings which are in some sense fusions or blendings of pleasure and pain; it experiences such feelings as hope, anxiety, despondency, despair, regret and sorrow. And, with the fuller development of mental structure, the adult man learns to know 'sweet sorrows', joys touched with pain, 'hope deferred that maketh the heart sick', and 'strange webs of melancholy mirth'; 'his sincerest laughter with some pain is fraught'; his darkest moments of abject failure are lightened by some ray of hope; his bright moments of triumph and elation are sobered by his abiding sense of the vanity of human wishes and the fleeting, unstable nature of all attainment. In short, the grown man no longer is capable of the simple feelings of the child, because he has learned to 'look before and after and pine for what is not'. With the development of his cognitive powers, his desires have become complex and of long range, and the simple alternation between pleasure and pain has given place to a perpetual ranging through the scale of complex feelings. These complex feelings are known in common speech as emotions. Adopting the terminology proposed by Shand, I have elsewhere discussed them under the general title 'the derived emotions of desire, prospective and retrospective (2, 3)'.

It would greatly conduce to clarity and precision if, in science, we should cease to give the general name 'emotion' to these complex feelings. The difficulty of distinguishing these complex feelings from the emotions proper and the common practice of confusing them arise from the fact that well-nigh all the strivings of the developed mind are qualified both by emotions proper and by complex feelings or 'derived emotions' blended in one complex whole or configuration.

To turn now to the emotions proper or the qualities of emotional experience: As the primitive appetition and aversion became differentiated into impulses directed toward more special goals and evocable by more special objects and situations, each specialized impulse found expression in some special mode of bodily striving with some corresponding complex of bodily adjustments facilitating and supporting that mode of bodily activity. Without accepting the James–Lange theory in an extreme and literal way, we must suppose that each such system of bodily adjustments is reflected in the experience of the striving organism, giving to each specialized mode of striving a peculiar and distinctive quality, the quality of one of the primary emotions; and that, when mental development reaches the level at which two or more of the specialized impulses come into play simultaneously, conflicting or cooperating, these primary qualities are experienced in the complex blendings that we call the secondary or blended emotions, such complex qualities as embarrassment, shame, awe, reverence, reproach.

Let me now contrast the complex feelings or 'derived emotions' with the emotions proper, primary and blended, bearing in mind that all the concrete emotional experiences of the developed mind are configurations in which are blended qualities of both kinds, qualities which we abstractly distinguish as the true and the derived emotions.

1. The complex feelings, like the simple feelings, arise from, are conditioned by, the degrees of success and failure of our strivings, and, like the simple feelings, they modify the further working of the impulses by which they are generated, strengthening and sustaining them in so far as the balance of feeling-tone is on the pleasurable side, checking and diverting them in so far as the balance of feeling is on the painful side.

The true emotional qualities, on the other hand, are prior to and independent of success and failure; they spring to life with the evocation of the corresponding impulses and continue to color the experiences of striving each with its distinctive tone, giving its specific quality to the whole configuration regardless of degrees of success or failure, actual or anticipated. And they have no direct influence upon the course of striving. As qualities of experience they are merely indicative of the nature of bodily adjustments organically bound up with each fundamental mode of striving; but in the developed mind they play an indirect part in determining the course of conation because, serving as signs of the nature of the impulse at work, they render possible to the self-conscious organism some degree of direction and control of these impulses.

2. The complex feelings, then, are dependent upon and secondary to the development of the cognitive functions. It is perhaps true to say that they are peculiar to man, though possibly attained in their simpler forms by the highest of animals. The true emotions, on the other hand, must be supposed to be of very much earlier appearance in the evolutionary scale. Throughout the major part of that scale they appear as mere by-products of the impulsive strivings of the animals. In man alone they become an

important source of self-knowledge and, therefore, of self-direction.

The introspective study of these emotional qualities has been much neglected by psychology, for the reasons that they do not readily lend themselves to experimental control, and that our nomenclature inevitably remains very inadequate. Yet the practice of such introspection brings great increase of facility in recognition of the nature of our conations; and such facility is of more practical importance than any other kind of introspective skill, not only because it greatly conduces to efficient self-direction, but also because it is a principal means to a better understanding of the motivation of conduct in general. It is not difficult to know that we desire (or are averse to) some particular end; the difficulty, theoretical and practical, is to know what is the nature of the impulse in which the desire is rooted, what tendency finds satisfaction in the attainment of such an end.

3. The named complex feelings (such as hope, anxiety, regret) are not in any sense entities and do not spring from special dispositions. Rather, each of the names we use in describing such feelings denotes merely an ill-defined part of a large range of feeling, the whole of which may be incidental to the working of any strong desire, no matter what its nature and origin. As the subject, moved by desire, passes through this range of complex feelings, each named part is experienced in turn, and in turn passes over into its neighbor quality; there is consequently no blending of such qualities.

On the other hand, each one of the true primary emotional qualities arises on the coming into activity of a corresponding conative disposition, which is an enduring feature of the mental structure of the organism; hence, each such quality is experienced only in association with an impulse or a desire of a specific type; and, since two or more such dispositions may come simultaneously into play, yielding cooperative or conflicting desires, the corresponding primary emotional qualities may be simultaneously evoked and may fuse or blend with one another in various intensities. Let me illustrate these contrasting features with examples. Hope is the name we give to the complex feeling which arises when *any* strong desire is working in us and we anticipate success; if new difficulties arise hope gives place to anxiety or despondency, but cannot under any circumstances be said to blend with despondency to yield anxiety; rather, as the circumstances become less favorable, the feeling rooted in our desire changes by imperceptible gradations from hope to anxiety and then to despondency. Contrast with this the emotion we call curiosity or wonder and its relations to the emotion we call fear. The emotion-quality wonder accompanies always, in some degree, the impulse or desire to explore and to become better acquainted with some object; it is never experienced save as an accompaniment of that tendency in action. The process of exploration leads to the better comprehension of the nature of the object and this in turn may evoke fear, a quality which accompanies always the impulse to shrink from, or the desire to retreat from, the object. But with the rise of this new impulse with its distinctive emotion-quality, wonder is not necessarily driven out or arrested; the impulse to explore may continue to work simultaneously with the impulse to retreat, and in this case we experience an emotion-quality in which we recognize affinity to both wonder and fear, and which we seem justified in describing as in some sense a blend of these two primary qualities.

References

1. McDougall, W., 'Purposive striving as a fundamental category of psychology', Presidential address to the Psychological Section of the British Association, 1924. Reprinted in *Science*, November 1924.
2. McDougall, W., *Introduction to Social Psychology*, Luce, Boston, 1910.
3. McDougall, W., *Outline of Psychology*, Scribner, New York, 1923.

6 R. Plutchik

The Evolutionary Basis of Emotional Behaviour

Excerpts from R. Plutchik, *The Emotions: Facts, Theories, and a New Model*, Random House, 1962, pp. 55–63, 108–15.

[. . .] The view to be presented here would not restrict the concept of emotion only to the primate level, the mammalian level, or even the vertebrate level; emotion should be conceived of as relevant to the entire evolutionary scale. This suggests that emotion should be related to some kinds of basic, adaptive, biological processes, a point elaborated below.

A second implication is that a decision about which emotions are primary and which derived should not depend only on adult introspections, even though introspections may be useful in providing additional insights into the internal stimuli associated with certain adaptive reactions.

Third, although emotions may depend for expression on the integrated action of certain neural structures, they cannot be identified solely in terms of neural structures, for these structures change considerably in the course of evolution, and the most primitive organisms have no nervous systems at all. Thus, if emotions are to be recognized at all evolutionary levels, they cannot be identified with particular body parts.

It follows that if emotions are not identified by the action of particular body parts or neural structures, then emotions must be recognizable in terms of total body reactions, that is, in terms of overall behavior. Even at the human level, it has been noted, people do not identify emotions in others by physiological means, by taking heart rate or blood pressure measurements; emotions are most easily recognized by what people do. If a man walks slowly, with head bent forward, speaks in a low monotone or hardly at all, does very little work and sits with a somewhat huddled posture, we are very likely to assume that he is sad or depressed, regardless of what he may say. Clinicians often know that a patient is angry or anxious though the patient is not aware of it or will not verbalize it. How often we tell someone *you look irritated* or *you look hurt*, or *you look happy*, on the basis of his facial expression, posture, movements, or general behavior. Thus it seems reasonable to conclude that the basic definition of emotion should be a behavioral one which does not depend on introspections or the existence of particular neural events.

One immediate problem posed by this view is that of distinguishing emotional behavior from all other kinds of behavior. Some psychologists have suggested that we do without the concept of emotion and think of all behavior simply in terms of changes of magnitude and direction. But this view has not received wide support; there seems to be need for some way of distinguishing certain special kinds of behavior as 'emotional'.

One solution, suggested by the first implication discussed above, is that emotion be related to some kinds of basic adaptive, biological processes. This criterion can provide a partial basis for distinguishing emotional behavior from other behavior.

To summarize, emotions considered primary should:
1. have relevance to basic biological adaptive processes;
2. be found *in some form* at all evolutionary levels;   DISAGREE
3. not depend for their definition on particular neural structures or body parts;   BUT THESE ARE DEF IMP.
4. not depend for definition on introspections (although they may be used);
5. be defined primarily in terms of behavioral data (or to use Tolman's phrase, in terms of 'response-as-affecting-stimulus').

It is implicit in this view that emotions are adaptive devices in the struggle for individual survival at all evolutionary levels.

Basic types of adaptive behavior

In the attempt to identify basic types of adaptive behavior, it is necessary to find terms which apply to all animals so that generalizations can be made. Scott, in his book *Animal Behavior* (1958), puts the matter in the following way:

When we compare the activities of a wider variety of species, we begin to see that certain kinds of behavior occur over and over again, and that these fall into a few general kinds of behavioral adaptations which are widely found in the animal kingdom. In doing this, we must meet a problem of language as well as that of careful description. What words can we use to say that two animals as unlike as elephants and spiders are doing similar things?

One clue to this problem is given by Murray (1954), who pointed out that the life processes of maintenance, development, reproduction, and expression require certain basic functions such as respiration, ingestion of food, excretion, defense, and so on. Similarly Turner (1957) has noted that:

There is only a limited number of modes of dealing with danger available to the individual that have proved of general applicability exploitable in phylogeny. With respect to stimuli arising from within the organism, survival is favored by expulsion or by isolation. With respect to stimuli referring to a source of (potential) danger arising from the outer environment, survival is favored by flight, fight, submission, reversal, and vocalization, in the order of apparent phylogenetic development.

Perhaps an extension and formalization of these ideas might provide a key to the basic types of adaptive behavior we are seeking.

Such an extension has been made by Scott, who documents with a great deal of evidence the concept that there are nine general types of adaptive behavior. These are described and illustrated below and their relevance for a theory of emotion suggested.

Ingestive behavior. – All organisms, in order to survive, must take in food in some form. This is as true for the amoeba as it is for man.

Shelter-seeking. – An animal tends to move about until it finds conditions favorable for its existence. Even paramecia will move close to the bodies of other paramecia, forming a group. Scott suggests that 'this is actually a very primitive type of social behavior, which can be called contactual behavior . . . and it is possible that higher types of social behavior had their origin in this simple adaptation.'

Agonistic behavior. – All organisms become involved at one time or another in a struggle with other organisms or with nature. Fighting or protective behavior is included under the term agonistic from the Greek root meaning 'to struggle'.

Sexual behavior. – Almost all animals show sexual activity in one form or another, ranging from contact and courtship to coition.

Care-giving behavior. – In higher animals once the young of a species are born there is usually a period of time during which they are comparatively helpless. During this time, nurturant or succorant behavior is provided by the adult members of the group. This is not necessarily parental behavior, since in some groups, such as the bees, care of the young is provided by the workers, who are sterile females. McDougall considered the parental drive one of seven basic instincts.

Care-soliciting behavior. – The young of many species show various kinds of behavior which may be interpreted as care-seeking. Young birds make cheeping sounds and hold their opened beaks in the air, and the young of most higher species engage in behavior which seems to elicit care-giving responses from the adult members of the group.

Eliminative behavior. – Many animals have special patterns of behavior associated with the elimination of waste products. Many birds, for example, flip their tail at the moment the feces are released so the material is tossed away. Dogs and cats will dig holes and bury their excrement, and so on.

Allelomimetic behavior. – This is defined as 'behavior in which two or more animals do the same thing, with some degree of mutual stimulation'. It is illustrated by the integrated flight of flocks of birds, by the migration of schools of fish, and by the grazing behavior of many herbivorous animals. It implies imitative behavior, although it is not clear to what extent such activity is learned.

Investigative behavior. – This is often called exploratory behavior and may be thought of as a method animals use for getting to know the environment. What learning theorists usually call operant behavior would probably be included under this heading. McDougall elevated curiosity to the status of an instinct and defined it as an 'impulse to approach and to examine more closely the object that excites it'.

Several important points may be made in reviewing these nine types of adaptive behavior. Some of them do not fit the criteria listed earlier for basic emotions or basic adaptive processes. Care-giving and care-soliciting behavior are found only in higher animals and are thus not applicable to all levels of evolutionary development. Allelomimetic behavior is found only in certain groups of animals and requires, in any case, highly developed sense organs for distance reception. Shelter-seeking behavior may be thought of as learned behavior that the higher organisms show; at lower levels, it is hardly more than a tendency to keep moving until external conditions are not too dissimilar from internal ones. It is really not a pattern at all.

Of the nine adaptive processes listed by Scott, therefore, only five fit our criteria. Of these, agonistic behavior should be considered at greater length.

Scott classifies both flight and fight under the general heading of agonistic behavior. These tendencies, however, are so different and are expressed in such different ways that it is desirable to provide separate categories for them. In fight behavior the tendency is to destroy the opponent or to destroy the barrier to the satisfaction of some need. In flight behavior there is the need to avoid being destroyed; the organism shows either escape behavior, withdrawal, contraction, or freezing. It is thus suggested that Scott's agonistic behavior be broken down into destruction behavior and protection behavior.

Two other modifications of Scott's classification should be made. An organism may eliminate not only at the anal end but at the oral end as well. When some noxious material is ingested, the body usually reacts by ejecting this material, or 'vomiting' it. At the human level, this is usually associated with the feeling of disgust. McDougall described this process as 'repugnance' and considered it a basic impulse. He called it the 'instinct of repulsion'. He noted correctly that this is another kind of protection response of the organism.

A different basic pattern is the reaction to loss or deprivation. This may perhaps be illustrated by reference to some human parallels. A man in love may tell his sweetheart that she fills his heart; an attractive child may elicit the comment from an adult that he could eat her up. Both imply a kind of incorporation of desired objects. If the pleasureful object is, in some sense, lost, then there results a pattern of reaction usually thought of as sadness or grief and which may be described in the general case as a deprivation reaction. It is suggested that the essence of this proto-type pattern is the ubiquitous fact of hunger and the organism's reactions to loss of food. Experiences of grief in human beings are often characterized in terms of feeling 'empty', 'lost', 'alone' or as if there is a 'gap' which cannot be filled. Only in recent years has some research been directed toward identifying the nature of this deprivation pattern in detail. Thus, to the list of behavior patterns Scott has presented, deprivation might be added.

There is one final addition to Scott's list of basic biological processes. Magda Arnold (1960) has marshalled cogent arguments for the view that most emotions involve an intuitive appraisal of a stimulus as good (beneficial) or bad (harmful). Now although evaluations of harm and benefit may be involved in emotions, it is very unlikely that all organisms can unequivocally evaluate all stimuli with which they make contact. Some period, extended or brief, is necessary before tissue damage occurs, or internal injury develops, or pleasurable sensations occur. During this initial period of direct contact with an unevaluated object, a pattern of behavior apparently develops which, at the human level, is usually called surprise. It is therefore suggested that a pattern of behavior called contact behavior or orientation be added to the original list.

It is thus possible to arrive at eight basic behavior patterns which may be found in some form at all levels of evolution, which do not depend on particular neural structures or body parts, which do not depend on introspections, and which are defined in terms of gross behavioral interactions between organism and environment. *It is suggested that these represent the basic dimensions of emotion applicable to all organismic levels. They represent the prototypes of all emotional behavior.*

The following list summarizes these basic prototypic[1] dimensions:

Incorporation. – The act of taking in or ingesting food represents a basic prototypic pattern of behavior indicating *acceptance* of stimuli from the outside world into the organism. Such stimuli

---

1. Prototype is defined as 'an original or model after which anything is formed; the pattern of anything to be engraved, cast, etc.; exemplar; archetype'.

may be thought of as generally being ~~beneficial or pleasurable~~ for the individual.

Rejection. – This represents a kind of riddance reaction. It is the prototype of behavior involved in getting rid of something harmful *which has already been incorporated*. It may take two forms, such as expelling feces or vomiting.

Destruction. – This prototypic pattern of behavior occurs when the organism contacts a barrier to the satisfaction of some need, and consists essentially *in an attempt to destroy the barrier*. If the barrier is another animal, it may be killed or it may even be eaten. At the lowest organismic levels the destruction of a barrier and the incorporation of food are fused into a single pattern which at higher levels is gradually differentiated. But only at the very highest levels, i.e. in man, is mass destruction carried out with no intention of incorporating the victims. And apparently only in man is the individual himself perceived as a barrier to the satisfaction of his own needs so that destruction is attempted in various ways against himself.

Protection. – The prototypic protection response occurs basically under conditions of pain, although it may later occur under conditions of threats of pain or destruction. It is an attempt to avoid being destroyed. An organism in such a situation retreats, if possible. If flight is not possible, it makes itself as inconspicuous as it can by freezing, playing dead, or contracting to the smallest possible volume. (An analogy might be a group of soldiers pulling back into a small, tight circle to provide the best defense possible.) Although the description of this dimension might seem to imply consciousness on the part of an organism, this is not what is meant. The protection response to a stimulus is a basic protoplasmic reaction found in all organisms from the amoeba to man. Needless to say, in the life of most animals, protection responses are more necessary and meaningful (and perhaps even more frequent) than in most other types, and thus they must play a central role in affecting all behavior.

Reproduction. – This term is used to represent the prototypic response associated with sexual behavior. Apparently at almost all animal levels, sexual behavior is associated with some form of pulsatile or orgastic behavior. Even the asexual reproduction of one-celled organisms has an intense pulsating quality as recorded by high speed photography. Pleasure is presumably associated with all forms of sexual behavior, and may be defined in terms of approach and maintenance-of-contact tendencies.

Deprivation. – The loss of a pleasureful object which has been contacted or incorporated is associated with a prototypic behavior pattern which, at the human level, is generally described as grief or sadness. The word deprivation is defined as the pattern of reaction to the loss of something possessed or enjoyed.

Orientation is the pattern of behavior which occurs when an organism contacts a new or strange object. This reaction is typically quite transient and exists so long as the object remains unevaluated in terms of harm or benefit, pain or pleasure. As soon as the object or stimulus is evaluated (without, necessarily, self-consciousness), this pattern of surprise changes to one (or more) of the other patterns. If the object produces pain, the pattern becomes protection; if it produces pleasure, the pattern may change to incorporation or reproduction.

Exploration. – This refers to the more-or-less random activities organisms use to explore their environment. The form of these activities depends a great deal upon the type of sensory endowment of the organism, some animals utilizing their tactile sense more than others. Paramecia alternate between going forward and back, while birds, who have excellent distance receptors, explore large portions of their environment at a glance. Exploratory activity seems to be spontaneous and almost continuous in most animals. It is prototypic of what humans call curiosity and play.

These then represent the eight prototypic dimensions of emotion: *incorporation, rejection, destruction, protection, reproduction, deprivation, orientation*, and *exploration*. These basic dimensions apply to all organismic levels from the lowest up to man. The terms used to describe them refer to overt behavior patterns or involve concepts like pleasure and pain which are definable in terms of overt behavior. [. . .]

These dimensions seem to represent bipolar factors or axes with destruction versus protection, incorporation versus rejection, reproduction versus deprivation, and orientation versus exploration. This becomes even clearer if we think of the names used to describe these primary emotions when expressed in humans. We think of joy as opposed to sadness, acceptance to disgust, anger to fear, and surprise to expectation. These designations are obviously tentative because of one very important fact, that is, the dependence on intensity of the names given to emotions. Thus the dimension of rejection would include such intensity levels as boredom, dislike, antipathy, disgust, repulsion, and loathing; the deprivation dimension, pensiveness, melancholy, sadness, and grief.

These two observations, that is, the bipolar nature of the primary emotions, and the implicit intensity dimension, suggest the need for some kind of structural model or analogue to represent the organization and properties of the emotions.

Such an analogue may be found in the theory of color mixture. McDougall (1921) noted this parallel many years ago:

> The color-sensations present, like the emotions, an indefinitely great variety of qualities shading into one another by imperceptible gradations; but this fact does not prevent us regarding all these many delicate varieties as reducible by analysis to a few simple primary qualities from which they are formed by fusion, or blending, in all proportions. Rather it is the indefinitely great variety of color qualities, their subtle gradations, and the peculiar affinities between them, that justify us in seeking to exhibit them as fusions in many different proportions of a few primary qualities. And the same is true of the emotions.

In order to develop this analogy, it is necessary to conceive of the primary emotions as hues which may vary in degree of inter-mixture (saturation) as well as intensity, and as arrangeable around an emotion-circle similar to a color-wheel. Primary emotions which are opposite each other on such an emotion-circle should be thought of as complementary in the sense that their mixture produces the psychic or biological equivalent of gray (which is obtainable by mixing complementary colors). There should be some kind of gradation of emotions around the circle, so that adjacent emotions are more similar than emotions which are more removed, just as adjacent colors are more similar than opposite ones. The analogy also implies that mixtures or combinations of these primary emotions in various proportions will produce all of the emotions which are known and described in life. Such a model should provide us with answers to the many questions that may be posed about emotions and at the same time should act as an integrator of facts already known, a predictor of new relationships, a stimulator of research, and an incorporator, that is, it should show relationships between apparently diverse areas.

In the process of developing the most effective model of the emotions there are likely to be many trials and errors. Such a model can be established only by a series of successive approximations.

The structural model

A first approximation to a structural model of the emotions is presented in Figure 1. It shows the eight prototypic dimensions

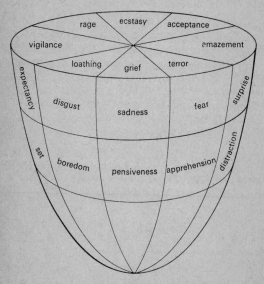

Figure 1 A multi-dimensional model of the emotions

arranged somewhat like the sections of half an orange, with the emotion terms which designate each emotion at maximum intensity at the top. The vertical dimension represents intensity, or level of arousal, and ranges from a maximum state of excitement to a state of deep sleep at the bottom. The shape of the model implies that the emotions become less distinguishable at lower intensities. If we imagine taking successive cross-sections, we keep duplicating the emotion-circle with progressively milder versions of each of the primaries.

The arrangement of emotions around this circle is designed to place similar emotions near each other, so far as is known. Several authors have commented on the similarity between joy and anger. Both are expansive, both involve outwardly directed activity, both involve vocalizations, etc. Other emotions which clearly belong together are surprise and fear, or joy and acceptance, or the negative emotions of grief and disgust.

This arrangement around the emotion-circle is still tentative, depending for confirmation upon various kinds of studies of similarity of emotions. The problem may be studied from the point of view of facial expressions in emotion, linguistic similarity of connotations of emotion words, and physiological patterns of expression. Some data on the first two points have been collected. [. . .] The eventual decision on the arrangement will also depend upon the kind of internal consistency provided by one grouping rather than another.

The question of the exact form of the emotion-solid is an empirical problem which can be answered only by studies of level of arousal of the primary emotions. Since this is a subjective problem as well as a behavioral and physiological one, any one study of intensity of the primary emotions will provide only an approximation to the structure. With this limitation in mind, the following study of the judged intensity of emotion words was undertaken.

Experiment 1: The judged intensity of emotion-terms. A list of synonyms for each of the primary emotion dimensions was compiled, using as many as could be found in both the unabridged dictionary and *Roget's Thesaurus.* The number of synonyms found for each dimension varied. Three of the four emotions with the most synonyms are negative or unpleasant emotions, i.e. disgust, fear, and grief, thus suggesting that we are able to make finer discriminations with negative emotions than with positive ones.

These lists of synonyms were then presented to a group of thirty college students with the following instructions:

Here is a list of words describing emotions. Some of the words (such as surprise and startle) mean very much the same thing, but indicate a different level of intensity of the emotion. Please examine the entire list of emotions, and rate them in terms of the degree of intensity that they represent, using a scale of 1 to 11. 1 means a very, very *low* intensity of the emotion. 6 means a *moderate* level of intensity of the emotion. 11 means a very, very *high* level of intensity of the emotion. You may use any number from 1 to 11.

The mean judged intensity was then obtained for each of the terms. These data are summarized in Table 1, where, since some overlap is found, only words representing clear-cut differences are presented, ranging from highest to lowest.

Five of the emotions show maximum intensities in the range of 9 to 10, while the dimensions of *incorporation* and *exploration* are both relatively low on the intensity dimension. None of the minimum intensities are below a value of three, thus implying that no discriminations are made between emotions at very low intensity levels.

These intensity values might provide an approximate estimate of the shape of the emotion-solid. It is important to recognize that maximum intensity values vary for each of the primary dimensions and that we cannot match all emotions for intensity, since the maximum value for the incorporation dimension is only about 4.

Figure 2 A cross-section of the emotion-solid

Table 1
The Mean Judged Intensity of Synonyms for each of the Eight Primary Emotion Dimensions

Dimensions							
Destruction	Reproduction	Incorporation	Orientation	Protection	Deprivation	Rejection	Exploration
Rage (9·90)	Ecstasy (10·00)	Admission (4·16)	Astonishment (9·30)	Terror (10·13)	Grief (8·83)	Loathing (9·10)	Anticipation (7·30)
Anger (8·40)	Joy (8·10)	Acceptance (4·00)	Amazement (8·30)	Panic (9·75)	Sorrow (7·53)	Disgust (7·60)	Expectancy (6·76)
Annoyance (5·00)	Happiness (7·10)	Incorporation (3·56)	Surprise (7·26)	Fear (7·96)	Dejection (6·26)	Dislike (5·50)	Attentiveness (5·86)
	Pleasure (5·70)			Apprehension (6·40)	Gloominess (5·50)	Boredom (4·70)	Set (3·56)
	Serenity (4·36)			Timidity (4·03)	Pensiveness (4·40)	Tiresomeness (4·50)	
	Calmness (3·30)						

Similarly, the orientation dimension has all of its emotion intensities ranging between 7 and 9; thus any of the forms of surprise occur at high intensity, if they occur at all. This is consistent with the various descriptions given in the previous chapter of surprise or startle as a sudden mobilization or orientation of the body in response to a novel stimulus.

Using these intensity judgements as a basis, it is possible to obtain groupings of emotion-terms representing the primary dimensions at nearly equal intensity levels. For example, rage, ecstasy, astonishment, panic, grief, and loathing all represent emotions judged to indicate intensity levels approximately between 9 and 10 on an 11-point scale. Anger, joy, surprise, fear, sorrow, disgust, and anticipation all represent medium levels of intensity somewhere between 7 and 8. The emotions of annoyance, pleasure, acceptance, timidity, pensiveness, boredom, and heedfulness represent low intensity levels of the primary dimensions, at about 4 to 5 on the 11-point scale. These groupings therefore represent approximate cross-sections of the emotion-solid and may be represented, as in Figure 2, for a medium intensity level.

References

ARNOLD, Magda B. (1960), *Emotion and Personality*, 2 vols., Columbia University Press.

McDOUGALL, W. (1921), *An Introduction to Social Psychology*, Luce.

MURRAY, H. A. (1954), 'Toward a classification of interaction', in T. Parsons and E. A. Shils (eds.), *Toward a General Theory of Action*, Harvard University Press.

SCOTT, J. P. (1958), *Animal Behavior*, University of Chicago Press.

TURNER, W. J. (1957), 'Some phylogenetic roots of human behavior', *Trans. New York Acad. Sci.* vol. 20, pp. 192–8.

Part Three Emotion in Depth Psychology

Freudian psychoanalysis also connects emotion with instinct, at least in the case of love and aggression where the emotion is the affect charge of the libido. But anxiety has a different status because it is experienced by the ego and aroused by threatening situations – a life-long remnant of the birth trauma. According to Rapaport, a prominent American disciple of Freud, anxiety is the expression of unconscious conflict. This view that some emotions are affect charges of instinct while anxiety is the product of conflict amounts to two different theories of emotion which have never been reconciled. Indeed, Freud adds still another dimension when he speaks of the pleasure principle, according to which pleasure is felt when tension is reduced, and unpleasantness when tension is increased.

For Jung, affectivity rests on instinctual forces as they act through the archetypal images. Archetypes are organized forces rooted in the unconscious, which direct conscious life. But emotions also form dynamic complexes around the archetypal nucleus, and it is unclear whether they have a dynamic aspect over and above the archetypal energy.

Neither Freud nor Jung was interested in a systematic theory of emotions but described them as they affect personality, which accounts for the different emphasis at different times. For this reason, discussions by their disciples (Rapaport, Hillman) give a more connected picture of their views than do their own writings.

7 D. Rapaport

The Psychoanalytic Theory of Emotions

Excerpt from D. Rapaport, *Emotions and Memory*, International Universities Press, 1950, pp. 28–33.

The Freudian concept of affects is not an unequivocal one. In Freud's early writings (1, p. 30; 2, p. 64), and in the early psychoanalytical literature in general (3), the concept of affect is similar to that advanced by Prince: affects are considered as *a* form or *the* form of psychic energy. Yet it would be erroneous to consider this the definitive Freudian concept of affects. A lack of conceptual crystallization in early psychoanalytic writings resulted in frequent mention of 'affective tone' (1, p. 31), as though affect were assumed to be a mere attribute of other psychic contents. A tendency to adopt a conflict theory also appears to be indicated in Freud's early statement that 'affects are inherited hysterical attacks'[1] in as much as these attacks are results of conflicts and their expression of an unconscious idea through the body shows a striking similarity to emotional expression. The new element implied here is that the conflict underlying both hysterical attacks and emotions is *unconscious*. This idea was further elaborated in *The Interpretation of Dreams* (5):

> We here take as our basis a quite definite assumption as to the nature of the development of affect. This is regarded as a motor or secretory function, the key to the innervation of which is to be found in the ideas of the Ucs (p. 521).

In the later essay on 'The Unconscious' (6) we read:

> The whole difference arises from the fact that ideas are cathexes – ultimately of memory traces – whilst affects and emotions correspond with processes of discharge, the final expression of which is perceived as feeling. In the present state of our knowledge of affects and emotions we cannot express this difference more clearly (p. 111).

1. 'I believe I was not wrong in regarding these [affective] states as the equivalents of hysterical attacks developed later and individually, and in considering the former as the normal prototypes of the latter' (4, p. 23).

Thus, affects regulated from the unconscious are defined as discharge processes of energies of instinctual origin.

It will be worthwhile to consider at this point the differences between the view that affects are energies and the view that affects are discharge processes of energies. Let us take a physical example. The kinetic energy of a gas manifests itself in a pressure which may result in the expansion of an elastic container or in the discharge of part of the gas through a vent, or which may be only indicated in a reading on a manometer. Physicists do not regard these manifestations or discharge-processes as being kinetic energy any more than they regard a falling stone as being gravitation. Apparently this stage of conceptual development has not yet been reached in psychology. Sherrington and many later investigators saw the problem of emotions as one of sequence: that is, whether the *feeling* or the *expression*[2] of emotions was prior in time, or whether they were simultaneous. The answer, it was considered, settled the problem of causation. If the physiological processes precede the psychological, then 'emotion felt' is only their 'cortical reverberation'; if 'emotion felt' precedes, then the feeling 'elicits' the bodily changes. This theoretical approach has not sufficiently explored the possibility that both 'emotion felt' and physiological changes concomitant with emotions may be manifestations of a common variable. This shortcoming also may probably be attributed to the fact that in the final analysis the dynamics of psychic manifestations are *unconscious*, and cannot be found by investigating interrelations of the data of physiology and the data of consciousness.

The Freudian theory of emotions states explicitly that the 'key to the innervation . . . of the emotions . . . is to be found in the ideas of the unconscious'. Whether emotions are psychic energies or discharge processes of such energies has not been stated with like unequivocalness. In the course of the development of Freudian theory, it became clear that the psychic energies called 'libido' or 'interest' are of instinctual origin:

. . . an instinct-presentation, and by that we understood an idea or group of ideas which is cathected with a definite amount of the mental energy (libido, interest) pertaining to an instinct (7, p. 91).

2. 'Expression' implies here motor as well as physiological changes.

It also became clear that affects are *one* representation of these energies, and that the (unconscious) ideas are another:

We have adopted the term *charge of affect* for this other element in the mental presentation; it represents that part of the instinct which has become detached from the idea, and finds proportionate expression, according to its quantity, in processes which become observable to perception as affects (7, p. 91).

The role of the unconscious in the emotional process was emphasized by the psychoanalyst Kulovesi (8) in his discussion of the James–Lange theory:

James states that between perception and emotion there lies the bodily expression; we must object to this, since between the perception and the bodily expression unconscious psychic complexes become active. These psychic complexes are mobilized when the perception touches upon an object that is in associative connexion with the complex (p. 393).

The psychoanalytic theory of emotions need not assume that the sequence of events in the development of an emotion is: perception – unconscious process – bodily process – 'emotion felt'. In a psychoanalytic theory of emotions, the unconscious process elicited by the percept may be followed in any sequence by the bodily process or by the 'emotion felt', or by only one of these, or by neither; for both are conceived of as manifestations of the same psychic process.[3]

The lack of agreement as to whether emotions are discharge-processes or energies is exemplified in Brierley's (9) recent paper. This author came to conclusions contrary to Freud's; she maintains that her findings 'contradict the idea that affect is itself a discharge and support the view that it is a tension-phenomenon impelling to discharge either in the outer or the inner world' (p. 259). The question of what are the discharge processes of the tension phenomena with which she identifies the affects is not answered; in the same article, however, we read a definition of 'affects' which is in harmony with Freud's point of view as repre-

3. The relation between 'emotional behavior' and 'emotion felt' becomes clearer if we keep in mind a theory stated by Freud in the 'Two Principles of Mental Functioning' (12). Here he maintained that thinking is experimenting at action with small amounts of energy; so are conscious processes in general and so is 'emotion felt'.

sented on these pages, and which characterizes affects as an 'index to the fate of the impulse':

Affect, as inferred from its expression and behavior, can be aroused by internal conditions or by external happenings. It is influenced both by internal need and by the nature of the response from the outer world with which this need is met. The affect manifested is, in fact, the index to the fate of the impulse and to the nature of the beginning psychic object-formation (p. 262).

This view of Brierley coincides with Freud's view of the nature of pleasantness and unpleasantness. Pleasantness is described by Freud (10) and by G. Jelgersma (11) as the experience of decreasing tension, and unpleasantness as the experience of increasing tension. Both Freud and Jelgersma resisted the temptation to enter into physiological speculations as to the nature of this tension – a temptation to which the general psychologist has often succumbed. Thus, pleasantness-unpleasantness, is described by them as the conscious manifestation – discharge into consciousness – of decreasing or increasing tension.[4]

In the recent development of the psychoanalytic theory of emotions the conflict theory has remained a mere implication; only in Federn's (13, 14) theory of affects did it become explicit. Concerning the origin of these, Federn states:

Affects, like object-interests, issue from the relation of the ego to something that stimulates it; in the object-interests the ego enters into relationship with a libido-cathexed[5] object, in the affects with a libido cathexed process within the ego itself. . . . Affects come about between two interacting ego boundaries[6] and differ according to the kind of drive-cathexis of the ego on these boundaries . . . e.g. the affect of shame comes about when an anxiety-charged ego boundary interacts with a sexually, especially exhibitionistically, cathexed ego boundary.

4. It is important to stress this because general psychological theory as well as psychoanalytic theory disregards 'pleasant emotions' and deals usually only with the unpleasant.

5. The term 'cathexis' in psychoanalytic theory refers to an amount of psychic energy attached to the ideas of a person.

6. 'Ego boundaries' is a term coined by Federn (13) to designate a division of psychic contents into those representing the 'ego' and those representing the rest of the world. This concept of the ego is not the usual one, but we cannot discuss it here in further detail.

Sorrow comes about when an object-libido cathexed ego boundary interacts with one cathexed by destructive drives (14, pp. 13–15).

Thus, according to Federn, when two different drive-cathexes confront each other, in other words conflict, affects result.

We have seen thus far that, according to the psychoanalytic theory, the psychic processes underlying emotions are unconscious; that affects were at one time considered as psychic energies by this theory, but were later viewed as discharge processes of psychic energies; and finally, that affects were viewed as expressions of instinctual conflict.

One may ask why the conflict-origin and the discharge-character of affects are not accepted more widely, for they would seem to agree with the general dynamic conceptions of our science and with the majority of observations. One reason that they are not so accepted – namely, the unconscious character of the conflict – has been already discussed; another reason may lie in the social-patterning, or conventionalization, of emotions. Concerning this Whitehorn (17) wrote:

For a good many years I have been interested in listening to patients' accounts of their emotions. At one time I naïvely supposed that I might learn thereby just how the patient was feeling, perhaps even be able to label 'the emotions' which he was experiencing. I still listen with great interest to patient's statements along these lines, but not with the expectation of discovering what 'emotions' he or she is really experiencing – rather with the hope of understanding in some measure the conventionalized scheme of symbols by which the patient tries to represent himself to himself and to others. Not only are the words conventional symbols; the motor patterns of behavior are also conventionalized. Sometimes such conventionalized patterns of behavior and the corresponding verbalizations are used with the deliberate intention of deceiving others, but this is not the phenomenon of which I now speak. I refer to the degree of conventionality in the patterning of behavior by which one reacts overtly in an emotional experience. My own observations would lead me to believe that in ordinary living these modes of behavior commonly called 'the emotions' are the modes of reaction by which one *resolves*, and in effect, *escapes from* the essential emotionality of the experience. That is to say, 'the emotions' as we know of them empirically in the clinic and in ordinary life are the expression of sentiments in whose development there has been a large measure of cultural or conventional training (p. 263).

According to Whitehorn's observations, emotional manifestations apparently become controlled and patterned under the pressure of conventions. Brierley's (9) view that emotions are 'tension phenomena' rather than 'discharge phenomena' becomes more understandable here, for conventionalization of emotions tends not to allow discharge of them but rather to dam them up. Landauer's conclusion (15), based on psychoanalytic observations, may contribute to the understanding of this mechanism. According to him, affects which are originally time-restricted and attack-like become continuous, because their release is effected by the constant stimulation of the super-ego.[7] He derived this conclusion from studies on anxiety,[8] and maintained that this conventional 'patterning', or 'secondary release by the super-ego' of the affect, creates a hierarchy of affects ranging from the free and untamed to the intellectualized and 'patterned'. It appears that all psychic activity is accompanied by an emotional discharge of a varying degree of conventionalization.

References

1. FREUD, S., and BREUER, J., 'On the psychical mechanism of hysterical phenomena', *Collected Papers*, vol. 1, London, Internat. Psychoanal. P., 1924, pp. 24–31.
2. FREUD, S., 'The defense neuro-psychoses', *Collected Papers*, vol. 1, London, Internat. Psychoanal. P., 1924, pp. 59–75.
3. LANDAUER, K., 'Die Gemütsbewegungen oder Affekte', in Federn-Meng, *Das Psychoanalytische Volksbuch*, vol. 1, Bern, Huber, 1939, pp. 134–59.

7. He writes:
'Are the affects really reactions? In children we still see them as such. But in later life anxiety is apparently continuous in the anxious-minded, the pessimist is permanently melancholy and the cheerful man consistently buoyant. How does an isolated reaction become a continuous state? Freud has solved this problem in the theory of the affects by demonstrating the function of the super-ego in their release. He illustrated his remarks chiefly from the example of anxiety' (p. 389).

In his more recent writings he [Freud] has only added two further basic notions to this general theory of the affects. In the first place he states that moods and feelings are constantly repeated reactions to the stimuli constantly applied by the super-ego. Hence the affective process, originally restricted in time, becomes more or less continuous. His second important thesis is that an affective attack is an inherited hysterical attack . . . (p. 407).

8. See also Freud, S. (4) and (16).

4. Freud, S., *The Problem of Anxiety*, New York, Psychoanal. Quart. P., 1936.

5. Freud, S., *The Interpretation of Dreams*, in A. A. Brill (ed.), *The Basic Writings of Sigmund Freud*, New York, Modern Library, 1938, pp. 179–548.

6. Freud, S., 'The unconscious', *Collected Papers*, vol. 4, London, Hogarth, 1925, pp. 98–136.

7. Freud, S., 'Repression', *Collected Papers*, vol. 4, London, Hogarth, 1925, pp. 84–97.

8. Kulovesi, Y., 'Psychoanalytische Bemerkungen zur James–Langeschen Affekttheorie', *Imago*, vol. 17 (1931), pp. 392–8.

9. Brierley, M., 'Affects in theory and practice', *Internat. Psychoanal.*, vol. 18 (1937), pp. 256–68.

10. Freud, S., *Beyond the Pleasure Principle*, trans. C. J. M. Hubback, London, Internat. Psychoanal. P., 1922 (*Jenseits des Lustprinzips*, 1920).

11. Jelgersma, G., 'Psychoanalytischer Beitrag zu einer Theorie des Gefühls', *Internat. J. Psychoanal.*, vol. 7 (1921), pp. 1–8.

12. Freud, S., 'Formulations regarding the two principles in mental functioning', pp. 13–21, in *Collected Papers*, vol. 4, London, Hogarth, 1925.

13. Federn, P., 'Die Ichbesetzung bei den Fehlleistungen', *Imago*, vol. 19 (1933), pp. 312–38; 433–53.

14. Federn, P., 'Zur Unterscheidung des gesunden und krankhaften Narzismus', vol. 22 (1936), pp. 5–39.

15. Landauer, K., 'Affects, passions, and temperament', *Internat. J. Psychoanal.*, vol. 19 (1938), pp. 388–415; *Imago*, vol. 22 (1936), pp. 275–91.

16. Freud, S., *New Introductory Lectures on Psychoanalysis*, New York, Norton, 1933.

17. Whitehorn, J. C., 'Physiological changes in emotional states', *The Interrelationship of Mind and Body*, Baltimore, Williams and Wilkins, 1939, pp. 256–70.

8 J. Hillman

C. G. Jung on Emotion

Excerpt from J. Hillman, *Emotion*, Northwestern University Press, 1961, pp. 59–62.

Jung, like Freud, has been writing about emotional phenomena for many years and, like Freud, has no single explicit theory of emotion. Both consider it of first importance and both understand it through that system of operations called the unconscious. But where Freud was influenced in his explanation by a neurological and biological background, Jung's first views on emotion take rise in psychiatry and his association with Bleuler.

> The essential basis of our personality is affectivity. Thought and action are only, as it were, symptoms of affectivity (1, p. 42; translation mine).

But where Bleuler continued to treat emotion or affectivity as a kind of molar, quantitative and generalized event, Jung, in this same early work, showed an interest in the differentiation of this general affectivity.

> The elements of psychic life, sensations, ideas, images and feelings, are given to consciousness in the form of certain entities, which if one may risk an analogy to chemistry, can be compared to a molecule (1, p. 43).

This mention of elements, this interest in structure, shows another influence on Jung, that of Wundt.

His early work on the association experiment and the theory of complexes treated emotion – and feeling – as an energetic, quantitative charge, the formal aspect of which was the idea or molecular group of ideas. To put it simply: the 'molecule' or complex was a form of energy, or formed energy. The energy appeared as the feeling tone, or emotional tone, of a pattern of ideas. The energy of the complex was the emotional tone which could be experienced as felt value, yet this emotional tone was not separable from the way in which the ideas or memory-images were associated. In this way, the energy and the pattern were dependent upon each other, as if two aspects of the same thing. This was demonstrated by the fact that resolution of complexes freed energy.

The energetic view of emotion, in spite of this emphasis upon the formal aspect, remained the dominant theme. The emotional tone of the complex was also called 'association readiness', that is, the energetic drawing power of a complex to increase its size and strength. The energetic point of view was also furthered by correlations with physical energy by means of the psychogalvanometer. Nevertheless, just as Jung did not identify emotion and energy, he also kept distinct physical and psychic energy. He also distinguished later between feeling and emotion (affect); unlike Bleuler and Freud who did not make this distinction.[1] In this way, the concept of emotion became separated out from a host of related concepts – feeling, psychic energy, physical energy, affectivity – and came to be a concept closely related to the concept of the complex, as in his later writings where the autonomy of emotion as a distinct entity is emphasized.

As a matter of fact, an emotion *is* the intrusion of an unconscious personality. The unconscious contents it brings to light have a personal character, and it is merely because we never sum them up that we have not discovered this other character long ago. To the primitive mind, a man who is seized by strong emotion is possessed by a devil or a spirit; and our language still expresses the same idea, at least metaphorically. There is much to be said in favour of this point of view (2, pp. 19–20).

And these distinct entities appear spontaneously out of the unconscious.

1. As H. Rohracher (*Einführung in die Psychologie*, 1951, p. 441) and R. Heiss (*Allgemeine Tiefenpsychologie*, 1956, p. 243) complain, neither psychology nor psychiatry – or philosophy – has been able to achieve a simply formulated demarcation between feelings and affects. Jung agrees (at least in his earlier work, *Psychological Types*, definition 'Affect') 'that no definite demarcation exists'; nevertheless he points the way for clarifying the two concepts. Feeling is a function of consciousness; as Harms says ('A Differential Concept of Feelings and Emotions', FE 50, p. 153) '. . . Ego control effects a phenomenological differentiation between them, relegating "feelings" to the actual Ego-controlled activity and "emotions" to the Ego-uncontrolled feelings; we possess our feelings but we are possessed by our emotions.' (Affects, for him, are Ego-uncontrolled willings, while Jung uses 'affect' and 'emotion' interchangeably.)

Emotions are not 'made', or wilfully produced, in and by consciousness. Instead, they appear suddenly, leaping up from an unconscious region (2, p. 10).

Jung takes up the autonomy of emotion in another passage in relation to the formation of complexes, where emotion is conceived under *two aspects*: *energetic force and image*:

Psychologically we should say, every affect tends to become an autonomous complex, to break away from the hierarchy of consciousness, and, if possible, to drag the ego after it. No wonder, therefore, that the primitive mind sees in it the work of a strange invisible being, a spirit. Spirit in this case is the image of an independent affect, and therefore the ancients appropriately called spirits also *imagines* – images (3).

A late statement makes explicit the double view of emotion held all along: 'Affectivity, however, rests to a large extent on the instincts, whose formal aspect is the archetype' (4, p. 34).

Here, instinct is both energy and formal pattern and provides the ground – both as energy and form – for emotion. Hence, it becomes apparent why certain forms, those which are archetypal, i.e. archaic, collective, universal, are so emotionally charged and give rise to emotional reactions. These forms or images are but the formal side of instinct.

Finally, Jung adds another aspect to his views in discussing the relation of emotion to extra-sensory phenomena and synchronistic events.

... an emotional state ... alters space and time by 'contraction'. Every emotional state produces an alteration of consciousness which Janet called *abaissement du niveau mental:* that is to say there is a certain narrowing of consciousness and a corresponding strengthening of the unconscious which, particularly in the case of strong affects, is noticeable even to the layman. The tone of the unconscious is heightened, thereby creating a gradient for the unconscious to flow towards the conscious. The conscious then comes under the influence of unconscious instinctual impulses and contents. These are as a rule complexes whose ultimate basis is the archetype, the 'instinctual pattern' (4, pp. 42–3).

Jung quotes Albertus Magnus to the same effect:

When therefore the soul of a man falls into a great excess of any passion, it can be proved by experiment that it (the excess) binds things (magically) and alters them in the way it wants, and for a long time I did not believe it, but after I had read the nigromantic books and others of the kind on signs and magic, I found that the emotionality (affectio) of the human soul is the chief cause of all these things. . . . [Alb. Magn., *De Mirabilibus Mundi* (no date), quoted by Jung (4, p. 45)].

With this passage Jung points to the fascinating question of the relationship between emotion and parapsychological events. He observes that emotion as a state of relative unconsciousness is a magical kind of behaviour altering the subject-object relation. [. . .]

We are left then with the problem of explanation. Let us conceive of emotion, following the views set forth here, as an autonomous complex or unconscious partial personality having both energy and formal quality, an organized dynamism rather like a 'trait'. The emotion would be located 'in' the unconscious. But the unconscious must be taken in Jung's sense of a collective unconscious, or objective psyche of archetypal constellations which transcends the categories of inner and outer. Then the unconscious would no longer be conceptually confined within the individual and emotion would belong to the unconscious aspect of an entire situation rather than only to the individual's subjectivity.

References
1. JUNG, C. G., *Über die Psychologie der Dementia praecox*, Halle, 1907.
2. JUNG, C. G., *The Integration of the Personality*, London, 1940.
3. JUNG, C. G., 'Spirit and life', *Contributions to Analytical Psychology*, London, 1928, pp. 89–90.
4. JUNG, C. G., and PAULI, W., 'Synchronicity: an acausal connecting principle', *The Interpretation of Nature and the Psyche*, London, 1955.

Part Four Emotion as Significant Experience

Even without dynamic overtones, emotion can be conceived as a significant experience. Krueger, the founder of the Leipzig School which grew out of the Gestalt tradition, thought that feelings and emotions represent the warmth, weight and significance that makes sensory experience important for the individual. He distinguished between 'Gestalt qualities' (perceived objects and situations) and 'complex-qualities' (the feelings and emotions attached to them), and between the feelings aroused by a part (i.e. a single object) and the feelings aroused by the experience-total (the total situation). For Krueger, emotions direct experience more than behaviour. His contribution, ill understood because his style makes it difficult to follow his thought, is important because of his insistence that sensory experience is interwoven with emotion and only in this combination forms the world as we know it.

Dumas distinguishes between emotional shocks (the perception of sudden physiological changes) and emotions proper, which may be either passive or active. He denies that emotions have a dynamic aspect and ascribes the experienced impulsion to physiological excitation – without, however, investigating the connexion between these physiological changes and the emotion. Similarly, he ascribes emotional shock to the conflict between opposite tendencies without showing how the arrest of motor tendencies can arouse either an emotional experience or produce physiological change.

Klages, who developed a 'science of expression' from the perceptual emphasis of Gestalt psychology, insisted that feelings provide the necessary connexions between the self, and its receptor and effector processes. This implies an emotional dynamism, but it is directed toward emotional expression rather than action. Thus emotions seem to function parallel with instincts which alone lead to action.

9 F. Krueger

The Essence of Feeling

Abridged from F. Krueger, 'Das Wesen der Gefühle', *Arch. f.d. ges. Psychol.*, vol. 65 (1928), pp. 91–128. Translated by M. B. Arnold.

Experimental investigation has always preferred to study homogeneous perceptions, accurately bounded and organized; yet such perception is merely the result of abstraction and appears comparatively late in individual development. As often as not it is the artificial product of the laboratory, completely alienated from life. Even Gestalt psychology has tried to describe psychological events in isolation; the conceptions so formed actually veil the character of wholeness in all genuine experience and lock the door to the world of feeling.

In reality, the experience of the normal person is composed of diffuse, barely organized complexes resulting from the interplay of all organs and all functional systems. Even when we observe particular experiences, they are usually not organized according to the intellectual definition of objects and situations, or even according to the physical stimulus, physiologically mediated. The different parts of experience are never as isolated as the parts of physical matter with its molecules and atoms. Everything distinguishable in experience is interconnected, embedded within a total-whole that penetrates and envelops it.

The experience-qualities of this total-whole are the feelings and emotions. – The organized parts in this totality also have such experience-qualities (or complex-qualities) related to feelings, the more so the less distinct a part is from the whole. The earliest and most natural way in which we experience a visuo-motor situation, a change in bodily position, in which we react psychologically, is determined by such complex-qualities, that is, determined by feeling-like states. This is true also for all seeking, finding, willing, recognizing, remembering, knowing, judging – in short, for all psychological activities.

Phenomenologically, all complex-qualities have something in common: they spread over all conscious awareness; they deny indifference, they have 'warmth' or 'weight'. This is especially true for the complex-qualities attached to large part-complexes. Everything actually experienced is embedded in simultaneously experienced feelings. They penetrate these part-complexes and fill them with warmth and inwardness.

Feelings of objectless excitement, elation or ecstasy are soon transformed into less organized part-complexes, e.g. the awareness of *what* excites me, *what* I hope, seek, or fear. Conversely, one set of events, the objects of my feelings, is always related to the other set, my feelings themselves. The concept of the 'feeling-like' is needed to indicate these phenomenological relations. Our theory describes (perhaps better than other theories) what feelings are and distinguishes them from all other kinds of experience by stating that *feelings are the complex-qualities of the experienced totality.*

What has been said above indicates that feelings have universality, variability and lability, and an abundance of qualitative nuances; this agrees with the facts as found by careful, unbiased observation.

The universality of feelings. – Whether experiences are organized or diffuse, whether they are simple or complex, the totality of experience always has its own particular quality though it may be more or less distinct. The awareness of an organized whole, a Gestalt, is itself always total. Indeed, that is so even if something is experienced as utterly chaotic, diffuse and unorganized. It is true that a part must be organized, delimited, to be distinct from other experiences, but there are levels of organization within the total experience which make it possible to experience simultaneous and successive multiplicity. Still, organization may be extremely loose so that it is possible to have a completely diffuse experience. Very likely, the duration and frequency of such unorganized states decrease with increasing civilization, though the conditions for their occurrence may occur more often.

The growth of large cities with their increasing density of population and traffic creates ever new opportunities for the mass of mankind to have some common emotional experience. The larger the number of people, the more unorganized are the mental events they experience. Sacred ritual, acts of passionate devotion can easily become the product of mass suggestion. Think of the excitement produced by sports events, the emotions aroused by movies, the furor unleashed by demagogues, the elation produced by drugs. On the other hand, the enthusiasms that totally engross us and endure for years become increasingly refined with increased civilization, as, for instance, the passion for music. Surely, all these events do not lack a special experience quality! Demagogues, movie moguls and prophets see more clearly than restrictive theorists that diffuse and chaotic situations necessarily arouse the strongest emotions, well-defined experience-qualities which often contradict any non-emotional form of experience. They suppress criticism, cancel out judgement and consideration, contrast with every type of analysis. Such states are called feeling-like in every language.

Genetically, many of these emotions are primitive. They are more often found among primitive peoples, young children and animals than in educated adults. On the other hand, organized forms of experience that grow out of true culture and penetrate even the most personal perceptions are always accompanied and interwoven with feeling. Religious devotion, or a work of art can take possession of our heart and tax all our powers. These, of course, are highly differentiated emotions not easily observed in the laboratory. But it is possible to reproduce the development of emotion in abbreviated form by suitable methods and observe its regularity. This *Aktualgenese* (actual genesis) demonstrates how isolated sensations, perceptions, memories, clear ideas, firm decisions – in brief, all organized experience – split off from diffuse emotional tendencies and always remain dominated by them. These experiences always remain embedded in the emotion which fills in the gaps, as it were, and forms the common background of all experience. Emotion is the maternal origin of all other types of experience and remains their most effective support. Whenever something happens to a living being, we always find an emotional mood. When there is a change in experience, the emotion also changes, either alone or together with other experiences, determining their course. This is what is meant by the 'universality' of emotion.

The ideal of the older psychophysics: to correlate changes in experience to exactly defined physical stimuli, stems from disconnected observation and stimulus-bound analysis. Today, behaviorism has made this old ideal almost the sole principle of psychological investigation. In reality, it can never be seriously applied to psychophysical events, least of all to emotions and feeling-like states. The totality of experience (and of bodily functions) defies such analysis. No constellation of stimuli can allow the prediction that any emotion, let alone a particular emotion, will actually be aroused. However, every change in our experience can become the occasion for any kind and any intensity of emotion. On the other hand, an actually experienced emotion will colour every simultaneous experience. If that is not taken into account, every psychological investigation will go astray.

The abundance of emotional nuances. – According to the rules of experiential combination, we would expect many more complex-qualities than there are qualities of the final, unanalysable parts of the experience complex. A tone perception, a cutaneous pain, a visual figure, a thought or a decision can remain the same, whether other sensations, memories, etc., are experienced at the same time or not. In contrast, the feeling experienced simultaneously never stands 'beside' another experience as does one sensation in relation to another. Feelings and emotions are influenced by every change in the experience content and its conditions (quality, intensity, duration, etc.). Here the smallest causes may have the greatest effects.

The variability and lability of feeling. – A chord of two notes can arouse a very different feeling if a third tone is sounded at the same time. If the third tone is disturbing or unsuitable in relation to one or both of the tones, the feeling aroused by the complex can change greatly. Feelings are always related to what goes on in experience at the same time or immediately before. Think of synaesthesias, of surprising insights or sudden hunches; think of the play of imagination: they are all determined by their relation to feeling.

The determination of limen has only been applied to experience complexes for the last few years. One of the best validated results has been that our differentiation of just noticeable differences (JND) is remarkably accurate. From experimental results we can derive the law that the change in total complexes is more exactly perceived than any change in their parts. The more organized, extensive and closed these complexes are and the more important the part is for the whole, the more accurate will be the judgement of JND. Methodological difficulties have prevented thus far the study of JNDs in feeling. But the context of observation and other facts permit us to extend our conclusions in the direction required by our view of feeling. Even primitive awareness reacts more accurately on the basis of emotional sensitivity than by means of part functions. It has been observed over and over that the smallest changes in experience are felt emotionally long before the change can be exactly described. (See 5, 7, 12, 13.)

The three main characteristics of the life of feeling are interrelated. The variability and intensity of feelings, their lability and quick adaptation to a variety of conditions as compared with sensory adaptation can be regarded as the dynamic counterpart of the static abundance in qualities. Both the dynamic and static aspects of feelings are necessarily related to their universality, which accounts for the fact that they are never absent in experience, that every change of events brings about more of an emotional than a sensory change; and finally, that emotional fluctuations seem to accompany the most diverse changes in experience.

Analysis versus totality of experience. – This leads to a better understanding of the contradictory character of psychological functions, which has occupied psychological thinking for a long time and is expressed most strikingly as a conflict between 'head' and 'heart'. Passionate devotion is diminished by intellectual activity, and vice versa. Such emotional commitment loses intensity and, in fact, merges into indifference if we abstract definite currents from the experience complex, if we judge, or make clear distinctions, or analyse the pulsing emotion into its elements. The same effect occurs if attention is focused sharply, if we remember, expect, or want something definite. These facts may be formulated into a general law: every dissection of the total experience destroys the whole and is functionally in discord with it. In other words, the more a mental part function becomes dominant, the more is the functional unity of the mind endangered.

Observation of both normal and pathological facts confirms this rule and justifies our method of comparing part complexes with the experience total, and both with the organization of experience. The opposition between total experience and attention to its elements has been observed in my experiments on *Zweiklänge* (3) and

Konsonanz (5). It was found that emotional impressions can only be observed in the beginning of each experiment because the rise of partial phenomena and their after-effects soon makes the feeling unclear, weakens or destroys it.

The dominance of the whole. – It has been pointed out before that changes in any part of the experience total usually result in a change in the total-quality, particularly in feeling. Thus the smallest changes in experience can be emotionally felt even when the elements of experience cannot be localized or identified at all. Who has not experienced that a mood suddenly became dominant or was changed, often into its opposite, when something (in itself perhaps quite unimportant) had changed in his background experience? Often we discover only after long search what it was that produced the change; and in many cases we never understand just why this mood was forced on us or why it disappeared.

These cases belong in the area of reciprocal action between the experience-total and its elements. Total-qualities and part-qualities have the tendency to adapt to each other. The emotional colouring of the part-whole penetrates the total-whole; on the other hand, the quality of the whole experience always depends on the qualities and the relations of its parts, as long as there is any organization at all. Thus far, accurate observation of these interrelations has been possible only in the organized experience of part-complexes, particularly in the field of sight and hearing. When dissonance is experienced, it can be shown that there is at least one out-of-tune chord in the tonal manifold even when it is not noticed as such. Its dissonance character is transferred to the clang and penetrates the total-whole of the experience in a feeling-like manner. (See 7.)

Newer experimental studies have provided many insights into the reciprocal relations between wholes and their parts. In general, it can be said that those part-functions dominate which significantly influence the quality and structure of the total experience; in short, it is the parts most closely related to the totality that become dominant. These are contour, in the visual as well as the figurative sense, i.e. anything that closes and limits an experience complex; rhythm in the broad sense; Gestalt characteristics; in general, the type of organization. If these parts possess decided membership character in the totality, and perhaps a pleasing shape (in the field of vision), these qualities act as dominant part-contents within the momentary totality. (See 12, 13, 14.)

If, in an exceptional case, a relatively unimportant part becomes dominant for a moment, this is usually a fleeting constellation that soon sinks back into its normal relationship to the whole. More exact analysis usually shows that this part has had an intimate connexion with the total-whole from the beginning. Often this is indicated at first by a feeling-like complex-quality of something confused, out of tune, annoying, which usually results in an urge to close the contour left incomplete, to re-establish order, to supply missing details, in short, to experience the whole as a complete and stable unit. This urge toward closure supplies most of the illusions of sense and memory.

And now that we understand the experience of part-complexes and their feeling-like quality, and also the total-whole and its function, we realize that feelings are always naturally attended to. They always dominate. Even the most neglected parts of an experienced whole always remain integrated with and embedded in the simultaneous feeling. Accordingly, even the most discordant inner events are directed by the feeling aroused by them. The emotion always urges to penetrate everything that goes on in us, to quench resistance or rechannel it, and to impose its own total rhythm throughout our inner life. Emotion always fills consciousness totally, but it may quickly change its character. Emotion gives direction to all our psychological activities. Anything recognized up to now as dominant factors of our mental life: the intensity of sensation which overpowers other part-experiences, the power of the concrete and extended, the force of duration, the compulsion of custom and habit, of closure and organization, all may be seen as corollaries to our principle of the dominance of the whole and so can be understood in a unitary manner.

Durable psychophysical structures. – Of all psychological functions, the emotions clearly have the greatest importance for life. Emotions are the products of the total psychophysical state and of the totality of functions; but emotions also maintain life in its fullness and regenerate it. Indeed, it is thanks to emotion that the tiny entities we know as living beings maintain themselves as psychophysical structures in the endless whirlpool of forces in the universe and so remain alive for a few hours, a few years, a few decades.

This point of view throws new light on the fact that human beings (and probably animals also) continually strive for new experiences. They play, take risks, and flirt with intoxication, for the sake of emotionally toned and motivated experiences. Whenever possible, they want to be inundated and overwhelmed by emotion. Even the sick cling to emotional warmth in the enjoyment of their pain. To quiet their longing for a vibrant life, the young indulge in pathos and sentimentality, while brittle adults rush into senseless activities or paralyse themselves by introspective self-criticism. As Nietzsche says, 'all joys long for eternity'. This is true for all emotions, though not always to the same degree.

However, the emotional life is highly labile, even fragile. This is particularly true of those emotions which have their roots in accidental constellations, contrary to structural determination (2, 10). They do not last but continually change and are swiftly blunted, they dissolve or turn into their opposite without any possibility of control. Man is not built for a succession of moods, still less for a succession of emotional outbursts.

It is an established fact, though it has not been sufficiently considered either in research or in theory, that different kinds of emotion become blunted in different degree. Think of an amusing witticism or a slapstick comedy; and in contrast, think of an attitude full of true humour and sparkle. Humour demands a harmonious combination of many gifts of mind and heart and creates an enduring attitude that can be maintained through troubles and difficulties. In the same way, the merely sensational can easily be distinguished from enduring sentiments of friendship, from the enthusiasm of artistic and creative work. A catchy tune is amusing for a while but soon loses its appeal and may gradually become annoying. But a Bach fugue or a painting by Rembrandt never stales because we discover ever new beauties in each. Finally, emotions do not become blunted with equal ease at every stage of development. Primitive peoples and children up to the age of eight or thereabouts can go on repeating the same simple joke that would bore an adult to death.

The problems discussed here can be investigated up to a point by experimental methods. Sander, for instance, has successfully investigated the actual genesis (*Aktualgenese*) of limited structures. He not only established the genetic primacy and the phenomenological and functional dominance of feeling but gained new insights into their structural conditions.

Fundamentally, what can unify these new and promising methods of investigation is the conception of the totality of inner experience, particularly the totality of emotional experience; secondly, the totality of functional integration; and thirdly, the totality of its psychophysical structural foundation. With our carefully refined methods, we dare not fall back into old ways of thinking far removed from totality and from genetic development. Part-experiences, necessarily isolated when examined in the laboratory, are in reality always embedded in more inclusive experiential units. They are always dominated by the total-whole we have recognized as emotional.

Much more frequently than would be expected according to present-day views, highly civilized people are inclined to behave purely emotionally, to give in to passion and ecstasy – although hardly in the laboratory. Of course, they do not remain in such a state for long because it would disturb the integration of the living being. A hangover follows every indulgence, the more severe, the more developed an organism and the more civilized its environment. Deliberately induced ecstasy makes a man unfit for life and damages the organization of mind and body. In contrast, the ecstasy of art, wisdom, or religion lends strength to life and warmth to the mind. Such passions are genuine experiences, full of fire and strength. They are structurally conditioned and so promote genuine structural growth. Organized experience, permeated by strong emotions, is a biological necessity. Even the most spiritual way of living depends on the body if it is not to lose its connexion with life.

All living beings are endowed from the beginning of life with numerous inherited adjustments to regularities in their environment. These inherited constancies of the psychophysical process interweave with a variety of acquired attitudes. They also interact with historically developed dispositions such as rites, institutions, mores, etc. I call these attitudes and tendencies part-structures. Their structural integration is the constitution, the personality, or character. Their direction is never absolutely fixed or they would be torn away from the ever developing structure of the living individual. They interact with one another and with the structural whole. All these structures are plastic – even the bones and teeth, the instincts, habits, and reflexes – and are changed by the shaping, restoring, and integrating powers of the total organism, individual as well as social. In disease, physical or emotional crises, in war and revolution this organization can fall apart and be destroyed.

What threatens the enduring life structure most is the conflict of structural dispositions among themselves, which we experience in depth like other structurally conditioned experiences (9, 10). Structurally conditioned experiences are value experiences as contrasted with momentary excitements; significant emotional insights and profoundly integrative thoughts, in contrast to fleeting hunches or opinions taken over from others; and decisions based on a sense of duty or responsibility. Such structural dispositions are realized whenever the individual is strongly convinced that his whole existence and the level of development he has achieved are at stake in his action. These profoundly emotional experiences are on an entirely different and deeper level than his normal life. They are entirely different from momentary emotions which have warmth and intensity but no depth. When an experience is not determined by values and value systems, when it remains without connexion to the central aims of life, it has a curious surface character that is immediately recognized. In contrast, the depth dimension of experience expresses the functional unity of life in phenomena of profound significance. These reflect the essence of life and so indicate the developmental stage of these dispositional structures, their requisites for growth and the conditions of their decline.

Profound inner experiences depend on the polarity of feeling. All growth in depth, all reorganization of the person and of society is brought about by opposition. It requires struggle and sacrifice, deprivation and suffering. Indeed, it may happen that the heart does not remain whole in severe conflicts of duty, in bitter wrestling for eternal salvation. Some hurt may remain and not be healed during the whole of a man's life; yet he will continue in his struggle, go on growing and feel blessed in his suffering.

Limited perceptions, as we produce, change and measure them in our laboratories, have their theoretical value. Though they are surface phenomena, their rich interconnexions can yield a rich harvest on thoughtful reflection. The whole always shines through the living parts if they are observed correctly. The admirable organization even of small bits of experience with their boundary tensions, all those part-phenomena whose regularities we are beginning to suspect, must become incorporated into the developing structure of life. Science has access to these developing structures through psychological study. Here we are on the inside, can draw on our own total experience, observe and describe it, can carefully compare, manipulate and combine different experiences. What has been conscientiously observed in this way will yield willingly to accurate conceptualization. Life itself seems to demand today more urgently than ever before that some of its life forms observe psychological events psychologically. We must ponder them as whole men, clear-eyed but humble before life's mysteries.

References

1. KLEMM, O., Sinnestäuschungen. Psychologie und experimentelle Pädagogik in Einzeldarstellungen. Leipzig, 1919.

2. KRUEGER, F., 'Der Begriff des absolut Wertvollen als Grundbegriff der Moralphilosophie', Leipzig, Teubner, 1898.

3. KRUEGER, F., 'Beobachtungen über Zweiklänge', *Philosophische Studien*, vol. 16 (1900), pp. 307–79; pp. 568–663.

4. KRUEGER, F., 'Zur Theorie der Combinationstöne', *Philosophische Studien*, vol. 17 (1901), pp. 186–310.

5. KRUEGER, F., 'Differenztöne und Konsonanz', *Archiv für die gesamte Psychologie*, vol. 1 (1903), pp. 205–75.

6. KRUEGER, F., 'Beziehungen der experimentellen Phonetik zur Psychologie', *Bericht über den 2. Kongress für experimentelle Psychologie in Würzburg, 1906*, p. 65.

7. KRUEGER, F,, 'Die Theorie der Konsonanz, Eine psychologische Auseinandersetzung, vornehmlich mit C. Stumpf und Th. Lipps', *Psychologische Studien*, vol. 1 (1906), pp. 305–87; vol. 2 (1907), pp. 205–55; vol. 4 (1908), pp. 201–82; vol. 5 (1910), pp. 294–411.

8. KRUEGER, F., Über Entwicklungspsychologie', Leipzig, 1915.

9. KRUEGER, F., 'Die Tiefendimension und die Gegensätzlichkeit des Gefühlslebens', Festschrift zu Joh. Volkelts 70. Geburstag, München, 1918.

10. KRUEGER, F., Über psychische Ganzheit', *Neue Psychologische Studien*, vol. 1 (1926), p. 1. (Auch separat erschienen.)

11. SANDER, F., 'Wundts Prinzip der schöpferischen Synthese', *Beiträge zur Philosophie des deutschen Idealismus*, vol. 2 (1922), pp. 55–8.

12. SANDER, F., 'Über räumliche Rhythmik. I. Mitteilung: Experimentelle Untersuchungen über rhythmusartige Reihen und Gruppenbildungen bei simultanen Gesichtseindrücken', *Neue Psychologische Studien*, vol. 1 (1926), pp. 123–58.

13. SANDER, F., 'Optische Täuschungen und Psychologie', *Neue Psychologische Studien*, vol. 1 (1926), pp. 159–66.
14. SANDER, F., 'Über Gestaltqualitäten', Sonderdruck des *Vortrags vom 8. internationalen Psychologenkongress in Groningen, 1926*.

10 G. Dumas

Emotional Shocks and Emotions

Excerpts from G. Dumas, *La Vie Affective*, Presses Universitaires de France, 1948, pp. 63–5, 78–90. Translated by Y. Bégin and M. B. Arnold.

Emotional shocks

What is an emotional shock, from a psychological point of view? We may be glancing through the obituaries in the newspaper, reading several names with complete indifference, until we come upon the name of a friend from whom we have not heard for some time and whom we believed in good health: we experience an emotional shock. Now what was it in that name that determined the shock? It cannot be the association of ideas or their dissociation, provoked by the death of our friend. The effect we experience is more immediate: it comes from the clash of many tendencies and habitual impulses (all assuming our friend alive), with the idea of his death. This whole complex, temporarily outside our awareness, has been suddenly aroused and broken up. And the more established, co-ordinated, and profound these tendencies, the stronger is the shock.

But this definition of emotional shock, which relates it to various degrees of surprise and astonishment, can separate this shock only conceptually from the emotion that follows it. In fact, the shock so defined is almost always accompanied by a trace of the emotion about to be aroused. Accordingly, we must talk of emotional shock as it is, followed by weak or strong, well-defined or vague emotions. We propose to distinguish three categories of shock, according to the intensity of the excitation and reaction.

The first category of shock includes the weak emotional shocks in which rather unspecified and indefinite respiratory and circulatory reactions correspond to weak affective states difficult to define, and to weak and unimportant stimulations such as the sound of a door banging, the crack of a shot, a laboratory experiment about which the subject is a bit dubious, an unknown person abruptly entering a room where someone is working. For animal subjects, such weak stimuli would be a whistle call, the crack of a whip, the sound of a shot.

The second category will include more intense emotional shocks. These can and often do precede secondary affective reactions such as more or less durable emotions of joy, sorrow, anger, fear, etc., and may prolong or even provoke them. We will consider these shocks at length.

With Ribot, we may distinguish in these shocks an increase of movement or its arrest. But we believe we should insist on the fact that the emotion proper, following upon these shocks and usually mingling with them after the first instant, may last in a chronic form, reappear in imagination, and become complicated by psychological and physiological reactions. For these reasons, emotions constitute an infinitely richer and more varied object for psychological study than the emotional shock.

Moreover, it should be noted that confused or clear imaginary schemes usually come after the initial shock and before the emotion. Consequently, the origin of the emotion is not only the shock but also a more or less rapid interpretation of its cause. Finally, in many cases, for instance when the shock was expected, the emotion can be aroused via its habitual processes and channels.

The third category comprises the most intense emotional shocks in which particularly intense experiences – scenes of carnage, mortal peril, being buried by an exploding shell – give rise to disturbances in circulation, respiration, motor activity, and equilibrium, to vegetative disorders, and often to reactions of intoxication, inhibition or exhaustion. Obviously, there are emotions behind all these intense emotional shocks, but the disturbance or general inhibition they create prevents the experience of the underlying emotions in all their distinctiveness.

Accordingly, there are two categories of affective states that are poorly defined because they are either too weak or too strong. These are very weak shocks and very strong ones. But shocks of medium intensity can and often do precede emotions properly so called. [. . .]

Weak emotions facilitate organic functions but strong emotions depress them. This can be used as explanatory principle provided we are satisfied with rough approximations. Confirmation can be found in the response of heart, stomach, intestines, glands and striated muscles, and may at least be suspected in endocrine changes. In general, it seems that the organism responds to an emotional experience with excitation, depression, arrest or paralysis, depending on the intensity of stimulation. Wundt (1900) was in accord with this general law as far as the striated muscles are concerned when he wrote: 'Violent emotions produce a rapid paralysis of numerous muscle groups; and weaker emotions produce excitation which is later replaced by exhaustion' (p. 286).

Between weak stimulation which results in faster or more energetic reaction, and violent stimulation which results in depression, there is room for strong stimulation which results not only in quick and strong response in every sphere but also in disturbed and paradoxical response. In this case, the emotional excitation does not follow its usual course but instead finds its way into unused channels and produces chaotic functioning, respiratory and circulatory irregularities, motor incoordination and excessive motor or secretory stimulation. [. . .]

It need not be emphasized that emotional shock, considered from the point of view of consciousness, is no more than the complex of clear or diffuse sensations corresponding to the local or general reactions which constitute its physical manifestations. To describe psychological shock, it would suffice to enumerate and order those among the above reactions that are conscious. Certainly, many would be found that are consciously experienced, from normal breathing to laboured breathing and respiratory arrest; from the arrest, acceleration, slowing, intensification and disturbance of the heartbeat, to the contraction of the cardia, the release of rectum and *sphincter ani*; from dryness of the mouth to loss of equilibrium and collapse. An ample harvest of evidence awaits the psychologist who would care to re-create such an emotional shock mentally, to imagine and to feel it, and could use in this mental reconstruction all the objective and organic details that might throw light on this phenomenon and give it content.

But whether these facts of organic consciousness are demonstrated or not, one cannot help but note how vague and imprecise they are, though they are numerous enough; and how restricted their domain in comparison to the vast field of totally unconscious organic changes that constitute the emotional shock.

There are so many organic changes in the smooth muscles of the viscera, in the glands, the excretions, in external and internal secretions, in the humoral balance of the blood, in the nutrition of the deeper tissues, that there is not one organ, not one tissue or cellular element of the bodily economy which escapes the organic effects of emotional shocks. Because of these changes, the emotional shock is a profound and complex biological fact in which the original psychological cause merely acts as the trigger. This biological fact concerns the neuro-vegetative as well as the cerebrospinal system, and in its upper reaches barely touches our conscious life. Its analysis reveals physical, chemical, toxic troubles over and above the properly physiological difficulties.

What remains to be mentioned at the end of this discussion are the emotional reactions of shock that are the most expressive according to expert opinion. Those are necessarily the most conspicuous reactions, particularly bodily and facial expression. Vascular, cardiac or peripheral changes can become expressive, for instance a complete or incomplete loss of consciousness that comes with the arrest or slowing of the heart, or the change in colour that comes with the variation in pressure and size of the arterioles. Cutaneous vasoconstriction produces pallor, and vasodilatation produces reddening of the skin, whether these reactions are active or passive.

Reactions linked to respiration and its changes are equally expressive, depending on the extent to which they can be heard or seen. For instance, when the expulsion of the breath is interrupted it can result in noisy expiration similar to a cry of fright; when there is a laryngeal spasm, the voice becomes strangled and can give out altogether. When the diaphragm is contracted intermittently, the voice becomes broken and gasping. [. . .]

The emotions. From the series of weak, medium and strong shocks we will now select for study the medium shocks and the emotions that may follow them. [. . .]

These emotions [. . .] are complex states composed psychologically of excited, depressed, embarrassed, demented, rebellious attitudes, sometimes followed by impulsion, as happens in anger and fear, but always accompanied by organic changes. Some of these changes seem to be localized, others diffuse; the corresponding conscious state may, accordingly, be pleasurable, painful, or a mixture of both.

This sensory and affective complex is not necessarily, as Ribot would have it, an 'organized' reaction of the affective life, for there are depressive emotions, for example certain sorrows and certain fears, in which the organization is weak if not absent altogether; on the other hand, emotions characterized by great excitement, as for instance certain joys, angers and fears, tend toward disorganization by their very nature. Despite these reservations it seems to us that each emotion represents an organic and psychological whole with a certain individuality and a certain psychological colouring – notwithstanding the diversity and often instability of its constitutive elements. Each emotion can be analysed as a whole, provided we do not let ourselves be deceived by the rigidity imposed on facts by language, and provided we do not elevate emotions to the status of entities.

According to André Lalande (1948), the affective states called emotion must be static, that is, any tendency toward a goal, toward action or the direction of action, must be excluded. We agree, and suggest that fear is an emotion because it is not a tendency to flee; and anger, because it is not an aggressive tendency – despite its violent disturbance expressing revolt or indignation.[1] This type of confusion has resulted in the mistaken notion of some psychologists who have thought that emotions are nothing but the affective aspect of particular instincts like the instinct of flight, aggression, repulsion or curiosity (see McDougall, p. 42ff.), and who thus have been obliged to exclude joy and sorrow from the list of emotions.

To account for the chronological sequence in the individual development of emotions, Ribot (1896) has distinguished five basic emotions: fear, anger, tender emotion, egoistic emotion, and sexual emotion. And he has asked a question which we would like to take up, particularly because we do not offer the same solution. He says:

Should joy and sorrow be considered as basic and specific emotions, comparable to fear and anger? One might be inclined to say so. Thus Lange [1895] has included them among the four or five simple emotions

1. Let us specify that the term 'static' is to be understood as the distracted or rebellious response of fear or anger, to the extent that these responses do not contain goal-directed impulses.

he has selected as typical and described. But I think the following reasons can be offered against that solution. No doubt joy and sorrow show every characteristic of emotion: movements and cessation of movement, organic changes and a state of consciousness that is *sui generis*. But if they are emotions, physical pleasure and physical pain must also be included among emotions, for they show some of the same characteristics. Moreover, there is an identity of nature between physical pleasure and joy on the one hand, physical pain and sorrow on the other. The only difference is that the emotion in its physical form follows an organic state, while in its mental form (joy, sorrow) it follows upon an image. In other words, it would be necessary to classify pleasure and pain – without qualification or restriction – among the basic and specific emotions. But these alleged emotions are obviously completely different from those discussed previously because of their character of generality. Fear is quite distinct from anger, tender emotion from egoistic emotion, and sexual emotion from the other four, by virtue of the specific character of each. Each emotion is a complex state, closed, impenetrable, independent, in the same way as sight is different from hearing, or touch from smell. Each of them expresses a particular tendency (defensive, aggressive, an attraction to something similar) and is organized in a particular pattern. In contrast, pleasure and pain express general conditions of existence; they diffuse and penetrate everywhere. There is pain in fear, in certain moments of anger and egoistic emotion; there is pleasure in sexual emotion, in certain moments of anger and egoistic emotion. These two states do not have a proper domain. By nature, emotion is particular, pleasure and pain are universal. Those are the reasons that prevent us from classifying pleasant and painful states as basic emotions (pp. 15–16).

On this page of our regretted master there are a few statements we would like to discuss so as to prevent confusion in the description and analysis that is to follow.

In the first place, Ribot, who favoured the notion that emotions are the affective aspect of tendencies, that anger is the instinct of self-preservation in its aggressive aspect, and fear the same instinct in its defensive aspect, would have been embarrassed by a classification of sorrow and joy (so devoid of any dynamic aspect) together with the other emotions. This, no doubt, is the *a priori* reason for excluding them. In the more specific reasons he develops he does not seem to distinguish sufficiently between pleasantness and unpleasantness on the one hand, and pleasure and pain on the other; and finally, between these and joy and sorrow.

We have mentioned before in what way the modalities of pleasantness and unpleasantness differ from the acute affective reactions of pleasure and pain with which they are generally but not necessarily associated, for certain pains are pleasant and certain pleasures can be unpleasant. Neither can pleasure and pain be confused with joy and sorrow. Even though our joys and sorrows, representing the response to tendencies that are in conflict, dissociated or readapted, have an organic repercussion, these pleasant or painful reactions cannot in any way be compared to pleasantness and unpleasantness. Elementary modalities cannot be identified with complex sensory and affective states like sorrow and joy.

No doubt there are joys and sorrows with a simple sensory and motor content that are very similar to the basic affective modalities. However, it is easy enough to distinguish the pleasure experienced on seeing a beautiful landscape from real joy, and the annoyance caused by hearing bad music from real sorrow. Paulhan (1887) says,

We may find the periwinkle a pretty flower, and the sight of it may arouse a certain not very keen pleasure; but Rousseau's [1898] cry on finding a periwinkle again, and the emotions this flower aroused, reveal affective phenomena very different from simple affective sensations (pp. 83–4).

It is not even possible to use diminutives for joys and sorrows to indicate experiences of this order. In cold fact, simple modalities cannot be confounded with complex reactions in which these modalities are but elements in the interplay of various tendencies. Indeed, the linkage between these modalities and emotions is loose at best, for there are pleasant melancholies as well as pleasant pains.

Pleasantness and unpleasantness are found in anger and fear, and in other passionate or emotional states. But sorrow and joy, pleasure and pain, as we have analysed them, are never found in those emotions. Only pleasantness and unpleasantness have the characteristic of generality (one could almost say with Ribot, of abstraction) that is never found in pleasure and pain. Joy and sorrow are emotions as specific and individualized as any other emotion.

To distinguish joy and sorrow from anger, fear, and from Ribot's other specific emotions, we could point out that joy and sorrow, instead of being linked to definite tendencies, as is anger or sexual emotion, simply accompany the interplay of our many and varied tendencies and spell out their triumph or failure; hence their greater frequency and less specialized character. On this topic, Larguier des Bancels (1921) has well said: 'While emotions like anger or fear have their origin in precise conditions and respond to strictly defined tendencies, joy and sorrow find at each moment and in the most varied circumstances an opportunity to manifest themselves. Perhaps there are men who have never felt anger or fear. But there are none who do not know sorrow or joy.' And he concludes, as we do, that sorrow and joy are reactions as typical and as specific as anger and fear.

And now we may ask, what is the psychological and physiological nature of these special responses we call emotions, which are always to some extent mixed with pleasantness and unpleasantness? [. . .]

There is a widely held opinion among physiologists that emotions can be distinguished better by bodily and facial expression than by vegetative changes. Some physiologists go so far as to insist that none of these changes can be considered characteristic for a particular kind of emotion. Hallion (1909), for instance, writes:

Cardiac and vasomotor reactions which I have studied intensively with Charles Comte are similar in every case. The same seems to be true, or at least very nearly so, of respiratory changes, explored carefully by a good many authors. To sum up, the observations on this topic and the very fact of contradictions among researchers give evidence of the inconsequentiality of most emotional reactions when expression is disregarded (p. 1560).

This is an important psychological and physiological question, which raises the problem of the nature of emotion and its organic or central conditions. We hope to provide at least some answers.

Since we will use the notions of excitation and depression constantly [. . .] we have to define them. We will speak of excitation, either in the psychological or organic order, whenever there is a change from minus to plus, that is, when ideas are more numerous, associations are faster, the affectivity richer; when motor reactions are more energetic, the pulse beat is quickened and strengthened, when respiration increases in depth or in speed, when secretions are increased, etc. We will speak of depression whenever there is a change from plus to minus in the reactions of our physiological or psychological organism. The norm used will be the habitual state of the organism rather than some abstract and general mean. However, without deviating from our general definition we shall have to distinguish between many forms of depression, from the depression resulting from inhibitory stimulation to that resulting from exhaustion or the reduction of habitual stimuli.

As excitation increases, it may happen that it can no longer be confined within its habitual pathways so that it comes close to disorganization in the physical as well as in the psychological sphere. But we do not consider it necessary to create a new term, such as agitation, which is sometimes used to indicate such a change; this would imply that the excitation changes its nature. It is sufficient to state that excitation may be organized or disorganized, depending on its intensity. These are purely quantitative definitions, the only ones that can be applied to excitation and depression. We will attempt to distinguish different modalities according to the emotions involved. But it is important to note that the initial definition calls only for very simple quantitative considerations of plus and minus.

Almost every expert in emotion, psychologist and physiologist alike, has used the notions of excitation and depression as above defined in attempting to classify emotions. Hallion himself has used this general division, despite his opinion as to the triviality of emotional changes. Darwin (1877) wrote that there are exciting emotions of which joy and anger are the most important, and depressing emotions among which he ranks sorrow and fear. This classification would be debatable if Darwin had not drawn on the notion of excitation and depression by admitting that there could be active joy and passive joy, depressed sorrow and excited sorrow, fear that excites and fear that paralyses; he had even seen that anger can be inhibitory or excitatory. But apart from the fact that he gave no physiological explanations, he did not draw the implications from his distinction that could further a psychophysiology of emotion. Indeed, he has made this distinction rather summarily and has seen neither its importance nor its general applicability.

What we call the active form of emotion is the form expressed in excitatory reactions. The most important of these is the excitation of the sympathetic nervous system. Its principal signs are, according to Cannon (1929), cardiac acceleration, hypertension, increase of tonus, horripilation, mydriasis, etc. These active forms are the ones to which the term emotion is most frequently applied because the motor element is always present and positive. These emotions come to mind when the psychologist is looking for a definition of emotion.

What we call the passive form of emotion is the form characterized by depressive reactions such as hypotonus, cardiac slowing, arterial hypotension. On the whole, these changes occur in the reverse direction from the preceding ones. It must now be decided whether the term emotion is appropriate for depressive reactions; we have adopted the view that it is, because the motor element seems to have the same importance whether it is expressed in negative or positive changes.

References

CANNON, W. B. (1929), *Bodily Changes in Pain, Hunger, Fear and Rage*, 2nd edn., Appleton.

DARWIN, C. (1877), *L'Expression des Émotions chez l'Homme et les Animaux*, trans. Pozzi et Benoit, Reinwald & Cie.

HALLION, L. (1909), 'De l'émotion. Problèmes Physiologiques', *Rev. Neur.*, vol. 2.

LALANDE, A. (1948), *Vocabulaire technique et critique de la Philosophie*, vol. 1, Presses Universitaires de France.

LANGE (1895), *Les Émotions*, trans. G. Dumas, Alcan.

LARGUIER DES BANCELS, J. (1921), 'Introduction à la psychologie', *L'Instinct et l'Émotion*, Payot.

MCDOUGALL, W. (1908), *An Introduction to Social Psychology*, Methuen & Co.

PAULHAN, F. (1887), *Les Phénomènes Affectifs et les Lois de leur Apparition*, Alcan.

RIBOT, Th. (1896), *La Psychologie des Sentiments*, Alcan.

ROUSSEAU, J. J. (1898), *Les Confessions*, Barbier.

WUNDT, W. (1900), 'Bemerkungen zur Theorie der Gefühle', *Philosophische Studien*, vol. 15.

11 L. Klages

The Life of Feeling

Excerpts from L. Klages, *Grundlegung der Wissenschaft vom Ausdruck*, Bouvier, 1950, pp. 61–7, 160–4; 6th edn, 1964. Translated by M. B. Arnold.

Perception of objects and so-called feeling tone. The participation of the perceiver may be different in degree, but is always essential to the production of impressions. Up to now it has been called 'feeling tone' and was supposed to 'accompany' the perception of an object and determine its value. Seen from this point of view, the origin of perception seems to be discoverable apart from its 'feeling tone'; and the so-called feeling tone seems to be an event produced in the perceiver by the finished perceptual picture, an event that does not correspond to anything in reality.

True, it is possible to distinguish the so-called feeling tone from the so-called stimulus. It is also true that there must be a stimulus when there is a feeling tone. Yet this view [. . .] is based on three errors: in the first place, stimulus and feeling are assumed to be separable. Secondly, the significance of the so-called feeling tone for the organization of the impression itself is neglected. And finally, reality is determined in a completely erroneous way. We [. . .] will content ourselves at this time to discuss the participation of the perceiver's life situation in the perception – which happens because every psychological change in the perceiver results in a change in perception.

The same section of the world will develop a different aspect, for the human being as well as for the animal, depending on whether the perceiver is young or old, healthy or sick, hungry or sated, rested or tired; whether he is male or female; whether he seeks or flees, hunts, fights, or plays; whether he is in a state of anticipation or indifference, fear, joy, or depression. Finally, it depends also on the kind and degree of the vital processes aroused in the past by this particular situation or similar perceptions.

In the little book *Streifzüge durch die Umwelten von Tieren und*

Menschen [. . .] Üxküll describes how the anticipation of an object in a certain place, the so-called 'anticipation picture' can obliterate the perception of an object really present (the memory picture) or change it into the object looked for. When Üxküll was a house guest in a friend's house, he used to find an earthen pitcher with water at his place on the dinner table. One day the butler put a glass carafe there instead. 'When I looked for the pitcher at dinner,' writes Üxküll, 'I didn't see the glass carafe. It was not until my friend assured me the water was there that various highlights dispersed over knives and plates collided in the air and combined to a glass carafe. . . . The anticipation picture obliterates the memory picture.' The opposite case is exemplified by a hungry toad which picked up a match stick after ingesting an earthworm. However, 'if it has just eaten a spider, another anticipation picture is present, for now it snaps up a bit of moss or an ant, and does not like it at all.' [. . .]

Anyone who has become used to this way of looking at things finds so many supporting pieces of evidence that he is surprised ever to have thought differently. An embarrassing encounter, a depressing period of life, falling in love, will significantly change the picture of the places where these events happened. When a murder was done in a room, there won't be many who know about it and would want to live there right afterwards, even though they are not aware of superstitious fear. And who would deny that the contrast of far and near [. . .] divides all perceptions into two classes of significance which reflect not only two opposing types of experience but also two opposing systems of motivation! Far places attract the man who likes to travel, his neighbourhood the homebody. The one flees the familiar and sees foreign countries at the price of security; the other flees the unfamiliar and finds in familiar places and things the warmth and security he needs. Only those blind to life could deny that the perceptual worlds of these two men are as different from each other as the unknown is different from the known. Actually, the mere mention of this contrast is enough to uproot the so-called naturalistic theory of perception, for no other contrast between perceptual facts shows such an essential opposition as does the known and the unknown. Banal though it may be, the proverb that 'the burnt child fears the fire' is true literally and figuratively. But consider: when the as yet unburnt child, full of anticipation, tries to grasp the flame, does he see the same flame the burnt child sobbingly runs away from? Must not the picture of the flame itself have changed after its significance has changed into its opposite, at least in one respect? Everybody knows that experienced people see the world differently from those inexperienced, but few realize that, in consequence, the world of the experienced must be different from the world of the inexperienced.

Primitive and advanced human perception [. . .] The animal perceives within its species-specific sphere everything that lives and moves. It perceives only those pictures that either enhance or threaten it. But even the primitive human being perceives everything for which he has receptor organs. In every picture, not only in those that promise weal or woe but in indifferent ones as well, he finds things that express themselves and, as it were, speak to him. Like the animal, he sees a world of significant units. But because these are no longer complementary to instincts, but throughout are pictures filled with life and value (as are those correlated with drives) his sensory world reaches far beyond the animal horizon and is filled with life of every kind and degree. His experiences with this world are as numerous as the events and happenings he can encounter in it. Moreover, since he perceives what lives and moves by virtue of his animal nature, and his horizon goes far beyond that of the animal, he must be able to perceive and recognize vegetative life as well as the whole inorganic realm. This new level of perception, so vast compared to the limited world of organic structures, now incorporates this small world and changes it profoundly. [. . .]

We have demonstrated that perception (including the experiences that enable the unicellular animal to respond appropriately to changes in the environment) is the combined product of two processes: sensory experience and vision. Sensory experience is an experience of resistance, permits only quantitative differences, and forms the basis of the experience of intensity and, in man, of comparison. Since it connects the perceiver only with things close by, sensation is blind and might as well not exist without vision. Only the combination of sensation and vision gives perceptual character to sensory impressions.

Vision also, though deeply rooted, needs the cooperation of sensory experience. If we define vision as seeing pictures, and understand it as including the occurrence of such pictures, then we have added a quality to perception which prevents confusing it with the perceiver. We distinguish two stages in the process of vision: the union with the event and the detachment from it, so that the event becomes visible as the appearance of an active object. While the mechanical process is merely the distinguishable link of a regular chain of events and never transcends the event, the function of detachment transforms the vital process (in man, in microbes, in the cells of the living body) into an experience of reception, and transforms the acting object into a reality that is connected with the perceiver yet does not occur in him but independently of him, and outside him. [. . .]

We know that there is no receptor process without an effector process, no effector process without a receptor process; there is no reception without reaction, no reaction without reception. The passive vision corresponds to active imaginative creation, the passive sensation corresponds to overt action (motivated by instinct). Since living polarities are never mirror reflections but always unsymmetrical, we can use this as a clue to the decisive difference between animal and man. In the whole animal world, vision is determined by sensation, distant fields by near-by objects, the picture of changing appearances by the picture of bodies in motion, and in the effector area, action by instinct. Accordingly, the moving animal body is really the embodiment of instinctual systems. As we move from unicellular animals [. . .] to birds and mammals, we notice an increase in the power of vision with a simultaneous decrease in the influence of sensation, until we could imagine a species that would come close to the point where sensation and vision would be in equilibrium. But there never is true equilibrium. As soon as it would be achieved it is transcended: even in primitive man, sensation is determined by vision, the near-by by the far distant, the picture of the moving body by the picture of changing appearances, instinct at first by magic, and later by creativity. This change is accompanied by the increasing dominance of sight and hearing over smell and touch.

On the essence of feeling [. . .] Feeling and emotion play a similar role in psychology as do hormones in biology because both connect different processes, or rather, different aspects of a single life process. On this basis, we will risk a schematic figure to facilitate the discussion. In Figure 1, the different aspects of the life process are indicated by different points: at left is the bodily aspect of the individual with the centres of receptive sensory experience (E) and the effector drive (D). At the right, the psychological aspect of the individual with the centres of receptive vision (V) and the

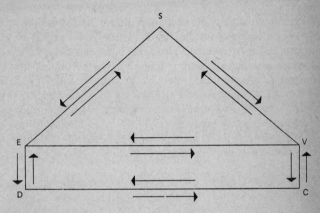

Figure 1

effector process of creativity (C). The point S is the self, the individual. The connecting lines with arrows going in opposite directions indicate the feeling aspect of life. (For the sake of simplicity, the connecting lines between S and D on the one side, and between S and C on the other have been omitted.) [. . .]

What is 'real' for the human being was originally on the outside and only much later inside the self. But the individual experiences the outside immediately via E and V, and mediately via C because drive without creativity would be impotent. And he deals with the outside as personal self on the basis of his vitality, thus always mediately; on the receptor side through a group of perceptual acts, on the effector side through a group of voluntary decisions. If the connexion between self and vital centres were sundered, the self would be deprived of reality. If the connexion between the vital centres themselves were broken, the vital unit would fall apart. It follows first of all that feelings and emotions are not only extraordinarily important but, indeed, absolutely necessary for the experience of reality. Secondly, it means that reality has affected the individual via V and E in connexion with D and C, to make it possible for feeling to 'respond' and often to dominate. Since the aspect of the inner life indicated by V and C has been lost in modern theories, it has been held erroneously that feelings are subjective. [. . .]

Seen from the psychological point of view, the individual is a microcosm. Seen as body, he is part of the universe. As part of the universe he has two different possibilities of living: either he gives in to innumerable temptations and disturbances from outside or he isolates himself as far as possible. As a universe in himself, a microcosm, he also has two possibilities: he can participate in the universe outside, or live within his own microcosm. According to our scheme, both possibilities imply that V is dominant, but in the one case it ranges far afield, in the other it remains stationary. In both alternatives, the depth of feeling is overemphasized. [. . .]

If the connexions of S with E and V are excluded (which represent the subjective aspect of feeling) it is clear that the individual will seem determined by his inner activities, living more in himself than in his environment, at least to the extent that feelings and emotions dominate E and V. Moreover, if the psychological aspect is emphasized as against the biological (whether through egoistic V or through pathological C), feeling will be dominated by mood qualities. If the bodily aspect is emphasized, feeling will be dominated by excitement. But whether a person is dominated by the mood of objectless depression or the enraged excitement caused by some object, he always lives more in himself than in his environment because in his depression he does not see things that might please him if he were calm, and because in his 'blind' rage he risks acting against his better intentions. Such are the examples that were used to validate the subjectivity of feeling. But we know why experience in itself need not mean experience for itself; and that the intensity of our feeling of reality depends entirely on the imaginative content of our inner life – we could say, on its world vision.

This intimacy of experience, which is the essence of feeling and distinguishes it from sensation and vision, will prevent us from trying to localize feelings. It follows that emotional expression (in contrast to instinctive action) has its aim in itself so that all expression is emotional expression. If we make the fantastic assumption that the aspect called feeling or emotion could be separated from all other states of the individual without lethal effect, we would find that such an individual would have no expression of any kind. His instinctive impulses would be no more than reflex movements, and his reflex movements would really not be reflexes but mechanical motions.

All joy implies an impulse toward opening of the self; all sorrow, an impulse toward retrenchment, closing the self off from the outside. To characterize both impulses we could now postulate an inclination toward the environment as characteristic for joy, and a turning away from it as characteristic for sorrow. Of course, there is no doubt that these aims are far more abstract than any instinctive aim because an instinct always results in approach to its natural object or withdrawal from it. Also, it is clear that even such general conditions would permit a great variety of expressive tendencies. Strictly speaking, an inclination toward the environment is different from approach, and a turning away from it, different from withdrawal. Thus an inclination toward and turning away from something could result in all manner of attitudes [. . .] but never in moving toward or away from it. [. . .]

Whether we consider in the impulsion of joy more the opening of the self or the inclination toward the outside, the wave of impulse rolls outward in a way which permits us to speak of a giving of the self, a diffusion of the self, and, when the impulsion is stronger, of a prodigality of self-giving. And whether we consider in the impulsion of sorrow more the self closing itself off or the self's withdrawal from the outside, in every case there is not only a paralysis of self-giving but a resistance of the self to such giving. This is true for all individuals, animals as well as human beings. But it is only a short step further to speak of a person's diffusion of self as a gift of self, and thus to define the aim inherent in joy as an urge to give. The opposed aim in the case of sorrow would not be an impulse to take or collect; it could only be defined negatively as an unwillingness to give. This, however, would involve only one possible result of the impulse to turn away from things.

Certain opposing motives of action are facilitated in opposite ways by joy and sorrow. Happiness leads to prodigality and displeasure to miserliness. When filled with joy, even the miser will forget to count pennies; and the prodigal will start to count them when he is depressed. [. . .] Every other kind of acquisitiveness, like the desire for power or superiority, ambition and vanity, the need to be important, they all are reduced by enduring joy and increased – not by sorrow which has some depth dimension – but by discontent which is essentially a surface phenomenon.

Part Five Emotion as Hypothetical Construct

A behaviouristic point of view makes it imperative to explain behaviour without recourse to conscious experience: emotion becomes emotional behaviour. This has its disadvantages because emotional behaviour is not always easy to distinguish from unemotional behaviour, especially on occasions when the individual is ill, delirious, or under the influence of drugs. Duffy tries to explain emotional behaviour as intense activation – but drugs also may produce intense activation, and so does strenuous exercise. Neither the problem of defining emotional behaviour nor the problem of explaining it is advanced by this expedient. Duffy has published several articles on this topic, which are included in her reference list. More recently, she has published a book in which the general implications of 'activation theory' are exhaustively discussed (Duffy, 1962).

Hebb is willing to use the term emotion if it is understood as a hypothetical construct with no experiential content. True to his objectivist premises, he explains emotion as incompatibility between phase sequences – a reduction of psychological facts to physical facts. This notion links his theory to earlier theories of emotion as disturbance. Hebb is best known for his book *The Organization of Behavior* (1949), which established him as a theorist of note. He has also published several excellent articles on his work with chimpanzees in the Yerkes colony in Florida, particularly on fear (quoted in his reference list).

References
DUFFY, E. (1962), *Activation and Behavior*, Wiley.

12 E. Duffy

An Explanation of 'Emotional' Phenomena without the Use of the Concept 'Emotion'

E. Duffy, 'An explanation of "emotional" phenomena without the use of the concept "emotion",' *J. gen. Psychol.*, vol. 25 (1941), pp. 283–93.

For many years the writer has been of the opinion that 'emotion', as a scientific concept, is worse than useless. In 1934, in an article published in the *Psychological Review*, she examined the various types of definition of emotion offered by psychologists and reached the conclusion that no one of these types of definition succeeded in describing a state or response pattern of the organism different in *kind* from other states or response patterns (3). 'Emotion' apparently did not represent a separate and distinguishable condition. Each definition purporting to describe such a distinguishable condition succeeded in describing, not a difference in *kind* of response, but merely a difference in the *degree* to which certain characteristics of response were manifest. Nor was there any criterion by which to determine *what particular degree* of a certain characteristic should be called 'emotion' and what degree should be called 'non-emotion'. Instead, the phenomena described appeared to occur in a continuum, or rather in a number of continua, since more than one aspect of behavior was involved in the description of 'emotion', and there was no indication as to what points on the continua represented the transition from 'non-emotion' to 'emotion'. The concept 'emotion' apparently referred to the extremes of certain continua of response, but it implied, not continuous variation in these phenomena, but a sharp break between 'emotion' and 'non-emotion'. In fact, 'emotion' was supposed to follow different principles of action from 'non-emotion'. The writer contended that the concept 'emotion' should be abandoned and the phenomena loosely referred to by this term should be studied in their own right as separate aspects of response occurring in continua rather than in discrete categories.

But, alas, the concept 'emotion' has not been abandoned.

Psychologists remain convinced that the term refers to a distinguishable category of response, and they persevere in the attempt to give this category more adequate definition. The descriptions of 'emotion' which have appeared since 1934 differ in no significant respects from those which had appeared prior to that time. The reading of these definitions has left the writer with a sentiment similar to that expressed by William James in regard to the classificatory descriptions of the separate emotions – that he 'should as lief read verbal descriptions of the shapes of the rocks on a New Hampshire farm as toil through them again'. Yet if psychologists continue to believe that 'emotion' exists there must be some reason for their belief. And the reason must be one which is not affected by the demonstration of the inadequacy of our present definitions of 'emotion'. That inadequacy merely spurs them to renewed efforts to describe in a satisfactory manner a category of response whose existence they do not question.

One reason for the well-nigh universal belief in 'emotion' is that every man has experienced a vivid, unforgettable condition which is different from the ordinary condition in which he finds himself. It may be more pleasant or more unpleasant, but it appears to have a unique quality which differentiates it from the general run of his experience. To this condition he gives the name 'emotion', and it would take more than the arguments of a misguided psychologist to convince him that he does not experience that which he knows so well he does experience. Hence, if a psychologist wishes to question the concept 'emotion' it is not sufficient that he show the inadequacies of the concept; he must offer in addition some explanation of the experiences which have been called 'emotion'. He must show that these experiences, which appear to be unique, are in fact merely manifestations in extreme degree of phenomena which are of very general occurrence, and which follow the same principles of action throughout the continua of their occurrence, rather than different principles of action during the condition called 'emotion'. To that task I now address myself.

The experience which is labelled 'emotion' is the conscious aspect of a response, or group of responses, which the individual makes to a stimulating situation which he interprets as having marked significance for himself, favorable or unfavorable. I think it will be agreed that the individual does not experience 'emotion' except in situations which are of significance to him. He is 'afraid' or 'angry' when he is threatened, or when his progress toward an important goal is blocked. He is 'joyful' or 'elated' when his progress toward an important goal is facilitated. Hence, 'emotion' is the individual's response to situations which promise well or ill for the attainment of his goals. The term refers to how the individual *feels* and how he *acts* when his *expectations* in regard to a situation are that it will, or it will not, permit him to reach some rather strongly desired goal. The strength or intensity of the 'emotion' is roughly proportional to the degree of importance of the particular goal to the individual, and to the degree of threat or of promise which the present situation bears with reference to that goal. However, it must be emphasized that the response of the individual, or the 'emotion' he manifests, is that which is appropriate to the situation as *he interprets it*, not that which would be appropriate to the situation in the opinion of other individuals. The 'emotional' response of the neurotic or the psychotic, for example, is frequently too much or too little for the situation as it is generally interpreted, but it is no doubt appropriate to the situation as it is viewed by the individual making the response. It follows, then, that the 'emotion' experienced in a given situation depends upon the nature of the individual's goals and upon the background of experience and quality of insight which he brings to bear upon the interpretation of the situation. Older children, for example, fear situations which younger children do not fear (6). Their expectations in regard to these situations are different.

Starting from the proposition that 'emotion' represents an adjustment of the individual, or a response to the stimulating situation as the individual interprets it, we may ask what are the characteristics of the response or adjustment which is called 'emotion'. In the first place, emotion represents a change in the *energy level*, or degree of reactivity, of the individual. The excited individual has an energy level which is higher, and the depressed individual an energy level which is lower, than that which he ordinarily experiences. By 'energy level' I refer to the degree of mobilization of energy within the organism, which Cannon (1) found to be very high during the excited 'emotions'; or to what Freeman (5, p. 326) has defined as 'the general organic background (neuro-glandular-muscular) which operates to sustain and energize overt phasic response'. Change in energy level appears to be the most characteristic feature of the condition called 'emotion'. It occurs as an adjustment to the stimulating situation. Situations which are interpreted as threatening or thwarting are characteristically responded to with increased energy, for by means of this increased vigor of response the individual may, in spite of difficulties, be able to reach his goal. Such vigorous response is frequently observed in 'fear' or 'anger'. Increase in the energy level of response is observed also, though perhaps to a lesser degree, in 'joy', for 'joy' is the response made when the situation suddenly changes, or is interpreted to change, in such a way that progress toward the goal is facilitated. Under these circumstances the individual either actually or imaginatively moves quickly forward to the attainment of his goal. The phenomenon is similar to that observed when the rat in the maze moves more quickly through the alleys at the end of his route and nearest to the food box, or when the human subject works most rapidly on the last of a group of problems which he must solve. The *energy level* of the individual's responses *increases*, then, both when progress toward his goal is blocked and when barriers to his progress are suddenly removed.

Under what circumstances do we find, not an increase, but a decrease in *energy level*? Characteristically, I believe, when the individual is making no attempt, or almost no attempt, to reach a goal. Such is the situation found in depression. When an individual's progress toward a goal is completely blocked by some circumstance which he interprets as an insuperable obstacle, he ceases to be active in relation to that goal. We say that he has 'given up', or that he is 'resigned', or that he is in a 'depressive stupor', depending upon the degree of departure of his activity level from that which is usual. This lack of responsiveness, this low energy level, may persist for a considerable length of time and may affect the individual's responses to other goals which are not in themselves unattainable. Because the individual has given up hope of reaching some highly desired goal, other goals have lost their appeal. There is no longer sufficient 'motivation' for normally vigorous action.

But we do not always find clear-cut instances of either striving with great effort to reach a goal or sinking into almost complete inactivity in relation to all goals. Sometimes the picture is confused. In agitated despair, for example, the individual has given up all hope of reaching a particular highly desired goal, but he has not become inactive. His energy level is high. In this case the blocking of progress toward a goal of primary importance has resulted, not in lack of interest in all other goals, but in great compensatory activity, as seen, for example, in attempts at revenge or suicide. This example and the others which we have cited illustrate the principle that the energy level of the individual will be high or low depending on whether he is or is not attempting to reach goals of great importance to him, or, in other words, according to the degree to which he is motivated.

But *all* behavior is motivated. Without motivation there is *no activity*. The conditions to which we give the name 'emotion' represent merely unusually high or unusually low degrees of motivation and consequently unusually high or unusually low levels of energy. We have no criterion, however, by which to determine whether a given energy level is high enough or low enough to be called 'emotion', and it would not be useful to employ such a criterion if we had it unless it could be shown that energy levels high enough or low enough to be called 'emotion' result in behavior different in *kind*, and not merely in *degree*, from that resulting from levels of energy intermediate between these extremes. The responses called 'emotional' do not appear to follow different principles of action from other adjustive responses of the individual. Changes in internal or external conditions, or in the interpretation of those conditions, always result in internal accommodations. The responses made are specifically adjustive to the situation and are not subject to classification into such categories as 'emotional' and 'non-emotional'. An example of this fact may be seen in some studies of the maintenance of the blood sugar level made by Silvette and Britton (8). It was demonstrated that changes which occur in the blood stream may be induced by any of a number of factors which affect the essential equilibria of the organism – by 'emotion', by intense physical activity, or by a change in temperature. There is no reason to conclude that the blood sugar changes occurring when the organic equilibrium was disturbed by so-called 'emotional' stimuli were any different from those occurring when the same degree of disequilibrium was produced by physical activity or exposure to cold.[1] All responses – not merely 'emotional' responses – are adjustive reactions attempting to adapt the organism to the demands of the situation. The energy level of response varies with the requirements of the situation as interpreted by the individual. Diffuse internal changes (especially in the viscera) are involved in the production of these changes in energy level. But continuous visceral activity, with accompanying changes in energy level, is a function of life itself, not merely a function of a particular condition called 'emotion'. We have in fact a continuum of response which has been artificially broken into the categories, 'emotional' and 'non-emotional'.

A second characteristic of 'emotional' responses is that they are frequently, if not usually, disorganized. The angry or fearful individual often fumbles in his movements and is confused in his thinking. His speech is frequently incoherent. The depressed individual, too, may manifest incoordination in speech, thought, and movement. However, disorganization of response is a function, I believe, not of a unique state or condition called 'emotion', but a function, though not an invariable one, of any behavior which occurs at a very high or a very low energy level. Since the term 'emotion' is applied to much of the behavior which occurs at high or low levels of energy, disorganization of response has appeared to be a distinguishing feature of 'emotion'. We have on record, however, a number of instances in which 'emotion' has been accompanied by no disorganization of response, and a number of instances in which disorganized responses have occurred under conditions not ordinarily called 'emotional'. Stratton (9), for example, has reported a case in which the 'emotion' aroused in a man by the sight of the flaming bathrobe of his niece caused him to think and to move with extraordinary speed and effectiveness. The heightened energy level produced by the situation resulted in

1. Silvette and Britton (8, p. 691) make the following observation: 'It is pertinent to emphasize that the influences of emotion on important chemical constituents of the body are essentially similar to those which are brought about by severe muscular exertion. Both motion and emotion result in release to the blood stream and degradation in the tissues of energy-supplying substances, and concurrent accumulation of the products of tissue oxidation or metabolites.'

this instance, not in disorganization, but in increased speed and force of action, with no loss in co-ordination. Some degree of disorganization of response has been found, on the other hand, in most situations where the adjustive response is not a well-established habit. It occurs frequently during the learning of a new motor skill or during the attempt to solve a difficult 'mental' problem. It is likely to occur in any type of situation in which the individual is too highly motivated, i.e. has too high an energy level. The over-eager golfer, teeing off, makes a poor shot. The enthusiastic child, speaking of something which interests him intensely, begins to stammer. Disorganized responses occur also when the individual is drowsy or fatigued. Under these conditions the energy level is usually too low for effective behavior. And, finally, disorganization of response occurs as a result of the physiological condition by glandular dysfunction or by the administration of drugs. It is apparent, then, that disorganized response is not peculiar to 'emotion'; nor is there any particular degree of disorganization of response which is called out *always* by 'emotional' stimuli. But most 'emotional' conditions, involving as they do unusually high or unusually low levels of energy, usually involve also disorganization of response, but the disorganization appears to be a function, not of 'emotion' *per se*, but of the *energy level* of the response, since disorganization is found at high and at low levels of energy which are not ordinarily called 'emotional'.[2]

A third characteristic attributed to 'emotion', and one which is generally considered most indisputable, is that 'emotion' involves a unique kind of sensation or quality of consciousness. Whatever may be said about the lack of uniqueness of 'emotional' *responses*, the individual is likely to feel that the *conscious* quality of 'emotion' is different from that which he experiences under any other circumstances. He describes 'a lump in the throat', or 'a turning of the stomach', or the heart's 'skipping a beat'. These sensations appear to him to be not merely different in *degree* but actually different in *kind* from those which he experiences on ordinary occasions. Sometimes, when he is 'emotional', he feels unusually helpless and confused. At other times he feels unusually powerful. So different are these feelings from his usual experiences

2. For a fuller discussion of *energy level* and of *disorganization of response*, see E. Duffy (4).

that he may report that he feels 'beside himself' with anger or with joy. Is it possible that a conscious state of this kind, one of the most vivid ever experienced by the individual, differs merely in degree, and not in unique quality, from the states of consciousness which make up most of our experience in everyday life? I think it is.

The subjective qualities of 'emotion' appear to derive from two sources: (a) awareness of the bodily changes which occur in the process of adjusting the energy level of the individual to the demands of the situation; and (b) awareness of the stimulus situation and of the set for response to that situation. 'Emotional' experience is merely the conscious counterpart of the adjustments which the individual makes to stimulating conditions which are of sufficient significance to cause a marked change in his energy level and his set for response.

Sudden and extreme changes occur in the viscera and in the skeletal muscles when the individual attempts to make a quick and extensive readjustment for which he is not 'set' or prepared. The *sudden* change in the situation demands a *sudden* change both in overt movement and in the processes supplying the energy for that movement. These sudden changes in physiological functioning are experienced by the individual as strange and vivid sensations which are described in such picturesque terms as those of the stomach's 'taking a flop' or the heart's 'being in the throat'. Such sensations occur only when the 'emotional' stimulus appears unexpectedly or when the *interpretation* of the situation abruptly changes. Situations which demand, not sudden readjustments, but more gradual readjustments, such, for example, as the change in energy level and in overt behavior which occur as the individual gradually comes to believe that he is exposed to danger, also produce changes in conscious experience which correspond to the changes in adjustive activity, but in these situations the individual is not conscious of sudden, violent changes in the viscera, for no such changes occur, since no sudden change in the stimulus situation requires them. When the energy level of the individual increases or decreases in marked degree, the individual 'feels' different from the way he does under ordinary circumstances; he experiences different sensations. If this change in energy level takes place gradually, is not too extreme, and persists for some time, he experiences a 'mood'; if it takes place in extreme degree or occurs suddenly, he is likely to experience an 'emotion'.

But the awareness of 'how the body feels' does not make up the whole of the conscious quality of 'emotion'. The bodily sensations have an external reference. They are viewed by the individual as having been *caused* by a certain situation. They are part of a more comprehensive whole which includes the *interpretation* of the *stimulus situation, expectations* of future developments in the situation, and the *set* of the individual for response to that situation. Without this characteristic context for the visceral sensations the individual who experiences visceral changes is likely to be uncertain as to whether or not he is experiencing 'emotion'. Experiments by Cantril and Hunt (2) and by Landis and Hunt (7) offer support for this point of view. Subjects to whom adrenalin was administered (which, of course, produced visceral changes similar to those occurring during the excited emotions) reported in some instances that they experienced 'emotion', in other instances that they did not experience 'emotion', and in a number of cases that they felt '*as if*' they were angry or '*as if*' they were afraid.

The conscious experience of 'emotion' appears, then, to be a complex which includes awareness of the stimulus situation and its significance, awareness of the set for response, and awareness of certain physiological changes which are occurring in the individual. But what 'non-emotional' state of consciousness is devoid of any one of these factors? And what characteristic quality if any one of these factors has been found to be present in 'emotional' states alone? The consciousness of these various aspects of the situation may be somewhat 'blurred' during 'emotion', especially during the *strong* 'emotions'; but disorganization is to be expected in both experience and behavior which occur at a very high or a very low energy level.

The 'unique' conscious quality attributed to 'emotion' appears to refer either to the pleasantness-unpleasantness aspect of *all* experience, and not merely of 'emotional' experience, or else to the vivid and unusual sensations experienced when sudden and extreme physiological readjustments occur, as they do when a sudden change in energy level is demanded. If it refers to the former, it may be said to represent a characteristic of consciousness itself and not a distinguishing feature of 'emotion'. If it refers to the latter, it may be said to represent the conscious counterpart of adjustive responses which differ from other responses in *degree* rather than in *kind*; hence the conscious experience must itself differ from other conscious states in degree rather than in unique quality. Changes in energy level, in degree of organization of responses, and in conscious state occur in a continuum. There is no point on this continuum where a 'non-emotional' energy level changes suddenly to an 'emotional' energy level; there is no point at which a 'non-emotional' degree of disorganization of response changes suddenly to an 'emotional' degree of disorganization; and there is no point at which a 'non-emotional' conscious state changes suddenly to an 'emotional' one. These characteristics of experience and behavior show continuous variation rather than separation into hard and fast categories. Extremes of the continuum are readily identified as 'emotion'; intermediate points offer difficulty in identification. For example, slight changes in energy level such as occur during 'interest' or 'boredom' usually leave the individual uncertain as to whether he is experiencing 'emotion'; extreme changes, such as occur in 'anger', are unequivocally identified as 'emotion'. The conscious quality of 'emotion', like other aspects of 'emotion', represents a variation in *degree* rather than a difference in *kind*.

I am aware of no evidence for the existence of a special condition called 'emotion' which follows different principles of action from other conditions of the organism. I can therefore see no reason for a psychological study of 'emotion' as such. 'Emotion' has no distinguishing characteristics. It represents merely an *extreme* manifestation of characteristics found in some degree in all responses. If there is any particular point at which a difference in *degree* becomes a difference in *kind* this fact has not been demonstrated. Yet in psychological description we deem it necessary to state that 'emotional' processes *also* follow laws already laid down for other kinds of behavior. For example, when we have shown that behavior in general shows the phenomenon of 'conditioning', we find it necessary to state that 'emotional' behavior *also* may be conditioned. When we have shown that motives affect the level of activity of the individual, we find it necessary to state that 'emotions' also may have this result. It would be more in accord with the facts to state instead that the energy level of an organism depends upon the degree and suddenness of the disturbance of its equilibrium by both internal and external factors, and that the responses made are specifically adjustive to the situation. Since situations show endless variation in their details, adjustments to those situations must show corresponding variation. They will not be readily classifiable, therefore, into 'emotion' or 'non-emotion', or into any of the categories represented by our names for the specific 'emotions'.

All responses, not merely 'emotional' responses, occur as adjustments to stimulating conditions. *All* responses, not merely 'emotional' responses, occur at some particular *energy level*. *All* responses, like 'emotional' responses, show *direction* toward a goal; and *all* responses manifest *discrimination*, or response to relationships. 'Emotion' is an adjustment made to a stimulating condition of such a kind that the adjustment involves a marked change in energy level. It involves, like other behavior, interpretation of the situation, or response to relationships. And from the goal-direction of the overt behavior, or of the set for response, are derived the classificatory divisions into the particular 'emotions', such as 'fear' or 'rage'. Its characteristics – its principles of action – are those of behavior in general. It has no laws or qualities of its own. It is futile, therefore, to look for an 'indicator' of 'emotion'. It is futile to inquire, '*What are the effects produced by "emotion"?*' For a so-called 'emotional' condition will *vary* in its effects, depending upon the *energy level* at which the behavior occurs, upon the adequacy with which *direction* toward the goal is maintained (or disorganization or response avoided), and upon the nature of the *response to the relationships* in the situation. Behavior not classified as 'emotional' also varies with variations in these three aspects of response. Instead of investigating 'emotion' *per se*, we could more usefully study variations in these three fundamental dimensions of behavior, determining the conditions under which such variations occur and the effects produced by their occurrence. Perhaps, when we formulate our questions better, Nature will be more obliging in her replies.

References
1. CANNON, W. B., *Bodily Changes in Pain, Hunger, Fear, and Rage*, 2nd edn, Appleton, 1929.

2. CANTRIL, H., and HUNT, W. A., 'Emotional effects produced by the injection of adrenalin', *Amer. J. Psychol.*, vol. 44 (1932), pp. 300–7.

3. DUFFY, E., 'Emotion: an example of the need for reorientation in psychology', *Psychol. Rev.*, vol. 41 (1934), pp. 184–98.

4. DUFFY, E., 'The conceptual categories of psychology: a suggestion for revision', *Psychol. Rev.*, vol. 44 (1941), pp. 177–203.

5. FREEMAN, G. L., 'The postural substrate', *Psychol. Rev.*, vol. 45 (1938), pp. 324–34.

6. JONES, H. E., and JONES, M. C., 'Fear', *Child. Educ.*, vol. 5 (1928), pp. 136–43.

7. LANDIS, C., and HUNT, W. A., 'Adrenalin and emotion', *J. exper. Psychol.*, vol. 39 (1932), pp. 467–85.

8. SILVETTE, H., and BRITTON, S. W., 'The comparative effects on carbohydrate metabolism of exhausting motive and emotive responses and exposure to cold', *Amer. J. Physiol.*, vol. 100 (1932), pp. 685–92.

9. STRATTON, G. M., 'The functions of emotion as shown particularly in excitement', *Psychol. Rev.*, vol. 35 (1928), pp. 351–66.

13 D. O. Hebb

Emotional Disturbance

Excerpts from D. O. Hebb, *The Organization of Behavior*, Wiley, 1949, pp. 236–45, 250–55.

Traditionally, emotion is an awareness, an event in consciousness. Here, perhaps more than anywhere else in psychology, a traditional interactionism (which is animism) tends to persist. The afferent excitation is thought to produce a feeling of awareness, *and that feeling then acts on the nervous system* – it must do so, according to such ideas, for it is the *feeling* that makes the subject sweat or tremble or run away, and the sweat glands and the legs are controlled by nerve fibers.

Just such an inconsistency of thought has led to an endless, and pointless, debate on the James–Lange theory of emotion. What James and Lange were accounting for, again, was that emotional feeling or awareness; they postulated that the awareness is a set of sensations, that the awareness follows and does not cause emotional behavior ('I see the bear, I run, I feel afraid'). Their critics proceeded to show that emotional expression is still there in the dog whose sensory processes have been interfered with, and thought this a refutation of the theory. But such an argument is totally irrelevant; James did not say that emotional *behavior* depends on sensations from the limbs and viscera.

It is equally irrelevant to show that emotional expression is centrally organized, in the hypothalamus. If James had raised the question at all, he must have assumed something of the sort; remember that what he denied was that consciousness intervenes between stimulus and response. Therefore, showing that the 'higher' centers of the cortex are not needed for the response is clearly support for his position. The extraordinary *non sequitur* of such criticisms, made by some very distinguished critics indeed, would not be possible if there were not the immutable idea that *only* emotional awareness or feeling can produce emotional response. If the response is there, the feeling must be also. Such logic, assuming James to be wrong first, in order to prove him wrong, is the clearest evidence of the hold traditional ideas have on psychological thought.

But we must get rid of the tradition both for scientific consistency and because psychological observers have been unanimous in denying that there is any special, fundamental category of consciousness that can be called emotion. 'Emotional experience . . . is a highly variable state [and] often partakes of the complicated nature of a judgement (Landis and Hunt, 1932). I have reviewed the evidence on this point elsewhere (Hebb, 1946a) and need not go into it again. Since it seems that the term emotion does not refer to a special kind of event in consciousness, and since in any case we must not slip into the inconsistency of treating an immaterial awareness as a causal agency, the term is not very useful in its traditional significance. At the same time, we must postulate that the disturbances of emotional behavior have a neural origin; and the term emotion still can be useful to refer to the neural processes that produce emotional behavior.

It is important to be clear that in this discussion 'emotion' is a reference to the hypothetical neural processes that produce emotional behavior; explicitly, it refers neither to an immaterial state of consciousness nor to the observable pattern of emotional behavior.

Emotion as a disorganizing influence

The third point to be clarified is the distinction between emotional disturbance and those processes (also called emotional) which are inherently organizing and motivating. A paper by Leeper (1948) has urged that all emotion be considered to have such an integrating function. He has expressed a commonly held point of view, and has at the same time I believe clouded the issue with which he dealt. His position demands consideration.

Leeper has shown effectively that regarding emotion as disorganizing has led some of us into an inconsistency, but he has proposed another inconsistency to take its place. He points out that others have first defined emotion as a disorganization of behavior and have then gone on to give mother-love as one example of emotion. This is certainly inconsistent. But how is it different logically from defining emotion as something that makes behavior more efficient and at the same time giving, as examples, the stage fright that ruins a performance, the anger that makes a boxer less skillful, and the mental depression that makes a man unable to earn a living? I must add at once that Leeper anticipated this criticism. He answered it by saying that, though emotion may sometimes disorganize, the disorganization is not characteristic because it occurs only (1) when emotion is extreme, or (2) when the emotion conflicts with some other motivation. As far as one can see, however, the first of these explanations depends on a mistaken use of analogy, the second begs the question.

1. It might be doubted whether emotion is disorganizing only when extreme. A touch of shyness or of self-consciousness, for example, may sometimes ruin one's conversational skills. Leave this to one side, however, and accept the assumption that only strong emotion disrupts behavior.

The idea that such an effect does not indicate the true nature of emotion depends on this analogy: An excess of salt or oxygen has toxic effects, 'but we do not use this as a means of determining the normal functions of such products'. The same logic, then, should apply to emotional processes (Leeper, 1948, p. 15). But we must really use the same logic. We must, that is, ask the same question in both cases. The question does not concern the 'normal function' of emotion, but what emotion *is*. No one doubts that fear has a useful function, aiding survival; the question is, how? Might fear not be a simple disrupter of behavior and still be useful, if the disruption is mainly of the behavior that gets us into trouble? Emotion could then be disorganization and still have its survival value, because the disorganization is selective, eliminating some actions and allowing others to take their place.

If we accept the analogy between emotion and salt we still can say that emotion is disruptive of behavior, that it generally has a useful function when it occurs in moderate degree and bad effects when there is too much of it – exactly as with salt or oxygen.

2. In discussing the stage fright that keeps a pianist from giving a good performance, Leeper says the emotion is not a disorganizer of behavior because, by itself it would produce only flight – a well-organized pattern of behavior. This seems to beg the question, since the pianist neither runs away nor stays to play well.

Leeper says it is not the emotion that produces his incoordinations, but the conflict. But if there were no conflict at all, would there be any emotion? Are the conflict and the emotion quite independent?

The difficulty here is clearest by Leeper's own criterion of 'organization'. He points out first that any directed behavior means the suppression of conflicting tendencies; so conflict is not *ipso facto* disorganization. The test is 'whether [an] interference is relatively chaotic and haphazard, or whether the suppressions and changes of subordinate activities are harmonious with some main function that is being served'. The trembling, palmar sweating, disturbance of breathing, and incoordinations of the pianist's fingers, obviously, are not harmonious with the main function being served – until he actually runs away. Could we regard his emotion as solely organizing even then? See what this implies. If we are really consistent in saying that any disorganization in emotion is accidental, that emotion is essentially an organizer only, then a well-organized avoidance is at least as much an instance of fear as an ill-organized one. Consequently, the pianist who anticipates the possibility of stage fright, and calmly decides to keep away from the stage, provides as good an example of emotion as the one that trembles before an audience. We have deliberately got rid of any criterion of emotion except that it 'arouses, sustains, and directs' behavior. We have equated avoidance and fear, aggression and anger. But these surely are not identical.

The upshot of such an argument is to broaden the category of emotion so much that it includes all psychological processes. We should then have to find another name for the distinctive event that – at present – is called emotional.

How are we to find some half-way point between this position and the one that Leeper has criticized so effectively? I think it is evident that Munn, Young, Dockeray, Woodworth, Landis, and so on (authors criticized for treating emotion as disorganization) were after all not as absurd as Leeper thought them; at the same time, he has made untenable the proposition that 'emotion' simply means a disruption of behavior.

A way out, I believe, can be found if we do two things: first, stop talking about emotions as a single, fundamental kind of unitary psychological process, and separate (1) those in which the tendency is to maintain or increase the original stimulating conditions (pleasurable or integrative emotions) from (2) those in which the tendency is to abolish or decrease the stimulus (rage, fear, disgust), including, however, depressions in which the organism may discover no way of escape from the condition giving rise to the emotion. Secondly, if it is assumed that stimuli in class 2 above are essentially disintegrative, it must also be recognized that the disintegration in rage or fear is often *incipient* or *potential* and likely to be successfully averted by the aggression or avoidance of the subject. [. . .]

The theory of emotion proposed by Watson (1924) is by now classical. It held that there are three innate emotions, rage, fear, and love: rage aroused by a restriction of physical movement, fear by a loud noise or sudden loss of support (and, presumably, pain), love by stimulation of the genitalia. These stimuli may then serve to condition others: if a child fears animals, it is because he has been scratched by a cat or knocked over, perhaps, by a friendly dog while learning to walk. As soon as one tries to apply this theory to the emotional disturbances that are actually observed in children, serious difficulty shows up; it is not really plausible, and it has been subjected to powerful criticism by Dennis (1940) on rage, by Jones and Jones (1928) on fear, and by Valentine (1930), also on fear. But it has been hard to document the criticism with experimental evidence, for two reasons. First, it is not safe or socially permitted to arouse a strong degree of emotion in human subjects for experimental study. Important as the topic is, consequently, we have surprisingly little exact information about the causes and consequences of human emotion – above all, of adult emotion. Secondly, when one studies emotion as it occurs socially, outside the laboratory, it is almost impossible to know the antecedent conditions as they must be known if one is to understand the present responses of the subject.

But neither of these objections need apply to the study of emotion in animals, and the chimpanzee fortunately has an emotional repertoire that is very like man's. The things that annoy us are apt to annoy him, and he shows his annoyance much as we do; his fears in some respects are astonishingly like man's – in what is feared, in complexity of the causes of fear, in the relation of fear to intellectual development, in resistance to extinction or reconditioning, and in the marked individual differences between one subject and the next. Even more, there are data on what were with practical certainty two cases of neurosis or psychosis in mature chimpanzees whose histories were known from birth or very early infancy, one born in the Yerkes Laboratories of Primate Biology and one captured in the first year of life. These animals of the Yerkes colony can be studied as human subjects cannot. Their histories are known in detail, being recorded in individual diaries. With these data, one is in a position to see just what complexity of response must be provided for in a theory of emotion, chronic as well as acute.

The causes of rage may have nothing to do with physical restraint of movement. When the chimpanzee Dita, in heat, would sit where he could watch her from the next cage but one, Don seemed calm (if not content); but he had a temper tantrum repeatedly whenever she left the outer cage for an inner room where he could not see her. When Mona had a noisy temper tantrum because Pan had stolen a peanut from her, Pan was finally enraged to the point of beating her up. A chimpanzee may be angered by a reproof, by being startled, or by being obliged to look at something unpleasant such as a model of a snake. These causes act 'spontaneously'; that is, the emotional disturbance does not have to be learned, any more than a human being must learn specially to be angry at disturbance of the peace, at being shown something nasty, or at being momentarily scared by a practical joker (Hebb, 1945) – although, as we shall see, a certain kind of learning, in infancy, may have to have been established first.

The causes of fear include not only loud noise or sudden fall, but snakes with which an animal has never had contact (this can be known certainly with some chimpanzees reared in the nursery), solitude, and the strange or mysterious. McCulloch and Haslerud (1939) have analysed such fears in a young chimpanzee reared quite apart from others, and were thus able to show that they are not necessarily acquired by 'social conditioning' or imitation. I discovered accidentally that some of the chimpanzees of the Yerkes colony might have a paroxysm of terror at being shown a model of a human or chimpanzee head detached from the body; young infants showed no fear, increasing excitement was evident in the older (half-grown) animals, and those adults that were not frankly terrified were still considerably excited. These individual differences among adults, and the difference of response at different ages, are quite like the human differences in attitude toward snakes, the frequency and strength of fear increasing up to the age of seventeen or so in persons who had never been injured by a snake (Jones and Jones, 1928). The increase fits in with the conception that many fears depend on some degree of intellectual development, and so with the idea that the range of such fears is characteristic of 'higher' animals like man and chimpanzee (McBride and Hebb, 1948).

The observations using detached heads were then followed up by others, using various stimuli: an isolated eye and eyebrow, a cast of a chimpanzee's face, a skull, a cured chimpanzee hide, an anesthetized chimpanzee.

Two things appeared: first, that such stimulation may be primarily a source of profound *excitation*, rather than specifically fear-producing; the excitation was usually followed by avoidance, but sometimes by aggression, and sometimes it produced a marked autonomic reaction combined with apparent friendliness. On occasion, a confusing mixture of all these reactions was seen.

Secondly, this primitive excitation appears to be fully parallel to the human emotional disturbance that may occur at the sight of a badly deformed face, in watching a major operation, dissection, or autopsy for the first time, or as a result of contact with a dead body (Hebb, 1946b). This human disturbance, like the chimpanzee's, is not specific – it may take the form of nausea, of vascular disturbance and dizziness, of disgust or fear, or may even facilitate anger (e.g. at 'desecration' of the dead). It is important to recognize individual differences of sensitivity to such experiences, and the loss of sensitivity with repeated exposure (which is presumably an effect of learning); but this does not mean that the responses are wholly learned. The evidence is very definitely to the contrary: the degree of excitation is likely to be strongest on the first exposure, provided certain *other* experiences have preceded. On the other hand, the disappearance of response with repetition must be an effect of learning, and I believe we must assume that it is learning also that establishes any integrated response to such stimuli, transforming a nonspecific emotional disturbance into an organized flight (disturbance plus a tendency to flight then constituting fear) or aggression (constituting rage).

147

The complex origin of emotional disturbance may be clearest in the infant fear of strangers. About the age of four months the chimpanzee reared in the nursery, with daily care from three or four persons only and seeing few others, begins to show an emotional disturbance at the approach of a stranger (Hebb and Riesen, 1943). The disturbance increases in degree in the following months. This is 'shyness' but may become much more violent than that term would usually imply. It commonly shows up in the human baby about the sixth or seventh month. (The age difference is in keeping with the fact that chimpanzee development generally takes only about two-thirds of the time for the corresponding human development.) Everyday experience tells us that shyness does not occur in the human child that is continually in contact with strangers; and that it is very strong, as a distrust or fear of 'foreigners' (even in adults) in isolated communities. We might then suppose that the excitation out of which the fear develops is aroused innately at the sight of a stranger, but extinguished if enough new faces are seen with no accompanying injury. But this supposition is wrong: there is definite evidence that the response is *not* innately established.

Dennis (1934) pointed out that human patients, congenitally blind and operated on to restore vision, have shown no emotional disturbance at the first sight of a human face. Chimpanzees reared in darkness, and brought into the light at an age when the response normally would be at its strongest, show not the slightest disturbance at the sight of either friend or stranger. *But* some time later, after a certain amount of visual learning has gone on, the disturbance begins to appear exactly as in other animals.

So it appears that the emotional disturbance is neither learned nor innate: a certain learning must have preceded, but given that learning the disturbance is complete on the first appearance of certain stimulus combinations. Dennis (1940) has also made it clear that tantrums are not learned, and still require that other things have been learned first. We are accustomed to think of any particular response as either learned or innate, which is apt to be a source of confusion in thinking about such things as far apart as an insightful act or neurotic behavior – is the response inherited, or acquired? The answer is, Neither: either Yes or No would be very misleading. The irrational emotional disturbances of man and chimpanzee are fully dependent on learning, but are not learned in the usual sense of the term. [. . .]

The aspects of emotional disturbance that mainly determine this treatment of the problem can be summarized as follows: (1) the great variety of causes of disturbance, ranging from an unfamiliar combination of familiar things (fear of the strange) or an interruption of sleep, to hunger, nutritional deficiency, or withdrawal of a drug from the addict; (2) the fact that a single cause may produce anger, fear, or nausea and faintness, in the same subject at different times, or in different subjects; (3) the great variety of expression even of a single emotion; and (4) the different ways in which the expression of emotion changes, as the subject is habituated to the stimulating conditions.

To account for item 1, it has been assumed that the emotion is a disturbance in the timing of thalamo-cortical firing – a disruption of the phase sequence when the subject is awake, of the intrinsic organization of cerebral activity when he is asleep. The disruption may be slight and brief, in this hypothesis, or extensive and prolonged; it may be produced by a conflict of phase sequences, by a lack of sensory support for the phase sequence, or by metabolic changes.

Now the question is, how far a second assumption can account for items 2, 3, and 4 listed above. This assumption was made earlier to account for the learning by a rat to choose a lighter door and avoid a darker one, in discrimination training. It is, in short, that a disruption of thalamo-cortical timing tends to prevent the recurrence of the phase sequence that led up to that disruption on previous occasions, because of the cyclical (anticipatory and recurrent) organization of the phase sequence. This is a mechanism of learning, and it is proposed now that it would account for the adaptive features of rage (emotional disturbance plus attack) or fear (the same thing plus avoidance), as learned behavior that is determined by the accompanying emotional disturbance. Particularly, it would account for the variability of the behavior and for the marked tendency of the emotional element itself to disappear as the originally disturbing situation is repeated.

Above and beyond the question of the intrinsic plausibility of the idea that flight, in fear, is a learned response (it may not be as implausible as it seems at first glance) is the apparent necessity of my first assumption, that emotional disturbance is a disruption of cerebral timing. If this is necessary, we must then find *some* way of accounting for the other aspects of emotional behavior. Let us look again, then, at the causes of emotional disturbance, which may be arranged in three classes.

Class I. Take as a starting point the infant chimpanzee's fear of the strange. It has already been seen that this is not innate, not a fear of what is totally strange, since the animal reared in darkness does not show it until vision in general has begun to have some 'meaning' for him (until it arouses phase sequences). Consider further that a familiar attendant *A*, wearing the equally familiar coat *B* of another attendant, may arouse the fear just as a complete stranger would. *A* causes no disturbance; *B* causes none; *A* and *B* together cause a violent emotional reaction. It is this sort of fact that makes it necessary to suppose that two phase sequences may interfere with one another. The first class of emotional disturbance thus is one caused by a conflict (which may be extended to the disruptive effect of pain stimuli and other 'unpleasant' sensory events).

Class II. Now a second case. It was for long heresy to suppose that there could be a fear of darkness. Darkness is a lack of stimulation (at least after the first few seconds in the dark); how can it arouse an emotional response? Fear of the dark is not likely to appear until the age of three or later in human children (Jersild and Holmes, 1935), and so the skeptic who thought that *his* child developed the fear without cause could be answered by the old appeal to ignorance: how can he be certain, with the varied unsupervised experiences a child must have in a three-year period? However, the violent avoidance of solitude by young chimpanzees (Köhler, 1925) is at least as marked as the human fear of the dark, and can be shown to be due only to the *lack* of the perception of companions. This then implies a second class of emotional disturbance: fear of the dark, fear of solitude, fear aroused by loss of support, and the emotional changes observed by Ramsdell[1] following prolonged absence of the normal auditory

1. Personal communication from Dr Donald A. Ramsdell, who was concerned to understand the high frequency of marked emotional changes which

stimulation. It would comprise also emotional disturbance due to contact with a dead body (which lacks warmth and the usual responsiveness); anger at the lack of social response in another person ('inattentiveness'), or a monkey's anger at not finding the particular kind of food reward he expected (Tinklepaugh, 1928); grief; homesickness; and so on.

That a conflict of phase sequences, or a lack of sensory support for the phase sequence, should produce any extensive disruption in the timing of cortical action is not a logically inescapable deduction from the schema of neural action presented in Chapters 4 and 5 [*not included in this edition*]. What the schematizing actually did was suggest the possibility, as something that would account for a similar effect of two so dissimilar causes and make the relationship between perception and emotional disturbance intelligible. The idea then seemed to gain strong support when it drew attention to another set of facts that is usually forgotten in

---

he observed in veterans following traumatic loss of hearing. He arranged experimentally to deafen himself, effectively eliminating airborne sounds for a period of three days. The results are described by Dr Ramsdell as follows, particularly with regard to the question whether the deafness would contribute to any neurotic or psychotic tendency:

'In my experience there was a definite increase of irritability and a desire to either withdraw from the field or, if held in the field, to "charge" into it. This would be comparable to being irritated with a friend, and either withdrawing without saying anything or "letting him have it". Such behavior would not be characterized by ideas of persecution nor suspicion of the friend. However, you might say that the desire to "charge" into a situation is such stuff as paranoia is made of, but for a true paranoid idea of persecution, the capacity for interpersonal relationship must be so weak that real suspicion can develop. Assuming then interpersonal relationships to be secure, I would say that deafness is accompanied by a feeling of perplexity and disorientation analogous to the fear of the dark or fear of solitude. Such a disorientation in one's social milieu need not necessarily involve paranoid disturbances any more than being in the dark would induce one to hear footsteps at his back. In my opinion, the feelings of personal inadequacies (impairment of the body image); irritability, and an exaggerated response to stimuli; and the wish to leave the field or, if held in the field, to "charge" into it, characterize the experience of deafness.'

I should like to draw attention also to Dr Ramsdell's suggestion that the emotional condition might lead to more than one overt pattern of response. This is relevant to the later discussion of the way in which different 'emotions' might develop from the same primitive disturbance.

discussing emotional theory. These facts concern the relationship of emotional disturbance to metabolic changes.

Class III. The third class of the causes of fear, rage, and so on though it was actually arrived at last in formulating these ideas, comes nearer than either of the others to being a necessary consequence of the neural schema. To the earlier discussion of the effects of chemical changes in the nutrient fluids that bathe the neural cell, showing that a disturbance of timing must result, I need add only that a large intracranial tumor, compressing blood vessels and interfering with blood flow, obviously could have similar effects; and also that asthma, or vascular disease, or an antigen acting to produce vascular spasm in intracranial vessels – any of these – might produce emotional disturbance directly, by affecting the amount of oxygen in the blood or the amount of blood that is supplied to neural tissues. Emotional changes are in fact frequently associated with all such conditions; and the one assumption that seems to provide a common ground for such varied sources of disturbance (including not only the metabolic changes in Class III but also the perceptual conflicts and perceptual deficits of Classes I and II) is the assumption that emotional disturbance is in the first place a disruption of the timing of neuronal activity in the cerebrum. This also accounts directly for the incoordinations of emotion. Until some better guess is made, we must see what can be done with the assumption; and this imposes the burden of accounting for the integrated and coordinated aspects of emotional behavior (Leeper, 1948).

Now this coordinated part of the behavior, in the unpleasant emotions, has one constant function. It is always such as to tend to put an end to the original stimulation (in the pleasant emotions, of course, this tendency is reversed). *Aggression*, in rage, tends to change the irritating behavior of another animal – by cowing, driving off, or killing the annoyer. *Flight*, in fear, tends to prevent or terminate noxious stimulation. *Avoidance* – turning the head away from an unpleasant sight, covering the ears, holding the nose, or withdrawing the hand, as well as actually running away – tends to stop the stimulation that arouses either an irrational fear of some inert object or the practically equivalent disgust. *Fawning* may be a manifestation of fear as much as flight, and so may the *desperate attack* of a cornered animal: and each is a possible way of putting an end to the emotion-arousing behavior of another organism.

Failure to respond, in shame, is a special case, in which one's own behavior is the emotion-provoking stimulus; the effect of the emotional disturbance is negative, preventing the recurrence of that behavior, but this is also in line with the present thesis, namely: All these effects may be achieved because *strong emotional disturbance tends to prevent the repetition of any line of thought that leads up to it*, and to eliminate the corresponding behavior. In some situations, a primitive, undifferentiated disturbance would develop into fear, where withdrawal is the only thing that ends the disturbance; in others, anger, when attack is the only effective behavior; in still others, either fear or anger might result, when either behavior would be effective, and which result happens would be determined by the animal's past experience as well as by his own inherited peculiarities. But in some situations, and for some subjects, no behavior might be discovered that would abolish the emotional disturbance; and the effect of learning in this case might be to reinforce the visceral disturbance and the incoordinations of the skeletal musculature, and – above all – the disorganization of the phase sequence, which is a disorganization of thought.

This is the point at which neurosis and psychosis enter the theoretical structure: they are (1) conditions of chronic emotional disturbance, or (2) ones in which emotional disturbance, in the past, has effected a lasting modification of the thought process.

References

DENNIS, W. (1934), 'Congenital cataract and unlearned behavior', *J. genet. Psychol.*, vol. 44, pp. 340–50.

DENNIS, W. (1940), 'Infant reaction to restraint: an evaluation of Watson's theory', *Trans. N. Y. Acad. Sci.*, ser. 2, vol. 2, no. 8, pp. 202–18.

HEBB, D. O. (1945), 'The forms and conditions of chimpanzee anger', *Bull. Canad. Psychol. Ass.*, vol. 5, pp. 32–5.

HEBB, D. O. (1946a), 'Emotion in man and animal: an analysis of the intuitive processes of recognition', *Psychol. Rev.*, vol. 53, pp. 88–106.

HEBB, D. O. (1946b), 'On the nature of fear', *Psychol. Rev.*, vol. 53, pp. 259–76.

HEBB, D. O., and RIESEN, A. H. (1943), 'The genesis of irrational fears', *Bull. Canad. Psychol. Ass.*, vol. 3, pp. 49–50.

JERSILD, A. T., and HOLMES, F. B. (1935), *Children's Fears*, Teach. Coll. Bur. Publ., New York.

JONES, H. E., and JONES, M. C. (1928), 'A study of fear', *Childhood Educ.*, vol. 5, pp. 136–43.

KÖHLER, W. (1925), *The Mentality of Apes*, Harcourt, Brace.

LANDIS, C., and HUNT, W. A. (1932), 'Adrenalin and emotion', *Psychol. Rev.*, vol. 39, pp. 467–85.

LEEPER, R. W. (1948), 'A motivational theory of emotion to replace "Emotion as disorganized response"', *Psychol. Rev.*, vol. 55, pp. 5–21.

MCBRIDE, A. F., and HEBB, D. O. (1948), 'Behavior of the captive bottle-nose dolphin, *Tursiops truncatus*', *J. comp. physiol. Psychol.*, vol. 41, pp. 111–23.

MCCULLOCH, T. L., and HASLERUD, G. M. (1939), 'Affective responses of an infant chimpanzee reared in isolation from its kind', *J. comp. Psychol.*, vol. 28, pp. 437–45.

TINKLEPAUGH, O. L. (1928), 'An experimental study of representative factors in monkeys', *J. comp. Psychol.*, vol. 8, pp. 197–236.

VALENTINE, C. W. (1930), 'The innate bases of fear', *J. genet. Psychol.*, vol. 37, pp. 394–419.

WATSON, J. B. (1924), *Behaviorism*, Norton.

Part Six Emotion as Interference

If emotion is neither permitted its own driving force nor connected
with an instinctive drive, it is often seen as the result of conflict, an
arrest of action tendencies, to account for its dynamic character.
This is true for Freud in the case of anxiety (Part Three), for Dumas
in his conception of emotional shock (Part Four), and for Hebb in
his notion of interference with phase sequences (Part Five). But there
are theorists who consider emotion itself as disorganized and
disorganizing. Claparède, for instance, suggests that emotions are
mixtures of adaptive and maladaptive reactions; the more explosive
the emotion, the more disorganizing it is. Feelings, on the other hand,
he considers as useful attitudes; emotional explosions follow only if
such useful adaptation is frustrated. Pradines goes one step further
by suggesting that complex feelings (sentiments) have a regulative
function, while emotions are an explosive and disordered form of
sentiments.

Emotion as disorganized response has had many supporters in
English-speaking countries as well. Leeper's critique was a timely
reminder that there are other than conflict-produced emotions which
have to be accounted for.

14 E. Claparède

Feelings and Emotions

Excerpts from E. Claparède, 'Feelings and Emotions', in
M. L. Reymert (ed.), *Feelings and Emotions*, Clark University Press,
1928, chapter 9, pp. 124–38.

The psychology of affective processes is the most confused chapter
in all psychology. Here it is that the greatest differences appear
from one psychologist to another. They are in agreement neither
on the facts nor on the words. Some call feelings what others call
emotions. Some regard feelings as simple, ultimate, unanalysable
phenomena, similar always to themselves, varying only in quantity. Some, on the contrary, believe that the range of feelings
includes an infinity of *nuances*, and that feeling always forms a
part of a more complex whole, in exhibition or in condition.
Certain psychologists regard physical pain and moral pain as
identical, while others separate them by calling one a sensation,
the other an emotion. Some regard pleasure and pain as two
phenomena, antagonistic but of the same kind, while others describe them as entirely heterogeneous. A number of pages might
be filled by simply enumerating the fundamental differences.

These differences are increased when one passes from one
language to another, since the lack of agreement about the facts
is then complicated by lack of agreement about words. What
French word is the exact equivalent of the word feeling? Does
Gemütsbewegung correspond exactly with emotion? And what
equivalent does one find from one language to another between the
words *Affekt*, *Gefühl*, *passion*, *douleur*, pain, affection, etc.?
[. . .]

The functional point of view

It is always advantageous, in my opinion, when one wishes to
study a psychological phenomenon, to begin the approach from
the functional angle; in other words, before trying to analyse it in
detail under a strong magnifying glass, as it were, to examine it

157

rather less enlarged, in order to take account of its functional value, its general part in conduct.

If we apply this principle of method to the study of affective phenomena, we ought to commence by asking ourselves: Of what use are feelings? Of what use are emotions? And, if this way of speaking should be found too finalistic, one can say: What are the situations in which feelings and emotions intervene, and what is the role played by these phenomena in the conduct of the individual?

It cannot be denied that the functional point of view has shown itself fruitful in psychology. Let us recall Groos's theory of play, which has shown the value of play in development, and the Freudian concepts, which have considered mental maladies from the point of view of their functional significance. I myself have considered thus sleep, hysteria, and also intelligence and will. Without doubt, the functional study constitutes only an introduction to a more complete study. Nevertheless, it has no slight value in making clear the path to follow.

The functional point of view then places the emphasis on conduct. Functional psychology demands less what the phenomena *are*, than what they *do*. It is thus closely related to behaviorism. It is clearly distinguished from it, however, since that which interests it is conduct, its laws, its determinism, and not the method by which one pursues the study of these laws. It is of very little importance to it whether these methods be objective or introspective.

Let us observe another advantage of the functional point of view: it brings to our notice problems which otherwise would not have been raised.

Distinction between feelings and emotions

From the analytical point of view, feelings and emotions are distinguished with difficulty. One needs but to open any book on psychology to see the confusion which reigns in this subject. Let us see if the functional point of view permits a clearer delineation of the two groups of phenomena.

Suppose we ask ourselves: Of what use, in everyday life, are feelings, and of what use are emotions? We are immediately tempted to give to these two questions very different answers:

Feelings are useful in our conduct while emotions serve no purpose.

We can, in fact, very easily imagine a man who would never feel an emotion, who would never experience a crisis of fear or of anger, and who would be none the less viable. But we cannot imagine a man deprived of feelings, of that range of affective *nuances* which permit him to estimate the value of things to which he must adapt himself, who would not distinguish between what is good for him and what is detrimental to him.

Observation shows us, on the other hand, how unadaptable emotional phenomena are. Emotions occur precisely when adaptation is hindered for any reason whatever. The man who can run away does not have the emotion of fear. Fear occurs only when flight is impossible. Anger is displayed only when one cannot strike his enemy. Analysis of bodily reactions in emotion points to the evidence that one does not make adaptive movements but, on the contrary, reactions which recall the primitive instincts. (Darwin has also shown this.) Far from being the psychic side of an instinct, as McDougall teaches, emotion represents on the contrary a confusion of instinct, 'a miscarriage of instinct', as Larguier des Bancels has said. And, as in emotion, we can prove not only the vestige of the ancestral reaction but also the confusion or insufficiency of the acquired reaction, so we can, perhaps, with more justice define emotion as a 'miscarriage of conduct'.

The uselessness, or even the harmfulness, of emotion is known to everyone. Here is an individual who would cross a street; if he is afraid of automobiles, he loses his composure and is run over. Sorrow, joy, anger, by enfeebling attention or judgement, often make us commit regrettable acts. In brief, the individual, in the grip of an emotion 'loses his head'.

Emotion, from the functional point of view, appears to be a regression of conduct. When, for one reason or another, the normal correct reaction cannot be made, then the opposite tendencies borrow the primitive ways of reaction. And these primitive reactions, rudiments of reactions formerly useful, may be contractions of the peripheral muscles as well as phenomena vascular, inhibititive, secretory, visceral, etc. Perhaps some of them have no biological significance (e.g. tears) and result only in the propagation of a nervous impulse which has not found its normal issue. Everyone has noticed that one weeps more easily in the theater than in real life, although in the theater one knows that the scenes in which one is taking part are fictitious, but in the theater the normal reactions are prevented from occurring.

And again, in these cases one can attribute to these phenomena a secondary function of discharge, an appeasement of the nervous system unduly excited.[1]

Peripheral theory of emotion

The James–Lange theory is the only one, to my mind, which explains the existence of specific bodily phenomena in emotion. In regarding the bodily phenomena as the result (and not the cause) of the emotion, the old theories made the emotion an entirely enigmatic process. Moreover, facts of great importance speak in favor of the James–Lange theory; the suppression of the emotion by the suppression of the peripheral phenomena according to James's observation; and also the production or the facilitation of certain emotional states by the consumption of poisons, alcohol, coffee, hasheesh, etc.

The peripheral theory of James and Lange raises, however, a very great difficulty. Why, if the emotion is only consciousness of peripheral changes in the organism, is it perceived as an 'emotion' and not as 'organic sensations'? Why, when I am afraid, am I conscious of 'having fear', instead of being simply conscious of certain organic impressions, tremblings, beatings of the heart, etc.?

I do not remember that anyone has sought until now to reply to this objection. However, it does not seem to me that it should be very difficult to do so. The emotion is nothing other than the consciousness of a form, of a 'Gestalt', of these multiple organic impressions. In other words, the emotion is the consciousness of a global attitude of the organism.

This confused and general perception of the whole, which I have formerly called 'syncretic perception'(1), is the primitive form of perception. In the case of emotional perception, we know well that it is more useful to know the total attitude of the body than

1. If organic phenomena are the bases for all emotions, it does not follow that all organic phenomena cause emotions. It is probable that many physiological phenomena (internal secretions, vasomotor modifications, etc.) are compensatory reactions of regulation, the function of which is to repair the disturbance caused by the emotion.

the elementary sensations composing the whole. There must be for an individual no great interest in perceiving the detail of internal sensations. What is above all important to an organism is action; the question then is whether it is aware of the general attitude it is showing to the environment. As to the 'internal sensations', their perception results especially from a theoretical interest, and perhaps, before there were psychologists in the world, each internal sensation, each kinaesthetic or muscular sensation was not, as such, an object of consciousness.

Many of the impressions which we receive are interpreted differently according to the direction of our interest. This is particularly true for tactile impressions, which sometimes are perceived as objective, sometimes as subjective. The experiment is very easy to make. Put your hand on the table. The same tactile impression is apperceived, according to the direction of your attention, sometimes as a 'tactile sensation', sometimes as 'a hard object', a table. If, at that moment, your interest is turned to yourself (for example, in the course of psychological experiment on tactile sensations), you feel your hand, but no longer the table.

It is the same thing in the case of emotion. When you are angry, turn your attention to the kinaesthetic sensations in your clenched fists, to the trembling of your lips, etc., but then you have no longer the consciousness of anger. Or permit yourself to become absorbed in your anger; but then you no longer experience distinctly the trembling of your lips, your pallor, or the isolated sensations arising from the different parts of your contracted muscular machinery.

What the consciousness seizes in emotion is, so to speak, the form of the organism itself – that is to say – its attitude.

This peripheral conception which regards the emotion as the consciousness of an attitude of the organism is, besides, the only one which can take account of the fact that the emotion is immediately, implicitly 'understood' by him who experiences it. The emotion contains in itself its significance. As far as we can judge by external observation or by our own memory, a child who for the first time experiences a great fear or a great joy or falls into an excess of anger understands immediately what has happened to him. He does not need experience to understand successfully the meaning of this explosion of his organism, as he does to understand the meaning of impressions which come to him by sight or by hearing, impressions which do not possess any immediate and implicit significance. But what is meant by 'understand'? Does not the 'understanding' consist essentially in the assuming of an attitude with respect to an object? If this is so, it is not astonishing that emotions should be implicitly understood, since they consist in the assuming of an attitude toward a given situation, this assumption of an attitude being itself due to hereditary and instinctive causes.

These last remarks allow us to understand not only how antibiological but also how antipsychological the 'central', classic concept of emotion is: 'we tremble because we are afraid, we weep because we are sad, we gnash our teeth because we are angry'. This concept is antibiological because it does not allow any significance to the organic reactions and because it makes these primitive reactions, evidently of reflexive or instinctive nature, the result of a purely intellectual perception, of a judgement which can be formulated as follows: The situation in which I find myself is dangerous or terrifying (fear) or it is sad (sorrow) or it is provoking to me (anger), etc.

This concept is also altogether antipsychological. It implies in fact that we can, by a simple intellectual perception of a situation in which we find ourselves, call it 'dangerous', 'terrifying', 'sad', etc. But 'dangerous', 'sad', etc., are not consciousnesses which are given us by means of the external senses, as are color or temperature. It is we ourselves who color the things or the external situations, by projecting into them the feelings which they arouse in *us* and which they excite by producing a reaction of our organism. A large dog or the dark is found terrifying by a child because they have aroused in him the reactions the consciousness of which is what we call 'fear'.

To say, as the classic theory does, that a situation arouses fear because we judge it to be terrifying, is either not to explain why we find this situation frightening, or to revolve in a vicious circle.

Indeed, how does an individual 'comprehend' that a situation is 'terrifying'? To comprehend, we have said, is to take an attitude toward things. To understand that a situation is 'dangerous', 'frightening', is to take, with regard to this situation, an attitude of flight or of protection. But this attitude of flight or of protection is precisely what is at the basis of the emotion of fear. In other words, to say with the classic theory that a situation makes you afraid because it is terrifying is to say that it makes you afraid because it makes you afraid. It is only revolving in a circle!

Functional concept of affective phenomena

We say that the emotion is capable of giving a significance to the situation which it arouses. This assertion demands examination. For, if the emotion is a deficiency in conduct, a poorly adapted act, how can it give a true meaning of things?

It must not be forgotten, however, if the emotion is an objectively poorly adapted act, it represents none the less a total of reaction having a biological significance. To an objective misadaptation may correspond a subjective significance. The attitude taken by the organism is without efficacy on the surrounding environment. It is none the less comprehended by itself; that is to say, it orients itself in a certain definite direction.

I believe that, in order to explain the paradox of an unadapted act which plays, nevertheless, a useful role – for one cannot deny that fear, shame, sorrow, joy have great importance in the life of man – it is more simple to make the following hypothesis. The emotion is a mixture of adaptive reactions and unadaptive actions, of which the proportions vary. The more the emotion takes the form of shock, of explosion, the more important is the share of the misadaptation as compared with that of the adaptation.

Considered from the point of time, the two parts of the emotional phenomenon habitually succeed one another. Sometimes the emotion begins with a shock, with unadapted reactions, which little by little readjust themselves toward a useful behavior. Sometimes on the contrary, the useful adaptation delineates itself at first, and if it is hindered in its termination, it is followed by an emotional explosion. Does not the observation of emotional phenomena in everyday life show us the presence of these two forms of affective processes?

That the emotion, when it is an explosive phenomenon, is not capable of influencing behavior usefully, seems to be shown by the following example, taken from among many others.

Here are two individuals passing through a forest at night. One, of emotional character, feels violent fear. The other remains calm.

They have to return another time, also at night, through the same forest. The frightened man will take precautions. He will carry a weapon, take with him a dog. The second will not modify his behavior. It is without doubt the affective experience of the first journey through the forest which has later modified the behavior of the first traveler. We can, nevertheless, ask whether it is the emotion, as such (considered as a disorder of the reactions), which has made this modification in the ulterior conduct. We can very well indeed imagine a courageous man who, in passing through this forest, ascertains that this crossing is not without danger, and makes this decision *without feeling the least emotion of fear*. His subsequent behavior will be, however, modified in the same manner as that of the man who was afraid; he takes with him a weapon, a dog. The comparison of the two cases shows that the fear as such has not played the role which it seems to have had.

What then has happened to the brave man? The crossing of the gloomy forest has excited in him diverse reactions of attention, of eventual defense; it has determined, in a word, an attitude of 'being on his guard'. Is it not the perception of this attitude which constitutes the 'consciousness of danger'? And can one not say, in the case of the man who is afraid, that it is this attitude of precaution which has modified his subsequent behavior in a useful way? This attitude was blended with the emotion or alternated with it, and one can say that it is not because of the emotion but in spite of it that the behavior has been happily modified.

Do not these reflections lead us to admit, besides the emotions, reactions which are distinguished from them by the fact that they are, themselves, adapted, and as a result capable of orienting behavior usefully. These reactions, these attitudes, and the consciousness that the subject possesses of them, we group together under the name of feelings.

Besides the emotion of fear, we should have then the 'feeling of fear', which it would be better to call 'feeling of danger' and which would consist of the consciousness of the defensive attitude. Besides the emotion of anger, there would be the 'feeling of anger', which it would be better to call 'combative feeling' and which consists of the consciousness of the offensive attitude and the attitude of combat. Besides the 'emotion of shame' – which seems to me to be a 'miscarriage' of the instinct to hide oneself – there would be the 'feeling of shame', which betrays the tendency to hide from the sight of others.

For the emotions of joy and sorrow, the corresponding feelings would then be the pleasant and unpleasant, pleasure and pain, as described by current psychology, and also would be only the consciousness of an attitude of the organism, an attitude positive or negative with respect to the present situation. Only, in the case of the pleasant and the unpleasant we have the case of particularly obscure phenomena, which represent surely a very primitive phase of the organic attitude, that phase in which the humoral processes still predominate over the nervous processes.

The concept which I have outlined seems to me to give an account of the various facts, and presents certain advantages, which I shall enumerate.

Reconciliation with the current concept of emotions

Our concept permits of a reconciliation to a certain extent of the peripheral theory with the current concept of emotions.

It is true, as the current concept affirms, that often fear does not arise in us until after we have first had a consciousness of the danger of the situation in which we find ourselves. Only, this consciousness of danger does not consist, as the classic theory supposes, in a purely intellectual judgement. According to our theory, it results in a 'feeling of danger'. Let us say then that the emotion of fear follows the feeling of danger; it follows if we cannot flee or protect ourselves in an effective way, that for the normal unrolling of behavior is then substituted a miscarriage of behavior. In its principle this way of looking at it, however, is profoundly different from the classic theory, since it considers that neither the emotion nor the feeling of danger is awakened immediately by the perception. The reactionary processes always intervene, as indispensable to the development of the affective phenomenon. It is the awakening of this process which warns us of danger. The emotion, then, appears only as a special phase of the reactionary process. The primitive reactions are substituted for the adaptive reactions when these are prevented from terminating in an act. In cases where the emotion appears quickly, as when we jump at a sudden noise, the James–Lange theory in its ordinary form retains its full value.

The following schema shows the theories about emotions, and will make more clear what we understand by them:

Classic theory	Perception – emotion – organic reactions
James–Lange theory	Perception – organic reactions – emotions
Modified peripheral theory	Perception – attitude (of flight), feeling (of danger) – organic reactions – emotion (fear)
Flight without emotion	Perception – attitude (of flight), feeling (of danger) – flight

Variety of feelings

Our concept also enables us to render account of the infinite variety of affective phenomena, feelings, and emotions. If the whole affective phenomenon is subjectively the consciousness of an attitude and objectively this attitude itself, we can conceive how infinite is the possible range of all of the attitudes. Even attitudes orienting themselves in the same general sense (for example, in the sense of the agreeable) can, nevertheless, differ between themselves in the relation of the quality, since these attitudes can be very different in form.

We now understand why the range of affective phenomena is indeed richer than a theory, such as that of McDougall, which would relate each emotion to a definite instinct, would foresee. In the first place, these are not emotions, but feelings (as those of danger, of aggression, etc.) which correspond to actual instincts. In the second place, as there are more affective *nuances* than definite instincts, one is obliged to admit that feelings may sometimes have for organic base reactions or attitudes intermediate to two or more instincts.

The concept here presented also permits us to understand that feelings and emotions are distinguished not only by their quality and their intensity, but also by their *depth*. The pain which a pin-prick causes me may be much more intense than the pain which is produced by the news of a shipwreck of a boat full of passengers, but the latter is assuredly a deeper pain. One may suppose that this 'depth' corresponds to a supplementary arousal of certain reactionary systems. Perhaps, however, once admitted that feelings of the same kind can differ among themselves in the relation of the quality, the depth resolves itself simply into a question of quality.

The 'transcendental revelation of feelings'

A peripheral theory of feeling also explains the kind of immediate comprehension which we have of feelings – a comprehension of which I have just spoken above with reference to emotion. All affective phenomena have for us not only a content but a value. While blue or red has for us no immediate value, no implicit meaning, pleasure and pain have a value, an inborn value. It seems that, in the affective consciousness, we are the beneficiaries of a really transcendental revelation. How can a little infant, just born, or a caterpillar on a leaf know that this is good and that that is bad; and how, receiving only *subjective* impressions, do they behave as if they know the *objective value* of impressions of good and bad? Here we have material for fine metaphysical discussions. For us psychologists, the mystery resolves itself remarkably as soon as we consider that if feeling has, to consciousness, a subjective value, it is because it corresponds, in behavior, to an attitude, to reactions, which have an objective value. The value perceived by consciousness corresponds to the value for life, for conduct. And one cannot go farther in the way of explanation, if one holds to the principle of psychophysical parallelism.

Intellectual feelings

Our theory of feeling has also this advantage – that it gives a place to intellectual feelings. The term 'intellectual feeling' has not a very definite meaning. In his *Psychology of Feeling*, Ribot includes under this name only surprise, astonishment, curiosity, doubt. Other authors add to these the general feeling which we have of the movement of our thought, of its success, or its impotence. To my mind, one can go much farther, and include among the intellectual feelings all those elements of thought which James calls transitive and which are not representations: conformity, implication, congruity, certitude, probability, and those thousands of relations which we have expressed in the words, *but, if, and, why, after, before,* the thoughts which we express by the words *future, past, conditional, negation, affirmation,* etc.

William James has very well seen all this. 'If there be such things as feelings at all, then, so surely as relations between objects exist *in rerum natura*, so surely and more surely do feelings exist by which these relations are known. There is not a conjunction or a preposition, and hardly an adverbial phrase, syntactic form, or inflection of voice, that does not express some shading or other of relations which we at some moment actually feel to exist between the larger objects of our thought. . . . We ought to say a feeling of *and*, and a feeling of *if*, a feeling of *but*, a feeling of *by*. . . .'

It is very curious that so illuminating a passage of William James, which contains in all its essence a fruitful psychology of thought, should have remained almost a dead letter for psychology. This results, no doubt, from the fact that psychology, under the reign of the associationist doctrine, has remained very definitely closed to biological thought, which alone, to my mind, is capable of rendering it fruitful.

It must be noted, however, that Ribot, in all his work, has insisted on the role of movements and of tendencies in behavior. To him, thought brings itself at last to account in movement. But even he has not seen the consequence which can be drawn from this concept, being in part fascinated by associationism. However, in his *Evolution of General Ideas* (1897, p. 94), he rallies to an opinion derived from the linguists – the opinion according to which the prepositions and the conjunctions express movements. 'The consciousness of these movements', says Ribot, 'is the feeling of the different directions of the thought.'

In my *Association of Ideas* (1903), where I have strongly combated associationism, I have revived James's idea and sought to develop it in biological terms. I consider here all intellectual feelings as corresponding to adaptive reactions or to attitudes of the organism. 'Cannot the body', I say (p. 317), 'be also the source of those numerous ideas which do not correspond, it is true, to anything in the external world which is capable of making an impression on the senses, but which can indeed be nothing other than the consciousness of the reactions of the body with regard to its environment?' I have applied this point of view to the 'comprehension' which brings itself back to an adaptation, and have considered the feeling of comprehension as 'the consciousness of the more or less complete adaptation which is produced'. With respect to the consciousness of relations, 'it suffices', I say (p. 369), 'to admit a different reaction according as the relation perceived is a relation of identity, of resemblance or of equivalence, of possibility or of necessity, of affirmation or of negation, etc. . . .

And, in fact, we do not behave the same with two things when they are different, or similar, or simply equivalent.'

We well perceive, when we see someone gesticulating as he speaks, that all thought is doubled by a moving manifestation. One can say that to think is to gesticulate internally, to outline the acts which the thought prepares and co-ordinates. This concept, I repeat, is the only one which takes account of the role of thought, of its dynamism. But the psychology of thought, in developing – with the Würzburg school – towards pure introspection, has lost at the same time its explicative value. For, whatever may be the descriptive value of phenomena, like *Bewusstheiten* or *Bewusstseinslagen*, one must agree that the description of these states does not explain at all how they influence in an adequate way the course of thought and of behavior. This is, by the way, what Binet has recognized in an excellent article, where he also brings together the 'mental attitudes' of emotion and feelings (2; see also 3 and 4).

If one considers all intellectual feelings to be the outlines of actions or of inhibitions, all is clear, since one can understand how movements can influence the one over the other, reinforce, oppose, or modify themselves in their respective directions.

There remains, however, one difficulty – that is to know why, while emotions and ordinary feelings seem to us to be 'states of our self', the intellectual feelings appear to be objective.

But is this exact? Very many intellectual feelings, such as certainty, doubt, affirmation and negation, logical constraint, etc., can indeed, according to circumstances, according to the direction of our interest at the particular moment, appear to us as objective or as subjective. On the other hand, are ordinary feelings really always subjective? We know how they easily objectify themselves. The aesthetic emotion objectifies itself in the beautiful, the emotion of disgust in the repugnant, etc. We say that an event (objective) is sad, joyous, shameful, comic, or disagreeable. When we declare that a task is painful, we place the pain in the task or in ourselves according to the context of our thought.

To my mind, the subjectivity or the objectivity of a content of consciousness is always the result of a secondary process, depending on the acquired experiences. In the beginning, our states of consciousness are neither objective nor subjective. They become little by little the one or the other according to the necessity of our adaptation to our physical or social environment.

Feelings and internal sensations

The functional concept developed above permits us to state what distinguishes feeling from internal or organic sensations, notably the sensations of hunger, thirst, fatigue, or synaesthesia. Often this distinction is not made, and people generally speak of the 'feeling' of fatigue or of hunger.

To my mind, the sensations of hunger, of thirst, of fatigue (and perhaps one might add to these those of pain) have no value in themselves; they are phenomena which derive their value only from attitudes, tendencies, movements, which they instinctively arouse, and it is the instinctive reactions which confer on them their value for the behavior of the individual. But these instinctive reactions are nothing other than the basis of feelings: feelings agreeable or disagreeable, of desire, of need.

The internal sensations are then states, contrasting with feelings which are attitudes. The internal sensations inform us about such and such states of our organism as our external senses inform us about such and such state of the surrounding environment. But it is by virtue of these feelings that we can estimate the vital value of the organic sensations.

If we seek to represent to ourselves in a purely physiological way, in making abstractions from consciousness, the function of the stimulations corresponding to internal sensations, and the function of the attitudes corresponding to the feelings, it is easy for us to see the functional difference between the two orders of phenomena. The stimulations have value for behavior only in so far as they determine the attitudes or the movements of the organism. One can, with different stimulations, obtain identical attitudes (as, for example, in the experience of Pavlov's conditioned reflexes). This shows us that the stimulation of an internal origin has something of the accidental with relation to the attitude while the attitude represents *itself* a vital value, because it is already an outline of behavior.

Feelings express in some way a relation. The relation between such a situation or such an object and our welfare (or, what comes to the same thing, the attitude which we should take with regard to it). The physiological basis of this relation is the attitude itself. Feeling is the consciousness of this attitude. On the contrary, sensations give us only the objects with regard to which we should take an attitude. In the cases of internal sensations, as those of hunger, of thirst, of fatigue, the object which they give us is *our own body*. It is through the relation to its own state that our body can take a certain attitude. We understand that we have here a very intimate relation between internal sensations and feelings, since they have this in common – that they both have their source in our body. But this does not prevent us from distinguishing them very well from the functional point of view. They are opposed the one to the other, as a reaction is opposed to the object which has aroused it.

I have spoken about the fact that internal sensations correspond to our needs. What is the internal sensation of kinaesthetic nature, such as tension or relaxation, excitement or depression, which Wundt regards as of an affective nature? To my mind, the same observations can be made here that I have made just above. These phenomena are, on the one hand, sensations, or, on the contrary, feelings, according to the context in which we examine them. When we examine them in *themselves*, as states of the organism, they are sensations, objects, which can be agreeable or disagreeable. When we examine them as dependent on the situation which arouses them (an exciting situation, or one calling for attention, etc.) they become feelings. In other words, considered as evaluated objects, they are sensations; considered as instruments of evaluation, they are feelings.

References
1. E. CLAPARÈDE, *Archives de Psychologie*, vol. 7 (1908), p. 195.
2. A. BINET, 'Qu'est-ce qu'une émotion? Qu'est-ce qu'un acte intellectuel?', *L'Année Psychologique*, vol. 17 (1911), pp. 1–47.
3. M. F. WASHBURN, 'The term "feeling"', *Journal of Philosophy, Psychology and Scientific Methods*, vol. 3 (1903), pp. 62–3.
4. E. B. TITCHENER, *Experimental Psychology of the Thought Processes*, Macmillan, New York, 1909, p. 176.

15 R. W. Leeper

A Motivational Theory of Emotion to Replace 'Emotion as Disorganized Response'

Excerpts from R. W. Leeper, 'A motivational theory of emotion to replace "emotion as disorganized response"', *Psych. Rev.*, vol. 55 (1948), pp. 5–21.

A discussion of current theoretical interpretations of emotion might have two values. Thus, first, it might have some value as a means of studying the theoretical efforts of present-day psychology. Second, it might have value because of the increasing interest of psychologists in many particular fields in which emotional processes play important roles.

Confronted with the problem of the limitations of psychology, psychologists rather oddly have been inclined basically to accept the criticism of outsiders – to wit, that the trouble with psychology is too much theorizing and too little factual evidence. This criticism, however, has not reflected any well-informed study. Actually, psychology now shows a one-sided development of an opposite sort. It has achieved a considerable maturity in its factual material and fact-gathering techniques. But it has failed seriously to make corresponding progress in its task of organizing the descriptive data into general principles or theories.

The problem of the nature of emotion, however, is worth discussing, not merely as a means of studying psychological theorizing, but also as a problem worthy of study in its own right. Psychologists are showing increasing interest in the extension of their work into such fields as psychotherapy, personality, child psychology, and social psychology. In all of such cases, if psychologists are to make a full contribution, they must develop some sound concepts of emotional processes, because emotion clearly plays an important role in personality disturbances, social prejudices, etc.

The disorganization concept as dominating current psychological theories of emotion

Even though psychologists have taken an increasing interest in such fields as were just mentioned, the discussions of emotion by psychologists of experimental background have had little application to such other fields. A chief reason for this is that such experimental-psychological interpretations of emotion have been dominated by the concept of emotion as disorganized (or disorganizing) response. This is so poor a generalization of the known facts that it has served as a serious obstacle both to good research work on emotional processes and also to efforts to apply practically the psychological concepts of emotion.

Admittedly, not all of the textbooks of psychology have presented the same theoretical interpretations of emotion. [. . .] However, [. . .] the doctrine of emotion as disorganized or disorganizing response is the favored doctrine in some of the most widely used books. [. . .]

[Thus] N. L. Munn's *Psychology* (4), in its chapter on 'Emotion', says this:

Perhaps as satisfactory a definition as can be given at the present time describes emotion as 'an acute disturbance of the individual as a whole, psychological in origin, involving behavior, conscious experience, and visceral functioning' (8, p. 60). [. . .] We say acute because emotion comes over us suddenly and, after a time, weakens and disappears. [. . .] We say disturbance because all but the mildest emotions disturb or upset whatever activities are in progress at the time of arousal. We say of the individual as a whole because when an individual is emotionally disturbed, he is disturbed all over (p. 263). [. . .]

An even more noteworthy example, however, is R. S. Woodworth's *Psychology* (7). [. . .] We find Woodworth using basically the same concept as the authors quoted above. Thus:

The degree of emotionality depends on how free the lower centers are at any time from domination by the cerebral cortex. Or, if we do not pin our faith to any particular theory of the brain action, we can say that activity is unemotional in proportion as it consists in observing and managing the situation (p. 438).

Emotion is [. . .] a stirred up state of feeling – that is the way it appears to the individual himself. It is a disturbed muscular and glandular activity – that is the way it appears to an external observer (p. 417). [. . .]

The practical life of relation dominates more and more over the emotional life, so that the child's behavior becomes less emotional as he grows older. A scale for emotional age, after the analogy of the Binet scale for mental age, would consist in large part of tests for *not* being afraid or angry or grieved or inquisitive over things which regularly arouse these emotions in the younger child (p. 432).

Emotion, in other words, is something to outgrow!

Cultural origins of the disorganization theory of emotion

One might wonder whether psychologists have originated this theory from their experimental evidence, or whether they are merely reflecting a concept which has developed from other origins. Rather oddly, several spiritual kin of this disorganization concept are easily found. They are family relations which many psychologists might wish to disavow. But they are there, none the less.

We commonly think of the period of Locke and Adam Smith and the French encyclopedists as the age of rationalism. It was the period in which man was held to be primarily and fundamentally a rational creature. Or, at least, it was believed that he *should* be a rational and intelligent creature. Only in the rational or intellectual functions did mankind reach its proper stature. The passions and like weaknesses of human life were unfortunately too often visible, but they were something to be overcome. They were something that made for traditionalism in religious thinking, for respect and deference to authorities, for inertia rather than scientific-mindedness.

We generally pride ourselves that we have come to realize the inadequacies of this rationalistic approach to human nature. We are probably justified in this pride to some extent, because in psychology we have come to realize the rather humble nature of human learning processes in many types of situations. But we should not claim too much difference in our theories, because the view that emotions are basically disruptive, and that a child properly should become 'less emotional as he grows older', could almost have been the doctrines of the old rationalists themselves!

Furthermore, when psychologists consider emotion as disruptive, they have another relationship that is even more surprising, especially in view of the resemblance of psychological thought to the doctrine of rationalism just mentioned. For, if any psychoanalytic thinker were asked whether his ideas are comparable to the rationalistic tradition, he would insist proudly that psychoanalytic thought has been the one really effective challenge to that earlier conception of human nature. He would say that psychoanalytic ideas are the opposite of rationalism.

Perhaps they are. But the psychoanalytic theory states that the ego – the ordinary conscious and pre-conscious part of the personality, the main workaday part of the personality – is a reality-recognizing and reality-manipulating part of the personality. The instinctive processes of the personality, with their emotional components, are not a part of the ego functions, but are a part, instead, primarily of the id, and perhaps to some extent of the super-ego. Not only that, but these instinctive tendencies, with their emotional aspects or components, are the trouble-makers in the whole personality of the individual. They are not things that are to be enriched and developed, if possible. They are nothing that gives reassurance and stability to the personality, but, at least in one sense, they are the disruptive factors in the life of the person!

A fine expression of this is given in Hanns Sachs' *Freud: Master and Friend* (5) when Sachs speaks of Freud as a courageous thinker. He says:

> To look at the Medusa's head is no parlor game. Freud – and this is the sum of everything that has been said in this chapter – was steady enough to stand firm when he perceived that we are not and never will become the masters of our own soul, even when he made the staggering discovery of what unholy stuff the unknown masters are made. He did not flinch when he had to look down, standing at the brink of the precipice. Most others who followed in his tracks got at first a fit of giddiness and had to hold on to him to steady themselves when the mountains seemed to reel. What could those do who were too proud to be supported by him and yet too weak to stand alone? They covered their eyes with their hands and slunk away (5, p. 123).

Now, really, what is Sachs saying by this? What were the facts which were so fearsome to contemplate? In a sense, of course, they were ideas antithetical to the rationalist tradition. They were ideas of intellect as dominated by emotional forces, and they were ideas that these emotional forces were threatening forces of sexual passion, hostility, terror, and the like. But, in this, do we have entirely an abandonment of, or contrast with, the rationalist position? Or do we, on the contrary, have here merely the rationalist disconsolately convinced against himself, still convinced that human life *would* be best if intellectual processes could be the undisputed masters of human life, but forced to admit that this fond hope is unfounded? There is, after all, no confidence here in emotional reactions, no idea of emotional processes as necessary for a full or wholesome human life.

There is still another intellectual relative of the disorganization theory of emotion. This third relative has resulted from the whole trend of modern technology. It is the sort of thing which Gustav Ichheiser (3) has emphasized when he has pointed out that some of the views which we are apt to regard as rather original insights of psychology are merely elaborations of ways of viewing life demanded by the social setting of modern psychology.

What I refer to is that our modern world most obviously is a world of skills, factual knowledge, and intellectual processes – or, in short, of non-emotional processes. At least this is the case at the end where goods are produced, as contrasted with the consumers' end of the process. Advertisers of course know that they have to appeal to emotional motives rather typically. But we take the view that, if anything, the folly of people's behavior as consumers (see the kinds of movies they demand, the kind of radio programs to which they listen, and the kind of newspapers they buy) merely indicates the superiority of the brains involved in production as compared with the inferiority of the emotions involved in consumers' behavior.

Nor is it merely in industry that the broader social scene tends to echo the suggestion that emotion is disruptive. In political life we speak of propaganda (in an unfavorable sense) as appealing to the emotions. We speak of rabblerousers as depending on appeals to emotion. We know that some very unfortunate political movement, from Ku Klux Klan to fascism and nazism, more or less frankly have built their programs on an emotional basis. In the field of religion we have seen that traditionalism and fundamentalism, often openly allied with emotionalism, have conflicted with other more intellectual tendencies which have sought to revise religious beliefs in the light of historical criticism, scientific knowledge, etc.

Consequently, when we question the doctrine that emotions are disorganizing, it is no straw man that we are considering. It is a view, instead, that has been rooted in our popular thought for several centuries. It appears in psychoanalytic thinking as well as in academic psychology. It is enormously strengthened by the fact that a highly technological society tends to share the view that intellectual processes are *the* worthwhile and appropriate human functions.

It does not condemn a concept in psychology, however, merely to point out that it resembles some concept in psychoanalysis or some concept naturally used in everyday life. We need to turn, therefore, to the question as to whether there really is justification for thinking of emotions as disruptive.

The disorganization doctrine as resting on undefined and wrongly interpreted terms

When we consider the pitfalls which beset the path of the scientist who is trying to develop an adequate theory, we are likely to find that there are two main pitfalls: (*1*) the risk that he will survey too narrow a range of facts when he is trying to formulate or evaluate some abstract proposition, and (*2*) the risk that he will use vague undefined terms or poorly defined terms, so that it will be hard for him to see whether he always uses his terms consistently and hard for him to see whether the available factual knowledge supports or contradicts the abstract statement he is considering. It is from these angles, now, that we need to examine the rather common view of emotion cited above. Let us consider first the matter of carefulness of definition and of consistent use of terms.

First of all, we may note that none of the above-mentioned authors has attempted to give a definition of such terms as 'disorganized' and 'disorganizing'. They are the key terms, or crucial terms, for such a theory. But the authors apparently have assumed that the terms are self-explanatory or self-defining, with their meanings sufficiently indicated by common usage or by the dictionary. But to proceed in this way is dangerous. It is the typical way in which sloppiness and inaccuracy sometimes slip into scientific theory. Where there are no explicit definitions of key terms, it is easy for thinkers to neglect significant factual data and it is easy to fall into inconsistent usages.

177

As an example of such inconsistent or shifting meanings, we find that these psychologists seem to speak as though the two terms 'disorganized' and 'disorganizing' (or 'disturbance' and 'disturb') are synonymous. Thus, Munn says that emotion may be defined as 'an acute disturbance'. Then, to explain this, he says, 'We say disturbance because all but the mildest emotions disturb or upset whatever activities are in progress . . .' (4, p. 263). Now either usage might be clearcut. We might say that the *disturbance* or *disorganization* of behavior is the emotion. Or we might say that the emotion is *what produces this disturbance*. Or, conceivably, we might say that emotion is both the disturbance and that which produces the disturbance of the previous processes. But there can be no claim to scientific thinking when, without explaining our gymnastics, we jump back and forth from one such contradictory usage to another. It is not Munn alone, either, who follows such a shifting usage. It is the typical thing with all of the authors quoted above.

The difficulty is not solely a matter of lack of definitions, however, but is a matter also of sticking consistently to the same definitions, because even when the implied meanings are fairly clearcut, there still exist contradictions in closely adjacent sentences. Careful thinking takes a lot of time, a lot of turning-over-and-over of the material. The disorganization theory of emotion has not received such careful thought. Let us consider Munn again. He says that '. . . all but the mildest emotions disturb or upset whatever activities. . . .' From this a student might reasonably assume that there are some (mild) emotions that do not 'disturb or upset'. But, when the student then tries to find out the definition of these emotions, he has to go back to the statement that emotions are 'an acute disturbance'. This is not acceptable, of course. A definition of a key term in psychology must cover the phenomenon as it appears in all degrees. [. . .]

Contradictions between the factual data and careful definitions of 'disorganized' and 'disorganizing'

The center of the whole discussion, then, obviously lies in the matter of what is meant by such key terms as 'disorganize' and 'disorganization' (or their opposites, 'organize' and 'organization').

First of all, it should be clear that these terms possess no connotation, properly, of 'good' or 'bad'. In fact, they have been used primarily because it was felt that they were terms which avoided any such value-judgements. This is a reasonable view. After all, an organized mob or an organized gang is not necessarily something good. So 'organized' must not be taken as meaning 'useful' or 'wholesome in its influence'. Instead, a system is 'organized' when one part of it is functioning harmoniously with other parts. Something is 'organized' when the parts fit, or dovetail, or are congruous with one another. And on the other hand, something is 'disorganized' when the subordinate parts operate at cross purposes with each other. Something has an 'organizing' influence in a system when it tends to produce order or co-operation or harmony between different subordinate parts or subordinate activities.

A qualification needs to be added, however. 'Organization' always is purchased at the price of interfering with what is inconsistent with the main basis of organization. For example, when we say that effective study or effective thinking is an 'organized' process, we need to recognize that the person's activity tends to inhibit or side-track some processes which otherwise would occur, or which were occurring previously. The person does not react to sounds which ordinarily would have diverted him; he fails to respond to a condition of hunger which is developing within him; he is side-tracking a number of competing interests. In the same way, even though we would say that a nation at war is more highly organized than a nation at peace, it also is true that factories often are required to give up their regular work, young men are taken from their schools and home life, many recreational activities are discontinued, and so on. The criterion of organization, consequently, is not a matter of whether there is some interference with preceding activities or with inconsistent subordinate activities. *It is the question whether this interference is relatively chaotic and haphazard, or whether the suppressions and changes of subordinate activities are harmonious with some main function which is being served.* Unless we adopt such a usage, the disorganization theorists must say that problem-solving thinking is an emotion, because clearly it disrupts preceding modes of response and also interferes with incongruous activities at the moment.

Is there any fault with the definitions just suggested? If there is, these various authors have not said so. As we have mentioned, they have simply let their main terms be undefined. It would seem, however, as though they would agree with the above suggestions. Let us see, therefore, whether the factual data are consistent with definitions which seem reasonable.

Rather commonly, the authors mentioned above have said that emotions involve disorganization of three aspects of life: visceral processes, behavior, and conscious experience. Let us examine, first, the asserted disorganization of visceral processes. The asserted facts are that when a person reacts with strong fear or anger (and in some other emotions, but not all) his digestion is slowed or stopped, his heart beats more rapidly, his breathing becomes more rapid, his blood is driven more extensively into the skeletal muscles rather than into the digestive organs, etc.

Is this to be understood as 'disorganization'? Do these subordinate visceral changes operate at cross purposes with one another, or do they dovetail in high degree? There is interference with digestion, of course. But, from the standpoint of the main function for which the organism is now prepared, is this interference with digestion a mark of disorganization, or is it more truly a mark of organization? In such matters, the disorganization theorists have not attempted to show that the different visceral reactions in fear and anger operate at cross purposes with one another! They have been content to refer to faster breathing, faster heartbeat, etc., as though such changes *ipso facto* are demonstrations of disorganization. But, carefully speaking, the person is organized during fear or anger. He is organized viscerally so that he can most naturally do something consistent with his fear or anger. What he is organized to do may be 'unwise' or 'bad'. But that is irrelevant. Viscerally, the 'individual as a whole' is not disorganized.

Behaviorally, is the person disorganized while afraid or angry? If he is, a football coach typically does some very unwise things, because he puts out considerable effort to get his men emotionally aroused (or even angry!). Of course, in some instances it is easy to demonstrate that such emotions as fear often handicap the behavior which the person (because of some other motive) wants to engage in. The pianist with stagefright, for instance, cannot play well. But the test of whether fear has an organizing effect on behavior is not the test of whether it tends to help produce some kind of behavior demanded by some other competing or conflicting motives of the person! The fear is tending to make the person avoid the platform appearance. It makes him seek for excuses to get out of such performances; it tends to make him flee even after he gets on to the platform. The stagefright, in other words, tends to organize behavior along lines consistent with that fear.

In the third place, *from the standpoint of conscious experience*, is there disorganization? Again our general factual knowledge denies any such assertion. When a person is strongly aroused emotionally, as in the case of a psychiatric patient, the conscious experience is not disorganized. On the contrary, a persistent, insistent mood prevails. The person finds it impossible to shake off a feeling of personal worthlessness or of discouragement or of danger or whatever. There may be some play of thought, it is true, within the limits of what is consistent with the emotionally-significant situation. But the conscious experience shows strong organization. In fact, a main difficulty with such clinical cases is that of helping the person to get any thoughts or feelings other than he usually has as a consequence of his most prevalent emotional response.

Several answers might be made to these comments, however. In the first place, the disorganization theorists might say, 'Yes, that may all be true, but there is a disorganization of the behavior and conscious experience that went before'. True enough. But every psychological process has this same effect. When the players in a symphony orchestra see the conductor come out on the platform, this perception causes a cessation of their preceding activity of talking, tuning their instruments, fingering special phrases, and so on. We could say that there is a disorganization of the behavior that was occurring before. But we do not say, because of this, that the musicians have now become emotional. All that we say is that there has been a change of activity and, if anything, a shift from a less organized condition to a more organized condition. When a challenging problem occurs to a scientist he tends to drop what he was working on previously. But we do not say that he is thus becoming emotional. In the same way, then, there is no basis for saying (unless we want to give up all effort at consistency of speech) that emotions are disorganizations because preceding activities are terminated and replaced by other activities.

In the second place, though, the disorganization theorists might say, 'Yes, but this shift involves a change from constructive or useful activities to foolish and inappropriate activities.' Maybe so. And, correspondingly, if we want to define emotions as 'foolish and inappropriate responses', this definition might harmonize with the facts to which we would thus be pointing. But, as we said above, the terms 'organize' and 'disorganize' are supposedly neutral with regard to value-judgements. They have appealed to psychologists, rather typically, because they seemed merely descriptive. Well and good, then, we must stick to our meanings. A shift from a wise behavioral organization to an unwise behavioral organization is not a shift from organization to disorganization.

In the third place, however, the disorganization theorists might say, 'Now we will play our trump card. Look at what happens when the person becomes *extremely* afraid or *extremely* angry. Then he wants to run, or he wants to call for help, and he cannot do it. He wants to win the football game, but his reaction is so over-intense that he is hampered rather than helped. The boxer becomes so angry that he loses his technical skill and fights ineffectively. What can you say about this – isn't this really disorganization, even in the sense that you defined above?'

In this type of case, indeed, the emotional process does seem to produce disorganization in significant degree. It interferes with reactions that would be consistent or harmonious with what is demanded by the emotion. But are such cases to be the means of deciding the function of emotional responses of all degrees of intensity? If so, there is a queer logic involved. In no other case do we decide on the properties of something by a like procedure. If we did, we would say, for instance, that the function of breathing is to disrupt psychological processes because the person who forces himself to breathe rapidly and deeply will find in a few minutes that he gets dizzy, he begins to tingle all over, and (as is used in electroencephalographic work) if he has a tendency to epilepsy, he will have a mild attack which can be recorded on the electroencephalograph. We do not determine the functions in the body of normal amounts of salt, iodine, fluorine, or any other material by discovering the influence of these same materials when consumed in extreme doses. We are interested, perhaps, in describing such effects also; but we do not use this as the means of determining the normal functions of such products. The same logic, then, should apply to emotional processes.

Let us now consider another slant on this matter. In the above discussion, in considering whether there is really evidence of disorganization in emotional activity, we have been talking only in terms of such emotions as fear and anger. But, although they have spoken somewhat hesitantly, the disorganization theorists have not applied their concept of emotion merely to such emotions. They have included, although to a relatively limited extent, what might be called positive emotions. For example, Dockeray says:

The satisfaction felt in a job well done, the pride of a father in his son, and the joy of meeting an old friend are relatively mild emotions as compared with the unpleasant experiences of dissatisfaction, disgust, or hate (1, p. 193).

Similarly, in his list of typical feelings and emotions, Woodworth includes joy, amusement, hope, courage, contentment, and love (7, p. 410). Shaffer, Gilmer, and Schoen, in their chapter on 'Emotional Behavior', include one section on 'delight, joy, and laughter' and another section on 'affection and love' (6, pp. 152-5).

If these are emotions, as the historical usage of the term would suggest, it would seem that they ought to occupy a rather significant place in these discussions. For one thing, unless we are to take an extremely pessimistic view of human life, we might well say that such 'pleasurable emotions' or 'positive emotions' are, in general, just as numerous and important in human life as are the 'unpleasurable' or 'negative' emotions. It is hard to see, therefore, why they secure merely passing mention and why such emotions as fear and anger are discussed as though they are the only valid prototypes of emotion.

However, even beyond this, if these positive emotions are to be spoken of as emotions, we have a right to ask the disorganization theorists to consider the question whether they also are interpreted as supporting the generalization that emotions disorganize the person viscerally, behaviorally, and in conscious experience. A scientific writer should be sensitive to empirical knowledge. As

Clark Hull has put the matter very clearly, '. . . wherever a generalization really conflicts with observation the generalization must always give way' (2, p. 12). But what we have in this matter is no such sensitiveness to accepted factual knowledge. Instead, we have the trick of Procrustes: The facts must lie down on a harsh bed of foreordained proportions, and if the facts do not fit, it is just too bad for the facts. [. . .]

Some fallacies which have obstructed the acceptance of a motivational theory

Our conclusion has been, therefore, that the whole framework of the discussion of emotion as disorganizing has been absurdly inadequate. It is not enough to leave the matter in this form, however. It is not sufficient to criticize such a concept adversely, because the question then would come, 'All right, but how else can we think about emotions?' This is a legitimate question. Indeed, if there were no alternative concept, we probably would not be inclined to object so strongly to what has been said.

To get some satisfactory alternative, we will need, of course, to get some agreement as to the subject-matter to be covered by such terms as 'emotion', and we will need to get some abstract statements about this subject-matter which will represent the best of our available factual knowledge.

To begin with, we can use the 'pointing' method of defining emotion. We can say that emotions are such phenomena as fear, anger, feelings of guilt, feelings of grief, affection, pride in the doing of good work, enjoyment of beautiful music, and enjoyment of companionship. Continuing our pointing, we may say that 'emotions' are to be seen, not merely in cases where these processes occur in intense form, but that emotion can exist, as Woodworth says, in all degrees of intensity.

We ask, then, what properties mark all of such a diverse collection of phenomena, at least when they are not carried to rare extremes. We have seen that disorganization is not characteristic. Hardly in any sense do we find any disorganization as a product of such emotions as affection or esthetic emotion. Even in such emotions as fear and anger we saw that disorganization occurs ordinarily merely as the price of achieving some dominating organization, and that consequently it is not truly disorganization.

In fact, we seemed to be moving toward the conclusion that, for all emotions, organization is the typical thing. Organization for what? Organization in what sense? When we come to this point, we have to decide whether to trust factual knowledge or whether to trust *a priori* conclusions. Our factual knowledge says that if you can arouse anger in a person you can increase the probability that his behavior will be directed and sustained in a certain direction. If you can arouse sympathy and friendliness, you will increase the likelihood that his behavior will be directed and energized in a different direction. The stronger the emotional process aroused (short of extremes that will perhaps run into qualitatively different effects), the more certainly will his behavior be governed in a way consistent with his emotional reaction. This is a principle which permits prediction and control of human behavior and conscious experience. It might be criticized of course, as being merely a vague, non-quantitative principle. Any principle is likely to have this character at the start. But that is no serious objection. Scientific work must proceed by a process of approximation and correction.

If this line of argument is sound, it means that emotional processes operate primarily as motives. It means that they are processes which arouse, sustain, and direct activity!

Or, at least, this is what it would seem that they are. But the doctrine of emotion as disorganized or disorganizing does not permit such a statement, even though the disorganization theorists have considered it as a possibility. Thus, P. T. Young makes this amazing statement:

... there are persistent, purposive activities which arise during emotional upset and which are a part of emotional behavior. Thus, fear is associated with impulses to escape, anger with aggressive attack, sexual emotion with fondling and caressing. Inasmuch as these purposive activities are integrated, they cannot be components of *emotion* – emotion being always disruptive – but they are a part of *emotional behavior*. Thus, emotional behavior includes both integrated components and the signs of disruption.

The association of certain purposive activities with emotional disturbance is not accidental. The psychological situation which arouses a disturbed state of fear evokes also the precipitate flight from danger. The situation which arouses the emotion of anger also produces aggressive behavior. Thus, organized and disorganized processes normally arise out of the same psychological situation (8, p. 401).

Now, where in modern science could one find a better example of the kind of thinking that marked the old scholastics – arbitrary definitions, subtle distinctions unsupported by empirical observations, and then deductive argument from those as unquestionable data! What an amazing thing this would be, if what Young asserts were true! In all of the higher animals there are evidently emotional reactions of fear, anger, affection, playfulness, and what not. And, by some mysterious alchemy, these occur at the same time that the organism struggles with unusual intensity and effectiveness to flee, fight, or whatnot. But these emotional reactions have nothing to do with these unusually-well-motivated actions which they accompany – in fact, though regularly correlated with such, they have exclusively a dragging or hampering influence. As Young insists, 'Emotion is always a disruption' (8, p. 400).

Munn argues in much the same way. He says:

There are several theories of emotion. . . . One, designated the *commonsense theory*, needs little discussion. It assumes that we perceive an emotion-provoking situation, have an emotional experience, and then behave emotionally – as if the emotional experience aroused or stimulated the visceral and skeletal reactions. To the man in the street this is obviously what happens. The psychologist, however, does not accept so naïve a view (4, p. 278).

This is all that he says about this 'commonsense theory'. But why is this commonsense view 'too naïve for scientific acceptance' (4, p. 282)?

Munn is relying, fairly surely, on the idea that any concept of mind-body interaction is naïve and unsound, and that therefore the psychologist cannot say that the conscious experience causes the reaction. Perhaps this is so, but if such is the case, it is equally unsound for him to discuss the James–Lange and thalamic theories as though they might provide some explanation of how certain physiological processes might explain the conscious experience of emotion, because any such theories involve the same assumption of mind-body interaction!

But, after all, in such a matter as this, we do not need to run into such difficulties. If we are willing to talk about conscious experiences, as Munn now is, we can simply state that we conceive of this conscious experience as an aspect of a larger happening or process, partly conscious in character and partly neurological or physiological in character (or partly susceptible to study by neurological or physiological techniques), which occurs under conditions that are presumably discoverable. The James–Lange theory asserts one hypothesis regarding the origins or conditions productive of this complex, partly conscious and partly neurological condition or event. The hypothalamic theory suggests another such hypothesis. But, in the same basic terms, it is quite a possible hypothesis that the perception of the emotion-provoking situation produces the emotional process (which may have a conscious aspect to it, and which may produce also an autonomic discharge, either directly or via some subcortical centers, and which may then be reinforced or supported by widespread bodily changes). And it is quite a possible hypothesis that this emotional process (perhaps as reinforced by interoceptive impulses from visceral reactions or proprioceptive impulses from general tonus changes) then operates to motivate behavior. In fact, from what we know, this seems to be decidedly the least naïve of the three theories!

One might well ask, 'On what basis, then, did Young and Munn decide that the emotional process is such a parasitic phenomenon, occurring at the same time at which unusually effective organization is needed, but operating solely to produce disorganization?' It may seem odd (and indeed it *is* odd in the work of persons as capable and careful), but the simple fact is that they had no basis other than the doctrinaire premise that emotions are always disruptive. For after all, by the same procedure, we could demonstrate that bodily drives such as hunger and thirst are always disruptive, basing our argument on the observation that a person's previous activities become disorganized when he becomes hungry or thirsty, his thinking becomes ineffective about other matters, he loses his ability, perhaps, to inhibit certain tendencies, etc. Then, confronted with the evidence that some very effective food-seeking occurs while the person is hungry, we could merely dismiss this with Young's type of argument, as by saying, 'The association of such adaptive and integrative activity with hunger is not accidental. The same situation which evokes the hunger also evokes the food-seeking activity. Inasmuch as food-seeking is integrated, it cannot

be dependent on hunger – bodily drives being always disruptive!'
The logic of such a statement would be exactly parallel to that
which Young has used with reference to emotion.

But, obviously, Young and the other workers have not argued
in this way about the bodily drives. Why, then, have they reasoned
in one way on one matter, and in the other way on the other matter?
The answer seems to be that in our thinking about emotion, perhaps because it has been relatively a neglected problem with
general psychologists, we have not been doing a reasonable
scientific job. We have been dominated by *a priori* conceptions
about emotion. Too commonly we have adopted, for all practical
purposes, a faulty representation of psychological functions which
was started back in the late 1700s – a division of psychological
processes into those of cognition, affection, and conation. The
view adopted by Young, Munn, and the others is essentially that
same view, that matters of feeling or emotion (or, affection) are
fundamentally different from matters of striving or motivation
(or, conation). But it is time that psychology issued a declaration
of independence from this antique tradition, and it is time that
this declaration of independence took the form, not merely of
change of words, but also of a rejection of the false dichotomy
between affection and conation which that eighteenth-century
view contained.

References

1. DOCKERAY, F., *Psychology*, Prentice-Hall, 1942, pp. xiv + 504.
2. HULL, C. L., *Principles of behavior*, D. Appleton-Century, 1943,
   pp. x + 422.
3. ICHHEISER, G., 'Why psychologists tend to overlook certain
   "obvious" facts', *Phil. Sci.*, vol. 10 (1943), pp. 204–7.
4. MUNN, N. L., *Psychology: The Fundamentals of Human Adjustment*,
   Houghton Mifflin, 1946, pp. xviii + 497.
5. SACHS, H., *Freud: Master and Friend*, Harvard University Press,
   1944, pp. 195.
6. SHAFFER, L. F., GILMER, B., and SCHOEN, M., *Psychology*, Harper
   & Bros., 1940, pp. xii + 521.
7. WOODWORTH, R. S., *Psychology*, 4th edn., Henry Holt, 1940,
   pp. xiii + 639.
8. YOUNG, P. T., *Emotion in man and animal: its nature and relation
   to attitude and motive*, John Wiley & Sons, 1943, pp. xiii + 422.

16 M. Pradines

Feelings as Regulators

Excerpts from M. Pradines, *Traité de Psychologie*, 6th edn, vol. 1,
Presses Universitaires de France, 1958, pp. 659–68, 675–83, 718–21.
Translated by Y. Bégin and M. B. Arnold.

Sentiments and affective sensations. Perceptual and associative
behaviour could not develop if the perceptual experience that
signals simple feelings were not loaded with semi-hallucinatory
images leading to motor dispositions that are adapted to the very
possibilities foreshadowed by perception. These dispositions are
not only motor, they are also affective in nature. As we said previously: 'The past builds a future which has something of the
liveliness of the present even when it remains indefinite; and which
moves us as if it were the present with varying perspectives none of
which is stable enough to hold our attention' (p. 227).[1] These
'images represent many possible stimuli and *move* us as if these
stimuli were real' – although they remain in the distance. '*In
imagination we see* these – in fact motionless – objects of sight and
sound change their place, their shape, their colour as well as their
sound; these *imaginary beliefs* determine our preparatory responses' (p. 228). Consequently, perception does not act merely
through the purely intellectual anticipation it produces but also
through the affective states that accompany it.

These affective states are not the *simple feelings* of physical
pleasure and pain . . . for these are connected with sensations of
contact that are fairly intimate; the images we are talking about
can only hint at the presence of things we cannot touch, of things
still in the distance. We are talking of feelings linked somehow
to images of physical pleasure or pain. This does not mean that
they retain nothing of these pleasures and pains. Perception would
be deprived of all action if it did not leave in us some remnant of
the power to act, inherent in the feelings it replaces. Perception
can inherit this dynamism because, in all physical pleasure and

1. [Page references refer to the 1958 edition of *Traité de Psychologie*.]

pain, perception constitutes an element distinct in nature but inseparable in fact from the pain/pleasure element.

Need, particularly, has seemed to us quite different from pleasure; and aversion is a defensive motor reaction to which painful feelings seem to be added rather than being inherent in it. The image of pleasure can move us, like pleasure itself, toward the object that promises it. And the image of pain can repel us, like pain itself, from what can dangerously injure us. We then have an *attraction* without pleasure – called *love* or desire – and an *aversion* without pain, called *hate*.

Thus we see *sentiment* in its most elementary form born of a feeling that is called *sensory* because it is linked to sensation. In one sense, sentiment is a *complex feeling*, for in its autonomous form it belongs to a higher and more complex level of behaviour than does a simple feeling. In another sense, sentiment could be said to be simpler than simple feeling, for its primary effect is to split up simple feeling and make one of its inseparable *elements* autonomous, namely the power to act which is inherent in sentiment but diffused in sensory feelings.

Sentiments and tendencies. However, we must not pretend that this dynamism can be transmitted without loss. Love and hate differ not only from sensory feelings but also from the physical *excitation* which is the common source of motor and affective elements of the original reaction and has given them the power to act. What we possess is loved differently from what we might possess. The cause of an actually experienced evil is treated quite differently from the eventual cause of a possible evil. But this loss of energy in *sentiment* is compensated by elements coming from another source, from properly perceptual factors. For perception is associative; and it associates not only ideas but forces. Association is cumulative energy.

Through association, a progressively enlarged experience is allowed to exert its influence on behaviour. It is fortunate that the actions made possible through association arouse energies which by their number and variety, if not by their brute force, can act as counterweight to blind impulse. Without it, instinct would never have given way to perceptual behaviour. These energies are affective. Because sentiment can absorb them, it can be considered a complex feeling. As we have said, sentiment owes this complexity to the mental *level* on which it operates. [. . .]

Sentiments as regulators. From the above comparison between sensory feelings and the feelings produced by perception it follows that sentiments appear to play the same regulatory role in life as does perception: they form the dynamic aspect of perception. They are the active forces which help us take advantage of the intellectual resources made available by perception. This notion has been developed by the Chicago school, which sees the function of sentiment as triggering adaptive motor responses; also by Pierre Janet (1928), who has been inspired by this school but in some ways has anticipated it. Indeed, the idea that sentiments are 'regulators of action' has been generally accepted in France, thanks to Janet, who explained that they are 'reactions to a given situation . . . organized and useful reactions'. Unfortunately, though he has deduced remarkable consequences from this notion, he has not followed it through with the desirable logic.

If sentiments are reactions to a given situation, functionally speaking, and are meant to regulate our behaviour accordingly, they must have a *circumstantial character* as does every situation. This character is the prime condition of their adaptive value. Seen from this standpoint, sentiments escape subjectivity, although we usually consider them as limited to the subjective world of the individual. But sentiments cannot be considered the *subjective aspect* of an activity that relates us to the external world. At the very least, sentiments are no more subjective than are sensations which produce perfectly objective impressions even of feelings. Similarly, sentiments provide a completely adequate rule of action *with regard to objects*. Since sentiments are circumstantial, objective and adaptive in a given situation, they appear to be different from tendencies (or inclinations) which are dispositions independent of circumstances and without precise orientation (which clearly distinguishes them from instincts). As a rule, tendencies are far removed from the changing world of objects and cannot provide a rule of action adequate to them. They cannot be said to be objective in the precise sense of the term. Of course, existential conditions do not always change, and it is possible to conceive of adaptive sentiments that remain stable in response to equally stable situations. But this is merely the exception that proves the rule: sentiments remain stable when circumstances are stable because they can adapt to circumstances which ordinarily keep changing. We can easily see that stability is desirable in those sentiments that enable us to live a social or at least a gregarious life. [. . .]

From the above discussion we can infer that sentiments have a circumstantial character. The current psychological trend mistakenly identifies sentiment with tendency and mistakenly sees sentiments as the stable elements of our emotional constitution.

At any rate, it is certain that many sentiments seem to be adaptive with regard to circumstances that by nature are changeable. As a result, they appear fleeting and variable. Moreover, it is to be expected that we should change most of our sentiments because they express our reactions to variable circumstances. The changeability of the affective life does not have the pathological implications ascribed to it. It is entirely normal that our emotions, from joy to sorrow, from confidence to discouragement, from fear and anxiety to hope and assurance, depend on how circumstances serve or frustrate our plans, and whether they require eagerness or reserve, resignation, prudence or distrust. It can hardly be denied that all our sentiments in their normal form are aroused by appropriate circumstances and specified by them. Yet people often think that sentiments are an exception in the affective life and confer stability on it. Though we ascribe stability to sentiment, it derives stability only from certain of its objects, as in the example of social sentiments discussed above. It seems obvious that sentiment directed toward others is stabilized according to their own psychological stability, and that our affective regulation takes account of the degree of firmness in their character. For this reason, the inexplicable change in sentiment toward stable personalities, which is sometimes seen, can be called pathological. However, change remains the natural principle of love and sympathy as well as of all other sentiments. It is a fact that this impulse, which carries us without specification toward a person of the other sex, or in general toward our *associates*, is specified only by knowledge. We love only those we find worth loving, and cease to love those who treat us inconsiderately. Morality can counsel different attitudes; but we are speaking of natural impulses. Sentiment, like instinct, is a weapon, a defence and a display: its functional value is closely tied to its plasticity. Properly directed observation will show that this plasticity of sentiment has been preserved in most people.

Disordered sentiments. What has deceived psychologists is misdirected observation. Disorder has often masqueraded as order, illness as health, perversion as nature. Sentiment is a naturally ordered phenomenon; but it can become disordered. The investigation of such *disorders* represents the most important part of a study of sentiments as well as of any general theory designed to include them.

There are four ways in which disorder can be introduced into sentiments: through fixation, passion, inversion, emotion.

1. *Through inappropriate fixation.* It is normal and natural to feel joy when there is a promise of happiness, sorrow at a threat of suffering or deprivation, anger at annoying behaviour, fear and worry in the face of danger. All these sentiments will disappear together with the occasions that have aroused them. In contrast, it is not normal to live in a state of perpetual joy, sorrow, irritability, worry and anxiety (though we exclude here the metaphysical anxiety which in sensitive people may be linked to their awareness of the enduring tragedy of our human condition). This existential anxiety has been exhaustively analysed by such philosophers as Kierkegaard and Pascal, and more recently in France by the psychologists Vialle (1933) and Lacroze (1938). However, there are people who are always cheerful or always depressed, always irritable and choleric, or timid and fearful. They have no need of special occasions to rejoice or grow sad, to become angry or to worry. These emotional dispositions may be innate like the diathesis to a certain illness, but that does not make them more normal. They may be elements of an individual's character, and form, as Dupré (1925) says, a *psychopathic constitution.*

But they may also be acquired through the influence of concrete events and so serve as a natural experiment showing the process by which sentiment can evolve from one form into another: from an affection that is adaptive, objective and circumstantial, to a purely subjective state indifferent to the necessity for adjustment and the prod of circumstances. René Dejean (1933) has published an excellent study of such transformations in soldiers of the First

World War. He has shown that their experience of mortal peril, of being wounded, of a series of tragic events, or the sheer continuity of danger, has produced a fear disposition capable of converting normal fighters into useless cowards. In contrast to the more usual habituation to danger which assures a kind of immunity to fear, this phenomenon seems to be the result of a veritable psychological *anaphylaxis*. According to Dejean, the continuous danger has sensitized the individual to the smallest additional threats, which now release an anxiety quite disproportionate to its cause. From now on, worry and anxiety are always present and so arouse the notion of danger, instead of danger arousing the emotion.

This functional maladjustment clearly appears as a state which creates the circumstances it is called on to ward off, as if there were an acquired need to function all the time – and so, out of due time. However, the normal adaptive character of sentiment is revealed even in such maladjustive processes which imitate the blindness of the normal adaptive processes we call habit and instinct. This makes us suspect, by analogy, that these maladaptive processes originate in a useful reactive mechanism which can be derailed and perverted through use. The living being is betrayed by the instruments he creates for his defence and so becomes their victim. The process functions in a vacuum; designed to react to an image of reality, it constructs a fantasy image out of appearances when there is no reality to draw on – in much the same way as a hen will sit on stone eggs. When a man is elated, he finds rapture in his dreams; when conceited, in triumphs; when depressed, he finds solace in his misery; and when bad-tempered, in the insults he has received. [. . .]

2. *Through passion*. Surely it is absurd to attribute passions even to the most evolved animals. Even children can only be called passionate to the extent that they show characteristically adult inclinations precociously. Thus it seems that passion can be validly regarded as tied to conditions of the affective life that are created by a specifically human mentality.

It cannot be denied that this will result in a transformation of sentiment. Not all sentiments may be amenable to such transformation, and it behoves us to look for the reasons: we don't speak of passionate joy, sorrow, fear; indeed, we hardly know what could be meant by these expressions. On the other hand, all passions are *impassioned*, or perhaps we should say *passionalized*, sentiments because they have acquired a character (of reason) which does not belong to the most common and never to the primitive form of sentiments.

Passion is a transformation of sentiment which is also a *stabilization*. This must be emphasized to prevent mistaking it for pathological stabilization. There is a difference between the two types of *disordered* stabilization. No doubt passion produces this disorder by making our goals rigid and immovable, despite moral or social reasons, despite interests of all kinds (personal, familial or collective), despite obstacles and even physical impossibilities which prevent their realization or should induce us to condemn even the thought of such goals.

For this reason, passion is a sign of disorganization, of *defunctionalization* of the sentiment so that sentiment is cut off from any consideration of object and circumstances and is made to live an intensely *subjective* life, unduly demanding, impervious to experience and blind to reality, for which it substitutes hallucinations.

But from another point of view, passion achieves the goal of adaptation for which sentiment is destined because passion begins to organize the sentiments themselves. Often our sentiments succeed in adapting us to things, only to disturb our internal adjustments. The wisdom of the ages has long recognized that the regulation provided by sentiments is far from ideal. Each sentiment pulls us toward its own side. In adapting us to circumstances, sentiments often manage only to tear us apart between divergent goals. Wisdom has always decreed that man should have some norms of conduct which transcend the influence of sentiments and have the power to forge a bond that is stronger than theirs. Such counsel is meant to guide man's step toward happiness which – define it as you will – has always implied conforming to his best adjustment. Passion surely works toward that end, whatever the value of the means it employs. This is what makes passion an affection playing the role of sentiment, but playing it against sentiment. It is an affection fostering concentration rather than dispersion; an affection with goals that are ignored by ordinary sentiments, which aim for objective adaptation without much care for subjective adjustment. In contrast, passion tends toward subjective and disregards objective adaptation. Sentiments permit adjustment to a thousand things but passion aims for one thing alone.

Enough has been said to show that passion implies the action of psychological factors of a totally new order. Since we have found no trace of their origin at the elementary level of mental life, only an investigation of the higher levels can provide an answer to the questions raised.

3. *By moral inversion.* Undoubtedly, self-interest has always been considered the most stable element of man's affective make-up. It seems to inspire almost all his actions, and all the sentiments that are called *base, gross* or *perverse* seem to stem from it. The usual classification of sentiments . . . usually refers to this group. And since there is hardly a more constant disposition than to love and serve ourselves, it is not surprising that psychologists have inferred that stability is a characteristic of sentiment.

But . . . this word 'egoism', in so far as it refers to any *psychological reality*, is more often than not a label that means nothing. When we withdraw the hand from the touch of a burning object, this act is usually ascribed to an instinct or an egoistic sentiment of self-preservation. But in fact it is nothing but a reflex excited by pain. Its adaptive value must be ascribed to a protective mechanism and not to a sentiment or tendency of any kind. In saying that such reflexes are stable we either commit an error – for they are always completely adapted to circumstances, and the response is always proportional to the stimulus and aims at fending it off by the most opportune means – or we are simply saying that these are protective reflexes, which does not imply any qualitative constancy in the affective states that accompany them. [. . .]

However, there is certainly a form of egoism which can be considered a sentiment; or better, the common form of many sentiments. This type of egoism is characterized by the remarkable stability of its action in most forms of human conduct. But this egoism . . . is not an expression of our psychological nature but a moral vice, that is to say a voluntary maladjustment. . . . Whenever the sentiment becomes stable (except when it conforms to stability in the object), it becomes maladaptive. However, such maladjustment may have a moral cause or it may stem from passion. It may also have its roots in routine or physical weariness. In this analysis we have described the first of these causes of maladjustment and have, we feel, indicated a basic process of maladjustment. In passion, the attachment to a variety of objects has been replaced by attachment to an invariable and unique *subject*. All the pleasures that come from being active are sacrificed to the sensory pleasure of activity. [. . .]

4. *By emotion*. The disorder of sentiment that is caused by emotion is certainly the type that is most interesting and most relevant to psychology proper. However, this disorder is not merely an *effect* of emotion, for emotion could be conceived without this disorder, as in general any cause can be conceived without its effects. This disorder is emotion itself. It defines and constitutes emotion. [. . .]

Emotions are disruptive by nature, which is why they are better considered as distinct affections rather than as a particular form of sentiments. This is perhaps what language intended by providing a special name; though it has not furnished a special name to distinguish disordered, egoistic or pathological sentiments from sentiments favoring adaptation. Among disturbing sentiments, only *passions* and *emotions* have been categorized separately according to vocabulary usage – and it seems that both deserve this attention. Whether egoistic or not, passions differ from sentiments in that they tend to lift sentiments to the level of reason. Emotions perhaps differ as profoundly in that they tend to lower sentiments to the level of reflex. At any rate, this is the definition and theory we will try to defend. . . .

However, this correlation itself is an indication that emotions as well as passions always have their origin in sentiments and that they must necessarily take form from these affections. In fact, what we call emotion is never anything but a kind of *crisis* of some sentiment (and often bears the same name). The emotion of joy or sorrow is but the explosive form of some affection. Sometimes, this affection comes before the emotion (when its cause is not absolutely new or when it encounters a special subjective predisposition). But in any case, the affection usually follows the emotion in the form of a *sentiment* of joy or sorrow in the strict sense of the term. What in one case provokes emotion might only arouse sentiment in moments less charged with *emotion* or in less emotional subjects. The death of a friend, particularly if not entirely unforeseen, may fill us with sorrow without provoking an emotional outburst. It could be demonstrated by similar examples that all cases of joy, fear, hope and aspiration or even of anger are not necessarily examples of emotion. The sentiment of anger can take shape or evolve in the form of an attitude of resentment or vengeance without ever provoking the affective shock which alone deserves to be called *emotion*. To repeat, it is possible in the same way to have a fear-sentiment, easily recognizable in the form of worry or distrust, without incapacitating emotional disturbance and without the agitation that denotes emotional fear, which is always akin to panic.

Imagination as the source of regulation through sentiment. Let us then return to the facts recalled at the beginning of this section. 'When perception appears in behaviour, it does not act only under the impulse of purely intellectual anticipation but also through the affective resources of certain states that accompany such anticipation.' Perception *regulates* action only through the *regulatory sentiments* it elicits. These sentiments inherit the energy contained in the physical affections of the earlier psychological stage. They both increase and decrease this energy, for the increase serves to compensate for the decrease. The prime error of Herbartian intellectualism has been not to recognize the *biological* character of imagination. By reducing it to purely intellectual elements, it has been separated from *sentiment* – without which imagination would remain inactive. Imagination and belief, one linked to the other, are the means by which memory images acquire their affective and active character. 'In imagination we see these – in fact motionless – objects of sight and sound change their place, their quality, and determine our reactions as *imaginative* beliefs.' Thus we *believe we see* things or events to come; and through our associative power of anticipation they appear as if present. Our life here and now is haunted and stirred by the phantoms that come from this imaginative and semi-hallucinatory source.

James and Lange seem to have misjudged the dynamic character of imagination to the same extent as their adversaries, though each has drawn different conclusions: while the Herbartians have cut imagination off from action, James and Lange have separated it from its dynamism. These positions follow inevitably from the principle they all defend. If imagination cannot be active, the active elements of sentiment must be reduced to a simple conflict of images, or its imaginative elements must be reduced to a simple awareness of our reactions, more or less intellectualized. The James–Lange theory rests entirely on the postulate that imagination cannot be active. Accordingly, its power must come from outside. These authors forget that what is *imagined* in terror, for example, is not a highly abstract *idea* of danger in general, but imminent personal danger beginning with a hallucination of the threatened evil. We *believe* this danger to be here and now. Why be surprised that a mode of knowledge capable of creating the hallucination of an actual physical evil – that is, the most common and most spontaneous source of our reflex actions – might be at the same time affective and active?

The disorder of the imagination-function and its emotional effects. If the Herbartians and their adversaries had understood that imagination has an inevitable influence on *sentiments*, they might have begun to realize that *emotions* also flow from imagination. Thus they would never have mistaken sentiments for simple conflicts between images, and emotion for a simple awareness of reactions. The adaptive nature of sentiment now becomes the key to the understanding of the *maladaptive* function of emotion and gives us an inkling of its inevitable nature. If what is merely imminent or possible is imagined as actually experienced, and what is expected becomes reality, a reflex reaction to this evil will then replace the thoughtful response of simply imagining the evil; a useless, premature, inopportune, even fatal 'riposte' will replace the simple 'parry'; reflex behaviour with all its simple-mindedness, stereotypy and blind impulsiveness will be substituted for deliberate plans for fight or flight that are appropriate to the situation. Such action will smother and suppress thinking or will not even let it happen, just as a stopper plugged into a fountain-head will stop the spray. So the tiger hunters mentioned by Lutfullah (in Dumas, 1932, p. 376) repeated the cry of pain 'Ho haï' of their companion who was carried away in the jaws of a tiger bounding out of the jungle, though they were unhurt themselves; so the convicts described by Gualino (in Dumas, 1932, p. 376) fell to the ground

199

with bent knees when their execution was announced, as if they bowed in advance before the fatal blow. We have noted this general effect of *cataplexy* produced by intense fear. Since it necessarily comes before the evil, fear should trigger movements that would lead to escape; and most of the time this is what happens (if common sense does not make them look useless from the start). In this case, sentiment manages to dominate emotion. But if emotion triumphs over sentiment, imagining the actual situation and its remaining resources will be overshadowed by the hallucination of the impending evil. The reaction to the experienced evil will be triggered off and finally lead to helplessness in the face of danger. Thinking itself, blocked by premature action, becomes impossible; the remaining resources are forgotten; and will power is replaced by reflex behaviour. The living being lives in the present instant. Memory evokes a future which is telescoped into the present so that time, the product of memory, is soon destroyed by its creator. This is the ruin, the collapse of a level of behaviour. It has been tripped up by automatic reflexes and has been *retransformed*. The living being assists at his own destruction as he becomes aware of the threat directed against what remains of himself. Emotion is a mental and motor disaster experienced by the subject who is its victim.

References

DEJEAN, R. (1933), *L'Émotion*, Alcan.

DUMAS, G. (1932), *Nouveau Traité de Psychologie*, Alcan.

DUPRÉ, E. (1925), *Psycho-pathologie de l'Imagination et de l'Émotivité*, Payot.

JANET, P. (1928), *Les Sentiments Fondamentaux*, Alcan.

LACROZE, R. (1938), *L'Angoisse et l'Émotion*, Boivin.

VIALLE, L. (1933), *Le Désir du Néant*, Alcan.

Part Seven Emotions as Organized Tendencies

Emotion could be considered a disorganized response only if it is denied any inherent impulsion. As soon as emotion is seen as inherently dynamic, it becomes a tendency leading to action. Arnold and Gasson point out that human action follows upon reflective as well as intuitive appraisal, but only the latter arouses emotion. Thus emotion can, but need not, lead to action. For Lazarus, however, emotions result from the 'cognitive activity of appraisal' (without distinction between reflective and intuitive appraisal) and consequently become coping processes.

Leeper follows up his critique of 'emotion as disorganized response' with a theory of emotion as motivating; indeed, he suggests that the emotional process is really a perceptual process, though not all perceptual processes are emotional. This formulation takes account of the fact that it is the perception of the situation that determines the emotion; but instead of distinguishing the factors that make a perception either emotional or indifferent (as Arnold and Gasson, also Lazarus, have done), perception comes to include even more functionally different aspects than it does in earlier formulations.

Young, finally, suggests that affective processes represent 'a kind of primitive evaluation'; they regulate and organize behaviour. Young has arrived at this conclusion on the basis of a long series of well-designed experiments on food preferences. Our selection is an excerpt of the relevant chapter in his recent book. However, he insists elsewhere in this book (as he did in his earlier writings – see Leeper, Part Six) that some affective processes, namely emotions, must be defined as persisting disturbances. Since all affective processes (of which emotion is a variety) are based on 'primitive evaluation', we would expect that this should hold for emotion as well; but Young does not make the connexion.

17 M. B. Arnold and J. A. Gasson, s.j.

Feelings and Emotions as Dynamic Factors in Personality Integration

M. B. Arnold and J. A. Gasson, s.j., 'Feelings and emotions as dynamic factors in personality integration', in M. B. Arnold and J. A. Gasson, s.j. (eds.), *The Human Person*, Ronald, 1954, chapter 10, pp. 294–313.

If emotions involve a double reference, both to the object and to the self experiencing the object, how can that functional relationship be formulated? And since that relationship represents the emotion, how can we define the term, how can we come to an adequate concept of emotion? In other words, what is an emotion? What is the difference between feelings and emotions? And what is the purpose or function of feeling and emotion in the economy of the living being, especially the human being? And finally, what is the role of emotion in relation to the self? How does it serve self-actuation and personality integration?

What is an emotion?

We suggest that an emotion or an affect can be considered *as the felt tendency toward an object judged suitable, or away from an object judged unsuitable, reinforced by specific bodily changes according to the type of emotion.*

The felt tendency. – This tendency is a vital response impelling toward suitable objects. We are *aware* of the attraction that draws us to the thing or situation which we have judged suitable for us. Moreover, the natural goal of that seeking tendency is something actually perceived or imagined. Therefore, an emotion will always occur when something is recognized as attractive or repulsive.

Judged. – The individual must perceive and judge the object in relation to himself (as suitable or unsuitable, good or bad for himself) before an emotion can arise. The emotion will follow this judgement, whether or not it is correct. In the animal, such judgement will be an estimate based upon sense knowledge and sense memory; in the human being, the present estimate always includes rational elements which have entered into the situation in the past and are recalled in the present. While it is obvious that this emotional response cannot occur at all unless the situation has been perceived and evaluated as to its effect on the individual, such evaluation is immediate, based upon a perceived similarity of this situation with situations in the past. In practice, there is no perceptible time interval between grasping the meaning of the situation and feeling the emotion appropriate to it, though there may be a perceptible interval between receiving a stimulus and grasping its meaning. That the emotion does depend on the evaluation of the situation, on its meaning for the individual, can be observed in a person's reaction to a sudden sharp noise: the startle reflex comes first, without any emotion; if the noise is recognized as that of a car backfiring, there is no further disturbance, but if the person discovers that it was a shot aimed at him, there will come fear with its accompanying physical sensations, which are very different from the sensations connected with the startle reflex.

Reinforced by bodily changes. – The simple felt tendency toward or away from something has a physiological accompaniment, consisting of organic changes. These changes are perceived in their turn and so continue to reinforce that tendency.

Specific changes according to type of emotion. – There is considerable evidence (Arnold, 2) that there are specific organic changes in fear, anger, and love.

An emotion is complete when there is the whole sequence described above, including the practical estimate of the situation, the reaction of wanting or dislike, the somatic expression and organic changes, and the awareness of these changes. An emotion is incomplete when there is an evaluation of the situation and resulting from it wanting or dislike, but no appropriate emotional expression or organic changes. This may happen if the neural pathways between cortex and thalamic centers are interrupted (by surgery, disease, or accident). Because we have defined emotion as the felt tendency toward or away from something which is merely reinforced by the appropriate bodily changes, it is possible in these cases to speak of emotion even though such emotion is not complete and the person neither shows nor is aware of emotional *expression* or organic changes. On the other hand, there may be the same organic changes as are ordinarily experienced during an emotion and the person may become aware of them – as happens, for instance, after adrenalin injection or in states of disturbed endocrine balance; the simple awareness of such a changed physiological state, however, cannot be called an emotion but should be called a feeling, indicating the response to changed functioning (see our discussion of feelings on page 209*ff.*).

Types of emotion

To discover the diverse types of emotion, we shall have to examine the objects toward or away from which the tendency is directed. The simple partiality toward that which is suitable could be called simple *love* (St Thomas's term, *simplex amor*), and the simple repugnance to something judged unsuitable or harmful, *hate*. Since the tendency away from something harmful is secondary to the tendency toward something suitable (for the harmful object threatens the possession of something suitable), love must be basic in all subject-object relationships, and hate and other avoidance emotions can only be a reaction to the actual or threatened deprivation of things loved.[1]

This tendency to respond emotionally has the same characteristics which we found in every other action tendency, namely, that it acts when conditions are favorable, and that it seeks an opportunity for action when none is given or when there are obstacles to its exercise. When conditions are favorable, the person simply *tends* towards the object or away from it; when they are unfavorable, he *contends* for or against it. In the first case, he acts

1. See also Allport's remark: 'So obvious is the priority of affiliative groundwork that one must perform contortions in order to give equal footing to the alleged aggressive instincts. By some psychoanalysts the feat is achieved by assuming that eating, perhaps the most conspicuous of the infant's activities, is a destructive act – "oral aggression", it is called. "Our primordial ancestors," writes one Freudian, "were cannibals. We all enter life with the instinctive impulse to devour not only food, but also all frustrating objects. Before the infantile individual acquires the capacity to love, it is governed by a primitive hate relationship to its environment." This statement precisely reverses the order of love and hate in ontogenetic development. Furthermore, it inverts the meaning of the act of feeding. When I devour roast beef it is not from hate but from love. Acts of incorporation into myself are, from my point of view, affiliative' (1, p. 152).

from an emotional *impulse*, in the second from an emotional *urge* or a *contending emotion*. There will be a simple tending toward, when the loved object is present, at least in imagination, or is easily accessible; a simple tending away from, when the repellent object is present at least in imagination, and easily avoidable. There will be contending when the loved object is attainable only with difficulty and the repellent object can be endured or evaded only with pain.

If the loved object is not present, that is, not possessed, but is easily accessible, simple love will become a *want* or *desire*. But if the loved object is neither present nor easily accessible, we feel the urge to overcome the obstacles to its possession, we *aspire* to it, we *hope* and *strive* for it. If the obstacles are judged to be insuperable, the urge to *despair* will overcome us. But if we gain the object we love, we rest and delight in its possession, we feel the impulse of *joy*.

On the other hand, if there is a threat of something harmful which can easily be evaded, we tend away from it, we feel *aversion* and *dislike*. If this threat is immediate and difficult to avoid, we turn away from it actively, we have the urge to flee, we feel *fear*. But if we judge that we can overcome that which threatens us, we contend with it, we show *daring*, we have *courage*. If something harmful is actually present and is frustrating and obstructing us, we have the urge to turn against it, we feel *anger*.

In this way, we can order emotions according to their aim as directed toward a suitable object and away from a harmful one, into *positive* and *negative* emotions; and according to their operation, their degree of impulsion, into *impulse emotions* and *contending emotions*.

The accompanying schematic table will show this twofold analysis of emotions according to the degree of impulsion, while the above analysis has been according to the object of emotion.

Basic emotions

1. Emotions differ according to their *object* (as it is suitable or harmful to the self). Therefore we distinguish

   positive emotions   (tending toward suitable objects)
   and **negative emotions**   (tending away from harmful objects)

2. Emotions differ according to their *operation*, the degree of impulsion. Therefore we distinguish

> **impulse emotions** (tending toward or away from an object when conditions are favourable)
>
> and **contending emotions** (contending for or against something when conditions are unfavourable)

	A. Impulse emotions	Emotion toward object as such (*whether present or absent*)	Object not present (*tendency toward or away from*)	Object present (*rest in possession*)
positive	Object suitable (*good*)	love	wanting, desire	delight, joy
negative	Object unsuitable (*evil*)	hate	aversion, dislike	sorrow, sadness

	B. Contending Emotions	Degree of difficulty	Object not present (*tendency toward or away from*)	Object present
positive	Object suitable (*good*)	if judged attainable	hope	
		if judged unattainable	despair	
negative	Object unsuitable (*evil*)	if to be overcome	daring	anger
		if to be avoided	fear	

Polarities in emotion

From a consideration of this scheme we come to see that opposite emotional attitudes can develop from one and the same emotion. Love is basic if understood as the tendency of all organisms to tend toward something suitable, to love it, want it, possess it.

But when we cannot attain that object, or when its possession involves some attractive, some repulsive aspects, we feel a different emotion according to the conditions which we judge to be attractive or repulsive, to be overcome or to be avoided. There is a polarity of emotions, either because they refer to different objects, suitable or unsuitable, or because they refer to the same object under different conditions, favorable or unfavorable, or because unfavorable conditions are either judged as yielding to attack, therefore to be mastered, or as insuperable, therefore to be avoided. We either love or hate, we either wish for something or strive to attain it, we either fight for it or give it up altogether. Therefore the emotion will differ according to precisely defined conditions which depend on the way in which the individual judges the situation.

This is a very different emotional polarity from the polarities discussed by Freud which occupy so important a role in the psycho-analytic system. Freud deals with such phenomena as the reversal of one emotion into its opposite (love into hostility); a transformation of a passive aim (to be looked at) into an active aim (to look at); or the reversal of a content (night into day). He assumes that these polarities are an inherent factor of the instinctual life; in particular, that our mental life is governed by three basic polarities – subject-object, pleasure-pain, activity-passivity. In each of these, one opposite pole may be replaced by another. Because the polarities are inherent in instincts, there is an implicit assumption that the reversal may occur at any time, may be set off by any chance occurrence, and is therefore unpredictable.

Our usage of the term 'polarity' approaches contemporary usage much more closely than does Freud's. For Freud, polarity in an emotion, for instance, implies two poles in the same thing, after the manner of a north and south pole in a bar magnet. For us, polarity means orientation in one direction rather than in another, after the manner of 'polarized light', which vibrates in only one plane.

That there are polarities we do not deny: what is good for us we love, what is bad for us we avoid. But one and the same object cannot at one and the same time and under the same aspects be both loved and hated by the same person. If we love something, we love it for its attractive, its lovable aspects. If we hate it, we hate it for its repulsive and unattractive aspects.

It is quite possible, of course, that one object has many aspects which are significant for us. One person may love another – but it would be more accurate to say he loves those features in another which give him pleasure, which enhance his personality, and which are in harmony with his own goals. He may also hate in him the things which repel him, which frustrate his goals, and which are a threat to his love of possession, his psychological stability, and his self-actuation. We never love another person's good looks and hate them at the same time. If his good looks attract us, the comparison with our own lack of attractiveness may displease us, but that is another aspect entirely. The more a human relationship depends on sensory appeal, the more ambivalent will it be; for on the sensory level many characteristics of the other person may be attractive, but some are bound to be repellent. Not only will there be a conflict between different sensory aspects; the sensory appeal may also come in conflict with other goals – for instance, the tendency toward stability and self-actuation. Similarly, if the relationship is not based on sensory appeal but on the satisfaction of one of the three basic tendencies, there will be a possibility of conflict and therefore ambivalence so long as these tendencies are isolated and not ordered in their proper hierarchy. Another person considered as a possession, or even as a means to self-actuation, is bound to disappoint us. While we love him for his promise, we shall hate him for his defection.

In general, the more a human relationship is based on sensory appeal, or appeal to isolated tendencies, the more ambivalent will it be. Only when it is based upon a common striving toward a common goal which is in harmony with man's final end, to which all other aspects of that relationship are subordinated, will there be love properly so called, love which is integrated, and undisturbed by hate, jealousy, or envy. Only on that level will it be love of a person rather than love of his physical or intellectual attractions. On that level, love becomes a sharing of the Good, and that sharing is the natural overflow of goodness which is inherent in the Good itself.

Feelings, moods, and emotions

In discussing the difference between feelings, moods, and emotions, we are well aware that this topic has been a vexing problem for psychologists. That feelings, moods, and emotions do not belong in the same class seems clear, but it is extremely difficult to distinguish them in such a way that their differences become definable. There are some feelings, for instance, which are called emotions when they become intense, and there are some emotions which are called moods when they last for a considerable length of time.

As a tentative scheme for distinguishing the three we shall classify feelings as *those affective states where the psychological reference is principally to the subject*. Pleasure and displeasure, then, would be the simple elements of sensory feelings, or, more precisely, they would be affective reactions to sensations. Gemelli, in a recent article (4), calls such feelings 'affective sensations', but we prefer the term 'sensory feelings' because this term makes it clear that we are dealing with feelings and not with sensations. Sensory feelings are different from sensations because one and the same sensation can be either pleasant or unpleasant for different persons; moreover, for the same person, that sensation may be sometimes pleasant, sometimes unpleasant; or the same sensation, judged pleasant at first, may become decidedly unpleasant if it is much prolonged.

We call these feelings *sensory* feelings because they are always the reaction not to an object as an object but to sense perceptions connected with the object. When we say that a color or an odor is pleasant, that a walk is pleasant, or dancing, or painting, the judgement we make is always a judgement of sensations, and the psychological reference is to the inner state of the individual. The feeling of pleasantness or unpleasantness is the result of a preceding awareness in the same way that an emotion is. But in the case of feelings, the question 'How does it affect me?' is answered by being aware how the particular object affects the individual's sensory and motor functioning and not how it affects him as a person. When a color is pleasant, it is really the sensation, or more accurately the *sensing* that is pleasant. When a walk is pleasant, it is the walking and breathing and looking connected with it that is pleasant. But since the walking and breathing and looking can be known as pleasant only because of the diverse sensations that inform us of the fact, it is correct even in this case to speak of pleasantness as a *sensory feeling* or an *affective reaction to sensa-*

tion. Thinking, imagining, and reasoning can also be smooth or difficult in their functioning, and will correspondingly be felt as pleasant or unpleasant.

The practical judgement preceding an emotion also answers the question 'How does it affect me?' but the 'me' in this case is not my functioning but my person. When I say the fragrance or taste of wine is *pleasant*, I do not necessarily want the wine; in fact, I may never take it. In tasting its fragrance, I possess the pleasant sensation and no possession of the object is asked for. But when I say I *like* wine, it means that I *do* want it when the occasion is given. The aim of the *emotion* (liking or simple love in this case) is possession of the object, while the *feeling* of pleasantness simply indicates smooth functioning in the subject. Hence, emotion aims at the object, feeling reflects the state of the subject.

For a sensory feeling to become an emotion it is necessary that the preceding judgement – how this sensation affects my functioning – should be followed by a judgement how the object which occasions the sensation affects me *as a person*. As an illustration, we quote a passage from Gemelli's above-mentioned article, which is an introspective report from one of his subjects in an experiment on pleasantness/unpleasantness.

The odor was disagreeable in itself, but the disagreeable sensation quickly disappeared when the stimulus ceased; immediately in my mind there arose a much greater repugnance, and different because it was not physical, causing an aversion to the source of the odor. I saw that this repugnance was caused in me by the memory of certain parasites, the smell of which had actually been presented to me as a stimulus. I also felt a strong movement of nausea, disgust, and repulsion (4, p. 211).

Here we see very clearly that first the *odor* was judged, then the *object* which possesses this odor. As soon as the object was judged as it affected the person, there came the tendency away from it which we have called emotion.

When there is a feeling state which is not ascribed to a particular sensation, but which reflects the total inner state, the total functioning, and this feeling state is protracted, we call it a *mood*. If we wake up in the morning feeling in a cheerful mood because all our powers are functioning smoothly, we find it easy to get up, to dress, to drive, and to work. Often, of course, the morning's cheerful or despondent mood may be the result of a dream, whether we remember the dream and the dream emotion or not. In that case, a disturbing dream, which provokes an emotion of sadness, will result in the physiological changes appropriate to the emotion which (in the case of sadness) will inhibit smooth functioning. Then the despondent mood next morning will be an indication of such hampered functioning. But a mood can also be the result of a *physiological* acceleration or retardation of functioning, as, for instance, in the euphoric mood of patients suffering from slightly febrile states such as occur in tuberculosis or the depression observable in some persons after taking massive doses of sulfa drugs which prevent cell nutrition.

Feelings and moods, then, are indicators of the smooth or difficult functioning of the organism. As such, they can act as danger signals to induce the individual to take steps toward re-establishment of effective physiological and psychological functioning.

The purpose of emotion

We have seen that feelings and moods serve as indicators of the inner state of functioning of the individual. He can, but need not, make use of them to correct unfavorable conditions of functioning.

Emotions, on the other hand, aim at the possession of suitable objects. They could be considered as instruments not only to reach particular objects but also to help us reach the perfection of our personality, the actuation of our potentialities in the possession of these objects. From even a cursory reflection upon our own experience it is evident that emotion can move us to action and can facilitate action. We pursue and achieve something we want very strongly without any feeling of effort; but we feel burdened by the effort we must expend to reach a goal we *ought* to reach, for which we do not care. The same thing is found in the speedup of action which comes with the exhilaration of daring or the impetus of anger and fear. Impulse emotions as well as contending emotions can be such instruments in the pursuit of our purposes. The possession of an object begins in desire, is achieved in action, and perpetuated by our joy in it. If ill befall us, we try to work clear of it, looking for something better.

It is an intricate matter to make clear how the negative emotions and the states brought on by them can facilitate action towards a goal. We must bear in mind that a 'negative' emotion and the 'negative' movement involved in it are in fact positive states – there is actually something going on. The movement is called negative because it is away from whatever provokes it. But this movement is not simply away from the undesirable object or state. It is reasonable to argue that this movement is as much positive (toward something) as it is negative (away from the undesirable), because even on the principle of sheer mechanical evolution of the organism, survival is the function of avoidance reactions. Thus the negative movement is always toward something better, not simply away from a present evil. It is true, of course, that the 'something better' is only dimly and confusedly known, while the object evoking the emotion is very clearly in the forefront of awareness. But what makes for survival is not the clarity of perception nor the fact of avoidance; it is rather the value of the movement for reaching its positive aim. 'Out of the frying pan into the fire' situations are exceptional and rare.

Moreover, the emotional reaction in negative emotional states is seldom the result of simply a single object or an uncomplicated state of mind. Sadness, which at first glance seems to be wholly depressing, has a positive bearing: a heading toward something – anything – constructive and elating. The case is somewhat more complex when the sadness comes from loss. Here we have a negative emotion reinforced and perpetuated by a contending emotion. We *desire* the lost good now unattainable, and are depressed by its *absence* now unavoidable. It is the contending emotion that keeps us *bound*, as it were, to the cause of our sadness. The whole problem of anxiety, sadness, and the negative emotions in general needs reinvestigation from this point of vantage. There is, however, a way of managing these negative emotions so as to facilitate action. There is a rational way of dealing with evil suffered which is called patience, just as there is a rational way of reacting to good denied or lost which is called longanimity or long-suffering.

This gives us some answer to the question whether the emotion, though a proper instrument for achieving the object toward which it tends, is necessarily a means for the integration of personality and for actuation of the person. The contending emotion coupled with sadness, as we said, keeps us bound to the good we have lost; in that sense, one purpose of the emotion is achieved. But the wellbeing of the person would require that he detach himself from the lost object which causes his sadness, and focus his attention on something else. Like every function, emotion is drawn toward its own objects. But also, like every other function, emotion can be organized so that it will tend toward the integration of the personality, provided that the person actively directs it toward rational ends.

Emotions, we have said, are aroused as the result of a value judgement, made primarily on the basis of sensory appeal or repulsion. But what is good for the human being cannot be judged solely on such a basis. It must be judged also on the basis of a rational evaluation. An object may be judged to afford bodily pleasure and satisfaction but be known as harmful from rational considerations. A chocolate bar may be very attractive to the diabetic, but he knows he will suffer if he takes it. Similarly, spring air and sunshine may arouse an intense desire in the student to skip lectures, but if he gives in to it he will defeat his hope of passing his examinations.

If, then, emotion is to be instrumental in self-actuation, the objects of emotion must be harmonized with the person's larger goal as a human being. If these objects are seen in their real value, if they are seen in the proper perspective of man's final end, then the judgement that they are suitable will be objective and well ordered.

We can discuss now in detail how emotions aid in personality integration and self-actuation. When the impulse-emotions simply tend toward objects, they will work as means for achieving possession, just as the impulse-emotions which tend away from harm work as means for retaining possession. Impulse-emotions, therefore, could be identified with the tendency toward possession which we have discussed earlier as one of the human being's three basic tendencies. The contending emotions or urges, on the other hand, act as means for establishing and stabilizing possessions, and also for establishing the self in its possessions, that is, for self-actuation. Contending emotions could be identified with the basic tendencies of the human being toward psychological stabilization (or security) and toward self-actuation.

Effects of emotion on the person

Every emotion is preceded by knowledge, evaluation, judgement, not on the speculative or intellectual level but on the practical level. This particular situation has been judged: What does it mean to me and what am I going to do about it? Following this judgement, there will be the emotional state accompanied by the appropriate muscular and glandular changes which are an integral part of emotional activity. Furthermore, emotion leads to motor action to achieve the desired object or to move away from impending danger.

The evaluative judgement requires sensation, imagination, and memory; it involves the intellect, too, because the factor of meaning is always present on the human level. Now the meaning of any particular situation is gradually built up, is the result of innumerable experiences of the person with similar objects or in similar situations. Since the emotional situation involves the activity of many powers, often of all the powers of the human being as they have been organized and ordered up to the time the emotional situation occurs, we find that not only are all the functions working simultaneously, but the total person, as he is here and now, is actively ordering and integrating the present situation into the total pattern of the personality as he progresses toward the self-ideal.

We can see now why the emotions play such an important part in the integration of personality. They are found in a setting which involves the whole person because an emotional state involves all his physiological and psychological activities.

Emotions as factors disturbing personality integration

In most of the literature, emotion is assumed to be a disorganizing factor in personality. True, Cannon (3) insisted that emotions had an emergency function, so they could not be said to be disorganizing altogether, but he pointed out at the same time that a state of emergency puts a burden on the organism which cannot be sustained for very long.

To correct this view, Leeper has recently suggested that emotions cannot adequately be explained outside a motivational framework. Though extremes of emotions may be disorganizing, he holds that normally emotions act 'primarily to arouse, sustain,

215

and direct activity' (5). This view is in agreement with our discussion in so far as we have stressed that emotion in its very nature is a tending toward or away from something, and will therefore lead to motor action and to the possession or avoidance of the object aimed at.

But it ought to be pointed out that emotion can act as a disorganizing factor as well, first when it is so intense as to overwhelm the individual, and secondly when its object is not in harmony with the person's rational goal. There is no doubt that extremely intense emotions are disorganizing, as Leeper himself admits. But perhaps it would be more adequate to call such emotions disabling rather than disorganizing, for they are disabling in the same way as response to excess stimulation is disabling. If an individual has an epileptic fit, his motor activity is excessive and disabling. If he is blinded by a strong light, he is temporarily disabled.

But the very intensity of emotional stimulation depends on our judgement how this particular object or this particular situation affects us. If it is judged dangerous, we are afraid, and this fear is a spur to escape. But if we judge that this danger situation is so threatening that flight is useless, we shall be overwhelmed by extreme fear, feel terror, and become incapacitated for flight. Whether or not fear becomes excessive will therefore depend on how dangerous we judge the situation to be.

But that judgement depends on other factors too. We may see that the danger is overwhelming, and yet not be overwhelmed by fear, provided only that the evil we fear is not the worst thing for us, no matter how important it may be in itself. Men have faced a firing squad with a smile on their lips, and martyrs have died with a shout of joy.

The intensity of an emotion, then, depends not only on how attractive or repulsive or dangerous we judge this situation to be, but also on how important this attraction is for us, how much we would mind having to put up with that repulsion, or how fatal for our real self this particular defeat would be. In other words, we can order and regulate the intensity of an emotion if we consider the emotional situation in its relation to our rational goal and to our final end. This will result in a proportional reduction in the degree of its affective appeal or repulsion. If we are successful, the danger will be judged less threatening, the attraction less compelling than formerly, because now it is seen only as important to part of us and not so important to our real self.

If, on the other hand, the object or situation is habitually judged as pleasurable or attractive regardless of its harmfulness to the person as a whole or its incompatibility with his properly organized life pattern, then desire may become intense and force action. In that case, emotion will not be so intense as to disable the person. He will go in the direction his emotion impels him but doing so will prevent the achievement of wider and more important aims.

Moreover, emotion acts as disturbing factor not only when it seemingly functions as a separate power pursuing its own aim. Personality integration can also be disturbed if emotions serve one of the three basic tendencies when these tendencies are not properly ordered.

A man may intend to remain an honest upright businessman. But he makes a lucky deal, becomes fascinated by easy money, gives in to his tendency to possession and finds before long that his taste for money makes him less careful to avoid shady deals. Or a father may intend to be a good companion to his children, but he is attached to his own stable way of doing things, and the children always interfere. As a result he gives in to his anger on every occasion and before long the children tremble when he tries to be kind to them.

Emotion may disturb personality integration even when it serves self-actuation. If a man becomes inordinately attached to his self-ideal, he will become fearful of anything that may threaten it, and will judge himself frustrated by every trifling incident. He will be fearful and aggressive in turn, and will worry and fret and spend his energy in emotions that will bring him no nearer to his goal. In such a case self is in the center of attention and the end result will be self-glorification rather than self-actuation. Only if the self-ideal is what it ought to be, and *influences the person as a motive rather than as a blueprint*, will emotion be saved from excessive self-reference and be an integrating rather than a disturbing factor.

Emotions urge a man toward particular goals and enable him to satisfy present-moment demands. But unless these demands are in harmony with the wider requirements of the total personality working towards self-actuation, their satisfaction will disintegrate rather than unify, will lead to inner conflict rather than healthy growth. If emotions are allowed free play, tempting a man toward any and every goal, they will first disturb and then prevent personality integration. For this reason, there has to be some emotional control.

Control of emotions

Though emotion normally leads to action appropriate to it, it is possible to go counter to the emotion, whatever it may be. But it is possible only when the goal we want to achieve is so important that we are willing to suffer to achieve it. Since emotions are instruments for attaining something beneficial and avoiding something harmful, their physiological components are so arranged that motor action will follow under pain of discomfort. Fear is intensely unpleasant; to act as fear prompts us to act, namely to flee, means to escape not only the external danger but the internal discomfort. Hope or longing for something difficult to attain is a torment when intense; to act as hope prompts us to act so that we achieve what we long for brings not only the possession of the longed-for object but also relief from emotional suffering. But to act counter to any emotion, to suffer fear, to deny ourselves the relief of attack, or the striving for something we long for, means not only giving up the object of the emotion but also enduring subjective discomfort. For this reason, acting counter to emotion is difficult; it is also unintelligent if the control of emotions can be achieved in some other way, for going against emotion means turning a help into a hindrance.

In animals, this possibility of going counter to emotion does not exist, nor is there any possibility of reducing the intensity of the emotion, or rather its persistence, by evaluating the immediate situation in the light of a more important goal. In animals, the estimate of the emotional situation is invariant because it is a sensory judgement depending merely upon the strength of the sensory appeal or repugnance. Of course, the strength of the affective appeal will be influenced by the animal's past experience, but the animal himself cannot do anything to change it. True, animals sometimes seem to act as if they could go counter to emotion. A dog has braved fire to save his master – but he does not quake with fear while he does it. His emotion is directed *towards* his master and *contends with* an obstacle in the way. His emotion always coincides with his action and nothing but a contrary emotion can interfere with it. That is why we have to train a dog for hunting in such a way that we counteract by his fear of punishment his tendency to tear and devour his prey; even the most intelligent dog will not train himself. A man may judge, for instance, that flying in a superannuated plane is danger- ous and will feel fear with all its symptoms: cold feet, trembling knees, racing heart; but he knows that the only way to save a badly injured man is to be flown to his assistance, so he will decide on flying in spite of his emotion.

The very characteristics which make emotion a fit instrument to achieve our object also make it difficult to control – namely, the fact that the whole organism is engaged in tending toward or away from a thing. There is not only a psychological *tendency toward*, or *wanting*, there is a physiological urge as well. The physiological changes which constitute that organismic wanting will continue, once started, and will become cumulative. That is the reason why a decision to act against an emotion be- comes more difficult as the emotion progresses.

Nevertheless, control is possible because reasonable decisions have a chance to intervene. We do not have to be forced by emotion, for most emotional situations have aspects which good sense rather than passion can assess. Now reasonable decisions follow good sense, not sheer emotional appeal, but to make the inter- vention of good sense effective it is easier to exercise it in the begin- ning rather than later on. Making a reasonable decision early in the situation will not eliminate emotional inclinations against the course of action decided upon, but it will lessen the attraction for the opposite course and reduce the pressure which emotion un- controlled can generate.

A decision may be made and carried out either *accompanied by* an emotional tending toward the goal, or *without* any emotion, or *against* an emotion. Only when we decide to do something which also attracts us will the action be felt as easy and pleasant. In the human being the decision to act is ordinarily based on rational judgement, but the emotion follows the prior evaluation which has revealed what satisfaction this may bring here and now. The object of an emotion may be anything which gives physical pleasure, intellectual satisfaction, or spiritual fulfilment. But the more intense the satisfaction which the object affords us here and now, the more intense will be the emotion.

If the desired object is judged rationally suitable but has sensory aspects which are undesirable, either there will be no felt emotion or the felt emotion will pull in the opposite direction. In deciding, for instance, to attack in battle, there is not only danger but also the appeal of physical combat and mastery. If the latter aspect is focused on, there will be the emotion of daring or courage which will make action easy and effective. But in deciding to stand up for one's convictions in writing or speaking to a large audience the element of combat is absent while the hostility of the audience or the disapproval of friends contains a powerful deterrent which makes such a course of action highly distasteful. In both cases we speak of courage, but only in the first case will it be an emotion in the strict sense of the term. Accordingly, action in the first case is easy, in the second it may be extremely difficult.

The only way, then, to have emotion as a help in achieving our aim is, first, to reach a certain detachment from appeals directed to the senses, and secondly, to discover in the rationally chosen objects whatever appeals to the whole man here and now. Then they will become important enough so that physical aspects become ancillary.

Suppose a student decides to become a physician. If he wants to achieve his end easily and quickly, he will first have to order all his other goals (especially those that have a strong sensory appeal) with reference to this end. He may play baseball or any other game, he may go to the theater, to concerts, the movies, but unless he comes to see that all these activities are less important than his profession, unless he comes to the point where he gladly gives up coveted pleasures in favor of a professional demand, he will find it extremely difficult to make progress in his profession. Only when he comes to develop genuine interest in medicine, when he comes to concentrate on it in such a way that he will find satisfaction and even exhilaration in overcoming difficulties, when he is able to feel the joy that comes from sharing his knowledge with others or helping them by his skill, only then will studying cease to be drudgery, only then will it be easy for him to succeed.

References

1. ALLPORT, G. W. (1950), 'A psychological approach to the study of love and hate', in P. A. Sorokin (ed.) *Explorations in Altruistic Love and Behavior*, Beacon Press, Boston.

2. ARNOLD, MAGDA B. (1945), 'Physiological differentiation of emotional states', *Psychol. Rev.*, vol. 52 (1945), pp. 35–48.

3. CANNON, WALTER B. (1927), *Bodily Changes in Pain, Hunger, Fear, and Rage*, 2nd edn., Appleton-Century-Crofts, Inc.

4. GEMELLI, AGOSTINO (1949), 'Orienting concepts in the study of affective states', *J. nerv. ment. Dis.*, vol. 110, part I, pp. 198–214, part II, pp. 299–314.

5. LEEPER, R. W. (1948), 'A motivational theory of emotion to replace "emotion as disorganized response",' *Psychol. Rev.*, vol. 55, pp. 5–21.

18   P. T. Young

Affective Processes

Excerpts from P. T. Young, *Motivation and Emotion*, Wiley, 1961, pp. 151–5, 166–70, 198–204.

Let us begin by postulating that affective processes have objective existence within the organism and that their nature and functions can be discovered.

Definition of the affective processes by their attributes. The affective processes can be defined objectively in terms of three attributes: sign, intensity, and duration.

1. *Sign.* – In laboratory situations, one observes that naïve animals develop approach-maintaining or avoidance-terminating patterns of behavior. If they develop the approach-maintaining pattern, I would assume that the underlying affective process is positive in sign. If they develop the avoidance-terminating pattern, I would assume that the affective process is negative in sign. If neither positive nor negative behavior develops, I would make no assumption concerning the sign of affective arousal.

It is important to note that the bare existence of adient or abient behavior is not a sufficient ground for inferring affective processes. Approach-maintaining and avoidance-terminating behavior may be habitual, automatic and affectively indifferent; but the *development* of approach-maintaining or avoidance-terminating patterns by *naïve animals* is the criterion for the sign of affective processes.

2. *Intensity.* – In addition to sign, affective processes differ in intensity, or degree. Affective processes vary along a bipolar continuum between the extremes of maximal negative and maximal positive intensity.

One way to demonstrate the relative intensity of affective processes is to give animals a brief-exposure preference test with foods. A brief-exposure test is recommended because with prolonged exposures the level of acceptability of test foods declines as the terminal state of satiation is approached.

In the brief-exposure test the animal is offered a series of choices between two test foods (A and B). The series of choices reveals whether a preference develops for one food (A) or the other (B). There is no way to force an animal to show a preference. Either a preference develops, with repeated choices, or it does not develop. Weak preferences, strong preferences, alternating preferences, and no preferences at all have been observed. In some tests the preference is obvious but, in others, statistical methods are needed to determine whether or not a particular body of data indicates a significant preference or a mutation of preference.

If both test foods are accepted, I would assume that the preferred food arouses a higher intensity of positive affectivity than the non-preferred. This is what is meant, objectively, by the statement that the preferred food is the more palatable. Again, it must be emphasized that the *development* of a preference in *naïve animals* indicates relative hedonic intensity and not the bare existence of a preference, since a preferential discrimination can be purely habitual and automatic.

3. *Duration.* – In addition to sign and intensity, affective processes differ in duration and temporal course. In so far as affective processes are induced by taste solutions, the duration of stimulation can be used to control the duration of affective arousal. The number of seconds that an animal is in contact with a food can be controlled or the number of individual licks of a fluid can be counted by an electronic device. The frequency and schedule of affective processes can thus be controlled.

With painful stimulations, it is also possible to control precisely the intensity, frequency, and schedule of presentations. In addition to direct stimulation, negative affectivity can be produced by frustration and conflict; but these conditions can be controlled less precisely than the conditions of sensory stimulation.

The hedonic continuum. The sign, intensity, and temporal changes of affective processes can be represented upon the hedonic continuum. Figure 1 shows this continuum extending from the extreme of negative affectivity (distress) to the extreme of positive affectivity (delight). Different intensities of affective arousal are represented by arbitrary units marked off upon the continuum. Midway between negative and positive affectivity is the range of indifferent, neutral processes and others that are weakly affective.

The arrows represent two opposed directions of hedonic change. The upper arrow, pointing away from the negative end and towards the positive end of the continuum, represents a kind of hedonic change that is of great importance in the organization of behavior. According to the hedonic hypothesis, neurobehavioral patterns are organized that minimize negative affectivity (distress) and maximize positive affectivity (delight). That is to say, organization

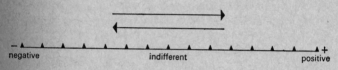

Figure 1 The hedonic continuum

is dependent upon hedonic change in the positive direction. Changes in the negative direction necessarily and frequently occur, and the lower arrow represents such changes. The total figure implies a principle of affective opposition or antagonism: there can be a change towards either pole but not a change in opposite directions at the same moment of time.

Although there are two opposed directions of change, there are, logically and psychologically, four main kinds of affective change that need to be considered: (1) increasing positive affectivity, (2) decreasing positive affectivity, (3) increasing negative affectivity, (4) decreasing negative affectivity. The first kind of hedonic change (increasing positive affectivity) is present when an animal tastes a sugar solution and organizes an approach-maintaining pattern of behavior. The fourth kind of change (decreasing negative affectivity) is present when an animal succeeds in relieving the 'distress' associated with an electric shock or reducing a need produced by dietary depletion. 'Distress reduction' is the hedonic equivalent of 'drive reduction' in the organization of instrumental behavior.

Changes in the negative direction occur under various circumstances. When an organism continues eating an acceptable food, the level of acceptability gradually declines as the final state of satiation is approached. Hedonic changes in the negative direction are also produced by shock, burns, cuts, shrill sounds, and similar conditions. When negative affectivity is present the organism tries to reduce it. The very attempt to escape from inducing conditions is the earmark of negative affectivity.

The distinction between sensory and affective processes. To a psychology that is limited by the concepts of stimulus and response the postulate of central affective processes may appear superfluous. I believe, however, that any theory of behavior which ignores the concept of affectivity will be found inadequate as an explanation of the total facts. There are facts which are difficult, if not impossible, to explain in strictly s–r terms.

Sensory processes convey specific information to the brain centers that make it possible for an organism to discriminate differences in spatial position, differences in time, quality, and perceptual configuration. Affective processes convey little or no information. In so far as they convey any information that relates to the organism's orientation, affective processes are primitive evaluations. A positive response indicates *good*, *pleasant*, '*green light*', and a negative response indicates *bad*, *unpleasant*, '*red light*'. Relative preferences indicate evaluations – '*better than*' or '*worse than*'.

The sophisticated evaluations of the artist are far removed from the primitive affective arousals. His affective processes depend markedly upon knowledge, information, training, and past experience. The appreciative judgements of an artist may be largely cognitive; yet at all levels of sophistication some degree of central affective process may be present.

The distinction between sensory and affective processes is seen clearly in the contrast between sensory and hedonic intensity.

If pairs of sucrose solutions are presented to rats briefly for choice, the animals select the higher of two concentrations in preference to the lower. Scale values based upon preference tests show that the level of acceptability is directly proportional to the logarithm of the concentration. Young and Greene (1953) found that this relation held all the way up the scale of concentrations.

From the facts about sucrose solutions one might be tempted to argue that *sensory* intensity or physical concentration of solution is the critical determinant of behavior. But difficulty with a purely sensory interpretation appears when one considers the relative palatability of solutions of sodium chloride.

Young and Falk (1956) ran a series of preference tests between distilled water and sodium chloride solutions of different concentrations, and between pairs of sodium chloride solutions. They found that need-free rats revealed an optimal concentration for sodium chloride within the range of 0·75 to 1·5 per cent. When concentrations were below this range, need-free rats preferred the higher concentration; when above this optimal range, they preferred the lower concentration. Within the optimal range there were marked individual differences in preference and there was much indiscriminate behavior. The experimenters concluded that there is a *range of acceptance* within which acceptability rises with increasing concentration of NaCl and a *range of rejection* within which acceptability falls as concentration rises. A similar result was obtained by Bare (1949), and others, who relied upon an intake method of studying acceptability of NaCl solutions.

It is clear, therefore, that with solutions of sodium chloride, hedonic intensity does not have a one-to-one relation with sensory intensity. *Sensory* intensity is an increasing monotonic function of concentration of solution; *hedonic* intensity is a discontinuous function of concentration.

Motivation and the affective processes

From every point of view the affective processes must be regarded as motivational in nature. First, affective processes are intimately related to the activation of neurobehavioral patterns. Second, affective processes regulate and direct behavior according to the principle of maximizing the positive and minimizing the negative. Third, affective processes have a specific role of organizing neurobehavioral patterns. They lead to the development of motives and evaluative dispositions that become relatively stable and permanent determinants of behavior.

The following sections will treat some of the ways in which the affective processes are related to the regulation and organization of behavior.

The regulative role of affective processes. Affective processes regulate the neurobehavioral patterns that organisms develop. If a rat, on the preference tester, develops a preference of A>B, I would assume that A is more palatable than B; if he develops a preference of B>A, I would assume that B is more palatable. If no preference develops, there is no basis for assuming a difference of palatability; the two test foods may be isohedonic or the animal may be dominated by position of the food, color of the container, or another factor that is not directly related to the foodstuff.

A preference test does not reveal the *absolute* level of affective intensity but only the *relative* levels associated with two incentives. This fact will be illustrated by data obtained in an experiment by Young (1947).

Preference tests were run with three pairs of test foods: (1) sucrose and casein, (2) wheat powder and casein, (3) sucrose and wheat powder. The percentages that indicate preference changed from test to test as the animals gained practice in the discrimination. These percentages are shown graphically in figure 2.

The percentages indicating preference were consistently highest for the first pair (sucrose and casein) where the *difference* in palatability is known to be the greatest. The percentages for the second pair (wheat powder and casein) were almost as high; and this agrees with the fact that wheat powder is just slightly below sucrose in level of palatability. The percentages were lowest for the third pair (sucrose and wheat powder) where the *difference* in palatability was relatively slight but the incentives themselves were of high palatability. A preference test, therefore, reveals only the *relative* affective intensities.

In the light of many such sets of curves, I make the assumption that affective processes have a regulative and organizing role. The relative intensities of affective arousals that are associated with two stimuli determine whether the animal will develop one preference or its opposite or no preference at all. Also, the *relative* hedonic intensities determine the rate of growth of a preferential discrimination when the frequency of repeating an affective response is held constant.

On the negative side of affectivity it is equally obvious that hedonic processes have a regulative role. The role is frequently that of inhibiting or blocking neurobehavioral patterns. To illustrate this point consider a bit of evidence in an experiment reported by Neal Miller (1956).

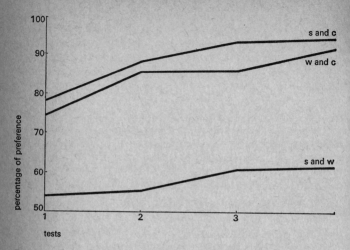

Figure 2 Curves of preferential learning for three pairs of test-foods. The top curve shows percentage of choices of sucrose in a test between sucrose (s) and casein (c). The middle curve shows percentage of choices of wheat powder in a test between wheat powder (w) and casein (c). The bottom curve shows percentage of choices of sucrose in a test between sucrose (s) and wheat powder (w). Each point plotted is based upon 360 choices – 12 rats, 30 choices per animal (from Young, 1947).

Miller was interested in measuring degrees of hunger by adding, progressively, different amounts of quinine to an acceptable food. He described the method as follows:

A series of bottle caps are countersunk on the periphery of a metal disc that is driven by a slipping clutch and escapement mechanism. The bottle caps appear immediately below an opening in the floor of a small cage that is arranged so that the rat can reach only 1 cap at a time. After a hungry rat has learned to drink a few drops of milk from each bottle cap as soon as it appears, it is presented at 30-second intervals with a series of 10 bottle caps, each cap containing 3 drops of milk, and each solution being adulterated with progressively increasing amounts of quinine hydrochloride ranging from concentrations of 0, 0·004 per cent, 0·008 per cent, to 1 per cent. For each cup that he cleans up, the rat receives 2 points; for each one started without finishing, 1 point; and for cups not touched, zero. The cumulative score has been found to be a sensitive and reliable measure of hunger.

The argument underlying this method is that the bitter taste of quinine hydrochloride inhibits ingestion and the degree of inhibition varies with the concentration of quinine in the solution. Consequently an acceptable food (milk) can be made unacceptable by addition of quinine; and the degree of hunger, Miller argued, can be measured in terms of the strength of the inhibiting agent.

Hence negative as well as positive affective processes have a regulative role in behavior. Affective processes determine what neurobehavioral patterns a naïve animal will organize and exercise, whether or not he will learn a particular pattern or preference, how many trials it will take him to learn a pattern up to some specified criterion of performance, how well a learned act will be performed and how frequently it will occur, what behavioral patterns he will inhibit, etc. But despite all this, I know of no evidence that affective processes *cause* learning. They have a regulative and organizing function and hence influence the neurobehavioral patterns that are learned. And, of course, we know that affective processes are not essential for human learning. Their main role is regulatory.[...]

Affective processes, however, must be distinguished from the stable conditions in the nervous system that are organized on hedonic (and other) principles. Through affective experience an animal develops stable organizations within his nervous system. He learns to run to places where sugar solutions can be found and to avoid places that yield electric shocks. He learns preferential discriminations – accepting one food and rejecting another. Through affective experience he builds up attitudes of liking and disliking, emotional dispositions, motives, and stable systems of value.

If a rat develops a positive orientation toward a sugar cup, this orientation can be taken as a mark of positive evaluation. If he develops a negative orientation toward a charged grill, this orientation can be taken as negative evaluation. Similarly, if repeated preference tests are given with the foods of a group, the animal will develop a *value system*. For example, if well nourished rats are tested with sucrose and wheat powder and casein, they develop a stable hierarchy of preferential values: sucrose is the most palatable, wheat powder is almost as palatable, and casein is the least palatable.

Such a value system is based upon affective processes. It has a stability and permanence (dependent upon the nervous system) that is independent of current affective arousals. The sign of an evaluative disposition is based upon the sign of the affective process aroused by the object. The degree of incentive value is related to the intensity of the primary affective arousal.

If an affectively neutral stimulus object, like an auditory click, is presented to an animal at the same time as acceptable food, the click acquires a positive incentive value. If this same physical click is presented to other animals with a painful electric shock, the click acquires a negative incentive value. If the click is presented without any hedonic accompaniment, it will be disregarded and become indifferent.

The facts indicate that almost any indifferent stimulation can become associated with an affective arousal. After an association has been firmly established, the erstwhile indifferent stimulation arouses or re-arouses an affective process. The general principle is this: *Any stimulus which occurs consistently, repeatedly, and contiguously with a primary affective arousal will tend to elicit a similar affective arousal.*

This principle applies not only to the gross difference between positive and negative affective processes but it applies also to hedonic intensity. For example, an object associated with a very sweet taste will elicit a stronger affective process than an object associated with a weakly sweet taste.

Affective arousals are conditioned to the stimulus-situations within which they occur but the stimulus-situations acquire incentive value by virtue of their association with affective arousals. This is essentially the mechanism of 'secondary reinforcement' or 'acquired reward'. It is not necessary to assume two kinds of conditioning – sensory and hedonic – but it is necessary to assume that stimulation evokes an affective process.

The incentive values shown in behavior can be changed by deprivation and satiation. For example, an unpalatable food, like casein, can become more highly valued than sucrose if rats are starved for protein. Again, the incentive value of water is low when animals are satiated but is greatly raised by deprivation of water. When incentive values are changed in these ways a stable value system may be disturbed and readjustments within the system are gradually made. A value system that has been well learned is more resistant to change than one in the process of formation. [. . .]

Statement of principles. The following statements should be regarded as tentative formulations and as a basis for experimental studies:

1. *Stimulation has affective as well as sensory consequences.* – Along with gustatory stimulation by sugar solutions, for example, there is a positive affective arousal which, by its very nature, is something to be prolonged and intensified. Along with painful stimulation there is a negative affective arousal which, by its very nature, is something to be terminated.

2. *An affective arousal orients the organism toward or against the stimulus-object.* – This goal orientation can be readily observed. For example, when a rat, in the course of exploratory activity, makes contact with a sugar solution he may pause for a moment, then continue to explore. Sooner or later, however, he returns to the solution and takes more. After repeated sips he becomes oriented toward the solution. If an experienced animal is forcibly delayed in his approach to the sugar cup, he shows a postural orientation toward the cup and approaches it quickly when released. He acts as if he expected or anticipated something. I would postulate a cognitive expectancy along with the affective arousal.

If an animal is offered a quinine solution, he fails to develop a positive orientation or an existing positive orientation is inhibited.

3. *Affective processes lead to the development of motives.* – An orientation toward the goal object instigates and regulates behavior and hence is a motive. The sign of an affective arousal determines whether an approach-maintaining motive or an avoidance-terminating motive will develop. This principle can be illustrated by numerous runway experiments in which animals acquire, through affective arousals, motives that lead to approach or to avoidance.

4. *The strength of a recently acquired motive is correlated with the intensity, duration, frequency, and recency of previous affective arousals.* – On the positive side, at least, the speed with which need-free rats approach a sucrose solution is related to the concentration, and to the duration, frequency, and recency of contact. With practice in running, however, the animals speed up as they approach their physiological limit. This speeding up with practice may level off and hence obscure initial differences due to affective arousals.

5. *The growth of motives is dependent upon learning as well as upon affective arousals.* – Learning of a simple pattern such as running down a straight alley or running back and forth upon the preference tester is dependent directly on exercise (practice, drill, training); but affective arousals play an essential role in organizing, activating, regulating, and sustaining the neuro-behavioral patterns that are learned.

It is necessary, therefore, to distinguish between learning through exercise (practice, drill, training) and the hedonic regulation of behavior. Affective processes regulate and organize neurobehavioral patterns in the sense that they determine what will be learned and what not; but such hedonic regulation and organization are not to be confused with learning through practice. Learning may be narrowly defined as a change in neurobehavioral pattern that depends upon exercise.

It should be pointed out that affective arousal is not necessary for human learning. To illustrate the point consider a subject who is instructed to memorize a series of nonsense syllables presented on a memory drum. The subject has an intent to learn. His instructional set furnishes adequate motivation for the task of memorizing. The learning proceeds whether the subject finds the task interesting, boresome, or affectively neutral. What appears necessary for learning to occur is the simultaneous excitation of contiguous neurons.

6. *The laws of conditioning apply to affective processes.* – Psychologists ordinarily describe conditioning in terms of s–r bonds, but this view is inadequate unless it can be made to include central affective processes.

An environmental situation, through conditioning, comes to arouse affective processes directly. To illustrate: If a rat is placed upon a piece of apparatus, he learns to respond to the stimulus pattern of his surroundings; but, in addition to the usual s–r patterns, the stimulus situation produces an affective arousal. If there is a positive affective arousal, the whole situation becomes hedonically positive so that the animal comes to react positively to environmental stimulus cues. If the situation is hedonically negative, the environmental stimulus cues come to arouse negative affectivity – call it distress, anxiety, fear, or whatever you will.

There is an internal conditioning of affective processes along with the usual conditioning described in s–r terms. By human analogy it can be said that the animal learns how to *feel* in the situation as well as what cognitive discriminations to make and what acts to perform.

I would postulate that affective conditioning is a contemporary event. Affective arousal does not act retroactively to influence, in some mysterious way, previous acts. The primary affective process is evoked directly, e.g. by the stimulation of pain nerves. Conditioned affective arousals develop according to the principles of frequency and spatiotemporal contiguity.

7. *Affective processes regulate behavior by influencing choice.* – Numerous experiments upon the development of food preferences show that the sign and intensity of affective processes influence choice. The development of a food preference between two acceptable foods indicates which food stimulus arouses the more intense affective process.

The acquisition of a preferential discrimination is not an instance of pure learning because affective processes determine whether one preference or its opposite will develop and, further, the relative hedonic intensities associated with two stimuli determine the rate of growth of a preferential pattern.

8. *Neurobehavioral patterns are organized according to the hedonic principle of maximizing the positive and minimizing the negative affective arousal.* This principle has a very wide range of application. It is seen most clearly in situations that involve choice. The stimulus associated with the more intense affective arousal dominates the preferential discrimination.

Functions of affective processes. In general, the affective processes have several important functions:

1. Affective processes have *activating* (energizing, driving) functions in that they provoke action. They lead the organism to do something.

Activation is dependent upon sensory stimulation (peripheral) and affective arousal (central). It is difficult to estimate the contributions of the peripheral and central factors. If an organism is painfully stimulated, the activation is dependent upon both the sensory (peripheral) and affective (central) processes. When a naïve rat for the first time tastes a sugar solution he does not appear to be greatly excited by it; but he does come back for more. When an experienced animal is placed in a situation that has repeatedly yielded sweet tastes, he moves promptly to the sugar solution and shows excitement if delayed. The facts suggest that activation comes from proprioceptive tension that is associatively aroused by the stimulus situation and the animal's goal set. Activation thus has a sensory as well as an affective basis.

2. Affective processes have *sustaining and terminating* functions. If the arousal is hedonically positive (like sexual excitement or the appetitive state produced by tasting honey), the induced patterns of behavior are sustained and repeated. If the arousal is hedonically negative (like that produced by electric shock, shrill tones, cold, bright lights, etc.), the induced patterns of behavior terminate the stimulation if possible.

3. Affective processes have *regulative* functions. At least they determine whether appetitive or aversive behavior will develop. They give a primitive kind of evaluation without providing specific information. They act like stop-go lights in traffic control.

4. Affective processes have *organizing* functions in that they lead to the formation of neurobehavioral patterns which tend to become learned. This organizing of neurobehavioral patterns through subcortical affective arousals is perhaps the chief function of affectivity.

Positive affective arousals tend to facilitate and negative to inhibit activities that were instrumental in producing them. Through a kind of primitive evaluation ('good' or 'bad') the organism is oriented towards or against certain kinds and intensities of stimulation. This organizing process is something very basic and widespread throughout nature.

Development of approach and withdrawal behaviour. In discussing Pavlov's principle of conditioning and the reflex-circle of Bok, Holt (1931) considered the origin of approach and avoidance patterns. He pointed out that certain reflex responses, e.g. reaching, go out to meet the stimulus, to get more of it. Adopting the terminology of the late Professor Warren, Holt designated these reflexes as *adient*. Adient behavior includes more than simple reflexes that maintain a pattern. Inquiring, examining, grasping, forward pressing, even predatory patterns, are *adient* in the sense that an organism goes out to get more of the stimulus, to approach it. The term *abient* designates reflexes the immediate effect of which is to give the organism less of the exciting stimulus. Behavior patterns that lead to escape, avoidance, removal of the stimulus, are *abient*. The term *abient* literally means turning away from the object, and *adient* turning towards the object.

In making his argument, Holt was strictly objective. He deplored terms with subjective implications such as 'pleasure' and 'pain' – terms found frequently in the works of J. M. Baldwin, Alexander Bain, Herbert Spencer, and other psychologists. Such terms, he wrote, are remnants of the ghost-soul type of psychology, and they have no place in a radical empiricism; they tend only to obscure the basic problems.

Although Holt refused to talk about pleasantness and unpleasantness, he was forced to take account of adience and abience because they are objective facts of observation. Holt pointed out that adient and abient reflexes are organized in the fetus and that they appear later in the infant as reflexes. A moot question in this connexion is whether some reactions of approach and withdrawal are dependent upon built-in or truly innate mechanisms. There is considerable evidence that they are.

Schneirla (1959), in a comprehensive review of the problem within comparative psychology, pointed out that there is a biphasic process of approach and withdrawal in all organisms from amoeba to man. He believes that stimulus-intensity is the controlling factor. All organisms, he wrote, tend to react positively to weak stimulation and negatively to intense stimulation.

While there is a good deal of evidence for Schneirla's thesis, I believe that *quality* as well as *intensity* of stimulation must be considered. The stimulus-quality producing a sweet taste, for

235

example, leads to the development of approach *at all intensities*. Also the stimulus-pattern may be important in releasing instinctive acts, as the work of Lorenz, Tinbergen, and other ethologists has shown. Schneirla, however, would interpret responses to stimulus-pattern in terms of intensity or change of intensity.

Going back now to Holt's view, I think that some principle of behavioral organization, other than Pavlov's principle of conditioning and Bok's principle of the reflex-circle, must be postulated to explain why an organism ever begins to respond so as to receive more of one kind of stimulation and less of another. The built-in bodily mechanisms are such that the taste of sweet leads to development of adient behavior and the taste of bitter to abient. Pain, when intense, leads to development of abience but in all sense departments there are many neutral stimulations that do not lead to approach or withdrawal.

Current research offers hope that some day we may be able to describe the neural mechanisms that regulate growth of adience and abience. In the meantime the growth of adient and abient patterns is a fact of observation. This fact would seem to imply some principle of organization related to affectivity.

Conclusion

The construct of affective arousal is supported by facts of human experience and by laboratory observations upon animal behavior. The affective processes can be represented as varying along a bipolar continuum extending from negative, through indifferent, to positive values. Affective processes vary in sign, intensity, and duration.

Affective arousals are motivating in the sense that they evoke action, regulate the course of behavior, and organize patterns of approach and withdrawal. They engender relatively stable systems of value within the organism.

The view that there are two dimensions of arousal – an activating and an hedonic dimension – is supported by physiological studies in electroencephalography and studies upon the physiology of 'reward' and 'punishment'. There are degrees or levels of activation and also degrees of positive and negative hedonic intensity.

Affective processes can be studied objectively and their functions determined. Affective processes have functions of activating behavior, sustaining or terminating activities, regulating the pattern of behavior, and facilitating or inhibiting instrumental acts. The main function of affective processes, however, is that of organizing neurobehavioral patterns of approach and withdrawal or organizing the bodily mechanisms that lead to positive and negative forms of activity.

References

BARE, J. K. (1949), 'The specific hunger for sodium chloride in normal and adrenalectomized white rats', *J. comp. physiol. Psychol.*, vol. 42, pp. 242–53.

HOLT, E. B. (1931), *Animal Drive and the Learning Process: An Essay toward Radical Empiricism*, Holt.

MILLER, N. E. (1956), 'Effects of drugs on motivation: The value of using a variety of measures', *Annals New York Acad. Sci.*, vol. 65, pp. 318–33.

SCHNEIRLA, T. C. (1959), An evolutionary and developmental theory of biphasic processes underlying approach and withdrawal, in M. R. Jones (ed.), *Nebraska Symposium on Motivation*, University of Nebraska Press.

YOUNG, P. T. (1947), 'Studies of food preference, appetite and dietary habit: VII. Palatability in relation to learning and performance', *J. comp. physiol. Psychol.*, vol. 40, pp. 37–72.

YOUNG, P. T., and FALK, J. L. (1956), 'The relative acceptability of sodium chloride solutions as a function of concentration and water need', *J. comp. physiol. Psychol.*, vol. 49, pp. 569–75.

YOUNG, P. T., and GREENE, J. T. (1953), 'Quantity of food ingested as a measure of relative acceptability', *J. comp. physiol, Psychol.*, vol. 46, pp. 288–94.

19 R. W. Leeper

The Motivational Theory of Emotion

R. W. Leeper, 'The motivational theory of emotion', in
C. L. Stacey and M. F. DeMartino (eds.), *Understanding Human
Motivation*, Howard Allen, 1963, pp. 657–65.

In all, I will discuss seven main points that I see as important for a motivational theory of emotion.

The first of these is the proposal that, when we talk about emotions, we ought not to think of them in the old introspective tradition, but as full psychological processes. That is, we ought to think of them as processes that might conceivably be studied as neurological or physiological processes; and, from another standpoint, as processes that have influences on the rest of psychological functioning. Or, to put the matter in negative terms, we ought not, I think, to conceive of emotions as merely the conscious aspect of some larger events. I am not proposing, on the other hand, that we ought to think of emotional processes merely in behavioristic terms. Sometimes emotional processes are conscious processes, and we may as well use our opportunities for subjective observation whenever this is helpful. On this first point, then, I am proposing that we ought to think of emotional processes in the same way that most psychologists regard concept-formation – that is, as a process that may be either conscious or unconscious, but that will have most of its properties the same in either case.

This is a different view from the Freudian view of affect or emotion. – This is surprising, because the Freudians certainly have been insistent, in general, that mental activity cannot be equated with conscious activity. But, with regard to affect or emotion, it seems that the Freudians unfortunately carried over the common-sense tradition that you cannot talk sensibly about a psychological process unless you conceive of it as a conscious process.

In the second place, and central to my whole proposal, is of course, the suggestion that emotional processes are motives. In fact, I would submit that, except as we use a motivation criterion, we cannot distinguish between some processes that we call emotions and some other processes that we do not think of as emotions.

But, now, is this actually a reasonable view? Do emotions actually function as motives?

To answer this question, we will need to look first at some processes which psychologists generally would conceive as motives, and ask what means we have for identifying such motives in human beings and animals. For example, take hunger. Can we infer a motive of hunger merely on the basis of some period of food-deprivation? Definitely not. An animal like a shrew has a terrific consumption of food and seems to need to eat almost continuously; a boa constrictor, on the other hand, might go for weeks after a really good meal before it would be inspired to search for any more food. No; basically we have to infer hunger on the basis of influences exerted by hunger on the rest of the life of the individual. One of the most vivid accounts of such influence has been given by Sir Ernest Shackleton, who, with his three companions, tried to reach the South Pole in the old, hard way back in 1909. These men were engaged in very strenuous physical exercise, they were living under conditions of intense cold, and yet they had only the smallest of daily rations.

As Shackleton reports, they thought and talked about food virtually all day long. They dreamed about it at night. They spent an enormous amount of time comparing notes on new recipes that they wished to use when they returned to civilization. They devised special rituals for dividing the food at each meal to insure that no one would get a smaller portion than another person. They gladly hauled their sleds with their food supplies on them, even though they were tired and might have wished for lighter burdens. Even aside from their conscious experience of hunger, these several influences are the means by which we would judge that they were tremendously motivated by a hunger for food. As a matter of fact, their example illustrates the point that the conscious aspect of motivation is not an essential attribute. These men were also strongly motivated to try to reach the South Pole. Each day, at every step and every choice point, instead of turning back to where they could find food, they were moving further and further away from their base camp to the goal that was dictated by what-

239

ever motives made them want to reach the South Pole. But it was only in the effects on the rest of activity, and not within conscious experience, that the other motives demonstrated that they were dominant over the motive to seek for food.

Now, if such influences on other psychological functioning are the means of inferring a physiologically-based motive, we need to ask whether these influences also come from emotional processes. That is, do emotional processes tend to dominate the content of thought, do they tend to determine what will be stressed perceptually, and do they make people willing to endure penalties or forego other satisfactions to reach goals resulting from emotional sources? Do emotional motives tend to lead to a learning of new means of acting that would serve such goals?

Suppose we examine a case of emotional reaction. Thus, suppose that you start on a drive with another person and that you quickly observe that he is a rather reckless and clumsy driver. You note, for instance, that he often misjudges when it is safe to pass other cars and that he often wanders across the middle line on the road even when other cars are coming toward him. What are the effects of the fear that gets aroused in you? Does your fear tend to focus your perceptual processes, making it hard to watch the scenery, just as it was true that the magnificent scenery of the Antarctic was wasted on Shackleton's men? Do you tend to engage in problem-solving thinking or trial and error activity trying to find some means to change the behavior of the driver or to extricate yourself from the situation? In all such respects, it would seem, the fear that is aroused in you is functionally equivalent, in its basic effects, to strong hunger. The same would be true of other emotions. Consider, for example, how much sacrifice and efforts at problem-solving a nation will engage in when it fears it is endangered by some other nation.

So, since emotions have the same fundamental effects that the physiologically-based motives have, we may call them motives. This is the most fundamental fact about emotions. It is our basic means to distinguish between emotions and other psychological processes of a non-motivational sort.

Often we tend to think of emotions as processes that are identified by physiological effects such as visceral reactions or galvanic skin response or the like. But such indices of emotion are not nearly as sensitive or efficient as the behavioral effects of emotions. The case is like that with regard to a qualitative food-hunger after some period with an inadequate diet. The behavioral indications of such qualitative food hunger come long before there are any physiological indications of dietary imbalance.

In the third place, now, if we are to conceive of emotional motives, we need to ask about the relation between emotional motives and motives more generally. What I am assuming is that all motives may be conceived of as two types that are spaced along some continuum. At the one end are the very clearly physiologically-based motives like hunger and thirst. Some of these are dependent on general tissue states. Others, like toothaches or pain from an electric shock or from a blow, are dependent on external stimulation. But, in these cases, the external stimulation is relatively intense and an interruption of the afferent impulses from the point of stimulation, as from the tooth, would bring the physiologically-based motive to an end. Emotional motives, on the other hand, depend on relatively more complex psychological processes. For example, consider the goslings that were studied by Tinbergen. These goslings showed an arousal of fear responses and hiding behavior when the silhouette of a hawk was passed over them, but they were unaffected when the same cardboard model was turned end for end and passed over them in such a way as to mimic the long-necked silhouette of a goose. In this case the perceptual reaction is apparently innate or instinctive, and yet we would call the process an emotional one.

In most cases, however, learned meanings are involved. Thus, suppose a person consults a physician about a certain symptom and is told that there is some chance that this might indicate cancer and that he should have an exploratory operation in another week. The physician might tell the person not to worry in the meantime and merely go about his usual life. But the effects of all the usual stimuli now are changed because of the person's complex processes of representation on his situation. So, while some emotional motives shade off from almost similar physiologically-based motives, most of them are markedly different, even though they do belong within the large classification of motives.

Some treatments of the topic of emotion propose that only the responses to serious frustrations are emotions and that, on the other hand, the processes involved in, or at the back of, healthy goal-oriented behavior are not emotions. There are differences, of course, between these two sorts of processes, and we need to study these differences. But this difference is not of such a character that we ought to speak of emotions as existing only in the one case. Or, at least, if we use a motivational theory of emotion, we would not speak in that way. For, in both cases there may be processes that depend, as I have just said, on complex representation of the life situation, and that also serve as the basis of goal-directed functioning. Consider a person, like a surgeon, who thoroughly enjoys his work, who believes that it has great value and that it is deeply appreciated by other persons. Such a person shows all the hard work, the willingness to forego other goals, the focusing of perceptions, and so on, that mark emotional processes or emotional motives. But the person who is deeply concerned about the threat of war, which is certainly a frustration effect, also has the same highly organized goal-directedness. It seems to me, therefore, that emotional processes are involved in both kinds of activity and not merely in the frustration case.

As the fourth point, now, I would like to suggest that, in the higher animals, including man, the most important motives are the emotional ones. At least, these are the motives that are particularly developed in the higher animals. They are the motives that take advantage of distinctive biological characteristics of the higher animals both on the side of their excellent distance receptors and on the side of their greater perceptual and learning capacities. Take a deer, for example. It can detect a very faint odor or sound that would indicate an enemy. But, what is important biologically is that the deer must do more than merely sense the presence of a cougar. What is important also is that the deer must be powerfully motivated in consequence of this, even though there is, as yet, no condition of tissue injury such as may later occur if the enemy is disregarded.

I do not mean that physiologically-based motives are unimportant in our lives. But, particularly when, as Maslow says, we have achieved some fairly adequate means of satisfying cravings for food, water and physical comfort, the main motives of our lives come to be emotional motives. We are strongly motivated creatures in modern society, but the motives that cause this fact are emotional processes. The emotional motives are the ones particularly that can be greatly modified by learning. They operate with reference to distant objectives as well as with reference to immediate ones. They can use very subtle cues. They are the ones, therefore, that particularly fit the requirements of human existence.

As a fifth problem, now, we ought to say something more about the nature of emotional processes. We have been considering the suggestion that emotional processes are motives. But what more about them? What are these processes that are emotional motives?

Particularly what gives rise to this question is the observation that emotional motives are relatively definite, precise processes. We tend to use broad terms that do not suggest this. When an elderly man picks his way carefully along an icy street, we say that he does this because of fear. When a person is reluctant to make a speech, we may say that his hesitancy is because of fear. And so on. But surely the one fear is quite different from another – the one man has a fear of physical injury; the other person has a fear, say, of being criticized or embarrassed. These don't seem like the same process. What is a fear process, then?

What I want to suggest, and I see this as perhaps the main new point of the present paper, though it may seem like a peculiar idea, is that emotional processes ought to be seen as one type of perceptual process. I don't mean that emotional processes *depend on*, *or come from* perceptual processes, though this also is true. I mean a more drastic statement – namely, that emotional processes basically and fundamentally *are* perceptual processes, just as apparent movement is a perceptual process.

Not all perceptual processes, of course, are emotional processes. Most of the processes that have been studied in research on perception have been about as nonemotional or nonmotivational as one could find, as in studies of reversible figures, influence of visual contours, and psychophysical effects. Such nonmotivational perceptions have been focused on for reasons of expediency. It is much easier to get subjects for experiments on comparisons of lengths of line than it is to get (or at least keep) subjects in a study of discrimination of strengths of electric shock. It is much easier to study simple visual discriminations than to study such complex matters as discriminations of the degree to which one situation is more embarrassing than another.

Because of such considerations of convenience or expediency, the psychologists doing research on perception have worked with these simple, nonmotivational examples of perception. They also have worked almost entirely with *conscious* perceptual processes, so that they could have the economies of introspective reports, rather than working also with unconscious perceptual processes. And, since they have worked with perceptions that were not motivationally significant, they have worked with processes that are very transitory in character.

But these considerations of expediency of early research efforts ought not to dictate our basic conception of perception. For, with many other examples of perception, the processes shade over into those that are more and more definitely motivational, either in an emotional sense or in a simpler physiologically-based sense. Thus, suppose that an infant who is being given a bath takes a bite from the cake of soap. Is this any less a perceptual effect because it is not a motivationally neutral process? Suppose a person receives an electric shock – is this any less a perceptual process because it is so painful and because the person tends strongly to translate his perception into overt action? Remember Tinbergen's goslings that saw the silhouette that had the rough shape of a hawk – was this process any less a perceptual process because of the added fact that it governed their behavior in the way characteristic of a motivational process? In fact, as Wolfgang Köhler has suggested in his address as president of the American Psychological Association in 1959, if a process is to have a motivational effect – that is, a goal-directing influence – it cannot be something as formless as a tissue state or a diffuse affect. It must be something that has a sufficiently precise and definite character that it can operate as a vector – with a direction – rather than merely somehow serve in an energy-releasing fashion.

One objection that this suggestion faces, of course, is that emotional processes often have only a vague conscious character. A person is despondent, say, or suffers from so-called 'free-floating anxiety', but cannot say what he is despondent about. And, many psychologists say, perceptual processes are of course an awareness or conscious experience of something or other. But, here again, we are following too narrowly a tradition dominated by considerations of expediency in early research. There is no reason why we should conclude, merely because so much work on perception has concerned merely conscious perception, that all perceptual processes are conscious. When clinicians work with cases of free-floating anxiety, they find that it is not formless and free-floating. It arises in certain situations characteristic for the given person and expresses itself in certain characteristic ways of dealing with those situations. As this indicates, a good portion of the perceptual processes that constitute some emotional processes are unconscious perceptual processes. But they still are fairly definitely structured processes – that is, perceptual processes.

To make this proposal more clear, I might compare perceptual processes to movies. The kinds of perceptions that we ordinarily experiment on are like the black and white movies. Then, from them, let us imagine that other movies might have more and more color added to them. The fact that such color has been added does not mean that such movies have any less precision of detail; that they are any less 'movies'. Or, as perceptions come to have more and more of a motivational character, or more specifically of an emotional character, this does not mean that they cease being dynamically organized neural processes, involving complex cortical activities. It does not mean, in brief, that they cease being perceptual processes.

If we held such a motivational theory of emotion – or, I suppose I should say, such a perceptual-motivational theory of emotion – what are some implications that would flow from it? I propose two such implications as the sixth and seventh main points of this paper.

In the first place, if emotional processes are perceptual processes, this suggests that, after the earliest period of life, emotional processes will exist in increasingly diverse and highly individualized forms. For, if there is one thing that marks perceptual processes in addition to their dynamic organizational character, it is their great susceptibility to modification by learning or experience. I think it is safe to say, much as Koffka did and as Hebb has been emphasizing, that the small infant has capacities for only the simplest kinds of perceptual organization. To the tiny infant, the face of the mother is probably indistinguishable from the faces of other persons. But, as the child develops, the perceptual mechanisms that were originally so indefinite become sharper and finer. The original neural mechanisms no longer exist. He can no longer perceive things in the undifferentiated way that he did originally. And, different persons learn different perceptual mechanisms. One person develops his perceptual mechanisms for one kind of music, another person for another kind. One person learns to recognize chimpanzee faces, another person picks his friends from his fellow human beings.

This is one of the points where a perceptual-motivational theory of emotion would differ most strongly from the view that Robert Plutchik has developed. For, as I understand it, he believes that emotions continue as primary, physiologically-given emotions even though they may get into new combinations that produce strikingly new effects. It seems to me that one of the main theoretical and empirical issues regarding emotion would be to determine which of these two hypotheses comes closer to reality.

Finally, another implication of a perceptual-motivational theory of emotion would concern questions of how emotional processes and emotional habits are changed. We have a lot of ideas about how emotions are changed, as by permitting 'emotional discharge', by 'making emotions conscious', by 'experimental extinction', and so on. There is some truth in all of these views. But, from the viewpoint that I have been proposing, I think we might say that, wherever any of such means is successful, an influence of a different sort has been responsible and that we would get more command over this problem if we could recognize what this more fundamental process is.

To explain this suggestion, let me use a small example of a non-technical sort, one taken from the little book by Katherine Forbes, *Mama's Bank Account*. In one chapter, the young girl who tells the story is described as sharing, with her aunts, a very unsympathetic and disparaging attitude toward one of her uncles. He had seemed solely preoccupied with himself. He lived in the most miserly fashion, even though it was thought that his work in buying run-down farms, building them up, and selling them had probably brought him a good income. There was bad feeling because he had sold certain family heirlooms brought over from Norway and apparently pocketed the money. The relatives granted that he had his troubles. They knew he had been somewhat crippled from childhood and had a bad limp, but they resented his seemingly entirely self-centered ways.

When he died, the family gathered at the funeral with some interest in the question of his estate. What they found, though, was that there was no money left – only a little notebook with a lot of entries such as these:

Jospeh Spenelli. Four years old. Tubercular left leg. $237. Walks.
Jamie Kelly. 9 years. $435. Walks.
Esta Jensen. 11 years. Braces, $121.
Sam Bernstein. Five years. Club foot. $452.16. Walks.

Now, when this additional material was met, there was a sharp and enduring emotional change as a result. Why? Not because there had been any lack of strength or practice with the preceding emotional reaction to this man. But because, instead, a new and more compelling perceptual organization had been developed which did not deny any of the previous factual knowledge, but which incorporated it into a more powerful and enduring perceptual organization.

To say this does not mean necessarily that any one means of psychotherapy is more effective than another. But it does suggest that, when psychotherapy is successful, we must look for the development of such new perceptual organizations as the basic happening. Experimental extinction procedures are effective only when they are suited to accomplish this; making an emotion conscious is effective only when it involves conditions that accomplish this; and so on.

As I see it, therefore, our approach to problems of emotion has been greatly hampered by our continuance in certain habits of thought that we carry over from the earlier days of psychology, as with the ideas that we ought to think of psychological processes merely in terms of what is conscious, and as those cases where we have failed to see similarities because we have been so impressed by differences that also exist. I might even suggest that we have been somewhat like the child who is asked, 'In what way are an orange and a ball alike?' and who insists, with admittedly some degree of justification, 'They aren't alike. You can eat an orange and you can play with a ball.' Admittedly there are differences between emotions and other motives; admittedly there are differences between emotional processes and other perceptual processes. But, I submit, we would open out some very useful conceptualizations if we would see that there are also major similarities.

20 R. S. Lazarus

Emotion as Coping Process

Excerpts from R. S. Lazarus, *Psychological Stress and the Coping Process*, New York, McGraw-Hill, 1966, pp. 53, 159–61, 250–3.

From our point of view, threat is the product of appraisal, and the action tendencies aroused by threat may be regarded as coping processes. Thus, for example, both anger and fear involve forms of coping with threat. Any such action tendency depends upon additional appraisals – for example, appraisal of the possibilities of escape as opposed to attack or of some other attempted solutions to the threat. To distinguish the latter kind of appraisal process from that producing threat itself, we employ the terms 'primary' for threat-producing appraisal and 'secondary' for additional appraisals related to the coping process. The final shaping of the reaction thus involves processes and conditions not germane to the production of threat itself, such as anticipations about the probable reaction of the environment to any behavioral response. [. . .]

Psychologists often appear to believe that the causes of behavior have been explained satisfactorily by reference to learning or by suggesting that the response has become connected to the stimulus configuration by conditioning. This is all well and good, for we agree that in higher animals the significance of a cue must be learned, and conditioning represents one of the theoretically conceived processes whereby the response gets connected with the cue. Still, on the basis of such a general statement of learning, we cannot specify the present conditions under which one or another type of coping process will occur. That is, we are not led to hypotheses about these conditions merely by casual reference to learning. In order for the reaction to occur, the individual must appraise the situation in a particular way based on what he has learned about certain cues, about what follows what. *The perspective in which action tendencies are viewed as coping processes that depend on cognitive activity assists us, as we shall see, to suggest factors in the stimulus configuration and within the psychological structure that influence the coping process and its manifestations.* [. . .]

Relations between primary and secondary appraisal

How is secondary appraisal related to the primary appraisal of threat? They should not be regarded as necessarily sequential even though the former depends on the latter. They may overlap in time, since features of the stimulus configuration relevant to secondary appraisal may be noted even before threat is appraised, as when long-standing awareness of road or street conditions determines what the individual does when suddenly confronted with the danger of floods, or they may occur simultaneously, as when the stimulus configuration contains information relevant to both threat and coping. While the information pertaining to the latter may be assimilated before or during the appraisal of threat as well as after, threat gives the secondary-appraisal process its poignancy and urgency. Without threat, cognitions of the secondary-appraisal process are purely intellectual. They have little or no mobilizing value. They are rather like 'cold perceptions'.

This interdependency without temporal ordering being necessary is also featured in Smelser's (1963) use of the logic of 'value-added' as employed in the field of economics (Samuelson, 1958). In our use here, a temporal order between primary and secondary appraisal is not implied, only that primary appraisal of threat is necessary to the full elaboration of secondary appraisal. The latter is meaningless without the former.

The best way to see the distinction between primary and secondary appraisal is to consider the factors that contribute to each. Out of a complex assortment of cues, some are relevant to threat appraisal, some are relevant to the action tendencies that are generated, and some are relevant to both. The cues for the secondary-appraisal process concern the consequences of any action tendency that might be activated in the face of the given conditions. The balance of power between harm and counterharm resources, the imminence of the confrontation with harm, the ambiguity of the threat stimuli, motive strengths and pattern, general belief systems about transactions with the environment, and intellectual resources contribute to primary threat appraisal. Factors contributing to secondary appraisal include the degree of threat, viability of alternative coping actions, the location of the agent or harm, situational constraints, motive strengths and pattern, ego resources, and coping dispositions. Although there is some overlap, essentially different kinds of information are involved in each. In effect, *the cues for secondary appraisal concern the estimated consequences of any action tendency generated to cope with the threat*.

To get a clear picture of the distinction between primary and secondary appraisal, it will be useful to see the sources of information that contribute to both kinds of appraisal in tabular form. The sources of information, or, to put it differently, the kinds of consequences appraised, determine the distinction. Table 1 provides a schematic arrangement of the two processes and the factors contributing to both.

We can make the distinction between the categories involved in primary and secondary appraisal clearer if we examine more closely the matter of balance of power in the production of threat and the role of degree of threat in coping. Degree of threat depends, in part, on a judgement by the individual about how much danger there is of some type of harm. If the harmful agency is seen as extremely powerful and the individual views his own resources as weak, threat is greater. Of course, other factors such as imminence and the strength of the motive that is engaged also play a role. Now, once threatened, coping processes are activated. Which ones? This now depends on the degree of threat, which is itself a complex function of the several factors influencing primary appraisal. We cannot fruitfully regard the balance of power as directly affecting secondary appraisal (although it does indirectly), since degree of threat is derived not only from this factor, but from other factors as well. Thus, it is better to say that degree of threat, which is itself based on a number of factors and is therefore a higher order abstraction, directly influences the individual's decision about what to do. A similar analysis can be made for the other factors that influence secondary appraisal. Motive strength is, of course, relevant to primary appraisal of threat as well as secondary appraisal. However, in the former case the issue being

Table 1
Sources of Information Contributing to Primary
and Secondary Appraisal

	Primary appraisal (based on nature of harmful confrontation)	Secondary appraisal (based on consequences of action tendencies)
Factors in stress configuration contributing to appraisals	Threat or nonthreat 1. Balance of power between harm and counterharm resources 2. Imminence of confrontation 3. Ambiguity of stimulus cues concerning harm	Coping 1. Location of agent of harm 2. Viability of alternative coping actions 3. Situational constraints
		* Degree of threat
Factors within psychological structure contributing to appraisals	1. Motive strength and pattern 2. Several belief systems concerning transactions with environment 3. Intellectual resources, education, and sophistication	1. Motive strength and pattern (because of potential sacrifices entailed in any action) 2. Ego resources 3. Coping dispositions

* Belongs neither in stimulus configuration nor psychological structure but is a complex, intervening product of both.

evaluated is the seriousness of the harm, while in the latter case it concerns what further harms (or sacrifices that must be paid) will come from employing some particular act of coping. In sum, *with primary appraisal, the issue is how much am I in danger from a situation; with secondary appraisal, the issue concerns how much am I in danger from anything I do about the threat or to what extent will any particular action relieve the danger*. Clearly, primary appraisals can influence secondary appraisals, and vice versa. However, the two sets of appraisal processes are each concerned with a different aspect of the problem and depend, to some degree, on different information.

As in the case of the primary process of threat appraisal, there is no implication that in secondary appraisal the individual engages in a lengthy reflection about the situation, although this may indeed occur. The process is often nearly instantaneous, although it is also commonly a symbolic process, especially in higher animals. Similarly, the individual need not be fully aware of the evaluations he is making, or of the factors that enter into them. And secondary appraisals need not be accurate reflections of reality or represent sound judgement any more than in the case of the primary appraisal of threat. [. . .]

Rationality, coping, and emotion

We have taken the position that threat reactions are linked to the process of coping with threat, and that in turn, both are the result, at least partly, of a process of secondary appraisal in which the situation is surveyed or evaluated in order to select an appropriate way of preventing or minimizing the anticipated harm. At first glance it would seem that this focus on appraisal places an undue emphasis on entirely cognitive processes in the psychodynamics of stress. It is as if the individual is continually making rational judgements about coping process, for example, which is viable, which contains the possibility of further threat, etc. The reason for this impression is that in this book emotions have been treated as consequences, rather than causes of reactions. It is common in psychology and in lay usage to blame emotions for the failures of adaptation, for irrational conduct. But here we have been saying that emotions like fear are the result, not the cause of cognitive activity. In emphasizing the importance of factors in the stimulus configuration – for example, in shaping the processes of coping and the threat reaction – we have made coping seem like a highly rational affair. How can this be justified? Is something wrong here? Can we no longer comprehend the obvious irrationality we see so often in human adaptation?

The psychological processes of stress are indeed cognitive, if by this is meant that beliefs, expectations, perceptions, and evaluations as well as learning and memory underlie the reaction to a threat stimulus. *But appraisal does not imply awareness, good reality testing, or good adaptation.* It implies only that thought processes are involved, not the kind of thought. A belief may be unwise, a perception inaccurate, a coping solution to threat primitive and unsuccessful, yet still be cognitive. In this way, coping can be based on cognitive processes, yet nonadaptive or even bizarre. The 'irrationality' does not come primarily from the intervention of emotions in thought processes, but rather from the fact that threat places the psychological system in jeopardy, and that the alternatives for dealing with threat are tied to motives, beliefs, and abilities, as well as to a complex set of stimulus inputs. Thus, what appears to the observer to be the most adaptive solution may be unacceptable to the individual in question. Because of his particular experiences and the psychological characteristics that this experience helped create, it may threaten him further or he may lack the resources for carrying out this solution.

It is true that one finds abundant clinical examples of individuals who have acted 'irrationally' under accompanying intense emotional disturbance. In court cases, where one person has killed another under such circumstances, it is standard practice to evaluate his mental state at the time of the act. Often it is argued that intense emotion totally disrupted the reality testing of the murderer and his ability to control the impulse. This is often accepted as the explanation of the deranged or antisocial act. A psychological tradition has grown up which makes emotional disturbance the cause rather than effect of maladaptive behavior.

However, since negatively toned emotion is an inevitable accompaniment or correlate of threat and coping, it only seems as though the emotion is 'causing' the trouble. It is not the emotion that is responsible, although we grant that emotion might also be a source of interference in adaptive thought. Rather, the culprit is the recognition of threat or danger and the secondary cognitions that underlie the effort to cope with it. The correlation between threat and emotion makes it easy to confuse cause and effect, especially since the emotional state is the most obtrusive feature of the entire psychological event.

A typical example of the tendency to blame emotion for irrational or unrealistic ways of thinking is a remark heard on television in an NBC White Paper entitled, 'Terror in the Streets' and telecast on 6 April 1965. The documentary program dealt with the widespread impression that crimes of violence have increased markedly, especially in relation to current racial problems. In a videotaped comment, an expert on the program pointed out that crimes of violence have not increased, but the statistics have been poorly interpreted and the public has been aroused into a mood which creates an unwarranted atmosphere of crisis. After he had made this statement, an interviewer asked him, 'Would you let your wife ride in the subway (in New York) at midnight?' The expert blocked on this question and finally commented that he was no different from the general public in his feeling of fear, upon which he added, 'This is an emotional reaction, not an intellectual one.' He proceeded to reinforce this analysis by noting that on rational grounds his wife would be in far more danger driving her own car. The reader might also have noted the similarity here to the reactions of people who fear flying, preferring to travel by car yet appearing to recognize that, statistically, there is more danger in the automobile. Their fear seems not to be assuaged by this recognition.

When the comment is made, 'This is an emotional reaction, not an intellectual one', it reflects the common viewpoint that emotion is responsible for irrationality or the lack of realistic thinking. The expert really is pointing out that thinking that the subway is unsafe is based on an unrealistic belief system, just as the belief that flying is more dangerous than driving is similarly out of tune with the facts. Such beliefs are reinforced by the tremendous publicity that is given to the occasional episodes of subway murders and plane disasters. We would restate the above comment as follows: 'This is an irrational reaction, based on incorrect facts, or on an incorrect assessment of the facts.' Emotion is indeed experienced with this assessment because the individual does believe that his wife is in great danger of assault in the subway. The fear is a consequence of this appraisal, not the cause of it, although this is not the way it is usually expressed colloquially. And, of course, the decision to take the car rather than the subway is a coping decision that is based on the explicit or implicit appraisal that there is more to be feared in the public conveyance than in the privacy of one's auto. To blame emotion for this decision is to focus on the wrong factor, since the emotion and the unwise decision can best be changed by altering the belief system on which the appraisal is made. When the individual says he 'knows' that the facts prove otherwise, he is really saying that others may think so, but in reality he believes that flying or traveling in the subway in New York is really more hazardous than driving an automobile. Or, alternatively, he believes both things at the same time, but he must make a definite behavioral choice.

Now perhaps this is what psychologists who speak of emotions systematically as hypothetical constructs are really saying, and we are merely restating it in a slightly different way. A hypothetical construct, such as anxiety, must not be thought of in systematic usage as causing anything at all, and it must be defined in terms of antecedent and consequent conditions. For convenience and for the moment, we can ignore the antecedent variables and focus on the consequences of having been made anxious or guilty. At other times, we can focus on the conditions that led to these different reactions. There is nothing wrong with this. Furthermore, just because the layman uses casual communication about emotion and the popular literature shows erosion of the meanings of the systematist, there is no reason to attack traditional theory itself, if it is clear and fruitful.

In the light of this we would say that the treatment of emotion as a hypothetical construct is clearly justified and corresponds to what we are saying here, as long as emotion (especially a single emotion such as anxiety) is not literally taken to be the cause of various forms of coping. The logical outcomes of the position we have taken and the position that emotion is a hypothetical construct are not basically very dissimilar, as far as we can see. The main difference lies in the emphasis on the cognitions that produce different emotional reactions and their coping aspects. For one thing, we have said that aspects of emotion are, in effect, the coping process. Secondly, instead of talking about conditioned reactions, for example, we have said that the coping process depends on a complex act of cognitive appraisal. This appraisal represents a kind of transaction between an individual with a particular psychological structure and a stimulus configuration.

Associative-learning conflict theory and our position agree, of course, that the psychological structure and the reaction are based on the historical considerations of learning. However, to speak of learning does not point us toward the variables of importance in this transaction which, in our view, derive from the question, 'What must the individual believe about a stimulus situation, and what does he think about the consequences of anything he might do with it, in order to react as he does?' It may be true that these variables can be translated back to associative-learning conflict theory terms because these terms are broad enough to encompass them and because both viewpoints share the conviction that the relationships depend upon learning. But the research problem in psychological stress is to identify in advance the variables that predict the total reaction and to develop rules about their interplay. Our purpose is not antithetical to traditional conflict, association-learning theory, but rather to amplify, to clarify, and to sharpen certain distinctions. We think that an explicitly cognitively oriented, phenomenological frame of reference such as ours can do this better and more fully than the more simple stimulus-response frameworks. That is, by the nature of the question that it asks, it can turn our attention more profitably toward the critical conditions of each form of reaction. Furthermore, it is not enough to predict relatively simple behaviors, such as avoidance and approach, since the pattern of stress reaction is complex and variable. We must be able to state under what conditions (external and internal) not only avoidance, but also attack, defense, and other forms of coping will occur, and when agreements or discrepancies between what the individual reports about his affective state and what he does will take place.

In short, to say that emotion does not cause these reactions, but is part of the reactions themselves, and to interpose appraisal, threat, and coping as intervening processes is not so distant logically from the more traditional view. *The main function of this departure is to emphasize the cognitions that underlie the various reaction patterns, to keep us away from oversimple analyses and the eroding of meaning that comes from adopting too literally the language of emotion as the intervening variable, to point up that there is not one process connected with the reaction but several, and especially to enable us to pinpoint the conditions within the psychological structure and in the stimulus configuration that must play a crucial role in the reaction.*

Psychologists have been increasingly recognizing the critical role of cognitive processes in the determination of emotional behavior. Prominent examples of this cognitive orientation to emotion are the work of Arnold (1960), the analyses concerning aggression of Berkowitz (1962), and the discussion of affect and emotion by Peters (1963). This orientation is part of a growing mood of psychological thought.

An important experimental study by Schachter and Singer (1962) also illustrates this trend to emphasize the cognitive antecedents of emotion. The basic procedure of their experiment was to inject epinephrine (an adrenal medulla hormone connected with emotion which typically results in marked evidence of autonomic nervous system arousal) into subjects under various conditions. All subjects were told the compound was a vitamin supplement, 'Suproxin', and that the purpose of the study was to evaluate its visual effects. In one condition, the subjects were accurately informed of the usual physiological effects of the injection, for example, pounding heart, shaking hand, and warm, flushed face. Subjects were reassured that the effects were mild and transitory. In a second condition, nothing was said about the side effects of the injection. A third condition involved misinforming the subjects about the effects, saying, for example, that their feet would feel numb, an itching sensation would be experienced, and that a slight headache might occur. A fourth condition involved the injection of a placebo, a saline solution, with no information given about possible effects.

Two additional conditions of great importance for the study of the antecedents of emotion were also introduced. Some of the subjects in the epinephrine-ignorant, epinephrine-informed, and placebo conditions were exposed either to a *social situation designed to induce anger or to one designed to produce euphoria*. These conditions were created by having a stooge act in a standardized fashion. He was introduced as another subject and sat with the subject while waiting for further tests. One kind of stooge acted in a silly, euphoric manner. The other type of stooge expressed anger at the injection treatment, and, building up to an intense display, ended in a rage in the presence of the subject.

Behavioral observations relevant to emotional state and self-reports of mood were obtained by the experimenters. In those conditions under which epinephrine was injected, significantly greater evidence of sympathetic nervous system activation was found than in the placebo condition. But the most important finding in the study was that the type of emotional reaction observed and reported by the subject depended upon the social manipulations produced by the 'angry' or 'euphoric' stooge. Those subjects exposed to the former reacted with anger, while those exposed to the latter reacted with a euphoric state, especially in those conditions where they were misinformed or not informed about the effects of the injection. In such cases no reasonable explanation was available of their bodily states, and they were more susceptible to the social influence. This influence also operated slightly less in the placebo conditions, giving some minimal support to the role in emotions that is played by autonomic arousal or activation.

In discussing their findings, Schachter and Singer (1962) write:

Given precisely the same state of epinephrine-induced sympathetic activation, we have, by means of cognitive manipulations, been able to produce in our subjects the very disparate states of euphoria and anger. It may indeed be the case that cognitive factors are major determiners of the emotional labels we apply to a common state of sympathetic arousal. (p. 397)

And further,

Let us consider the implications of our formulation and data for alternative conceptualizations of emotion. Perhaps the most popular current conception of emotion is in terms of 'activation theory' in the sense employed by Lindsley [1951] and Woodworth and Schlosberg [1954]. As we understand this theory, it suggests that emotional stages should be considered at one end of a continuum of activation which is defined in terms of degree of autonomic arousal and of electroencephalographic measures of activation. The results of the experiment described in this paper do, of course, suggest that such a formulation is not completely adequate. It is possible to have very high degrees of activation without a subject either appearing to be or describing himself as 'emotional'. *Cognitive factors appear to be indispensable elements in any formation of emotion.*[1] (p. 398)

We feel that the logical and empirical case for cognitive processes as necessary antecedents of emotion is even stronger than

1. Italics supplied.

that made by Schachter and Singer (1962). In their experiment, the emotion is first stimulated by the injection of epinephrine and then given its shape or content by social contagion and a cognitive process of labeling. This injection procedure limits the conclusions that can be drawn about emotion in the normal life situation. In most life situations of emotional production, there is no artificial booster given to ensure a high state of autonomic activation. The individual perceives and appraises a situation relevant to his welfare, and this appraisal is a crucial antecedent to the emotional reaction. The appraisal encourages an action tendency with respect to the stimulus. Activation will indeed occur, but the activation follows, it does not precede, the cognition about the situation. It is true that the individual may have been previously activated, as, for example, when he is in a state of high motivation or drive. But the fundamental thing that generates an emotion is the cognitive activity of appraisal and the impulses it generates. The argument applies, of course, to psychological stress just as well since the latter deals with the negatively toned emotions.

References

ARNOLD, MAGDA B. (1960), *Emotion and Personality*, 2 vols., Columbia University Press.

BERKOWITZ, L. (1962), *Aggression*, McGraw Hill.

LINDSLEY, D. B. (1951), 'Emotion', in S. S. Stevens (ed.), *Handbook of Experimental Psychology*, John Wiley & Sons, Inc., pp. 473–516.

PETERS, H. N. (1963), 'Affect and emotion', in M. H. Marx (ed.), *Theories in Contemporary Psychology*, The Macmillan Company, pp. 435–54.

SAMUELSON, P. A. (1958), *Economics: An Introductory Analysis*, 4th edn., McGraw-Hill Book Company, pp. 187–8.

SCHACHTER, S., and SINGER, J. E. (1962), 'Cognitive, social, and physiological determinants of emotional state', *Psychol. Rev.*, vol. 69, pp. 379–99.

SMELSER, N. J. (1963), *Theory of Collective Behavior*, The Free Press of Glencoe.

WOODWORTH, R. S., and SCHLOSBERG, H. (1954), *Experimental Psychology*, Holt, Rinehart and Winston, Inc.

Part Eight Expression and Recognition of Emotion

The older literature on the recognition of emotional expression has concentrated on the recognition of photographs of posed facial expression (Féléky, 1914; Langfeld, 1918; Sherman, 1927); the conclusion, that emotions cannot be reliably recognized, can be attacked on the ground both that static poses do not reflect the dynamic character of emotion, and that the emotions portrayed depend on the (unknown) talent for mimicry possessed by the person who posed for the photographs. Recently, there has been renewed interest in this problem and its experimental investigation (see Schlosberg, 1941, 1952, 1954).

The two selections in this section have been chosen because one of them (Michotte) offers evidence that the recognition of emotion is based on movement rather than frozen facial expression, even if such movement is entirely schematic; and the other (Spitz) is a summary of careful clinical observations on the development of emotional expression in the infant, which complements an earlier review of emotional development in childhood (Bridges, 1931) which for long was the only one.

References
BRIDGES, K. M. B. (1931), *The Social and Emotional Development of the Pre-school Child*, Routledge & Kegan Paul.
FÉLÉKY, A. M. (1914), 'The expression of emotion', *Psych. Rev.*, vol. 21, pp. 33–41.
LANGFELD, H. S. (1918), 'The judgment of emotion by the facial expression', *J. abn. Psychol.*, vol. 13, pp. 172–84.
SHERMAN, M. (1927), 'The differentiation of emotional responses in infants', *J. comp. Psychol.*, vol. 7, pp. 265–84.
SCHLOSBERG, H. (1941), 'A scale for the judgment of facial expressions', *J. exper. Psychol.*, vol. 29, pp. 497–510.
SCHLOSBERG, H. (1952), 'The description of facial expressions in terms of two dimensions', *J. exper. Psychol.*, vol. 44, pp. 229–37.
SCHLOSBERG, H. (1954), 'Three dimensions of emotion', *Psychol. Rev.*, vol. 61, pp. 81–8.

21 A. E. Michotte

The Emotional Significance of Movement

A. E. Michotte, 'The emotional significance of movement', in
M. L. Reymert (ed.), *Feelings and Emotions*, Mc-Graw Hill,
1950, pp. 114–26.

I would like to take the opportunity provided by this second
Symposium organized by Dr Martin L. Reymert to report on some
observations relative to the psychology of the emotions. They are
observations which I was able to make with my students in the
course of some research on the perception of 'functional connections' and on the perception of causation.[1] I do not intend in this
paper to make an exhaustive study of the question nor a critical
discussion of the opinions of other authors, but only to put forward
an idea in general outline which was suggested to me by my
experimental work.

I

First of all, let us recall how these experiments were carried out.

By means of special technical equipment we made two (or
more) little colored rectangles, 1 cm. long and 0·5 cm. wide, move
along a horizontal slot 15 cm. long and 0·5 cm. wide (same width
as the rectangles). We could stop these objects at any position on
the slot or we could move them at any given moment. Moreover,
we could change the direction, extent, and speed of movement at
will and thus obtain an infinite variety of kinetic combinations.

As for the results, the essential data, as far as concerns us here,
can be summarized as follows. Certain combinations of visual
stimuli, well defined as to the initial distance between the objects,
the commencement of their movement, their speed, etc., caused
certain specific impressions, for example, the impression 'that
an object *A goes toward* an object *B*', 'that *A pursues B*', 'that *A
joins B* and *unites itself* to it', 'that *A bumps B*', 'that *A chases* or

1. See the following: Michotte (1941, 1946); Sampaio (1943); and
Knops (1947).

repels B', 'that *A distorts B* by exerting pressure on it', 'that *A pulls B*,' 'that *A goes to find B* and *take it away*', 'that *A pushes B* with follow up.' This kind of event we call 'functional connections' in order to stress the fact that one actually *sees* some change occurring in an object 'in function' of another.

It is most important to remark that the production of these phenomena is essentially dependent on the *system* of stimulation and that every notable modification of this system brings about a change in the nature of the connection (principle of concomitant variations). So when object *A* is halted after reaching object *B*, and *B* moves in its turn, an impression of 'throwing' can be produced; but it depends both on the relative speeds of the two movements and on the length of time the objects are in contact. The impression is very clear when the movement of *B* is slower than that of *A*; but when the relative speeds are reversed an entirely different impression arises. In the same way, a contact of a few hundredths of a second is sufficient to destroy the impression.

Here is another example: the impressions of 'approaching' and 'departing' occur only when the distance between the two objects is within certain limits, which we call the 'radius of action' and which vary with the speed of the moving object or objects. Beyond this distance the two objects cease to be connected.

The characteristic impressions with which we are dealing must therefore be considered as *Gestalten*, as specific kinetic structures corresponding to the action of a group of successive stimuli on the eye. In other words, we are dealing in this case with primitive phenomena and not at all with 'meanings' which under the influence of acquired experience could be attached to simple impressions of motions merely juxtaposed in space and time.

This opinion is confirmed by many other facts which it is pointless to set down in these pages, and which one can find set forth in detail elsewhere (Michotte, 1946).

While we were doing these experiments we noticed a rather peculiar fact, which at first we considered simply rather curious, but which was repeated so often and with such insistence that it became a factor of some importance to us, and one worthy of serious discussion. Our subjects did not content themselves with merely describing in an objective fashion what they saw in the apparatus, saying, for example, that they saw '*A pushing B* forward', but they often had an obvious tendency to complete these indications by comparisons with human or animal actions, comparisons which implied emotional states, attitudes, tendencies attributed to the objects. The letters *A* and *B* did not then signify the little rectangles as such, but took on the value of names of persons, and the experiments gave rise to interpretations of this nature: 'It is as though *B* was afraid when *A* approached, and ran off'; or '*A* joins *B*, then they fall out, have a quarrel, and *B* goes off by himself'; or again 'It is like a cat coming up to a mouse and suddenly springing on it and carrying it off.'

This kind of behavior frequently occurred in a quite spontaneous way, and in any case the least suggestion was usually all that was needed to elicit such a response.

Why was this? Why this tendency to translate the phenomena into terms of human or animal conduct? This was a problem.[2]

It is evident that our knowledge of the emotional states and tendencies of other people is based necessarily on their perceptible reactions, that is to say their words, facial expressions, gestures, or even a simple movement of their eyes. Moreover, these manifestations do not usually remain confined to the individual in whom they are produced, as would be an expression of joy or sorrow whose cause was unknown to the onlooker. Rather they seem to be connected to something, some animal or person. The person who is annoyed because he has tripped on a stone gives the stone a kick; if someone meets a friend he shakes his hand or grasps his arm. And on the other hand, these reactions are often followed or accompanied by other reactions on the part of the objects; the stone is sent flying, the friend returns the gesture of affection.

In all these cases, then, the observer is faced with a scene or an event in which two objects (two people or one person and a thing) take part, each moved in relation to the other. Such situations

---

2. By alternately lengthening and shortening the sides of a small rectangle it is possible to give an extraordinarily vivid impression of vital, immanent movement in the object; it then takes on an appearance analogous to that of a living animal, a caterpillar, for example. This 'artificial animal' can replace one of the rectangles in the experiments described, and then the interpretations in an emotional sense come even more naturally. We did not deal with this type of experiment in the present work, precisely in order to avoid as much as possible anything in the appearance of the object which would favor such interpretations. See Michotte (1946, p. 175*ff*.).

correspond in principle to the scheme of our experiments, and it is thus quite understandable that they may eventually evoke the idea of human behavior.

However, the fact is none the less strange if we consider that the movements used in our experiments consisted generally of simple translocations of inert objects, while human conduct expresses itself especially, it would seem, by language, by the play of facial expression, and by an infinity of extraordinarily complicated gestures. And further, even if we admit the possibility of such an evocation, it still remains to be seen why it is *in fact* produced with such frequency.

This calls for a few comments. Let us remember first of all that emotions and tendencies can be divided roughly into two groups, according to whether they present an *integrative* or *segregative* relationship to the person who experiences them with the thing, person, or event which is their object.

Sympathy, friendship, and love belong evidently to the integrative class. In their most perfect form do they not result in identification, union, possession? On the other hand, antipathy, disgust, hate, and fear are obviously of the segregative type. One feels poles apart from such and such a person, a certain thing is repulsive to us. We fear the presence or approach of such an individual or event.

Again, the motor reactions corresponding to the first group usually result in an approach, which may manifest itself in a simple glance, or by the fact of positioning oneself close to another, or by establishing a contact more or less pronounced, more or less prolonged – a grasp of the hand, a kiss, an embrace. It appears also in the fact that one carries on one's person the objects to which one is particularly attached, refusing to leave them. This happens often with children who will not leave their favorite toys, even taking them to bed with them.

The characteristic reactions of the segregative emotions naturally present the opposite attributes. We move away from the person we do not like. We remove, sometimes violently, the objects which displease us, sometimes even breaking them.

Now these truths are just common sense, and it would no doubt be pointless to mention them except for the fact that they make us see one thing which is important from our point of view, namely, that *the physical reactions which correspond to the emotions fulfill in fact the conditions of stimulation which are necessary to produce in an observer the kinetic structures of the kind that we have studied.* Thus the 'affectual' reactions will have the effect of producing in the observer the impression that one individual is 'going toward' another (once the distance between them comes within the radius of action), and they will induce the formation of new perceptual unities presenting various degrees of integration as a result of the juxtaposition, contact, or association of movements (law of common fate). Similarly, the physical reactions of the segregative emotions will give rise to definite impressions of departure, repulsion, etc.

Let us add that some of the kinetic structures we observed showed a simply indifferent reaction, as when an object moved close to another without its motion being modified in relation to that of the other (for instance, when an object simply appeared to pass in front of or behind another). And this again can find an obvious application to certain types of human relations.

It must nevertheless be remarked that the integration and segregation produced in the perceptual field are extremely equivocal when considered in isolation, in the abstract. It is clear, for example, that global unities are not found exclusively in the emotional field; nor, in this domain of the emotions, are they limited to the external manifestations of friendship and love. They can occur in quite contrary situations, as by the contact of a hand-to-hand struggle or by biting which are the manifestations of anger or hate. Similarly, segregation can correspond equally to anger and to disgust or fear. Yet the emotional interpretations given by the subjects were much more specific and, moreover, were in general agreement with each other.

That is because integration and segregation take on different characteristics according to the different conditions in which they appear. Everyone will admit that the kinetic structure corresponding to an embrace is quite different from that of a struggle, and this also was the result in our experiments. A 'contact', for example, varies considerably according to the nature of the preceding or following phase.

In a general way, speed plays an important part in this respect. Rapid movement gives the impression of 'violence' as opposed to the 'gentleness' of slow movement. A sudden slackening of speed or a momentary pause in movement gives it a mark of 'hesitation'. Sudden and repeated variations of direction, or even merely of speed, give the impression of 'nervousness' or 'agitation', etc.

Here is a general outline, rather condensed, which gives some details on this point. The main combinations are shown.

I. Object *A* alone moves and joins *B*.
   A. The contact thus established is static.
     1. When the movement is rapid, the impression is that there is a violent clash and that the two objects become welded together.
     2. When the movement is slow, one gets the impression that *A* goes gently to join *B* and unites itself to it.
   B. The contact is of short duration.
     1. When the movement is rapid, the impression is that *A* strikes *B*.
     2. When the movement is slow, the impression is that *A* simply touches *B*.

II. Object *B* begins to move after being reached by *A*, while *A* stops.
   A. The contact is of short duration.
     1. When *A*'s movement is more rapid than *B*'s, the impression is that *A*'s contact throws *B* forward. This can be interpreted in the sense of a reaction of anger.
     2. When *B*'s movement is the more rapid the impression is that the contact releases the departure of *B*. The movement of *B* appears as autonomous and when quick enough often gives the impression of 'flight'. This flight is considered as motivated by *A*'s touch and interpreted in the sense of a reaction of fear. This is further accentuated when *B* starts to move before contact and reacts at the mere approach of *A*.
   B. The contact is of sufficient duration to allow the two objects to form a global unity.
     1. The impression produced is often interpreted in the sense of a momentary agreement between two accomplices who meet, but which gives place to a disagreement followed by separation.

III. Object *B* begins to move after being touched by *A*, and the two continue to move at the same speed and in the same direction in juxtaposition.
   A. There is no pause at the moment of contact.
     1. The impression is that *A* draws, carries off *B*, takes it with it.

When the movement is slow and uniform, the association is 'gentle', 'friendly'. Rapid movement, on the other hand, gives an impression of violence; and if there is rapid acceleration after contact, following on a fairly slow approach, there is an impression that one carries off the other by brute force; this further takes on the character of a veritable kidnapping when the direction of movement is reversed at the moment of contact. The interpretations to which this can give rise are obvious.

B. There is a momentary pause after contact.

1. When the two objects then begin to move off again, the impression is one of 'going together', the unity being naturally accentuated by the similarity of their kinetic properties (law of common fate). And when this group of two objects disappears behind a screen, it not infrequently suggests a story – a lovers' rendezvous, or two accomplices going into hiding together.

This outline, though far from exhaustive, is sufficient to show to what degree the totality of stimuli and their combinations specify the kinetic structures to which they give rise; and it is easy to see how one can thus form little 'scenarios', little stories without words, which are very easy to interpret. Further, I think it would be very interesting, especially from the point of view of the projective technique, to go on to make systematic observations concerning the nature and frequency of the interpretations of such scenarios, particularly among children.

I would now like to stress one or two points in all that has been said up till now. First, in order to understand fully all that has been said, one must determine more precisely the parallel which exists between certain characteristics of the subjective aspects of the emotions on the one hand, and the characteristics of the corresponding motor reactions on the other. We have spoken several times of the 'system of stimuli'. This is obviously formed by light rays in a certain position in time and space which strike the retina of the observer; it could be defined by stating the geometric form of the images on the retina, their position in relation to the topography of the retina, the nature of the light rays, their degree of energy, the movements of the images, their direction, speed, and extent. In this way we could describe very exactly what happens in the eye of the observer during our experiments and also when he observes the motor reactions typical of certain emotional situations.

But it is obvious that such a chart, though no doubt very precise, would be no guide at all to what actually happens in the perceptual field of the observer. He sees a certain person approach another in a friendly way, embrace him, etc. And let me repeat, this is not just a 'meaning' *attributed* to the literal, step-by-step translation of a table of stimuli; they are primitive, specific impressions which arise in the perceptual field itself. One cannot stress too much this most important point. Thus, I do not think it is superfluous to examine in further detail the example, just quoted, of a person who approaches another in a friendly way.

The impression of 'approaching' is obviously caused by the lessening of the distance between the retinal images of the two objects; but the impression is really much more than a simple perception of 'diminution of distance'. In fact it contains elements which are absolutely alien to the world of stimulation. The movement perceived is polarized; that is to say, it is put in connection with a definite object, that which the other approaches. This polarization is a variable of the movement, distinct from direction, and only appears, as we have seen, within the limits of the radius of action (Michotte, 1946, p. *54ff.*). In other words, an 'objective' diminution of distance becomes an 'approach' only within these limits. Further, this impression is elective, for in a complex perceptual field the lessening of distance between two objects is necessarily accompanied by an increase of distance between the moving object and others; yet the impression of 'going toward *B*' is never accompanied by the simultaneous impression of 'going away from' these others. This fact alone would be sufficient to bring out the difference that exists between the system of stimuli and the structural organization of the perceptual field. There seems to be some incompatibility between the simultaneous presence of impressions of 'going toward' and 'going away from' in the case of the same object. It is something analogous to the distinction between 'figure' and 'background', where contour belongs exclusively to 'figure'.

Further, as we said before, the character of 'going toward in a *friendly* way, *gently*', and likewise the character of violence are connected with the speed. Yet gentleness and violence are obviously properties which are in qualitative opposition, while the physical differences of speed are purely quantitative.

This is only one example of the differences between the characteristics of the perceptual structure and those of the system of stimuli, but they could be shown to be present in all the cases quoted in the course of this work. And that confirms the essential conclusion – that analogy between the characteristics of the emotions felt by the agent and those of his emotional motor reactions exists only in regard to the kinetic structures aroused by those reactions in the perceptual field of the observer.

In order to drive home this conclusion still further, let us look at our example again. Let us suppose that there are three objects (three persons, for example) all in sight of each other – *A*, *B*, and *C*. *B* feels attracted by *A* and goes gently toward him, but remains indifferent to *C*. As far as the retinal images are concerned, there is a diminution of the distance between *A* and *B* and an increase in the distance between *B* and *C*. If the impressions were the literal translation of the stimuli the situation would be absolutely ambiguous – *B* approaching *A* could be a manifestation of friendship, *B* moving away from *C* could be a sign of antipathy or fear (which emotions, *ex hypothesi*, do not exist). But in point of fact, because the structural organization is determined by various factors (radius of action, etc.), only the approach and union come into the perceptual field of the observer, and the impressions he receives actually correspond to the sentiments of the agent.

In short, the principles which govern the structural organization of perceptions come into play, and the emotional reactions of the agent evoke specific kinetic structures in the observer, the characteristics of which correspond at least partially to the emotions of the former. So certain typical traits of the affective activity of the agent are reproduced in the observer by means of his perceptual activity. It is in this sense, and only in this sense, that one is justified in talking about 'expressive behavior'.[3]

But the perceptual reconstruction is, of course, only fragmentary. It only gives a sort of scheme of the emotional structure. The observer does not 'live' exactly the same experience as the agents. But this scheme can be completed, dressed up in a way, either by

3. On the expressive behavior, see the admirable pages which Köhler as early as 1929 wrote on the subject (Köhler, 1929, p. 234*ff*.).

the recollection of former affectual states which the observer has experienced and which correspond to the same scheme or by the reliving of those states, which then become fused with the data of the perceptual activity and can be 'projected' into the agent. This may perhaps cast some light on the difficult problem of 'empathy'.

One final point must detain us for a moment. We have just spoken of the possibility of evoking affectual states by means of certain structural schemes of the perceptual activity. Such evocation is evidently at the foundation of the interpretation in terms of emotions or tendencies which appeared in our experiments. The fact that this occurred is most instructive. It proves that it is the kinetic structures as such, the combinations of movements, which are above all effective; and it proves that the nature of the moving object is quite secondary *from this point of view*. How could one otherwise explain the fact that experiments with little inert rectangles could suggest the idea of emotional reactions? In fact, the surprising thing is that the nature of the object did not paralyze the evocative mechanism entirely, whereas apparently the only effect it had was to give the process an artificial aspect, which found expression in such words as 'It's as if', which occurred constantly in the descriptions.

As for the kinetic structures themselves, it must be mentioned that though they varied greatly, they were extraordinarily simple compared with those which correspond to the emotional reactions of men in real life. Yet in spite of this, their power of evocation was considerable. I think the necessary conclusion is that they must be considered as constituting a *fundamental* aspect of human action as it appears to an observer. The core of the matter, so to speak, is in the integration and segregation. These processes are enriched and take on an increasingly specific character according to factors of a kinetic, spatial, and temporal order, a few examples of which we have examined. In ordinary life, the specifying factors – gestures, facial expressions, speech – are innumerable and can be differentiated by an infinity of nuances. But they are all *additional refinements* compared with the key factors, which are the simple kinetic structures. And our experiments bring out precisely this point, that phenomena of this kind are of themselves sufficient to enable us to identify and differentiate a large number of human reactions. Naturally this does not exclude all possibility of erroneous interpretation, but it is sufficient, to a large extent, to enable us to judge the relations of human behavior in a great many circumstances.

This is an important fact from a biological and social viewpoint; for the mutual reactions of two individuals (men or animals) are often the essential element in a situation in which other individuals are present, the element which determines the reactions of the latter. So an aggressive or a friendly attitude on the part of one person toward another may eventually cause a reaction on the part of an observer or observers. Furthermore, the conditions of visibility are often deficient; any detailed perception is prevented by the distance, light, or by some other reason or, in the lower animals, by an inferior degree of development of the sense organs. But even in these cases the general outline of the behavior as shown in the simple kinetic structures enables us to be fairly sure of perceiving the nature of the social situation.

Finally, in concluding the first part of this paper, let me underline the fact that all the considerations developed above bring out in a striking way this point: that the motor reactions of men and animals, *when related in certain ways with other objects*, are of great importance as *expressive behavior*. This is perhaps a point which has not generally received all the attention it deserves in the psychology of emotion, owing to too exclusive a concentration on the study of the reactions of the organism as such, without taking account of the *perception of its relations with its environment*.

II

In the foregoing pages, we put outselves exclusively in the position of the observer. It now remains to say a few words on what happens in the case of the agent, the person who experiences the emotions. And I think that in this matter also our experiments will suggest some ideas.

What we have said on the subject of the integrative or segregative character of the emotions shows immediately that we are justified in taking them as functional connections on the same footing as the visual phenomena of throwing, drawing, pursuit, etc. It is evident that an emotion toward a thing, animal, or person establishes some form of liaison between the object and the subject whom it affects. Emotion is a modification of the subject *in regard to* these objects. Joy, sorrow, fear, and anger are undoubtedly states belonging to the person who experiences them, but they are states with a characteristic type of connection with their cause, a connection which differs qualitatively according to the kind of emotion experienced.

If we look at the emotions from this point of view, then, and in an abstract and very general way, they can be classed in the same group of phenomena as the visual kinetic structures.

Their similarity is even clearer when we examine the matter more concretely. It has always been noticed that certain motor reactions of the subject contributed largely in determining the subjective aspect of the emotional states; it is such an obvious fact that popular wisdom has consecrated it by introducing into the terminology reserved for the affectual life a considerable number of expressions whose primary meaning is purely spatial and motional. I have selected a few of these expressions:

Ceci se traduit en particulier dans certaines formules habituelles du langage, et tout d'abord dans le mot même 'd'émotion', c.à.d., 'mouvement' de l'âme. Puis, il y a cette infinité d'expressions courantes telles que: j'ai été saisi, cela m'a frappé, je me suis senti *envahi* par la tristesse, je me sens *transporté* de joie, je suis *empoigné*, cela me perce le cœur, je me sens *aplati* ou *abaissé*, cela me *coupe* bras et jambes, je me sens *dilaté* d'espoir, je me sens *porté vers*, cela est *repoussant*, je suis *écrasé* par la douleur, cela est *attirant*, cela m'a *donné un choc*, etc. (Michotte, 1946, p. 270).

It must be noted that all these phrases really express kinetic structures of the type that we have studied, with this difference, that the former were visual, while these belong mainly to the realm of somesthesia. But they are very frequently rather complex and include visual elements. Here is an example:

Ainsi, quande une personne avance brusquement le poing dans la direction du visage d'une autre et que celle-ci fait un mouvement instinctif de recul, on retrouve une situation tout à fait analogue à celle du lancement. Le poing de l'assaillant constitue l'objet *A* et le corps du 'patient' l'objet *B*; les mouvements exécutés de part et d'autre se réalisent approximativement en continuité temporelle; ils ont la même direction; et la polarisation du second est évidemment inversée (Michotte, 1946, p. 271).

In this case the first step in the incident is visual; it consists in the perception of the approaching motion of the assailant's fist. This may be followed by a tactual impression of contact and of pain; and finally the recoiling motion of the person attacked is perceived under a tactual-kinesthetic form. But all of this is integrated into one global structure.

Another example would be that of manifestations of affection – beginning with the perception of a person approaching with outstretched hand, this visual phase being followed by tactual contact, and then by the complex tactual-kinesthetic impressions of a mutual embrace. The conditions in which these episodes take place are naturally such as to create again a single structure in which the two persons are integrated; and again the unity so formed will be the greater according as the surfaces in contact are greater, the pressure more accentuated, the synchronization of movements more perfect (law of common fate).

There is no doubt that, in general, everything that has been said above about the formation of visual kinetic structures of integration and segregation, with their manifold nuances, applies equally to somesthesia. Nor, on the other hand, is there any doubt that the kinetic structures established in this domain play an important part in the subjective aspect of the emotions. But here a new problem arises. If the perceptual structures as such are similar, how does it happen that when they are exclusively visual the person in whom they are found is just an *observer;* while when they are somesthetic (at least predominantly) the person in whom they are found is an *agent*? At first sight this is a real enigma; for the somesthetic structures are in principle quite as 'sensory' as the visual and consequently belong by right to the domain of perception; and yet they no longer appear as the '*expression*' of an emotion (point of view of an observer), but as *constituents* of the emotion which is experienced (point of view of the agent).[4]

This is connected with the fact that they appear as reactions of

---

4. Of course I do not mean to say that the somesthetic structures are the sole constituents of the emotions, in the sense of the James–Lange Theory. On the contrary I hold that the emotional experience as lived by a man is much richer in content and especially that it has an extremely important intellectual aspect. But that does not imply any denial of the most important role played by somesthesia in qualifying and shading the emotions.

the *ego*; it is *I* who repels, who embraces, who avoids, etc. For the observer the reactions which he witnesses are conveyed by an object distinct from himself; it is that person whom he sees over there who goes toward the other and shakes his hand. In the case of the agent, on the other hand, the action is not that of another person, nor is it properly speaking the action of his own body (as a thing); it is *himself* who acts in such a way toward such and such a person or thing or who feels this affective reaction for this person or thing. And this 'himself' is lived in the action, in the emotion even, without any separate 'support'. This is true for emotion considered as a global state, but it is verified equally, needless to say, in its properly kinesthetic aspect. How is that possible? Opinions differ on this point; but in my opinion, the essential fact is that the sensory modality which intervenes in what it has been agreed to call the kinesthetic impressions is so imprecise, so lacking in 'consistency', that it is overshadowed by the formal aspect of the structure, the form, which is thus in a 'pure' state, so to speak, without any supporting object, and which alone is apparent. Action and passion (which intervene in the emotions) are thus experiences *sui generis* in which the 'ego' is lived immediately (Michotte, 1946, p. 205*ff.*).

Nevertheless, it must not be forgotten that the ego is more or less extensible and includes various zones. The most superficial, no doubt, is what we call our possessions, then come the clothes we wear, and then our bodies, in which again we must distinguish between the surface and the internal organs which are nearer to the inmost ego. (And in this connection it should be noticed how the reactions of affection and love manifest themselves in a tendency toward contact on the part of these organs.) Finally, there is the inmost ego; and it is precisely this one which is lived in action and passion; it is the ego of our thoughts, of our mental attitudes, of our desires; and these latter also intervene as factors of integration when there is community of aspiration or as factors of segregation when there is divergency of opinion or sentiment.

The ego, however, constitutes only one of the poles of emotion. Since emotion is considered as a 'functional connection', it must link this ego to something else. In other words, the emotions usually have an object, and it is of some importance to determine what this means. Must we, for example, envisage the question in a purely intellectualistic sense, and conceive this term 'object' as being only the object of thought? I think not, at least as regards the tactual-kinesthetic aspect of emotion or even emotion as a global state which is 'lived', 'experienced'. For if these phenomena are considered as global structures, it is clear that we must be dealing here with the integration of the object into a global form. So to return to the example quoted above, the approach of the assailant's fist takes place in such a way that the characteristic impression of causality must be produced, one must have the impression that it is the approach of the fist which *causes* the recoil. In other cases, the situation in which the emotions are activated will be such as to arouse impressions like 'drawing along'. 'coming from', etc. All these impressions are characteristic of certain structures and they include the object, just as they do in the case of visual perceptions; they simply express the fact that we are dealing with functional connections, that is, as we have said repeatedly, with changes which are produced 'in function of'. And in these conditions it is not surprising that we should spontaneously attribute our emotions to certain events as to their source or cause (Michotte, 1946, p. 269*ff*.). That is simply the result of the nature of a certain type of structural organization, and there is no reason to suppose that it will not take place in animals as well as in men.

But no doubt the matter is more complex in man, for he is not merely a being which 'feels', but also one which 'thinks' and 'knows', so the emotions he experiences usually have an intellectual aspect. On to the *felt connection* is superimposed the knowledge of the *abstract relation* implied in that connection. A man 'feels' himself attracted or repelled by an object, and at the same time he 'is aware' of the attraction or repulsion, he 'knows' it is happening. Whatever be one's opinion about the nature of thought, this is an unavoidable distinction, and one which is of some importance in practice. It is one thing to 'feel' someone going away from you, relaxing his grip, and to experience a sort of wrench, more or less painful; it is quite another thing to 'tell oneself', to 'be aware' of this separation, for this brings a wave of recollection of the past, of foresight into the future. The present experience then ceases to be a transitory episode limited to the moment; it is inserted into the much wider framework of a whole life, and this in its turn has repercussions on the emotional state itself, irritating it or eventually deadening it, according to circumstances.

As I said at the beginning, the ideas propounded in this paper originated in incidental observations made in the course of experiments which did not deal with the emotions. So, many of these ideas must be considered as mere suggestions, which might, I think, form a starting-off point for a more thorough critical discussion and form a basis for interesting experimental research.

References

KNOPS, L. (1947), 'Contribution à l'étude de la naissance et de la "permanence" phénoménales dans le champ visuel', in *Miscellanea Psychologica Albert Michotte*, Éditions de l'Institut Supérieur de Philosophie, Louvain, Nauwelaerts, Paris, Vrin.

KÖHLER, W. (1929), *Gestalt Psychology*, Liveright.

MICHOTTE, A. (1941), 'La causalité physique est-elle une donnée phénoménale?', *Tijdschrift voor Philosophie*, vol. 3, pp. 290–328.

MICHOTTE, A. (1946), 'La perception de la causalité', *Études de Psychologie*, vol. 6, Éditions de l'Institut Supérieur de Philosophie, Louvain, Nauwelaerts, Paris, Vrin.

SAMPAIO, A. C. (1943), *La Translation des Objets comme Facteur de leur Permanence Phénoménale*, Louvain.

22 R. A. Spitz

Emotional Development in the Infant

Excerpts from R. A. Spitz, 'Ontogenesis, the proleptic function of emotion', in P. H. Knapp (ed.), *Expression of the Emotions in Man*, International Universities Press, 1963, pp. 43–7, 54–9.

Emotions proper involve consciousness. During the first weeks of life conscious perception, in the sense in which psychoanalysis defines the term, is not present. At this time practically all activities of the neonate are uncoordinated and undirected, because a central volitional – that is, conscious – steering organization has not yet emerged. Physiological activities are the exception; they become increasingly coordinated and integrated into a functioning totality. But *intentional* skeletal musculature is not yet integrated under the direction of a *central steering and coordinating organization* and will only become so in the course of the subsequent months. It is this central steering organization to which we assign psychological functioning, both conscious and unconscious.

This organization, which we call the ego, will enable the infant to perceive his emotions and to relate their expression to sensations experienced and to stimuli received. It comes into being, at least in a rudimentary fashion, around the third month. Before this organization begins to function, I am unwilling to speak of emotion proper, only of its precursors. Even after the beginnings of the central steering organization are established, specific emotional expressions are still only loosely linked to specific types of experience. The infant's expression can still be interpreted (or understood) only in the context of an ongoing situation. In a certain measure, that remains true throughout a great part of the infant's first year.

It appears, then, that specific facial expressions as expression of emotions become meaningful as a result of a linkage. The linkage takes place between a specific facial expression and a specific experience, a coordination comparable to that which takes place in the conditioned reflex. The refinement and the

279

progressively increasing specificity of the expression itself are acquired in the course of development. A great deal of research remains to be done in order to learn how this coordination is achieved. The fact that the negative expression is present from birth shows that it is inborn. It is presumably of phylogenetic origin and has survival value. The demonstration of this proposition is one of the objects of the present paper.

The expression of pleasure is the next one to appear; in the infant its most conspicuous example is the smiling response. Beginning with the third month of life this is produced in response to a Gestalt signal, which comprises certain salient features of the human face. The constituent parts of this Gestalt are the eyes, the nose, and the forehead; moreover, the whole configuration must be in motion (Spitz and Wolf, 1946).

It should be clearly understood that I am referring exclusively to the smiling *response* and not to random activity of the facial muscles, which may look like a smile. The facial movement of smiling is probably present from birth – my earliest motion picture record for such a smile is of a three-day-old infant. This smile 'movement' is a discharge phenomenon which occurs randomly; it cannot be reliably elicited by repeating the specific situation in which it had been observed, nor by situations which are the opposite of those eliciting the negative 'displeasurable' expressions.

Among the few positive manifestations at birth, 'turning toward' is the most relevant for this discussion. I consider 'turning toward' as a positive expression because of its survival value, which is demonstrated by its phylogenetic history (Spitz, 1957). It is provoked primarily by eliciting the sucking reflex. In the third month of life this turning-toward response develops into reciprocity with the adult: the infant responds to the adult's face with a smile. I have considered this to be the expression of a positive *emotion* for the following reasons:

1. After the smiling response has been established, it ceases to be random and becomes stimulus specific. Beginning with the third month of life, it will be produced reliably in situations which have the specific character of initiating a need gratification. This linking of the smiling response to certain stimuli which adults would consider pleasurable or gratifying will continue throughout life in an unbroken line.

2. Conversely, the smiling response will not be manifested in situations which would provoke responses or emotions of unpleasure, such as pain, rage, anger, or boredom, in the adult.

3. The physiognomic characteristics of the smiling response are those of 'turning toward'.

4. Finally, when in the third month of life the infant achieves the smiling response, he has also achieved conscious perception and has become capable of rudimentary mental operations. This is evident not only from the smiling response but also from all his other volitionally directed, intentional activities.

The psychological concomitants of the smiling response at the level of the third month throw a new light on my findings about some responses at birth. They permit the conclusion that, from the viewpoint of structure, negative excitation at birth is fundamentally different from the turning-toward response. Negative excitation behavior is a nondirected, random, unspecific emergency behavior, in response to any stimulus *quantitatively* strong enough to break through the stimulus barrier. The turning-toward behavior, on the other hand, is specific, nonrandom, and occurs in response to a specific discrete stimulus. It is not a response to quantitative but to *qualitative* differences. At birth this is the only directed response to stimuli qualitatively differentiated from the surround. The turning-toward response has a positive value for survival. Consequently I feel justified in considering it one of the first positive behavior patterns in the infant, though not a psychological one.

Though the turning-toward response is present already at birth, it is questionable whether this applies also to the avoidance reaction. However, we know that the latter will soon emerge in the course of development, although its phenomenology has not been investigated in sufficient detail. We do not know when manifestations of unpleasure – e.g. screaming and random violent movements, which denote negative excitation – are transformed into movements of withdrawal and flight. In other words, we are unable to say at what point of infant development expression of unpleasure are replaced by expressions of *fear*.

The inception and the sequence in the structuring of the expression of negative emotion parallel the development of the smile. In the neonate stage, negative experience results from a break-through of the stimulus barrier (either from inside or outside) and is responded to by increase of random activity, rise of tonus, and vocalization. In the subsequent weeks, though expression of negative emotions is still triggered by the quantitative factor of a break-through of the stimulus barrier, a qualitative factor is added. The stimuli for such a break-through become ever more specific. It becomes increasingly evident that this behavior of the infant will arise mostly in the hunger situation or in situations of intestinal discomfort. These are need situations, requiring discharge through gratification to insure survival. The development which now sets in adds *secondary needs* to the primary survival-insuring ones; I will call these secondary needs '*quasi needs*'.

By the third month, the circumstances leading to an accompanying need gratification proper also begin to become specific. When they are withheld, the infant responds as if he were being deprived of physiological need gratification. In concrete terms, the infant now insists on being cuddled, on physical contact, on the presence of the adult.

By the fourth month of life, the infant reacts by screaming when the gratification of this quasi need is withheld, that is, when the adult leaves after playing with him; just as he reacts by smiling when the adult approaches him. It is at this point that the precursors of emotion are transformed into emotion proper. No other object (thing) will provoke these responses at the same age, though, of course, straightforward need deprivation or need gratification will.

It is regrettable that we do not yet possess findings on physiognomic differentiation between the infant's behavior when subjected to the frustration of a quasi need (such as the contact with the adult being interrupted), on the one hand, and the expression of fear resulting from the anticipation of pain on the other (Darwin, 1872). [. . .]

In the neonate the expression of emotion most in evidence is the one in response to unpleasure, caused by the unconditioned stimulus. This is in manifest parallel to the first stage of the food-recognition reaction, in which the response is to the nipple in the mouth. This would lead one to believe that later, more advanced expressions of unpleasure also develop in a straight genetic sequence from the original situation. But this does not seem to be the case.

In the weeks following birth the unconditioned stimulus of *somatic* pain, discomfort, etc., elicits manifestations of unpleasure, predominantly undirected and random. However, unequivocally clear manifestations of unpleasure in response to psychological stimuli do not develop in direct genetic derivation from these. To my mind, the first unequivocal psychological manifestation of unpleasure in the infant occurs when he begins to cry when left by the adult with whom he had been in contact. This behavior appears after the third month of life and is the counterpart of the smiling response of which I have spoken above.

This unpleasure manifestation can only be understood if we assume that the infant has integrated into the inventory of his need gratifications the *presence* of the adult as a quasi need. Accordingly the infant will react to the adult's moving away by expressing negative emotion in anticipation of being deprived of the gratification of this quasi need. There obviously is a parallel between this 'negative' expression of emotion in response to a *receding* person, and the 'positive' behavior manifested to the approaching person in the food-recognition response as well as in the smiling response. [. . .]

Unpleasure experiences of two fundamentally different kinds will be expressed by superficially similar behavior patterns:

1. A form of unpleasure in response to the unconditioned stimulus of pain and discomfort. The response to this is an uncontrolled behavior which will change very little in the course of development.

2. A form of unpleasure in response to psychological stimuli. This response is not present from birth. It has to be acquired by developing a *quasi need* on the one hand, and the *proleptic function*, that is, the function of anticipation, on the other. Both the need and the function are developed in the framework of object relations, primarily as the result of need gratification. Once the function to anticipate pleasure is acquired, it becomes possible for the child to perform also the psychological operation of anticipating unpleasure when *losing* the object. The infant displays this anticipation through the facial expression of negative emotion.

At this level at the age of three to six months of life the

anticipation of unpleasure has acquired a *signal* function, the function described by Freud in *Inhibitions, Symptoms and Anxiety*. The expression of this emotion increasingly acquires the function of communication. This communication comprises two bits of information, which are channeled in opposite directions:

1. The first is the mounting tension of the emotion. This is similar to the conditions leading to the break-through of the stimulus barrier. It is experienced as a danger signal, an information which is transmitted centripetally to the incipient ego of the three- to six-month-old infant.

2. The facial and behavioral expression of the same emotion. This is perceived by the surround as a communication. Though it is at first not intentional or directed, it nevertheless transmits information centrifugally.

At this stage the two components do not yet constitute an apparatus of the ego. They are not established as a discrete functional continuum, interconnecting with the different aspects of the personality. In the course of the following three months, these connections will be formed. They will become ever more suitable for triggering adaptive measures of the ego and for communicating with the surround. This process leads to the establishment of specific emotions firmly linked with their appropriate expression. The final outcome of this process is, in one instance, the 'eight-months anxiety'.[1]

The eight-months anxiety marks the inception of an important stage in the child's development. It lends itself particularly well to the exposition of several psychological processes. In the present context I am discussing that aspect of the phenomenon which illustrates the next step in the ontogenetic development of the expression of emotion. Through the study of this step we gain insight into the further vicissitudes of what originally was an undirected state of excitation. For in the eight-months anxiety we can observe how the subjective experience of emotion follows a different path from that of emotional expression. In what follows I will show how the *emotion* of anxiety (i.e. felt anxiety) assumes a centripetally directed function; at the same time the *expression* of the same emotion becomes effective in a centrifugal

1. For the description and discussion of this phenomenon see Spitz (1946, 1950).

direction. The part directed to the inside acts as a danger signal, mobilizing the pleasure-unpleasure agency (Freud, 1926); thus the resources of the personality are marshaled in the service of defense against mental helplessness.

The other part is channeled into the efferent nervous system and sets in motion the gamut of the expressions of this particular emotion. These expressions serve as a communication to the outside: to the surround, to the libidinal object. They are perceived by the outside world as a sign of helplessness or as a signal, that is, as an appeal for help.

The successive stages of this development, beginning with the break-through of the stimulus barrier, are:

1. the unspecific, undirected, total emotional responses in the first three months of life;

2. the progressive integration of emotional responses with their facial and behavioral expression in the course of the next three months on the one hand; their serving as a communication to the outside on the other;

3. the establishment, in the third quarter of the first year, of a definitive link between felt emotion as a signal for the ego and the expression of emotion as a communication to the surround.

The process of organizing the original discharge into recognizably different expressions linked to specific emotions is initiated and carried on through the exchanges between child and mother in the course of object relations. The unfolding of the individual child's object relations parallels closely the ontogenesis of the expression of his emotions.

When infants are deprived of object relations, their emotional expression remains on the archaic level of the first months of life (Spitz, 1946). The expression becomes rigid and vacuous. But when object relations are close and gratifying to mother and child, then the expression of emotions unfolds in a variety of patterns and eventually becomes a means of communication in the framework of object relations.

The proposition of the role of object relations in the ontogenesis of the expression of emotion is further borne out by two different observations: (1) the chronological sequence in the successive stages of the positive smiling response, which parallel those of the first specifically psychologically motivated expression of negative emotion; (2) the range of expressions accompanying the emergence of the eight-months anxiety in the second half of the first year.

As to the first: the response of smiling, the expression of pleasure on perceiving the Gestalt signal of the human face appears approximately one month earlier than the response of unpleasure on being left by a partner. In other terms, a partner, at least in the form of *a pre-object*, has to be established as a result of object relations before the consequences of the loss of this pre-object can be anticipated. It is gratifying to find this argumentation confirmed by the facts of observation.

In regard to the second confirmatory evidence, we find that the phenomenon of the eight-months anxiety varies in a wide range, and is dependent on the nature of the individual child's object relations. In my observations of psychopathological deviations in the first year of life, the appearance of the characteristic anxiety was significantly delayed and even completely absent when certain forms of inappropriate object relations were present during the preceding months. On the other hand, the eight-months anxiety was replaced by uncontrollable manifestations of panic and fear in those cases in which object relations were extremely inadequate or the infant had been deprived of them altogether.[2]

Eight-months anxiety of the usual kind varies a good deal in its intensity. This phenomenon has not been sufficiently explored up to now.[3] The reason for this is that it requires thorough investigation of children in private family homes, in itself a major project. Added to this is the fact that children vary in their congenital frustration tolerance and that as yet we have no instrument suitable for evaluating this tolerance in the neonate.

2. Two different sets of circumstances can lead to this end result. One is a separation of the infant from his object at a critical age, resulting in a mourning process with regression to earlier, and often archaic modes of functioning and adaptation. I have discussed this picture elsewhere (1946) and called it *anaclitic depression*. The second is the picture of infants raised from birth in institutions without opportunity to form any object relations whatsoever. Here the response remains unspecific, as in response to the unconditioned stimulus – a quantitative response, be it to the experience of pain or to the interruption of quiescence. I described this condition under the name of *hospitalism* (1945).

3. But see Benjamin's (1961) careful investigations and his distinction between 'stranger anxiety' and 'infantile separation anxiety'.

We may say in conclusion that the ontogenesis of the expression of emotions is a function of the nature of the individual child's object relations as much as of the unfolding of an inherited Anlage. To the psychoanalyst this finding is not unexpected. We were aware for a number of years and have been able to demonstrate (Spitz, 1946) that the expression of pleasure is developed from an innate Anlage in the course of the exchanges with the human object. We now find a similar sequence obtaining in regard to the expression of negative emotions. These also develop from an innate Anlage, from disorganized, decompensated response to the breakthrough of the stimulus barrier, through object relations to the expression of negative emotions in response to the loss of the pre-object and from there to the signal of anxiety.

I cannot discuss the further ramifications of the expression of emotions. Enumerating them as they appear in the course of the first year of life already shows that they also are differentiated in response to specific object relations. I need only mention jealousy, envy, possessiveness, demanding attitudes, anger, rage, love, amusement, laughter, boredom (yawning and fatigue), not to speak of the chronologically later, increasingly subtle expressions of doubt, hesitation, quizzical attitudes, trust and mistrust, and a whole gamut of others.

References

BENJAMIN, J. D. (1961), 'Some developmental observations relating to the theory of anxiety', *J. Amer. Psychoanal. Assn*, vol. 9, p. 4.

DARWIN, C. (1872), *The Expression of Emotions in Man and Animal*, Philosophical Library, 1955.

FREUD, S. (1926), *Inhibitions, Symptoms and Anxiety*, Standard Edition, Hogarth Press, 1959, vol. 20, p. 87.

SPITZ, R. A. (1945), 'Hospitalism. An inquiry into the psychiatric conditions in early childhood', *The Psychoanalytic Study of the Child*, International Universities Press, vol. 1, p. 53.

SPITZ, R. A. (1946), 'Anaclitic depression: An inquiry into the genesis of psychiatric conditions in early childhood, II', *The Psychoanalytic Study of the Child*, International Universities Press, vol. 2, p. 313.

SPITZ, R. A. (1950), 'Anxiety in infancy', *Int. J. Psychoanal.*, vol. 31, p. 138.

SPITZ, R. A. (1957), *No and Yes*, International Universities Press.

SPITZ, R. A., and WOLF, K. M. (1946), 'The smiling response', *Genet. Psychol. Monogr.*, vol. 34, p. 57.

Part Nine **Neurophysiological Aspects**

The neurology and physiology of emotion has aroused a great deal of interest in the last few decades. Particularly, the investigation of the neural structures activated during emotion has progressed apace. Cannon's thalamic theory, our first selection, was the first attempt to develop a theoretical scheme of the role played by the brain, even though it offered no more than a rough opposition between the thalamus (responsible for the emotional *quale*) and the cortex which has always been assumed to mediate cognitive processes. The next milestone was Papez' theory which described an emotional circuit and specified the participating structures. From then on, research studies multiplied to such an extent that it became more difficult from year to year to discover a pattern that might allow theoretical integration. Delgado's paper gives a good idea of some of the research methods used and the solid results achieved over the last few years. My paper, 'Neural Mediation . . .', is an excerpt from my book *Emotion and Personality*, in which I attempt to integrate the neural and behavioral results of these studies and to formulate a theory of brain function in emotion.

The physiological changes in emotion have been investigated as well. Cannon's 'emergency theory of emotion' was formulated in 1915 and accepted unquestioningly for the next thirty years. In 1945, I published an article based on my own work and that of others in which I questioned the emergency theory; this article was later extended and incorporated in chapter 7 of the above-mentioned book. The selection in this volume is an excerpt from this chapter.

23 W. B. Cannon

The Thalamic Theory of Emotion

Excerpt from W. B. Cannon, 'The James–Lange theory of emotions', *Am. J. Psychol.*, vol. 39 (1927), pp. 115–24.

In his discussion on the cerebral processes accompanying emotion, James (1884) argued that either there were special centers for them or they occurred in the ordinary motor and sensory centers of the cortex. And if in the ordinary centers, according to his postulate, the processes would resemble the ordinary processes attending sensation. Only that and full representation of each part of the body in the cortex would be needed to provide a scheme capable of representing the *modus operandi* of the emotions. Object – sense organ – cortical excitation – perception – reflexes to muscle, skin and viscus – disturbances in them – cortical excitation by these disturbances – perceptions of them added to the original perceptions; such are the occurrences which result in the 'object-emotionally-felt'. The strict alternative, however, of cortical processes *or* special centers we need not accept. There may be cortical processes *and* special centers. Whether such is the arrangement we may now consider.

1. *Emotional expression results from action of subcortical centers.* – In a paper published in 1887 Bechterev argued that emotional expression must be independent of the cortex because at times the expression cannot be inhibited (e.g. laughing from tickle, grinding the teeth and crying from pain), because visceral changes occur which are beyond control, and because it is seen just after birth before cortical management is important. Furthermore, he reported that after removing the cerebral hemispheres from various kinds of animals appropriate stimulations would evoke corresponding responses of an affective character. Noxious stimuli would cause the hemisphereless cats to snarl, the dogs to whine, to show their teeth and to bark; gentle stimuli (stroking the back) would cause the cats to purr and the dogs to

wag their tails. Since these effects disappeared when the optic thalamus was removed, he drew the conclusion that it plays a predominant role in emotional expression.

In 1904 Woodworth and Sherrington proved that many of the physiological phenomena of great excitement would appear in cats from which the thalamus had been wholly removed by section of the brain stem at the mesencephalon. Strong stimulation of an afferent nerve was required to evoke the 'pseudaffective' responses. Although these observations tended to lessen the importance of the thalamus as a center, recent experiments have again emphasized its dominance. In 1925 Cannon and Britton described a pseud-affective preparation – a cat decorticated under ether anesthesia – which on recovery displayed spontaneously the complete picture of intense fury. Further study by Bard (1928) showed that this sham rage continued after ablation of all the brain anterior to the diencephalon. Only when the lower posterior portion of the thalamic region was removed did the extraordinary activities of the preparation subside. These results clearly point to the thalamus as a region from which, in the absence of cortical government, impulses are discharged which evoke an extreme degree of 'emotional' activity, both muscular and visceral.

The evidence just cited is confirmed by observations on human beings. As has been pointed out elsewhere (Cannon, 1927) when the cortical processes are abolished by anesthesia, emotional display may be most remarkable. During the early (excitement) stage of ether anesthesia, for example, there may be sobbing as in grief, or laughter as in joy, or lively and energetic aggressive actions as in rage. The surgeon may open the chest to perform other oper-ations of equal gravity, while the patient is pushing, pulling, shouting and muttering; a few minutes later the conscious patient will testify that he has been wholly unaware of what has happened. It is when 'laughing gas' has set aside the cortical functions that the subjects laugh and weep. Similar release of the mechanisms for emotional expression is indicated in the depression of cortical activity during acute alcoholism. In all these conditions the drug acts first as a depressant on the highly sensitive cells of the cortex, and thus lessens or temporarily destroys their control of lower centers; only when the drug becomes more concentrated does it depress also the lower centers; but before that stage is reached the lower centers, released from the cortical dominance as in the surgically decorticated animals, show forth their functions in free play.

Consistent with the experimental and pharmacological evidence is the evidence derived from pathological cases. In certain forms of hemiplegia the patients may be incapable of moving the face on the paralysed side; if suddenly they are affected by a sorrowful or joyous emotion, however, the muscles, unresponsive to voluntary control, spring into action and give both sides of the face the expression of sadness or gaiety (Roussy, 1907). These cases occur when the motor tract is interrupted subcortically and the optic thalamus is left intact. The opposite of this condition is seen in unilateral injury of the thalamus. A patient described by Kirilzev (1891) moved symmetrically both sides of his face at will, but when he laughed in fun or made a grimace in pain the right side remained motionless; at autopsy a tumor was found in the center of the left optic thalamus. This localization of the central neural apparatus for the expressions of pleasure and pain has interesting relations to emotive phenomena commonly seen in so-called 'pseudo-bulbar palsy'. In such cases there is usually a bilateral facial paralysis, with one side slightly more involved than the other. Voluntary pursing of the lips as in whistling, or wrinkling of the forehead, or making a grimace may be impossible. The intractable facial muscles, however, function normally in laughing or crying, scowling or frowning. These well-executed expressions come in fits and are uncontrollable and prolonged. One patient is described who started laughing at 10 o'clock in the morning and continued with few pauses until 2 in the afternoon! Tilney and Morrison (1912), who have reported on 173 recorded cases of the disease, found such fits of crying and laughing in seventeen per cent of the cases, crying alone in sixteen per cent, and laughing alone in fifteen per cent. The fits appear as a rule without any of the usual provocations and most frequently are inopportune. The patient may have all the appearances of being convulsed with laughter, yet may not experience any of the feeling which the motions of face and body indicate. Such cases are attributed by Brissaud (1894) to lesions of a special part of the cortico-thalamic tract which free a portion of the thalamus from the cortical check. It seems probable, as later evidence will suggest, that afferent thalamo-cortical tracts are also defective. Finally, cases of 'narcolepsy' are known in which emotional expression is nearly nil; gibes and insults which enrage or infuriate the normal person are usually quite without effect. In some of these cases, examined *post-mortem*, were found tumors on the under side of the diencephalon, often affecting the whole hypothalamus.

All these observations, experimental and clinical, consistently point to the optic thalamus as a region in which resides the neural organization for the different emotional expressions. The section in James's discussion headed 'No Special Brain Centres for Emotion' must be modified in the light of this accumulated information. The cortex at one end of the nerve paths as a reflex surface and the peripheral organs at the other end as a source of return impulses make too simple an arrangement. Between the cortex and the periphery lies the diencephalon, an integrating organ on the emotive level, a receiving and discharging station, that on proper stimulation is capable of establishing in stereotyped forms the facies and bodily postures typical of the various affective states. That all afferent paths leading towards the cortex have relays in the diencephalon is a fact of great significance in explaining the nature of emotions.

2. *Thalamic processes are a source of affective experience.* – The relaying of all sensory neurones in some part of the optic thalamus has been stressed by Head (1921) in his important clinical studies. He and Holmes (1911) attributed to this region a sort of consciousness, an 'awareness'. The effect of anesthesia in abolishing consciousness while leaving emotional expression (thalamic in origin) undisturbed would seem to contradict this view. But even if consciousness is associated only with events in cortical neurones, the important part played by thalamic processes is little disturbed thereby. The relays of sensory channels in the thalamus and the evidence that disturbances in that region are the occasion for intensely affective sensations are all that we need for understanding its relation to the nature of emotions.

Head (1920) has cited numerous cases of unilateral lesions in the thalamic region in which there is a marked tendency to react excessively to affective stimuli; pin pricks, painful pressure, excessive heat or cold, all produce more distress on the damaged than on the normal side of the body. Agreeable stimuli also are felt keenly on the damaged side; warmth stimuli may evoke intense pleasure, attended by signs of enjoyment on the face and exclamations of delight. Again, affective stimuli, such as the playing of music and the singing of hymns, may arouse such increased emotional feeling on the damaged side that they may be intolerable. Affective conscious states have an influence on the damaged side similar to stimuli from the surface receptors. This extravagant influence of affective stimuli, whether from above or below, Head attributed to release of the thalamus from cortical inhibition. It is not an irritative effect, he argued, because it persists for long periods, well after all the disturbances due to the injury have subsided. And since the affective states are increased when the thalamus is free from cortical control, Head's conclusion is that the essential thalamic center is mainly occupied with the affective side of sensation.

We are not in a position to consider the evidence that the positions and tensions of skeletal muscle make the differentia of emotion. It will be recalled that, although James belittled this element in his theory, his supporters have stressed it, especially since the visceral element proved inadequate. The thalamic cases provide a means of testing the contribution from skeletal muscles, for the feeling-tone of a sensation is a product of thalamic activity, and the fact that a sensation is devoid of feeling-tone shows that the impulses which underlie its production make no thalamic appeal.

Head found that his patients reported marked differences in the feeling-tone of different sensations. A tuning-fork may have no effect, whereas patriotic music is felt intensely on the damaged side. All thermal stimuli make a double appeal, to the cortex and to the thalamus. Unselected tactile stimuli act similarly. On the other hand, *sensations which underlie the appreciation of posture are entirely lacking in feeling-tone.* Precisely those afferent impulses from muscles and joints which James and his supporters have relied upon to provide the extra-visceral part of the felt-emotion are the impulses which lack the necessary quality to serve the purpose! The quality of emotions is to be found, neither in returns from the viscera nor in returns from the innervated muscles.

A theory of emotion based on thalamic processes

The foregoing discussion has disclosed the fact that the neural arrangements for emotional expression reside in subcortical centers, and that these centers are ready for instant and vigorous discharge when they are released from cortical restraint and are properly stimulated. Furthermore, the evidence is clear that when these centers are released the processes aroused in them become a source of vivid affective experience. That this experience is felt on only one side in hemiplegic cases is a peculiarly happy circumstance, for in the same individual the influence of the same affective stimulus can be observed under normal conditions and compared with its influence when given free rein.

The neural organization for an emotion which is suggested by the foregoing observations is as follows. An external situation stimulates receptors and the consequent excitation starts impulses towards the cortex. Arrival of the impulses in the cortex is associated with conditioned processes which determine the direction of the response. Either because the response is initiated in a certain mode or figure and the cortical neurones therefore stimulate the thalamic processes, or because on their centripetal course the impulses from the receptors excite thalamic processes, they are roused and ready for discharge. That the thalamic neurones act in a special combination in a given emotional expression is proved by the reaction patterns typical of the several affective states. These neurones do not require detailed innervation from above in order to be driven into action. Being *released* for action is a primary condition for their service to the body – they then discharge precipitately and intensely. Within and near the thalamus the neurones concerned in an emotional expression lie close to the relay in the sensory path from periphery to cortex. We may assume that when these neurones discharge in a particular combination, they not only innervate muscles and viscera but also excite afferent paths to the cortex by direct connexion or by irradiation. The theory which naturally presents itself is that the *peculiar quality of the emotion is added to simple sensation when the thalamic processes are roused*.

The theory just suggested appears to fit all the known facts. Its service in explaining these facts may be briefly summarized.

When the thalamic discharge occurs, the bodily changes occur almost simultaneously with the emotional experience. This coincidence of disturbances in muscles and viscera with thrills, excitements or depressions was naturally misleading, for, with the role of the thalamus omitted from consideration, the obvious inference was that the peculiar quality of the emotion arose from the peripheral changes. Indeed, that inference is the heart of the James–Lange theory. The evidence presented in the foregoing pages shows that the inference is ill-founded; the sensations from the peripheral changes, contrary to James's view, are 'pale, color-less and destitute of emotional warmth', whereas the thalamic disturbances contribute glow and color to otherwise simply cognitive states. The theory now proposed explains how James and Lange could reasonably make the suggestion which they made. The lack of factual support for their suggestion requires another account of emotional origins. This is provided by the evidence that thalamic processes can add to sensation an aura of feeling.

One of the strongest arguments advanced for the James-Lange theory is that the assumption of an attitude does in fact help to establish the emotional state, which the attitude expresses. 'Sit all day in a moping posture, sigh, and reply to everything with a dismal voice, and your melancholy lingers.' On the contrary, 'smooth the brow, brighten the eye, contract the dorsal rather than the ventral aspect of the frame, and speak in a major key, pass the genial com-pliment, and your heart must be frigid indeed if you do not gradu-ally thaw!' Persons who have tried this advice have testified to its soundness, and have been convinced, therefore, of the truth of the claim that the moods have followed the assumed attitudes. Not all agree, however, that mimicking the outward appearance of an emotion results in the emotion itself. James suggested that the explanation of the discrepancy lay in variations of involvement of the viscera in the artificial expression. As shown above, however, the visceral changes offer only unreliable support for that idea. Again the processes in the thalamus offer a reasonable and simple explanation. As the cases reported by Head have shown, emotions originating from memories and imagination affect more intensely the half-thalamus that has been released from motor control than they affect the normal half. This shows that cortical processes may start thalamic processes and thus arouse an affective return from that portion of the brain. And if in addition a typical emo-tional attitude is assumed the cortical inhibition of the thalamic neurones with reference to that attitude is abolished so that they have complete release. Under such circumstances the enacted emotion would have reality. On the other hand a purely cortical mimicry of emotional expression without thalamic involvement would be as cold and unaffective as some actors have declared it to be. Whether the emotion results or not, the thalamic theory of the source of feeling offers a more satisfactory explanation of the effects of assumed postures than does the James–Lange theory.

The cases of release of the thalamus from cortical control on one side, with accompanying ipsilateral intensification of emotional tone, present an insurmountable obstacle to the James–Lange theory. Neither the thoracic nor the abdominal viscera can function by halves, the vasomotor center is a unity, and the patients certainly do not engage in right- or left-sided laughter and weeping. The impulses sent back from the disturbed peripheral organs, therefore, must be bilaterally equal. For explanation of the unsymmetrical feeling we are driven to the organ which is functioning unsymmetrically – i.e. the thalamus. It is there that the suggested theory places the source of the emotions.

Another serious difficulty for the James–Lange theory is the evidence that the emotion increases in intensity although the expression is checked. Indeed, there are psychologists who maintain that the emotional state lasts only so long as there is inner conflict between the impulse to act and the hesitant or prudential check on that impulse. So long as the check prevails, however, the organic changes supposed to be the source of the feeling are suppressed. How then can there be felt-emotion? Two answers to this question may be found in James's argument. First he denies the objection. 'Refuse to express a passion,' he wrote, 'and it dies.' 'Count ten before venting your anger, and its occasion seems ridiculous.' On the other hand, he appears to admit that a pent emotion may operate disastrously. 'If tears or anger are simply suppressed, whilst the object of grief or rage remains unchanged before the mind, the current which would have invaded the normal channels turns into others, for it must find some outlet of escape. It may then work different and worse effects later on. Thus vengeful brooding may replace a burst of indignation; a dry heat may consume the frame of one who fain would weep, or he may, as Dante says, turn to stone within.' There is no intimation that vengeful brooding, being consumed by a dry heat, and turning to stone within are not emotional experiences. Instead of recognizing them as such, however, James stressed the importance of training for repression of emotional display. These rather equivocal and indecisive comments leave untouched the common testimony that intense fear, for example, may be felt, with a pathetic sense of helplessness, before any overt act occurs, and that scarcely does the appropriate behavior start than the inner tumult begins to subside and the bodily forces are directed vigorously and effectively to serviceable ends. The difficulties of the James–Lange theory in meeting this situation are obvious. If there is a double control of behavior, however, both the inner conflict with its keen emotional accompaniment and the later partial subsidence of feeling are readily explicable. The thalamic patterned processes are inherent in the nervous organization, they are like reflexes in being instantly ready to seize control of the motor responses, and when they do so they operate with great power. They can be controlled, however, by the processes in the cerebral cortex, by processes conditioned by all sorts of previous impressions. The cortex also can control all the peripheral machinery except the viscera. The inhibited processes in the thalamus cannot set the organism in action, except the parts not under voluntary control, but the turmoil there can produce emotions in the usual manner, and possibly with greater violence because of the inhibition. And when the cortical check is released, suddenly the conflict is resolved. The two controls formerly in opposition, are now cooperative. The thalamic neurones, so long as they continue energetically active, provide the condition for the emotion to persist, as James claimed it does, *during* the manifestation. The new theory, therefore, not only avoids the difficulty of the James–Lange theory, but accounts satisfactorily for the poignancy of feeling in the period of paralyzed inaction.

In relation to the double control of the response there is another point that may be emphasized. McDougall (1923) has objected to the James–Lange theory on the ground that it is admittedly concerned with the *sensory* aspect of emotion; it pays little or no attention to the always present and sometimes overwhelming *impulsive* aspect of the experience. The localization of the reaction patterns for emotional expression in the thalamus – in a region which, like the spinal cord, works directly by simple automatisms unless held in check – not only accounts for the sensory side, the 'felt emotion', but also for the impulsive side, the tendency of the thalamic neurones to discharge. These powerful impulses originating in a region of the brain not associated with cognitive consciousness and arousing therefore in an *obscure* and *unrelated* manner the strong feelings of emotional excitement, explain the sense of being seized, possessed, of being controlled by an outside force and made to act without weighing of the consequences.

Finally, the view that thalamic processes add feeling-tone to sensation meets satisfactorily a difficulty which the James–Lange theory encountered in explaining the 'subtler emotions'. James had to assume indefinite and hypothetical bodily reverberations in order to account for mild feelings of pleasure and satisfaction. If a warm test tube, however, is capable of yielding keen delight on the damaged side in a case of thalamic injury, it is clear that almost any object or situation which can rouse thalamic processes can add affective quality to sensation. And just as a stimulus can become conditioned for a certain motor or glandular response, so likewise a stimulus can be conditioned for the patterns of neurone action in the thalamus. When that stimulus recurs the emotion recurs because the pattern is activated. In such manner we may consider that richness and variety of our emotional life are elaborated.

References

BARD, P. (1928), 'A diencephalic mechanism for the expression of rage with special reference to the sympathetic nervous system', *Homer J. Physiol.*, vol. 84, pp. 490–515

BECHTEREV, W. (1887), 'Die Bedeutung der Sehhügel auf Grund von experimentellen und pathologischen Daten', *Virchow's Archiv*, vol. 110, pp. 102–322.

BRISSAUD, E. (1894), *Leçons cliniques*.

CANNON, W. B. (1927), 'Neural basis for emotion expression', *Wittenberg Symposium on Feelings and Emotions*.

CANNON, W. B., and BRITTON, S. W. (1925), 'Pseudaffective medulliadrenal secretion', *Amer. J. Physiol.*, vol. 72, p. 283.

HEAD, H. (1920), *Studies in Neurology*, vol. II, p. 620.

HEAD, H. (1921), 'Release of function in the nervous system', *Proc. Roy. Soc.*, vol. 92b, p. 184.

HEAD, H., and HOLMES, G. (1911), 'Sensory disturbances from cerebral lesions', *Brain*, vol. 34, p. 109.

JAMES, W. (1884), 'What is an emotion?', *Mind*, vol. 9, pp. 188–205.

KIRILZEV, S. (1891), 'Cases of affections of the optic thalamus' (Russian), reviewed in *Neurologisches Centralblatt*, vol. 10, p. 310.

McDOUGALL, W. (1923), *Outline of Psychology*, p. 328.

ROUSSY, G. (1907), *La Couche optique*, p. 31.

TILNEY, F., and MORRISON, J. F. (1912), 'Pseudo-bulbar palsy clinically and pathologically considered', *J. ment. nerv. Diseases*, vol. 39, p. 505.

WOODWORTH, R. S., and SHERRINGTON, C. S. (1904), 'A pseudaffective reflex and its spinal path', *J. Physiol.*, vol. 31, p. 234.

24 J. W. Papez

A Proposed Mechanism of Emotion

Excerpt from J. W. Papez, 'A proposed mechanism of emotion',
Arch. Neurol. Psychiat., vol. 38 (1937), pp. 725–43.

The work of Cannon (1927, 1931), Bard (1929, 1934), Penfield
(1933, 1934), Ranson (1934) and others has greatly advanced
knowledge of the functions of the hypothalamus. In the light of
these researches the connexions of the hypothalamus to the medial
wall of the cerebral cortex gain a new significance. The following
discussion presents some anatomic, clinical and experimental data
dealing with the hypothalamus, the gyrus cinguli, the hippocampus
and their interconnexions. Taken as a whole, this ensemble of
structures is proposed as representing theoretically the anatomic
basis of the emotions.

It is generally recognized that in the brain of lower vertebrates
the medial wall of the cerebral hemisphere is connected anatomi-
cally and integrated physiologically with the hypothalamus and
that the lateral wall is similarly related to the dorsal thalamus
(Herrick, 1933). These fundamental relations are not only re-
tained but greatly elaborated in the mammalian brain by the
further development of the hippocampal formation and the gyrus
cinguli in the medial wall and of the general cortex in the lateral
wall of each cerebral hemisphere.

The main steps in the phyletic history of these structures are
clearly represented in the various classes of vertebrates. It is not
surprising, therefore, to find that the literature on this fascinating
subject presents on the whole a congruent account. Step by step,
the structures of the medial wall become differentiated into the
hippocampal formation, which establishes the first efferent connexion of the cortex, namely the fornix, with the hypothalamus,
and as the adjacent cingular cortex appears, it receives, *per contra*,
an afferent connexion from the hypothalamus. Step by step, the
lateral wall above the pyriform cortex becomes differentiated into

the lateral nonolfactory cortex, which through the medium of the internal capsule maintains its afferent and recurrent connexions with the nuclei of the dorsal thalamus. The histories of the two walls of the hemispheres owe their disparity and distinctive structure to two totally different kinds of integration – the hippocampus and the cingular cortex participating in hypothalamic activities and the lateral cortex in the general sensory activities mediated by the dorsal thalamus. It is also noteworthy that in both systems two way connexions exist between the cortical and the thalamic level.

The account which follows will be concerned chiefly with the reciprocal connexions which exist between the hypothalamus and the gyrus cinguli and hippocampus. Its chief purpose is to point out that these connexions may mediate by means of the cortical circuit the important function commonly called emotion.

The term 'emotion' as commonly used implies two conditions: a way of acting and a way of feeling. The former is designated as emotional expression; the latter, as emotional experience or subjective feeling. The experiments of Bard (1929) have demonstrated that emotional expression depends on the integrative action of the hypothalamus rather than on that of the dorsal thalamus or cortex, since it may occur when the cerebral hemispheres and the dorsal thalamus are totally removed. For subjective emotional experience, however, the participation of the cortex is essential. Emotional expression and emotional experience may in the human subject be dissociated phenomena. Hence, emotion as a subjective state must be referred to the higher psychic level. Concerning the theory of emotion based on diencephalic processes, Bard (1934) wrote:

As we have seen, every relevant experimental fact points away from the periphery and directly toward the brain as the site of the processes which determine whether or not a stimulus shall give rise to emotional feeling. What is the nature and the locus of these all-important central processes?

Cannon (1927, 1931) and also Dana (1921) have proposed the theory that emotion results from the action and reaction of the cerebral cortex and the diencephalon. This theory, unlike the James–Lange theory, has considerable experimental support and takes into account anatomical and physiological facts ignored by the older view. First of all, there is the evidence that at the base of the diencephalon are located the neural patterns responsible for emotional behavior, mechanisms capable of independent discharge but normally held in check by the cerebral cortex. At the same time the cerebral cortex is the immediate site of emotional consciousness, and, as we have seen, emotional experience and emotional expression may be dissociated by disease or surgical intervention. But we know that thalamic processes are a source of affective experience, that bodily sensations such as are sometimes associated with emotion may be thalamic in origin. Well-established anatomical facts show that, with the possible exception of the olfactory, all sensory impulses are interrupted at the thalamic level before gaining the cerebral cortex, and Head's (1920) studies suggest how there may be regrouping of corticopetal impulses in the thalamus. Cannon's theory has its basis in these facts and it proposes that, at the same time that the diencephalon discharges downward the motor impulses which produce the emotional behavior, it discharges upward to the cortex impulses which throw into action the processes which underlie emotional consciousness.

In order to make clear at the outset the general anatomic picture which I wish to propose as the probable corticothalamic mechanism of emotion, a diagram has been constructed, showing its main features (figure 1). I shall start with the hypothalamus, the three parts of which are illustrated. The pars optica is connected through the infundibulum with the pars neuralis of the hypophysis. The tuber cinereum is connected downward with the lower sympathetic centers. In the human brain a large tract can be seen passing down, ventral to the red nucleus. The pars mamillaris is connected in an efferent way to the cortex of the gyrus cinguli. The pars mamillaris also receives afferent connexions from several other sources, the most prominent being the fornix from the hippocampal formation.

As the figure shows, it is the mamillary body which bears the main hypothalamic relations to the cerebral cortex. This is a two way connexion in the nature of a circuit through the cerebral cortex, at the upper level, and through the mamillary body, at the hypothalamic level. In this circuit impulses may be incited at two points: the cerebral cortex and the hypothalamus. Incitations of cortical origin would pass first to the hippocampal formation and then down by way of the fornix to the mamillary body. From this they would pass upward through the mamillothalamic tract, or the fasciculus of Vicq d'Azyr, to the anterior nuclei of the thalamus

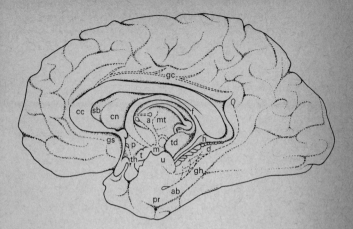

a	anterior nucleus	gc	gyrus cinguli	pr	pyriform area
ab	angular bundle	gh	gyrus hippocampi	sb	subcallosal bundle
cn	caudate nucleus	gs	gyrus subcallosus	t	tuber cinereum
cc	corpus callosum	h	hippocampus nudus	td	tractus mamillotegmentalis
cp	cingulum posterius	m	mamillary body	th	tractus hypophyseus
d	gyrus dentatus	mt	mamillothalamic tract	u	uncus
f	fornix	p	pars optica hypothalami		

Figure 1 Medial view of the right cerebral hemisphere, showing the hippocampus and its connexion with the mamillary body through the fornix and also the connexions of the mamillary body to the anterior thalamic nuclei and thence to the cortex of the gyrus cinguli. In this specimen an unusually large exposed (nude) hippocampus is seen

and thence by the medial thalamocortical radiation (in the cingulum) to the cortex of the gyrus cinguli.

The central emotive process of cortical origin may then be conceived as being built up in the hippocampal formation and as being transferred to the mamillary body and thence through the anterior thalamic nuclei to the cortex of the gyrus cinguli. The cortex of the cingular gyrus may be looked on as the receptive region for the experiencing of emotion as the result of impulses coming from the hypothalamic region, in the same way as the area striata is considered the receptive cortex for photic excitations coming from the retina. Radiation of the emotive process from the gyrus cinguli to other regions in the cerebral cortex would add emotional coloring to psychic processes occurring elsewhere. This circuit would explain how emotion may arise in two ways: as a result of psychic activity and as a consequence of hypothalamic activity.

The hypothalamus is accessible to both visceral and somatic sensory impressions from many peripheral sources, and it is well known that emotional coloring, or affect, may be associated with all sorts of sensory experiences of bodily and receptor origin. Most of the afferent receptor systems evoke sensations with characteristic qualities, perceptions, etc., which at the conscious level are accompanied by a more or less distinctive affective tone. The question arises as to how these afferent sensibilities, which pass through the dorsal thalamus and then by way of the internal capsule to the cerebral cortex, are capable of acquiring emotional coloring. Physiologic results imply that the emotive process is mediated by the hypothalamus, and anatomic data suggest that it is the mamillary body which sends the excitations to the cortex of the gyrus cinguli.

It has been aptly said that the hypothalamus is the recipient of the vague and undefined impressions from many bodily sources which in their totality represent afferent material capable of influencing the regulative functions of the hypothalamus. It is not yet generally recognized that there are primitive sensory centers in the ventral thalamus, the chief connexions of which appear to pass to the hypothalamus. These primitive receptive centers in the ventral thalamus (subthalamus) are known as the pars ventralis of the lateral geniculate body, the nucleus praegeniculatus, the pars ventralis of the medial geniculate body, the reticular nucleus and the nucleus of the mamillary peduncle. These primitive centers receive certain terminals from various afferent systems: For example, the optic tract ends in part in the pregeniculate nucleus and in the pars ventralis of the lateral geniculate body; the acoustic system ends in part in the pars ventralis of the medial geniculate body; the spinothalamic and trigeminothalamic tracts end in part in the reticular nucleus, and the medial lemniscus appears to contribute fibers to the nucleus of the mamillary peduncle.

These nuclei of the ventral thalamus send to the hypothalamus diffuse fiber connexions, some of which are better known as the supraoptic decussations. They end in general in the pars optica and the tuber cinereum, the regions which regulate visceral activities and emotional expression. However, the pars optica and the tuber are connected with the mamillary body, which also receives afferent connexions through the medial bundle of the forebrain, the mamillary peduncle and the fornix. Thus, the mamillary body is the ultimate recipient of various afferent excitations, which reach the hypothalamus especially through the afferent centers of the ventral thalamus.

It is thus evident that the afferent pathways from the receptor organs split at the thalamic level into three routes, each conducting a stream of impulses of special importance. One route conducts impulses through the dorsal thalamus and the internal capsule to the corpus striatum. This route represents 'the stream of movement'. The second conducts impulses from the thalamus through the internal capsule to the lateral cerebral cortex. This route represents 'the stream of thought'. The third conducts a set of concomitant impulses through the ventral thalamus to the hypothalamus and by way of the mamillary body and the anterior thalamic nuclei to the gyrus cinguli, in the medial wall of the cerebral hemisphere. This route represents 'the stream of feeling'. In this way, the sensory excitations which reach the lateral cortex through the internal capsule receive their emotional coloring from the concurrent processes of hypothalamic origin which irradiate them from the gyrus cinguli.

References

BARD, P. (1929), 'The central representation of the sympathetic nervous system as indicated by certain physiologic observations', *Arch. Neurol. Psychiat.*, vol. 22, pp. 230–46.

BARD, P. (1934), 'Emotion: I. The neuro-humoral basis of emotional reactions', in C. A. Murchison, *A Handbook of General Experimental Psychology*, Clark University Press, chapter 6, pp. 264–311.

CANNON, W. B. (1927), 'The James–Lange theory of emotion: A critical examination and an alternative theory', *Amer. J. Psychol.*, vol. 39, pp. 10–124.

CANNON, W. B. (1931), 'Again the James–Lange and the thalamic theories of emotion', *Psychol. Rev.*, vol. 38, pp. 281–95.

DANA, C. L. (1921), 'The anatomic seat of the emotions: A discussion of the James–Lange theory', *Arch. Neurol. Psychiat.*, vol. 6, pp. 634–9.

HERRICK, C. J. (1933), 'Morphogenesis of the brain', *J. Morphol.*, vol. 54, pp. 233–58.

PENFIELD, W. (1933; 1934), Wesley M. Carpenter Lecture, 'Influence of the diencephalon and hypophysis upon general autonomic function', *Bull. New York Acad. Med.*, vol. 9, pp. 613–37; *Canad. M.A.J.*, vol. 30, pp. 589–98.

RANSON, S. W. (1934), 'The hypothalamus: Its significance for visceral innervation and emotional expression', *Tr. Coll. Physicians Philadelphia*, vol. 2, pp. 222–42.

25 J. M. R. Delgado

Emotional Behavior in Animals and Humans

J. M. R. Delgado, 'Emotional behavior in animals and humans', in
L. J. West and M. Greenblatt, *Explorations in the Physiology of Emotions*,
Psychiat. Res. Report no. 12, Amer. Psychiat. Ass., 1960, pp. 259–66.

Study of emotions in animals cannot include the experiential side
of feelings because animals cannot tell us how they feel. The expressive side of what we call emotions, however, can be observed
as special patterns of behavior. For example, if a cat shows its
teeth, hisses, raises its hair and evinces tachycardia, pupillary
dilatation, etc., we can infer the existence of an emotional state:
anger. It is true that the inference is not reliable because anger may
exist without motor (or autonomic?) manifestations and vice
versa. However, study of emotional expression and bodily changes
constitutes a most useful tool for exploring the physiology of
emotion if we keep in mind its limitations.

Emotions evoked by electrical stimulation of the brain

Defensive-offensive responses produced in unanesthetized cats by
electrical stimulation of the perifornical zone of the hypothalamus
were demonstrated by Hess twenty-five years ago (17). Well-
coordinated and well-oriented attacks were evoked and some
effects persisted after the end of the stimulation. Increased motility
and flight were elicited from areas of the lateral hypothalamus,
while decreased activity, motor deficit, atonia, and sleep could be
induced by stimulation of the ventral nucleus of the thalamus.
As shown by Ranson (27) and his school, motor and autonomic
effects resembling rage could be evoked by electrical stimulation of
the hypothalamus. Several other authors have confirmed and
extended these experiments showing the participation of mesencephalon, diencephalon, and rhinencephalon in the integration
of emotional reactions (2, 9, 12, 13, 22, 23, 24, 28, 29, 32). In these
studies, however, it was difficult to decide whether or not the
electrically evoked external behavioral manifestations reached

consciousness. Decorticated animals indeed may exhibit emotional hyperreactivity (1, 15), and Masserman (26) has demonstrated that hypothalamic stimulation in the cat evokes pupillary dilatation, piloerection, and other signs of sympathetic activation without disturbing a feeding situation. Masserman's experiments also showed that stimulation of the hypothalamus did not establish conditioned reflexes. Several authors concluded, therefore, that electrical stimulation of some cerebral structures, such as hypothalamus, produced a pseudoaffective reaction, i.e., external manifestation of emotional behavior without emotional awareness of the animal (14).

Awareness of evoked emotional behavior

In contradistinction to the results of hypothalamic stimulation, other cerebral structures seemed to play a role in both behavioral manifestations and subjective experience of emotions. We observed this in the monkey during a study of cerebral structures that probably integrate pain perception (7). It was known that noxious stimulation such as electrical shock applied to the feet evoked a pattern characterized by defensive-offensive movements, snarling, vocalization, autonomic manifestations, and anxiety. In our study we attempted to ascertain the cerebral structures responsible for these effects. In awake monkeys we found that a similar pattern could be evoked electrically from lateral tegmentum, central gray, posteroventral nucleus of the thalamus, crus of the fornix and posterior hippocampus. We soon realized that after a few stimulations of these areas the monkeys showed signs of anxiety when they were brought into the testing room. Sight of the restraining chair and preparations for the experiment increased the anxiety of the animals, who tried to bite and escape and sometimes vocalized. They seemed to *remember* unpleasant experiences of previous experiments. This contrasted sharply with our experience with other animals in which motor areas, frontal lobes, cingulate gyrus, putamen, or pulvinar were electrically stimulated; repetition of these experiments had made the monkeys easier to handle and we saw no signs of anxiety.

If it was true that animals were aware of and remembered centrally evoked emotions, then it should be possible to establish conditioned reactions. New experiments were therefore designed to study cerebral areas which might control both emotional behavioral manifestations and subjective experiences. In cats with implanted electrodes electrical stimulation of tectal area, lateral nuclear mass of the thalamus, and hippocampus was paired with a flickering light or a 2,000 cycle sound. The cats could stop the brain stimulation by turning a wheel; after 16-92 pairings they learned to turn off the stimulation when the flickering light or sound started. When the habit was established the light or sound consistently evoked wheel turning even in the absence of cerebral stimulation. In other experiments it was proved that emotional disturbance evoked by electrical stimulation of these brain structures could establish escape responses, motivate trial and error learning and the performance of instrumental tests, and teach hungry animals to avoid food (9). In monkeys it was also demonstrated that conditioned avoidance responses could be induced by electrical stimulation of pallidum, amygdala, nucleus ventralis posteromedialis of the thalamus, etc. (10). Specificity of the effect was proved by failure to produce conditioning when sensorimotor cortex, pulvinar of the thalamus, putamen, substantia nigra, and other structures were stimulated.

With respect to their roles in evoking emotional behavior the cerebral structures we studied could be classified in three groups: (*i*) unrelated to emotions: motor cortex, pulvinar, substantia nigra; (*ii*) related to external behavioral manifestations of emotion but not to emotional experience: hypothalamus; (*iii*) related to both behavioral manifestations and emotional experience: some points of the hippocampus, posteroventral nucleus of the thalamus, tectal area, central gray.

The surprising fact was that our experiments showed that some depth structures did induce conditioning while the cortical areas did not. This casts some doubt upon the essential role of the cerebral cortex in conditioning. It is true that electrical stimulation of points in the depth of the brain does not rule out a possible activation of the cortex; but the fact remains that emotional awareness and conditioning have been evoked by direct subcortical stimulation.

Another experimental result should be emphasized. Fear-like responses evoked in cats and monkeys by electrical brain stimulation persisted without fatigue as long as the stimulation was applied. In contrast, motor effects evoked by cortical excitation fatigued after a few seconds or generalized into a convulsion. Otherwise friendly and docile cats growled and attacked any approaching object during fifteen minutes of tectal stimulation and returned suddenly to a friendly mood as soon as stimulation ceased. This resistance to fatigue of structures related to emotional behavior is of great theoretical and practical interest.

Inhibition of behavior

Inhibitory areas in the central nervous system have been repeatedly demonstrated. The inhibitory effects of the reticular system were first described by Magoun and Rhines in 1946 (25) and later by the Magoun school and many other authors. The existence of cortical areas with inhibitory functions, the 'suppressor strips' described by Dusser de Barenne and McCulloch (11), is controversial (4), but at least in some experimental conditions inhibition of movements has been shown. Arrest reactions characterized by cessation of motor activity and preservation of postural tonus have been obtained by electrical stimulation of the intralaminar thalamic nuclei, anterior cingulate gyrus, and hidden motor cortex (6, 20, 33). A somnagenous zone has been described by Hess (18) in the ventral nucleus of the thalamus. In all these studies a general inhibition of the animal, especially of the motor activity, has been described, but little attention has been paid to behavior.

In our experiments in unanesthetized monkeys with implanted brain electrodes we have seen that different aspects of behavior may be inhibited by electrical stimulation of some cerebral structures. This was not a systematic investigation but the following types of inhibition were indicated by our studies and were recorded by colored 16 mm. moving pictures. They are presented here as a basis for discussion and to orient future research.

1. *Motor activity*. – In monkeys trained to pull in and overturn one cup in response to a high tone to avoid a shock, and another cup in response to a low tone to obtain food reward, electrical stimulation of the anterior commissure, ansa peduncularis, pallidum, and putamen inhibited the learned response and the monkeys sat in the testing cage with small movements of the head but without responding to either stimulus. As soon as the stimulation stopped the animals moved quickly to the food cup (10).

2. *Dozing*. – Stimulation for five minutes or more of the septal region induced dozing in the animals which sometimes continued for fifteen minutes after the end of the stimulation. During this time the animals could be roused but they soon dozed again without further stimulation (30). It should be emphasized that the septal area is far from the somniferous zone described by Hess (18).

3. *Arrest reaction*. – The animal suddenly stopped motor activity but maintained postural tonus. This effect has been observed often and very dramatically in cats (5), but only rarely in monkeys, by stimulation of motor pathways under area 4.

4. *Hypotonic reaction*. – The arrest of motility was accompanied by a progressive loss of muscular tonus. The animal lowered its head, and if strapped to a chair its arms and legs hung flaccid, or if free on a stage the monkey slowly lay down on the floor. In either case the animal was not responsive to external stimulation. Previously learned conditioned responses were not performed, and even electrical shock to the feet was ineffective. The animal was not aggressive, and even the mouth could be safely touched. We have evoked this effect by electrical stimulation of the anterior cingulate gyrus and different points of the reticular system.

5. *Specific inhibition of aggressiveness*. – This effect was induced by electrical stimulation of some points of the head of the caudate nucleus. It was characterized by closure of the normally open mouth of the threatening monkey and a loss of aggressiveness, without lessening of motility or motor response to sensory stimulation, the animal giving the impression that it was well aware of its surroundings. For example, monkey Linda was an aggressive female who was always ready to bite anything and had to be handled with gloves. As soon as the caudate was stimulated she closed her mouth and was no longer interested in biting; if we put an object close to her or our hands near her mouth she rejected them, pushing them away or turning her head aside, showing good coordination. As soon as stimulation stopped the animal was as dangerous, or more so, than before the stimulation, trying to bite anything within reach.

6. *Specific inhibition of interest in food*. – Monkeys love bananas which they grab and eat voraciously. Electrical stimulation of some points of the septal area, however, abruptly stopped the monkey's

interest in food; the animal dropped the banana, stopped chewing and even spat pieces of it from its mouth. Interest in food resumed as soon as stimulation ceased. In monkeys restrained only by a belt which allowed freedom of movement around a testing table we have seen an animal push aside a banana and walk away during septal stimulation only to come anxiously back looking for it as soon as the stimulation ended. These effects were reliable on different days in the same monkey and were specific because they were evoked by electrical stimulation of only one or two contacts from the total of 12 to 42 present in each animal. In one monkey three points in the septal area only two mm. apart evoked consistently: (*i*) a hypotonic reaction, (*ii*) a specific inhibition of the interest in food, (*iii*) no effect, showing the specificity of the functional localization of the described response.

Electrically evoked emotion in humans

Demonstration through extensive animal experimentation of the innocuousness of cerebral electrodes and the need for new diagnostic and therapeutic methods in cerebral illness led us and others (3, 8, 16, 21, 31) to implant leads in human patients. This provided an exceptional opportunity to investigate the external manifestation and subjective experience of emotions that could be induced by direct stimulation of the brain. In our studies the conversation of the patient with the interviewer was tape-recorded and synchronized with recordings of cerebral electrical activity and the instant of applied stimulation. The general procedure was explained to the patient, but he did not know when stimulations were applied. Results were analysed and statistically computed to determine their meaning (19). Significant increase in the number of spoken words and friendly remarks was elicited in one epileptic patient by stimulation of the inferolateral cortex of the frontal lobes. Increase of friendliness as a result of brain stimulation was also observed in two other cases. In a thirty-six-year-old female epileptic electrical stimulation of the temporal lobes was accompanied by expressions of pleasure, giggling, laughing, humorous comments, and the frank remark that she enjoyed very much 'pleasant tingling sensations of the body'. In another patient electrical stimulation of the depth of the frontal lobes consistently evoked movements of the head and body; the patient looked around with an expression of 'fear' which was recorded in color motion pictures. The patient expressed the feeling of some unknown threat or imminent danger, without reporting pain or other unpleasant sensations. Stimulation of the motor cortex in other patients evoked movements of which they were aware but no modification of mood or emotional reaction that could be detected. Visual and auditory hallucinations were evoked by stimulation of the temporal lobes in several patients who were surprised by these unfamiliar sensations. *Déjà vu* phenomenon, i.e., a feeling that a present sensation evoked by cerebral stimulation was a repetition of some previous experience, was regarded as intrusive but amusing rather than disturbing the subjects.

Experimental results reported in this paper indicate that electrical stimulation of cerebral structures through implanted leads can modify emotions and behavior in animals and humans; we hope that diagnostic and therapeutic benefits will derive in future from their use.

Summary

Emotional behavior may be induced in cats and monkeys by electrical stimulation of the brain. Experimental evidence suggests that cerebral structures studies can be classified in three groups: (*i*) unrelated to emotions: motor cortex, pulvinar, substantia nigra; (*ii*) related to external behavioral manifestation of emotions but not to emotional experience: hypothalamus; (*iii*) related to both behavioral manifestation and emotional experience: part of the hippocampus, posteroventral nucleus of the thalamus, tectal area. Conditioning may be induced by electrical stimulation of structures of the last group, but not by the first two.

Evoked fear-like responses did not fatigue for fifteen minutes, in contrast to motor responses evoked by stimulation of precentral cortex which fatigued in a few seconds.

The following types of inhibited behavior were evoked in monkeys by electrical stimulation of specific areas: (1) inhibition of motor behavior, (2) dozing, (3) arrest reaction, (4) hypotonic reaction, (5) specific inhibition of aggressiveness, (6) specific inhibition of interest in food.

Objective and subjective manifestation of friendliness, pleasure and fear were evoked in conscious patients by electrical stimulation, proving that experiential and expressive aspects of emotion can be artificially induced by excitation of specific cerebral structures.

References

1. BARD, P., *Psychol. Rev.*, vol. 41 (1934), p. 309 (Part I); p. 424 (Part II).
2. BARD, P., and MOUNTCASTLE, V. B., *Res. Publ. Ass. nerv. ment. Dis.*, vol. 27 (1948), p. 362.
3. BRAZIER, M. A. B., SCHRODER, H., CHAPMAN, W. P., GEYER, C., FAGER, C., POPPEN, J. L., SOLOMON, H. C., and YAKOVLEV, P. I., *EEG clin. Neurophysiol.*, vol. 6 (1954), p. 702.
4. CLARK, G., *Quart. Chicago Med. Sch.*, vol. 10 (1949), p. 14.
5. DELGADO, J. M. R., *Amer. J. Physiol.*, vol. 170 (1952), p. 673.
6. DELGADO, J. M. R., *Amer. J. Physiol.*, vol. 171 (1952), p. 436.
7. DELGADO, J. M. R., *J. Neurophsiol.*, vol. 18 (1955), p. 261.
8. DELGADO, J. M. R., HAMLIN, H., and CHAPMAN, W. P., *Conf. Neurol.*, vol. 12 (1952), p. 315.
9. DELGADO, J. M. R., ROBERTS, W. W., and MILLER, N., *Amer. J. Physiol.*, vol. 179 (1954), p. 587.
10. DELGADO, J. M. R., ROSVOLD, H. E., and LOONEY, E., *J. comp. physiol. Psychol.*, vol. 49 (1956), p. 373.
11. DUSSER DE BARENNE, J. G., and McCULLOCH, W. S., *J. Neurophysiol.*, vol. 4 (1941), p. 311.
12. FULTON, J. F., *Frontal Lobotomy and Affective Behavior*, Norton, 1951.
13. GASTAUT, H., *J. Physiol. Path. gén*, vol. 44 (1952), p. 431.
14. GELLHORN, E., *Physiological Foundations of Neurology and Psychiatry*, University of Minnesota Press, 1953.
15. GOLTZ, F., *Arch. ges. Physiol.*, vol. 51 (1892), p. 570.
16. HEATH, R. G. (ed.), *Studies in Schizophrenia*, Harvard University Press, 1954.
17. HESS, W. R., *Beiträge zur Physiologie d. Hirnstammes*, I.G. Thieme, 1932.
18. HESS, W. R., *Das Zwischenhirn*, B. Schwabe, 1954.
19. HIGGINS, J. W., MAHL, G. F., DELGADO, J. M. R., and HAMLIN, H., *Arch. Neurol. Psychiat.*, Chicago, vol. 76 (1956), p. 399.
20. HUNTER, J., and JASPER, H. H., *EEG clin. Neurophysiol.*, vol. 1 (1949), p. 305.
21. JUNG, R., REICHERT, T., and MEYER-MICKELEIT, R. W., *Dtsch. Z. Nervenheilk.*, vol. 162 (1950), p. 52.
22. KAADA, B. R., *Acta physiol. Scand.*, vol. 24 (1951), suppl. 83, p. 285.
23. LASHLEY, K. S., *Psychol. Rev.*, vol. 45 (1938), p. 42.
24. MACLEAN, P. D., and DELGADO, J. M. R., *EEG clin. Neurophysiol.*, vol. 5 (1953), p. 91.

25. MAGOUN, H. W., and RHINES, R., *J. Neurophysiol.*, vol 9 (1946), p. 165.

26. MASSERMAN, J. H., *Psychosom. Med.*, vol. 3 (1941), p. 3.

27. RANSON, S. W., *Trans. Coll. Physns Philad.*, vol. 2 (1934), p. 222.

28. RANSON, S. W., and MAGOUN, H. W., *Ergebn. Physiol.*, vol. 41 (1939), p. 56.

29. RIOCH, D. McK., and BRENNER, C., *J. comp. Neurol.*, vol. 68 (1938), p. 491.

30. ROSVOLD, H. E., and DELGADO, J. M. R., *J. comp. physiol. Psychol.*, vol. 49 (1956), p. 365.

31. SEM-JACOBSEN, C. W., PETERSEN, M. C., DODGE, H. W., Jr, LAZARTE, J. A., and HOLMAN, C. B., *EEG clin. Neurophysiol.*, vol. 8 (1956), p. 263.

32. SPIEGEL, E. A., MILLER, H. R., and OPPENHEIMER, M. J., *J. Neurophysiol.*, vol. 3 (1940), p. 538.

33. WARD, J. W., and LEQUIRE, V., *Anat. Rec.*, vol. 106 (1950), p. 256.

26 M. B. Arnold

Neural Mediation of the Emotional Components of Action

Excerpt from M. B. Arnold, *Emotion and Personality*, vol. 2,
Columbia University Press, 1960, pp. 82–102, 169–200.

[. . .]

An object or a situation is perceived, appraised, and liked or disliked; and . . . this liking or disliking arouses a tendency to approach or withdraw, to deal with this thing in some particular way. Hence, we have defined emotion as the felt tendency toward something appraised as good (and liked) or away from something appraised as bad (and disliked). According to our conception, the limbic system mediates liking or disliking, while the hippocampus seems to initiate the recall of memories, and also the impulse to a particular action. The relay from the hippocampus seems to touch off the whole action pattern of a given emotion, everything that goes into making it fear or anger or love. This would imply that the various action patterns have to be organized and synchronized before they can be relayed to the motor cortex and so lead to actual movement.

We hope to show that these action patterns are organized in the cerebellum and relayed to the frontal lobe (see Figure 1). While the appraisal for action, as we have described it, implies that a specific action is already decided on when relays start from the hippocampus, the overall pattern of body and limb movements, of head, eye, or hand movements, complete with endocrine changes and autonomic adjustments, cannot be coordinated in that structure. And it is only when the urge to action is felt all over, when the child strains toward the mother with its body as well as with eyes and arms, that we can say emotion is actually *experienced* as an *action tendency*. Even when the emotion is not strong enough to lead to immediate movement or action, whenever it is felt at all, it is felt in this way: as an urge to a specific kind of action which propels whatever limbs or muscles are necessary toward the thing wanted or away from the thing feared.

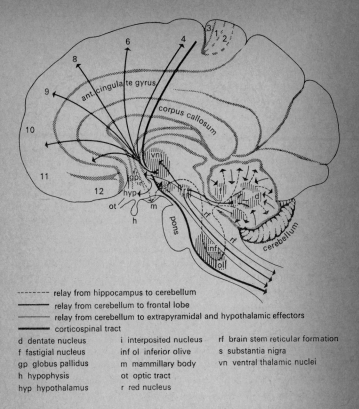

relay from hippocampus to cerebellum
relay from cerebellum to frontal lobe
relay from cerebellum to extrapyramidal and hypothalamic effectors
corticospinal tract

d dentate nucleus	i interposited nucleus	rf brain stem reticular formation
f fastigial nucleus	inf ol inferior olive	s substantia nigra
gp globus pallidus	m mammillary body	vn ventral thalamic nuclei
h hypophysis	ot optic tract	
hyp hypothalamus	r red nucleus	

Figure 1 The action circuit. When an action is intended, relays go from hippocampus to mammillary body, connecting with brain stem and cerebellum. From the cerebellar roof nuclei, the organized action pattern is relayed (*a*) via ventral thalamic nuclei to the frontal lobe, connecting with corticobulbar and corticospinal tracts, (*b*) via globus pallidus to extrapyramidal pathways, (*c*) via globus pallidus to hypothalamic neurosecretory nuclei. Both projections from the cerebellum send descending tracts directly to the spinal cord

The experiencing of emotion as a tendency to a particular action seems to be mediated by the structure which receives the fully organized and patterned relay; and that, we think, is the premotor area in the frontal lobe. Its connexion with the motor area ensures that the felt urge to action will lead to overt movement as soon as it is appraised as suitable or, when the emotion is sudden and intense, even before it is so appraised. We propose to show that the frontal lobe (with the sole exception of the olfactory bulbs and olfactory association area on the orbital surface) serves motor functions in the widest sense of the term. By motor functions we mean not only the actual innervation of motor cells, but also the felt impulse to action, including the impulse to look or listen or attend to something. The prefrontal area, which, we have argued, serves the registration of motor impulses, and the limbic motor area, which serves the appraisal of movement and motor impulses, can also be counted as serving motor functions.[1]

We would suggest that the cerebellum serves to amplify and organize the neural impulses received from the hippocampus and to coordinate them into a pattern for specific action. In this way, a pattern of movement is set which includes varied and often complicated motions, autonomic changes, and the facial and postural expressions that go with a given emotion. The structure of the cerebellum is admirably fitted for this task: it consists of numerous folia of cortex folded over the medullary white fibers, almost like the leaves of a book. The large majority of all incoming neural impulses go to the cerebellar cortex which has the same structure throughout all its parts (and such homogeneous structure is another argument for the suggested uniform motor function). All impulses leaving the cerebellum start from the roof nuclei (masses of gray cells in the upper part of the white matter) and proceed via the superior cerebellar peduncle (or brachium conjunctivum) and smaller accessory tracts to brain stem and thalamus. A descending limb turns downward at the level of the red nucleus and distributes to the reticular formation in midbrain and medulla oblongata (see Figure 1).

In the cerebellar cortex, there are sheets of large Purkinje cells which send out many branches to neighboring cells. Thus a neural

1. It is perhaps necessary to mention here that this hypothesis of frontal lobe function is not the result of unsupported speculation but was chosen after exhaustive study of relevant research as the only one that will fit experimental evidence and agree with clinical findings. The hypothesis has to be stated at this point to make it possible for the reader to follow the thread of the argument. Supportive evidence will be given as the argument develops.

impulse can induce the discharge of many neurons at once, so-called 'avalanche conduction'. In this way, impulses from the hippocampus-fornix system can be amplified and distributed to every cerebellar area, controlling the muscles in every limb that are necessary for a given movement. When the cerebellum is removed in animals, uncoordinated (ataxic) movement is still possible, but it is awkward and extremely effortful. [. . .]

Cerebellum and emotional patterns. – An emotional pattern always includes a motor pattern activated in so-called 'emotional expression'. Emotions are reflected in face and posture even if they do not lead to action. When more intense, they urge to specific movements: in anger a man may strike, when afraid of a blow he may shield his face with his arm. We would expect that the emotional pattern, like every action pattern, would be organized and amplified in the cerebellum.

This is confirmed by Sprague and Chambers (1955), who found that destruction of the dentate nucleus of the cerebellum markedly reduces the response to pain in trunk and limbs of the same side, while destruction of the auditory region on both sides greatly reduces startle. In fact, after destruction of the auditory areas in the cerebellum, the animal no longer paid any attention to noises which he had quickly investigated before. These authors point out that earlier investigators had reported increased sensitivity to touch, pain, auditory, and visual stimuli when the cerebellum was stimulated: the animals would howl, cry, snarl, back away, try to escape, cringe, or wildly lick and bite their own body. More recently, Zanchetti and Zoccolini (1954) produced outbursts of sham rage in placid decorticated cats by stimulating the fastigial cerebellar nuclei through implanted electrodes. These emotional outbursts were abolished by coagulation of rostral midbrain structures, apparently because the lesion had interrupted the pathway from thalamus to midbrain and cerebellum. These reports surely suggest that the emotional response to sensory stimuli (that is, the tendency to emotional action) is exaggerated by stimulation of the cerebellum and reduced or abolished when such stimulation is prevented.

The initiation of action

We have suggested that the choice of action is mediated by the hippocampus which sends neural impulses to the cerebellum, to be amplified and organized into a coordinated pattern. This synchronized impulse pattern is next relayed to the ventral thalamus and frontal lobe. On arrival of impulses in the premotor area, we believe, the urge to action is experienced and can be appraised as suitable or unsuitable when compared with remembered earlier actions. The relay of this impulse pattern from the cerebellum to the frontal lobe will be our next concern. [. . .]

Emotional expression always engages the whole body. When emotion is intense, it throws the whole body into violent action which makes finely coordinated limb or finger movements impossible. When only a mild emotion is felt (e.g. interest or alertness), the activation is similarly diffuse but will now facilitate action rather than disturb it. Since the whole body is active in emotional expression, the emotional tendency to action should be mediated via the relay from the medial cerebellar zone to the midbrain and the globus pallidus. Actually, electrical stimulation of the fastigial cerebellar nucleus in the medial zone has produced an outburst of rage; and patients with shaking palsy (in which the globus pallidus or its connexions with the cerebellum degenerate) have an expressionless, mask-like face and none of the automatic expressive movements of normal people. In contrast, destruction of the dentate nucleus (lateral zone) has reduced the response to painful stimulation in the limbs on the side of the lesion (Sprague and Chambers, 1955) which seems to show that the lateral zone organizes the reaction to pain from local stimulation.

The felt impulse to action. – The relays from all the zones connect with the premotor cortex (area 6), some via hypothalamus and striatum, others via the thalamus. We are suggesting that the premotor area mediates the experience of an urge to action which includes movements of the whole body and also discrete movements of one or both arms and hands.[2] In this area, both types of movement, mediated by different pathways, seem to be combined and experienced as an urge to coordinated action. When area 6

2. If the relays to the premotor cortex mediate an impulse to action, the relays from the premotor to the motor cortex may prime the motor cells for action while the direct relays from the ventral nucleus of the thalamus may activate them. Lashley points out that 'there are many bits of evidence which suggest that a neuron must be excited by several or many axon terminations in order to be fired' (Lashley, 1952, p. 544).

is stimulated electrically, contralateral movements are evoked, very similar to those evoked from the corresponding area of the motor cortex, though they are less discrete. These movements have a longer latency than those evoked by electrical stimulation of the motor cortex, with which the premotor cortex is connected. They seem to be produced via area 4, although the extrapyramidal pathways may have a share in them, providing background adjustments. At any rate, when the motor cortex is destroyed and the premotor cortex is then stimulated, there is a slow movement of the whole body while head and eyes are turned to the opposite side, similar to the slow movement evoked by stimulation of the medial cerebellar zone. Destruction of the pyramids does not interfere with these movements, but undercutting of area 6 abolishes them (Fulton, 1951b).

Stimulation of the lower portion of area 6 on the level of the motor representation of mouth, lips, tongue, and glottis, has evoked chewing, swallowing, smacking of lips, and grunting. Once started, these movements, like the slow body movements evoked from more dorsal points, may persist for some time. When area 6 is isolated from the motor cortex by a cut, this response persists; hence these movements also seem to be carried out via the same extrapyramidal pathway.

From area 8 (the so-called 'frontal eye field', which has a cortical structure almost identical with the premotor area) electrical stimulation produces movement of both eyes in the same direction, either left or right, up or down. This seems to indicate that eye movements also may be part of the total body movement, in which case they are mediated over an extrapyramidal route; but there may also be a deliberate looking, mediated via the motor cortex and the corticobulbar fibers. According to our conception, the relay from the cerebellum would prime the motor nuclei of the eye and other cranial motor nerves for action, while the two effector pathways, the cortico-bulbar tract and the extrapyramidal fibers from area 6 and globus pallidus, would activate them.

Psychologically speaking, excitation of the premotor area together with area 8 would mean that an impulse is felt to reach for something or to look at it or to make some other movement. When these areas are damaged, we would expect that man or animal could no longer feel an impulse to move the affected limb. Several reports show that this is actually the case. After one 'frontal eye field' was removed in a monkey, the animal showed what was called a 'visual agnosia' in one half of both visual fields. When a banana was brought into the affected half of the visual field, the monkey seemed to see the banana but made no move to reach for it, though he avidly took and ate it as soon as it was brought into the normal half of his visual field (Fulton, 1951a). Another monkey, whose left frontal eye field was destroyed, did not take a banana he saw on the right side but took a peanut instead which was held out to him on the left side. (Monkeys always prefer bananas to peanuts, as did this monkey before the operation.) However, banana and peanut had to be shown at the same time, one on each side of the animal, before this disability could be observed (Pribram, 1955). In every case, the difficulty was temporary, probably because area 6 was preserved. We believe that this was not a visual agnosia but rather a lack of any impulse to move on the right side. This seems confirmed by another report (Stenvers, 1953). A patient with a tumor in the right frontal lobe which destroyed the motor cortex (hence produced a paralysis in his left arm) and also destroyed area 8 could not take an object shown within his left visual field though his right arm was not paralyzed. When walking in the woods, he was unable to keep from walking into trees on his left side, even though he saw the trees clearly. Here as in the case of Pribram's monkey, no impulse to move either toward or away from anything on the left side was felt, and thus obstacles on that side could not be avoided.

Appraisal of the action impulse. – Unless an impulse to action is evaluated as appropriate in some sense and is liked, it would have as little chance of gaining attention and leading to action as a sensation that leaves us completely indifferent. If our earlier notion of a system that mediates the appraisal of sensations and action impulses is correct, we would expect the action circuit to connect with this system in its journey from hippocampus to motor cortex. More than that, we would expect that it is the fully organized pattern of action impulses that is appraised as good. Consequently, the connexion with the system mediating appraisal (what we call the 'estimative system') should be provided after the relays from the hippocampus have been organized in the cerebellum.

This actually seems to be the case. Cohen and associates (1958) have shown that the projection from the interposited and dentate nuclei of the cerebellum to the ventral thalamus (connecting with the frontal lobe) also goes to the centrum medianum, one of the intralaminar nuclei; and the projection from the fastigial cerebellar nuclei is relayed not only to the ventral thalamic nuclei connecting with the frontal lobe, but also to the midline and intralaminar nuclei, which are part of the estimative system. The former pathway crosses over to the opposite side and makes discrete movements of arm, hand, or leg possible. The latter projection goes to both sides, mediating activity of the whole body. We have suggested that this projection connects with the extrapyramidal motor pathway which also serves emotional expression and action.

Apparently the primitive liking or interest in any movement whatever is mediated by the thalamic nuclei of the estimative system, which is responsible for the attractiveness of desire, just as it is responsible for the pleasantness of sensations. But to estimate whether this particular desire, the impulse to this particular action, is suitable or appropriate in the light of memories of similar actions, seems to require the cortical region of the estimative system, the anterior cingulate gyrus. This area connects with the hippocampus and so allows the recall of relevant visual, auditory, and other sensory memories necessary for correct evaluation.

Thus the estimative system seems to mediate a distinct quality of experience. It seems organized analogously to the sensory and motor systems in that the experience it mediates (liking and disliking) is consciously felt as soon as impulses reach the thalamus. But a correct appraisal on the basis of memory is possible only when impulses in this system reach the cortical receiving stations, the limbic areas. Unlike the sensory and motor systems, the estimative system does not provide accurate localization. By virtue of its connexions with the sensory system we are able to appraise a particular object or experience as beneficial or harmful, so that we like or dislike it. Its connexions with the somesthetic system in particular make it possible to realize that a given part of our body is giving us pleasure or pain, but this localization is not always precise. Electrical stimulation of the anterior cingulate gyrus seems to induce an appraisal that a movement of trunk or legs is suitable or unsuitable (by virtue of the connexions from the motor areas for trunk and legs); stimulation of the posterior cingulate gyrus, an appraisal that sensations from these bodily regions are pleasant or unpleasant (by virtue of the connexions from the sensory regions for trunk and legs). The movements actually made, intended to continue or change the appraised action and to prolong or avoid the appraised sensations, will include the parts of the body that are involved in action or sensation but may not necessarily remain the same whenever the same points in the limbic cortex are stimulated. [. . .]

Autonomic accompaniment. – The involuntary muscles also have their share in the general mobilization for action. The active skeletal muscles must be provided with additional oxygen by increased blood flow at a time when the inactive inner organs need less oxygen. Hence, there will be a vasodilatation in skeletal muscles and a constriction in smooth muscles. When strong emotion urges to action, the autonomic changes are even more pronounced. There may be tremor, flushing or pallor, increased or decreased blood pressure, depending on the emotion and the action pattern to which it urges. There will also be endocrine activation, reinforcing and completing the emotional pattern. We will discuss these endocrine changes in connexion with the various different emotional action patterns.

It would seem likely that the circuit which mediates the impulse to action will also mediate the autonomic and endocrine changes that go with it. Certainly, blood pressure and respiratory changes have been obtained from the limbic areas which, according to our scheme, constitute the first links in the circuit: Wall and Davis (1951) have obtained blood pressure changes on stimulating the anterior cingulate gyrus, the insula, and also the sensorimotor and orbital cortex in anesthetized monkeys. In waking animals, autonomic changes have been observed together with emotion on stimulating the limbic system and the hippocampus (Kaada, 1951). Further along our proposed action circuit, in the brain stem reticular formation, the hypothalamus, and midbrain, electrical stimulation has also evoked blood pressure changes and other autonomic responses at widely scattered points. According to Rioch:

The diffuse scattering of the descending pathways . . . is rather striking. It suggests that there are not separate, single vasopressor, vasodepressor, pupillary, pilomotor, sweat, etc., centers in the hypothalamus, but instead that the type of localization in the hypothalamus, subthalamus and midbrain is of complex patterns of behavior, e.g. . . . rage, fear and fighting, female oestral behavior, etc. Evidence from localized electrical stimulation in the mesencephalon and remaining diencephalon of decorticate cats support such a conclusion (1940, p. 284).

If autonomic changes are mediated by neural relays that are incorporated into the various action patterns, it would seem likely that these relays run via both pyramidal and extrapyramidal routes. Various research findings admit such an interpretation.

For instance, it has been shown that stimulation of the motor cortex induces a psychogalvanic response (PGR) which is abolished by section of the cerebral peduncles (Wang and Lu, 1930), but not by destruction of the hypothalamus. This means that the motor cortex may receive relays from the hypothalamus initiating the PGR, rather than that the hypothalamus receives relays from the motor cortex and relays them to spinal centers. And Landau (1953) found that stimulation of the medullary pyramidal tract produced sweating, changes in blood pressure and pulse rate, contraction of pupils, nictitating membrane and bladder, and also piloerection. Hence it seems that the motor cortex and pyramidal tract relay impulses to autonomic motor nerves just as they do to somatic motor nerves. [. . .]

Not only the PGR but other autonomic changes also seem to be mediated via cortical areas, and probably are relayed over both pyramidal and extrapyramidal pathways. For instance, gastric peristaltic movements occur on stimulation of area 8 (Davey *et al.*, 1949) and inhibition of peristalsis on stimulation of area 6 (in recently fed monkeys; Sheehan, 1934). We would suggest that these movements occur when food is perceived, focused on, and wanted. Salivation occurs under the same circumstances and can also be induced by stimulation of area 8. An inhibition of peristalsis ordinarily occurs when there is a strong impulse to action, which demands muscular activity and so a reorganization of the bodily economy. The impulse to action is duplicated by stimulation of area 6.

Stimulation of the orbital surface of the brain induces respiratory arrest and changes in stomach motility (Babkin and Speakman, 1950; Kaada *et al.*, 1949) which seem to be the autonomic changes that go with eating. These changes also occur when something is smelled, appraised as good to eat, and is about to be eaten. Stimulation of the orbital cortex, the olfactory association area, could produce these changes.

Vasodilatation and constriction. – From a great deal of evidence in this area it is possible to infer that dilatation or constriction of blood vessels is brought about when a pathway is excited which runs from the midbrain via the hypothalamus to the frontal lobe. It is generally agreed that both dilatation and constriction of blood vessels is produced via sympathetic fibers. When these fibers are excited, the blood vessels constrict, the more intensely, the stronger the excitation. When these fibers are not excited, the blood vessels relax. But the blood vessels of skeletal muscles seem to be innervated by special sympathetic vasodilator fibers that are cholinergic in function and actively dilate the vessels; the diameter of such dilated vessels is much greater than mere relaxation could accomplish. These sympathetic vasodilator fibers are excited whenever striped muscles are innervated, that is, whenever there is any movement (Lindgren and Uvnäs, 1955; Folkow, 1955).

Eliasson and his co-workers have found that there are two regions in the medulla oblongata which induce such dilatation of blood vessels. The area in the ventrolateral part of the medulla induces active (bilateral) dilatation of blood vessels in the muscles,[3] and is connected with the supraoptic region in the hypothalamus and with the motor cortex (Lindgren and Uvnäs, 1955; Eliasson *et al.*, 1952, 1954). A cut several millimeters deep behind the optic chiasm which extended several millimeters beyond the midline on both sides did not eliminate these changes when the supraoptic area was stimulated. This seems to indicate that the pathway relays in the direction from the midbrain to the hypothalamus and motor cortex rather than in the reverse direction as the authors assume; for it was interrupted behind the point of stimulation, yet the lesion did not abolish the response. It seems likely

3. But *contraction* of vessels in skin and internal organs, and hence a *rise* in blood pressure.

that vasodilator impulses together with motor impulses are relayed in the action circuit from the hippocampus to the cerebellum, hypothalamus, and frontal lobe, and that they finally connect with the motor cortex and pyramidal tract (cf. McQueen et al., 1954). This is confirmed by Wall and Davis (1951) who report that vascular responses to stimulation of motor and sensory cortex are unchanged after destruction of the hypothalamus but disappear when the pyramids are sectioned. [. . .]

When the uncus, temporal cortex, and amygdala were removed on one side in animals, stimulation of the cingulate gyrus on the opposite side reduced the blood pressure changes by 90 per cent; stimulation of the cingulate gyrus of the same side reduced them by 10 per cent. Hence Wall and Davis suggested that the pathway mediating these changes runs from the cingulate gyrus via the anterior temporal cortex to the sympathetic effectors. We would assume that the route is rather from the cingulate gyrus via the cingulum to the hippocampus, brain stem, and frontal lobe; when activated it arouses an emotional action tendency (startle or fear). When the uncus, temporal cortex, and amygdala are removed, danger can no longer be imagined and will not induce fear. Even after removal of the amygdala, stimulation of the cingulate gyrus, which – according to our scheme – mediates the appraisal of action, may induce the animal to stop moving or to change his action, but now the new activity can no longer be guided by imagination, and so emotion will be mild and action feeble. Removing the anterior temporal lobe with the amygdala seems to exclude imagination and the action impulses and autonomic changes induced by imagination.

Of course, autonomic reflexes can occur independently of emotion, hence independently of the action circuit we have described. The blood pressure and respiratory mechanisms that function reflexly apparently need only an intact connexion between afferent and efferent fibres in the medulla oblongata. But when these functions are influenced by emotion and action, this influence seems to be exerted via the action circuit. The pyramidal connexion seems to mediate the autonomic changes necessary for discrete movements while the extrapyramidal connexion seems to mediate the autonomic changes of the body as a whole, as required for emotional expression and action. [. . .]

Patterns of action

There are various patterns of action: there are actions rooted in a hormonal change that leads to seeking a particular kind of object appraised as good, thus arousing instinctual desire and culminating in instinctual satisfaction. Next, there are *emotional action patterns* which take their origin in the appraisal of something perceived or imagined as beneficial or harmful, arousing various emotions and leading to appropriate actions. Among them, we have most information on fear and anger, and shall confine our discussion to these. There are also action patterns that are initiated on the basis of a *feeling* rather than an emotion, of a reaction to something appraised as beneficial or harmful *for our functioning*. Since some experiences felt as unpleasant have profound effects on the body, the pattern of action designed to avoid them includes equally strong countermeasures. [. . .]

By mapping out these various action patterns in detail, we hope to lay a foundation for our discussion of the peripheral effects of emotions and feelings. [. . .]

Emotional action patterns. In emotions proper (as distinguished from the desire that accompanies instinctual actions) the physiological changes follow upon perception and appraisal instead of preceding them.

Anger. – Reactions of anger with defensive posture, lashing of tail, extension of claws, hissing, spitting, retraction of ears have been induced in cats by electrical stimulation of the periaqueductal gray matter of the midbrain, the perifornical area of the hypothalamus, and the medial preoptic and ventral septal region. These reactions ended in well-directed attack upon any object near (Hess, 1956; Hess and Akert, 1950). Rage has also been produced by stimulation of the amygdaloid complex, of various limbic areas, and of the hippocampus (Kaada *et al.*, 1953), as well as by stimulation of the fastigial cerebellar nuclei (Zanchetti and Zoccolini, 1954).

Apparently, anger or rage is mediated via the action circuit, which relays impulses from limbic areas to hippocampus, cerebellum, thalamus and hypothalamus, caudate nucleus, and frontal lobe. The tract from the hypothalamus to the caudate nucleus seems to run more dorsally than the fibers mediating relaxation, since damage to the basal aspect of the brain rostral to the optic chiasma, and of the posterior orbital surface, has evoked attacks of rage (Spiegel *et al*., 1940), which implies that the tract mediating rage must be intact, the pathway mediating relaxation, interrupted.

The urge to fight seems to be experienced when relays from the caudate nucleus and ventral thalamus arrive in the premotor cortex, thus mediating the impulse to attack with teeth and claws. The autonomic changes accompanying anger (change in blood pressure, heart rate, etc.) seem to occur when impulses arriving in these cortical regions stimulate sympathetic motor neurons via pyramidal and extrapyramidal connexions. In addition, these connexions stimulate the secretion of noradrenaline from the adrenal medulla. The secretion of noradrenaline is increased during anger.

The secretion of saliva and gastric hydrochloric acid seems to be stimulated at the same time. French and associates (1954) have found that daily electrical stimulation of medial points in the hypothalamus in an area from preoptic to postmammillary region produced gastric ulcers in monkeys within thirty days. These monkeys became irritable and agitated and showed acute malaise. This would suggest that anger and worry may stimulate the action circuit in a similar way to wanting food and eating it, at least in man and monkey.

As soon as a man appraises something as annoying and feels anger (whether he expresses it or not), he immediately imagines what to do to fight effectively, even if all he does is use bad language. Such motor fantasies seem to be mediated via the amygdala and the frontal association areas, and reinforce the anger and attack as well as directing it. Finally, anger and attack are registered as motor engrams and so facilitate future anger and future aggressive action. This promotes not only the gradual development of an emotional attitude (irritability), but the gradual tracing of the marks of anger in face and posture.

Fear. – The impulse to escape is similarly organized into a co-ordinated action pattern. Hess found that running and escape was induced by electrical stimulation of a region about two milli-meters from the midline in the posterior hypothalamus and sub-thalamus, extending backward and upward to the pretectum and tectum, a region close to the pathway for anger (see Gloor, 1954).

In fact, this 'flight' region seems to extend not only backward but forward to the caudate nucleus and the frontal lobe, for Ingram *et al.* (1954) report that stimulation of the caudate and dorsomedial thalamic nuclei have produced searching and apprehension in animals. It seems reasonable to postulate a 'fear' circuit that can be excited by an appraisal that 'this is dangerous, to be escaped', and runs from the hippocampus via the lateral ventral thalamic nucleus to the premotor and motor areas, mediating the urge to flee; and via the anterior and medial ventral nuclei to the prefrontal cortex, serving the registration of the flight pattern. The autonomic changes can be touched off via the hypothalamic branch of the action circuit (which includes the adrenaline-sensitive fibers), running over the caudate nucleus to the premotor and motor areas, but connecting also with extrapryamidal pathways. Since electrical stimulation of 'flight' points in the hypothalamus results in increased adrenaline secretion (Folkow and Von Euler, 1954), relays from the hypothalamus seem also to connect with sympathetic fibers to the adrenal medulla. Finally, fear is accompanied by increased adrenocortical secretion, induced by the discharge of ACTH from the anterior pituitary gland – a discharge apparently initiated by relays from the caudate nucleus via the pallidohypothalamic tract to the hypothalamus and pituitary gland.

Our conception of the circuit activated in fear can explain some puzzling findings. W. W. Roberts (1958) reported that electrical stimulation of the posterior hypothalamus of cats, just rostral to the mammillary bodies, produced a 'flight' reaction with alerting, looking around, searching, and attempted escape. The cats quickly learned to *escape* such stimulation by climbing through an opening to the other side of the apparatus, but they did not learn to climb through the opening to *avoid* stimulation. Cats given an electric shock through the bottom of the cage or stimulated in other parts of the brain (mainly in the somatosensory areas) learned not only to escape such stimulation but to avoid it before it was given.

It would seem to us that a stimulation of 'flight' points in the posterior hypothalamus induced a generalized impulse to run. The cats followed this impulse as long as they felt it. When the current was turned off, they no longer felt the impulse and stopped. They could not learn to avoid the stimulation because they never felt an impulse to escape until the current was turned on. When other points in the brain were stimulated (particularly in the soma-tosensory areas), there was an appraisal for action and emotional arousal. Stimulation appraised as bad, to be escaped, was *feared* and could be avoided.

Stimulation at points along the last link of the action circuit, between brain stem and frontal lobe, will produce a felt impulse to action. This impulse will be appraised (hence, the looking around) but given in to when the stimulation continues and the impulse continues to be felt. Since the animals see nothing that could prevent running, they follow their impulse and run.

The reaction to feelings. Feelings as well as emotions may arouse a desire for action. An intense light is avoided by shutting the eyes; an unpleasant sound may drive a person out of a comfortable room; and too warm or too cold weather arouses a variety of desires, for anything from a long cool drink to a mink coat. Most feelings present no special problem because the sequence from perception to appraisal, feeling and the desire for action is much the same as in emotion. [. . .]

Deliberate action. Now that we have discussed instinctive and emotional action patterns as well as the overt reactions to feelings of pleasantness and unpleasantness, let us look at deliberate actions, actions that seem to be prompted neither by emotions nor by feelings. A child may practice the piano without any desire to do so. Even if he likes to play, there is no immediate pleasure attached to hitting one key after the other. The pleasure comes with the virtuosity of his performance, or the conviction of some-thing well done, or the joy in sound and harmony. In any case, the child is not attracted to each finger movement before he makes it, nor does he follow an instinctive pattern automatically. The decision to practice, to play well and with expression, is a rational decision. The emotion he expresses during his performance is an emotion that flows from an aesthetic appreciation of the music, not from an intuitive judgement that the finger movements are pleasurable.

In deliberate actions (and they comprise the large majority of our daily activities) we must depend on a judgement that is not in-tuitive to arouse an impulse to do something that may or may not be pleasant. Whatever may be the explanation for such rational judgements and deliberate actions, it is such judgements and actions that distinguish man from the brute. [. . .]

There is a difference between animal and human actions. An animal is guided to action by an emotional impulse, based on the estimate of the effect of this thing here and now. The human being judges not only on this basis but also on the basis of abstract and long-range considerations. An animal or a young child can appraise a particular kind of food as good or bad, and select an adequate diet accordingly. Animals and young children may also be tempted by specially tasty morsels to overeat, or to acquire food habits that result in some nutritional deficiency. In both cases, they act according to sense judgement, the sheer intuitive appraisal of what is good or bad here and now. But the older child and the adult can decide to abstain from certain foods (and do so) because they want to avoid undesirable consequences (e.g. overweight) or because their health requires dieting. In such a case, the human being employs reflective judgement in addition to sense judgement. He must initiate an action impulse that is contrary to his immediate preference by considering the rational alternative, finding it good and thus wanting it. [. . .]

Deliberate action is undertaken on the basis of a practical judgement of what is the appropriate thing to do. Since this judgement is the extension of an immediate intuitive appraisal (sense judgement), it could be mediated over the same circuits as sense judgement. The resulting action impulse, like the action impulse resulting from sense judgement, seems to be similarly mediated by neural relays from the hippocampus to the cerebellum and the frontal lobes. Such an impulse to deliberate action is usually called a 'will impulse' to distinguish it from the immediate unwitting attraction to something emotionally appealing. The human being is a unit; he cannot will something without having any desire for it. What is reasonable is also desirable, even though something else may be vastly more attractive and not very reasonable. There are degrees of attraction and degrees of reasonableness of an action; but seldom, if ever, is an action dictated either by emotion or by reason alone. The more attractive a course of action, the more effortless will it be because the emotional impetus, springing uncalled from the intuitive appraisal, carries us into action. The less attractive a course of action, the greater will be the conscious effort necessary to carry it through, not because it is difficult to move the necessary muscles, but because the emotional impulse, the desire that provides the tendency to action, is almost too feeble to organize the movement. Thus we must attend to the action over and over to arouse enough desire to go on with it. According to our analysis, emotion without any reflection will lead to impulsive acting out, to an action that is hardly human, while a will impulse without any desire could not produce action at all.

References

BABKIN, B. P., and SPEAKMAN, T. J. (1950), 'Cortical inhibition of gastric motility', *J. Neurophysiol.*, vol. 13, pp. 55–63.

COHEN, D., CHAMBERS, W. W., and SPRAGUE, J. M. (1958), 'Experimental study of the afferent projections from the cerebellar nuclei to the brainstem of the cat', *J. comp. Neurol.*, vol. 109, pp. 233–59.

DAVEY, L. M., KAADA, B. R., and FULTON, J. F. (1949), 'Effects on gastric secretion of frontal lobe stimulation', *Ass. Res. nerv. ment. Dis. Proc.*, vol. 29, pp. 617–27.

ELIASSON, S., LINDGREN, P., and UVNÄS, B. (1952), 'Representation in the hypothalamus and the motor cortex in the dog of the sympathetic vasodilator outflow to the skeletal muscles', *Acta Physiol. Scand.*, vol. 27, pp. 18–37.

ELIASSON, S., LINDGREN, P., and UVNÄS, B. (1954), 'The hypothalamus, a relay station of the sympathetic vasodilator tract', *Acta Physiol. Scand.*, vol. 31, pp. 290–300.

FOLKOW, B. (1955), 'Nervous control of the blood vessels', *Physiol. Rev.*, vol. 35, pp. 629–63.

FOLKOW, B., and VON EULER, U. S. (1954), 'Selective activation of noradrenaline and adrenaline producing cells in the cat's adrenal gland by hypothalamic stimulation', *Circ. Res.*, vol. 2, pp. 191–5.

FRENCH, J. D., PORTER, R. W., CAVANAUGH, E. B., and LONGMIRE, R. L. (1954), 'Experimental observations on "psychosomatic" mechanisms. I. Gastrointestinal disturbances', *AMA Arch. Neurol. Psychiat.*, vol. 72, pp. 267–81.

FULTON, J. F. (1951a), *Frontal Lobotomy and Affective Behavior*, New York, Norton.

FULTON, J. F. (1951b), *Physiology of the Nervous System*, 3rd edn, New York, Oxford University Press.

GLOOR, P. (1954), 'Autonomic functions of the diencephalon: a summary of the experimental work of Professor W. R. Hess', *AMA Arch. Neurol. Psychiat.*, vol. 71, pp. 773–90.

HESS, W. R. (1956), 'Beziehungen zwischen psychischen Vorgängen und Organisation des Gehirns', *Stud. Gen.*, vol. 9, pp. 467–79.

HESS, W. R., and AKERT, K. (1950), 'Symposion über das Zwischenhirn', *Helv. Physiol. Pharm. Acta*, suppl. 6, p. 80.

Neurophysiological Aspects

INGRAM, W. R., KNOTT, J. R., and PIRSCH, J. G. (1954),
'Electroencephalographic and behavioral effects of stimulation of
certain points in diencephalon and forebrain in unanesthetized cats',
Anat. Rec., vol. 118, pp. 392.

KAADA, B. R. (1951), 'Somato-motor, autonomic, and
electrocorticographic responses to electrical stimulation of
"rhinencephalic" and other forebrain structures in primates, cat and
dog', *Acta Physiol. Scand.*, Suppl. 83, vol. 24, pp. 1–285.

KAADA, B. R., PRIBRAM, K. H., and EPSTEIN, J. A. (1949), 'Respiratory
and vascular responses in monkeys from temporal pole, insula, orbital
surface and cingulate gyrus', *J. Neurophysiol.*, vol. 12, pp. 347–56.

KAADA, B. R., JANSEN, J., Jr, and ANDERSEN, P. (1953), 'Stimulation
of the hippocampus and medial cortical areas in unanesthetized cats',
Neurology, vol. 3, pp. 844–57.

LANDAU, W. M. (1953), 'Autonomic responses mediated via the
corticospinal tract', *J. Neurophysiol.*, vol. 16, pp. 299–311.

LASHLEY, K. S. (1952), 'Functional interpretation of anatomic patterns',
Res. Publ. Ass. Res. nerv. ment. Dis., vol. 30, pp. 529–47.

LINDGREN, P., and UVNÄS, B. (1955), 'Vasoconstrictor inhibition and
vasodilator activation – two functionally separate vasodilator mechanisms
in the skeletal muscles', *Acta Physiol. Scand.*, vol. 33, pp. 108–19.

MCQUEEN, J. D., BROWNE, K. M., and WALKER, A. E. (1954), 'Role
of the brainstem in blood pressure regulation in the dog',
Neurology, vol. 4, pp. 1–13.

PRIBRAM, K. H. (1955), 'Lesions of "frontal eye fields" and delayed
response of baboons', *J. Neurophysiol.*, vol. 18, pp. 105–12.

RIOCH, D. McK. (1940), Discussion in 'The hypothalamus and central
levels of autonomic function', *Res. Publ. Ass. Res. nerv. ment. Dis.*,
vol. 20, pp. 283–4.

ROBERTS, W. W. (1958), 'Rapid escape learning without avoidance
learning motivated by hypothalamic stimulation in cats', *J. comp.
physiol. Psychol.*, vol. 51, pp. 391–9.

SHEEHAN, D. (1934), 'The effect of cortical stimulation on gastric
movements in the monkey', *J. Physiol.*, vol. 83, pp. 177–84.

SPIEGEL, E. A., MILLER, H. R., and OPPENHEIMER, M. J. (1940),
'Forebrain and rage reactions', *J. Neurophysiol.*, vol. 3, pp. 538–48.

SPRAGUE, J. M., and CHAMBERS, W. W. (1955), 'Evidence for sensory
function of the cerebellum in the cat', *Anat. Rec.*, vol. 121, pp. 369–70.

STENVERS, H. W. (1953), 'Clinical features of pyramidal and
extrapyramidal disorders', *Folia Psychiat.*, vol. 56, p. 943.

WALL, P. D., and DAVIS, G. D. (1951), 'Three cerebral cortical systems
affecting autonomic functions', *J. Neurophysiol.*, vol. 14, pp. 507–17.

WANG, G. H., and LU, T. W. (1930), 'Galvanic skin reflex induced in the
cat by stimulation of the motor area of the cerebral cortex',
Chin. J. Physiol., vol. 4, pp. 303–26.

ZANCHETTI, A., and ZOCCOLINI, A. (1954), 'Autonomic and
hypothalamic outbursts elicited by cerebellar stimulation',
J. Neurophysiol., vol. 17, pp. 475–83.

27 M. B. Arnold

Physiological Effects of Emotion

Excerpt from M. B. Arnold, *Emotion and Personality*, vol. 2, Columbia University Press, 1960, pp. 205–28.

[. . .]

The connexion of emotion with various autonomic changes was first systematically investigated by Walter B. Cannon. Like his predecessors in the field of emotion, Darwin and James, Cannon assumed that the physiological changes occurring during emotion will facilitate emotional action. Cannon's investigations were restricted to animals; cats and dogs tied to the animal board or enraged by pinching their tail; or cats confronted by a barking dog. The most impressive aspect of emotional behavior seemed to be the great expenditure of energy during fight or flight. Accordingly, Cannon suggested that emotion serves emergency action.[1] He ascribed the physiological changes he observed to sympathetic excitation and adrenaline secretion, and concluded that the function of the sympathetic nervous system is to prepare the body for emergency action.

The emotional responses . . . may reasonably be regarded as preparatory for struggle. They are adjustments which, so far as possible, put the organism in readiness for meeting the demands which will be made upon it. The secreted adrenin cooperates with sympathetic nerve impulses in calling forth stored glycogen from the liver, thus flooding the blood with sugar for the use of laboring muscles; it helps in distributing the blood in abundance to the heart, the brain, and the limbs (i.e. to the parts essential for intense physical effort) while taking it away from the inhibited organs in the abdomen; it quickly abolishes the effects of muscular fatigue so that the organism which can muster adrenin in the blood can restore to its tired muscles the same readiness to act which they had when fresh; and it renders the blood more rapidly coagulable. . . . In short, all these changes are directly serviceable in rendering the organism more effective in the violent display of energy which fear or rage may involve (1932, p. 228).

1. Cannon's 'emergency theory of emotion'.

Thus Cannon claims that emotion (as exemplified by fear and rage) energizes the organism. Sympathetic excitation and the secretion of adrenaline in emotion produce physiological effects which account for the increase in energy.

Doubts and difficulties. – It is true that fear urges to precipitate flight, rage to violent attack, and thus both emotions could be said to '*energize*' the organism. But this impulse to action is mediated over central pathways and is not necessarily the result of the simultaneous excitation of peripheral sympathetic pathways or the accompanying adrenaline secretion.

When immediate escape from danger is not possible, when danger continues and fear with it, there is a persistent desire to escape but no facilitation of any action that can be undertaken short of flight. On the contrary, there is a peculiar difficulty of acting which may become a downright inability to move or speak. In stage fright, for instance, thinking as well as speaking become more and more effortful, movements become forced, stiff, and ungainly. The many symptoms of sympathetic excitation seem to aggravate the situation: hands and feet are cold and trembling, the heart is racing, the tongue seems to stick to the roof of the mouth, the knees are so weak that it is difficult to stand or walk. The same incapacity to move or think is exemplified by pilot trainees who 'freeze to the controls' on their first pilot flight.

This difficulty may occur even when there is a chance to escape, and may result in complete paralysis of action, for instance, in the moment just before an automobile collision when quick action might still avert it. Psychologically speaking, in these cases fear has turned into despair: the appraisal that this must be escaped has turned into the appraisal that this is so overwhelming that it cannot be escaped. It is the feeling of powerlessness and incompetence which gives ground for such a change of appraisal, and this feeling of powerlessness seems to come with fear.

Animal experiments show the same reduction of activity during persistent fear. Hall (1941), for instance, found rats less active when exposed to the 'open field', a large, open, well-lighted enclosure. These rats showed many signs of fear. They refused to touch the offered food and kept close to the walls. More recently, Tseng (1942) has confirmed this marked reduction of activity in fear situations, and Richter (1951) reported that wild rats reacted to a series of poisoning attempts either by ceasing to eat and starving to death, or by a marked and unusual immobility. The rats either sat, stood, or hung from the wire mesh of the cage, always in the same position, never moving or running around. Richter thought that this immobility was the result of 'an ever-present fear of being poisoned'. Mahl (1949) also found a reduction of activity in dogs when he gave them electric shocks daily for some time. They gradually became less active, slept less, and began to posture in odd ways. Arnold (1944) found this immobility in rats exposed to intense sound; it could be duplicated by the injection of adrenaline in dosages comparable to the secretion during fear.

Reduction of activity occurs not only in acute fear but also in chronic fear, as shown by Richter's rats and Mahl's dogs. It can apparently be transmitted from generation to generation. Hall's specially bred 'emotional' strain of rats (which showed symptoms of fear rather than of other emotions) were both less active and less aggressive than normal rats. Neurocirculatory asthenia, which apparently is indistinguishable from anxiety neurosis, seems to have a high familial incidence and reduces the patient's activity (Cohen and White, 1951). Such patients have complained that they could not do much work or take normal physical exercise. These facts seem to indicate that fear does not always aid action but may hinder it if the danger continues and the fear is extreme or becomes chronic.

Cannon explained the harmful effect of chronic anxiety by pointing to the difference between a temporary emergency in which all the resources of the organism are thrown into the breach and long drawn-out emergency states that eventually exhaust these resources. This analogy implies that resources are withdrawn from the economy of the organism for defense in the same way as consumption is curtailed during war. However, in the economy of a country, the raw material needed for weapons really is withdrawn from home consumption; but in the organism, the accumulated 'war matériel' can only be muscular energy or, more precisely, the assimilated food which provides it. As long as that is available, it can be used for any kind of muscular activity, peaceful or defensive. If it is true, as Cannon says, that sympathetic excitation and adrenaline secretion provide muscles with available glycogen, help in the utilization of blood sugar, and abolish the effects of muscular fatigue, this action should aid in muscular activity of every kind, not merely when muscles are used for flight. Either the sympathetic system and adrenaline facilitate the assimilation of energy-giving materials, as Cannon maintains (and then it is hard to explain why they should not do so continually); or they dissipate these materials (and then they will do so even in an emergency and cannot be said to 'energize' the organism).

To decide between these two alternatives, we propose to examine the evidence that led Cannon to his concept of emergency action. But before we do so, we must distinguish between the central effects of fear and its peripheral effects.

Fear and emergency action

In discussing the various action patterns observed in emotion, we have suggested that fear is an action tendency mediated by a special pathway within the general action circuit. When this pathway is activated, the experience and expression of fear with the urge to escape seem to occur. The electrical stimulation of this pathway induces violent action, which has led Hess (1949), for instance, to suggest that this region is an 'ergotropic zone'. Since adrenaline and noradrenaline seem to be synaptic transmitters in the hypothalamic link of the action circuit (see Vogt, 1954), an injection of either of these drugs should stimulate the action circuit.

We have attempted to show that this circuit sends relays to the motor cortex, which would suggest that its stimulation by adrenaline should facilitate muscular contractions. Several investigators have reported that large doses of adrenaline and noradrenaline lower the convulsion threshold and prolong convulsions (Hall, 1938; Keith and Stavraky, 1935; Minz and Domino, 1953). On the other hand, small doses of adrenaline seem to depress activity and suppress convulsions (Gellhorn *et al.*, 1939; Arnold, 1944). It seems likely that large doses stimulate the central circuits before the peripheral effects of adrenaline have time to develop, while small doses are not sufficient for central stimulation. This inference is supported by Minz and Domino's finding that these hormones prolong convulsions even when adrenergic blocking agents have reversed the rise of blood pressure produced by adrenaline and reduced the rise of pressure caused by noradrenaline. Here the peripheral effects of adrenaline were prevented without changing its central effects.

Fear or adrenaline injection excites a pattern of relays in the action circuit which includes not only impulses to somatic motor nerves but also impulses to fibers in the pyramidal and extra-pyramidal pathways that connect with vasomotor and other sympathetic nerves. This excitation of the sympathetic nervous system is intensified by the simultaneous secretion of adrenaline from the adrenal medulla (Cannon, 1915, 1932). It is this peripheral effect of fear or adrenaline which Cannon believed responsible for the energizing action of fear. Of necessity, this effect develops slowly and lasts for some time; it should increase and become cumulative if fear becomes chronic.

Rogoff and Stewart (1926) challenged Cannon's method of adrenaline determination in excited animals and claimed that the physiological changes during fear are the result of sympathetic excitation rather than adrenaline secretion. Since adrenaline is secreted when the sympathetic splanchnic nerves are excited, and later studies have invariably confirmed that the adrenaline content of the blood is increased during fear (Darrow and Gellhorn, 1939; Milhorat and Diethelm, 1947; and others), it can be taken for granted that fear induces both sympathetic excitation and adrenaline secretion, though it is possible that many of the effects Cannon ascribed to adrenaline are produced by the stimulation of sympathetic nerves (Celander, 1954). We now propose to show that the physiological effect of sympathetic stimulation and adrenaline secretion is such that it can account for the depression of activity found in chronic fear.

Physiological effects of adrenaline. – Cannon's conclusion that adrenaline (and therefore fear) prepares the organism for fight or flight was based, first of all, on the earlier observation by many clinicians that the adrenal glands are necessary for muscular activity. If they are removed, there is a gradually increasing muscular weakness which finally ends in prostration and death. Cannon also referred to Oliver and Schäfer's results (1895) which showed that an extract from crushed adrenal glands in-creased and prolonged the contraction of normal resting skeletal muscle. Finally, Cannon himself found that adrenaline injection or perfusion restored the size of muscular contractions in fatigued nerve-muscle preparations. From these observations Cannon concluded that adrenaline secretion in the intact organism is necessary for proper muscular functioning, especially during emergencies (cf. Cannon, 1915).

When Cannon first proposed his theory, adrenaline was believed to be the only secretion produced by the adrenal glands. Since then, a great deal of research has established that the adrenal cortex also secretes hormones. In fact, it is the adrenal cortical hormones or some of their fractions that are essential for life and maintain muscular strength. If adrenal cortical extract is supplied, animals survive normally after removal of the adrenals though adrenaline secretion is now impossible.

Not suspecting that the adrenal cortex also secretes hormones, Cannon and his co-workers frequently used bilaterally adrenalectomized animals together with animals which had one adrenal removed and the other denervated. They did not always list the data for these animals separately, and so the deficits noticed after exclusion of the adrenal cortex may have been ascribed to the lack of adrenaline secretion. After the discovery of adrenal cortical hormones, research was almost exclusively concerned with these hormones without attempting to re-evaluate conclusions from work in which adrenal medulla and adrenal cortex had been equated.

In a recent review, Ramey and Goldstein (1957) pointed out that the practice of Cannon and his co-workers to 'treat as indistinguishable bilateral adrenalectomy and unilateral adrenalectomy must indicate that the additional procedure of extensive sympathectomy is protective in nature'. But on the whole, they accepted Cannon's conclusions concerning the effect of adrenaline secretion, without accounting for the contradiction. When the effect of adrenocortical secretion is taken into account, some of Cannon's conclusions may have to be modified. For instance, the ablation of one adrenal may impair muscular power temporarily until the adrenal cortex of the remaining gland enlarges and compensates for the loss. It makes a difference whether the temporary loss is ascribed to a deficit in adrenaline secretion or a reduction in the output of adrenal cortical hormones. For this reason, it seems advisable to examine the evidence in detail, at least where it is relevant for our purpose.

Adrenaline and muscular contractions. – In their original articles, Oliver and Schäfer reported that they used extracts from the whole gland for their experiments, though in some of them they used extracts from the adrenal cortex and the medulla separately. When they injected the equivalent of 1 to 2 grains of fresh gland into a frog, they found a gradual arrest of all movement. When the muscle was electrically stimulated, it contracted; but the relaxation period after each contraction was greatly delayed. A larger dose had the same effect in a rabbit. These authors suggested that the adrenal gland (or at least the medulla) must have a secretory function (not an excretory function, as had been thought up to then), and that it was probably important for 'maintaining the tonicity of the muscular tissues in general and especially of the heart and the arteries' (1895, p. xiii).

But delayed relaxation after contraction is not synonymous with improved muscular performance. The increase in tonicity may contribute to cumulative general muscular *tension*, both in smooth and striped muscles, but is not evidence that adrenaline or medullary extract improves phasic contraction. This 'increase in tonicity' in the frog and rabbit was compatible with near-abolition of all reflexes and apparent paralysis. Such delayed relaxation might account for the catatonic immobility of Richter's rats and Mahl's dogs during chronic fear. We know that general muscular tension is higher in anxiety neurotics (Jacobson, 1934) though their work capacity is reduced.

Cannon's own work showed that the injection of adrenaline, either before or during work, does not increase work capacity, and adrenaline perfusion does not increase the contraction of rested skeletal muscle. Conversely, the bilateral removal of the adrenal medulla or of the sympathetic nervous system does not reduce work capacity in animals (Campos *et al.*, 1928; Cannon, 1932; Harris and Ingle, 1940). In fact, Harris and Ingle found that demedullated rats showed a slight but significant increase in performance. Campos and co-workers (1928) found that adrenal denervation on one side and removal of the other adrenal eventually produced better performance and longer endurance. According to their work curves (pp. 686, 688), exhaustion sets in earlier and work decreases after adrenaline injection – which corresponds to Harris and Ingle's results. Moreover, Brouha *et al.* (1936) found that performance was reduced for about six weeks after removal of one adrenal and demedullation of the other. This is about the time required for the growth of additional adrenocortical tissue to compensate for the loss of one adrenal.

In a later investigation, Ingle and Nezamis (1949) found that the work performance during faradic stimulation of the hind legs of adrenalectomized rats was proportional to the amount of adrenal cortical extract given intravenously. Injection of glucose markedly improved performance but adrenaline in small doses had no effect. In larger doses it suppressed work. Apparently, the injection of adrenaline does not prevent fatigue or increase performance in the intact animal; in fact, large doses decrease performance and increase fatigue. Conversely, the absence of adrenaline secretion or sympathetic stimulation does not impair muscular work; in fact, it may actually enhance it.

There is direct evidence also that adrenaline reduces muscular contractions. Gellhorn, Darrow, and Yesinick (1939) found that adrenaline in small doses diminishes or prevents insulin convulsions, even though the blood sugar remains low; it also prevents or reduces metrazol convulsions. Darrow and Gellhorn (1939) reported that adrenaline in physiological concentration reduces somatic hyperexcitability; it prevents sound-produced seizures in susceptible rats and also in rats made susceptible by strychnine injections (Arnold, 1945). Qualitatively, it was observed that adrenaline injection reduces muscular tension and results in flaccidity and sometimes in prostration, even when given in physiological amounts. It also abolishes or prevents strychnine convulsions (Arnold, 1942). Gellhorn (1953) suggested that such reduction of muscular contractions is a peripheral effect while adrenaline facilitation is a central effect. And Mohme-Lundholm (1953) has shown that this relaxing effect of adrenaline occurs because glycogen is broken down into lactic acid and is unavailable for muscular contractions. Drugs inhibiting such breakdown prevented not only the formation of lactic acid after adrenaline injection, but also the usual adrenaline inhibition. This breakdown of glycogen to lactic acid requires some time before it will inhibit muscular contractions; massive doses of adrenaline seem to exert their stimulating effect on central circuits before the peripheral effects have developed sufficiently to inhibit muscular activity.

We would suggest that central stimulation in fear produces increased muscular contractions, representing a 'readiness to act' which is expressed as heightened muscular tension. Gradually, the peripheral effects of sympathetic stimulation in fear make it difficult for the muscles to respond with strong phasic contractions; consequently, there will be reduced work capacity yet increased muscular tension (e.g., in anxiety neurotics; see Jacobson, 1934). Excessive sympathetic stimulation (e.g., in terror) seems to make it impossible for the muscles to respond even with tonic contractions; instead, there will be flaccidity and prostration.

There are some findings, however, that have always been considered convincing evidence for an energizing effect of adrenaline: Cannon showed that adrenaline increases muscular contractions in the fatigued nerve-muscle preparation, and Campos and co-workers found that exhausted dogs began to work again on a treadmill if given small doses of adrenaline. It could be objected, of course, that these findings are of purely pharmacological interest. The normal organism could not secrete adrenaline when fatigued because intense exercise completely exhausts the adrenal medulla (Cameron, 1936). Nor could fear and sympathetic excitation occur at this point, because the readiness to react emotionally is severely curtailed in exhaustion. This is illustrated by the feeble response of rats to teasing after a sound-produced seizure, and also by Campos et al.'s report that they could not arouse 'excitement' in exhausted dogs.

Though the renewed capacity to work after adrenaline injection cannot be used to prove that fear or adrenaline energizes the rested organism, the sheer fact requires an explanation. We have suggested that the injection of adrenaline activates the central circuit mediating fear, and will induce increased muscular activity. In complete exhaustion, when the adrenal medulla is depleted, a moderate dose of adrenaline might be expected to activate this circuit without stimulating the sympathetic nervous system sufficiently to depress muscular contractions. If, on the other hand, a large dose is given, enough adrenaline will be present to produce violent excitement and eventually peripheral symptoms. According to Campos and associates, a large dose of adrenaline (from 0·04 milligram per kilogram up) injected into exhausted dogs produced excitement, increased fatigue, and prevented further work.

The recovery of contraction in the fatigued nerve-muscle preparation after adrenaline injection or perfusion can be explained by the fact that adrenaline in weak concentration augments the effect of acetylcholine, and so improves transmission across the myoneural junction. Luco (1939), for instance, reported that small doses of adrenaline produce a fleeting depression of a fatigued muscle stimulated through its nerve, which is followed by a secondary augmentation. Since large doses of adrenaline produced only depression, and this depression was prevented by ergotoxin (which blocks sympathetic effects), the depression seems to be the primary (adrenergic) effect, while the secondary augmentation seems to result from improved cholinergic transmission. Bülbring and Burn (1940) reported similar findings and showed that this secondary augmentation of muscle contractions after adrenaline was accompanied by a fall in blood pressure, indicating that sympathetic stimulation had ceased.

In a careful review, Burn (1945) showed that adrenaline in weak concentration increases the action of acetylcholine, both in the central nervous system and in the ganglia of the sympathetic system. In strong concentration, cholinergic transmission is depressed. In other words, the improved muscular contractions after small doses of adrenaline are the result of a transmission of cholinergic impulses which is activated or potentiated by adrenaline. When too much adrenaline is present, muscular contractions are inhibited. Burn suggested that the paralysing effect of fear may be the result of increased adrenaline secretion which inhibits muscular activity.

Cannon discovered that transmission in sympathetic postganglionic nerves is mediated by two adrenaline-like substances which he called 'Sympathin E' and 'Sympathin I'. The former excites, the latter inhibits. Later research has shown that these two kinds of neurohumors roughly correspond to two different hormones secreted by the adrenal medulla but also found in the brain and in sympathetic ganglia, noradrenaline and adrenaline. Of the two, only adrenaline potentiates acetylcholine action, but both hormones seem to stimulate the action circuit. Adrenaline was secreted by the adrenal medulla when points in the hypothalamus were stimulated which induce the 'flight' pattern; and noradrenaline was secreted on stimulation of an area from which Hess has reported 'rage' reactions (cf. Folkow and Von Euler, 1954).

Now let us turn to the mechanism by which adrenaline or sympathetic nervous system stimulation was thought to help put the body on an emergency footing.

Adrenaline and the circulation. – Cannon held that adrenaline produces vasoconstriction in the viscera and in the blood vessels of the skin, but vasodilatation in skeletal muscles. Thus adrenaline secreted during emotional excitement would drain the blood from the viscera where it is not needed and shift it to the limbs where it is.

The initiation of movement is accompanied by a dilatation of blood vessels in the active muscles which is mediated over sympathetic *cholinergic* nerves. This is a central effect that occurs with any movement, long before the adrenaline secreted during fear could begin to act. In the resting muscle, adrenaline decreases the blood flow (Gellhorn, 1943). With larger dosage, adrenaline can produce vasoconstriction even in active muscles (Luco, 1939). Injection of acetylcholine into the mesenteric artery produces extreme dilation, while the injection of small doses of adrenaline produces an initial dilatation (because it potentiates acetylcholine) and later constriction; but larger doses of adrenaline, or the injection of noradrenaline, results in constriction (Celander, 1954). Thus the primary effect of both adrenaline and noradrenaline seems to be vasoconstriction.

The effect of sympathetic stimulation or adrenaline on blood flow in skeletal muscle is still controversial. But the view that such stimulation increases the blood flow seems to be based on inference from Cannon's theory as much as on actual evidence. For instance, it is held that the reduced blood flow in the hand during fear and pain is the result of vasoconstriction in the skin which masks the dilatation of blood vessels in the muscles (Selye, 1950, p. 504). But adrenaline, noradrenaline, and sympathetic stimulation produce vasoconstriction even in the skinned limb (Celander, 1954), and blood flow in the resting forearm is increased after sympathectomy or blocking of sympathetic nerves. Adrenaline injected into an artery in doses large enough to increase the blood pressure also reduces the blood flow in the forearm (Harpuder et al., 1947).

The rate of blood flow depends primarily on the force with which the heart pumps blood into the arteries. When the arteries are constricted, the blood pressure will rise correspondingly, provided the heart action remains constant. But during sympathetic stimulation, the rise in blood pressure does not necessarily parallel the constriction of blood vessels because the heart muscle probably cannot maintain an unchanged cardiac output (Celander, 1954). In addition, it is known that both adrenaline and noradrenaline impair the capillary walls so that fluid and proteins are lost to the surrounding tissues (Gellhorn, 1943; Ramey and Goldstein, 1957); the peripheral resistance drops and blood flow decreases. This is confirmed by Freeman and co-workers (1941) who found that the continuous intravenous injection of adrenaline (0·0034 to 0·1164 milligrams per kilogram per minute) in dogs resulted in increased blood pressure and decreased rate of blood flow. The mucous membranes gradually became pale until limbs and ears were cold and had a doughy feel, the pulse was thready, the blood flow in the ear veins was very slow, the blood dark, and the dogs eventually died in shock. If this is the result of an infusion not greatly exceeding the adrenaline secreted during fear,[2] we cannot assume that intense and long-continued fear will have an energizing effect. Far from having beneficial effects in surgical shock, sympathetic stimulation or adrenaline infusion can produce shock. Total sympathectomy, on the other hand, *prevents* shock from hemorrhage in dogs (Freeman et al., 1938), as does procaine block of the adrenal nerves in man (Parkins et al., 1941). Neither the sympathetic nervous system nor adrena-

2. In dogs whose sympathetic nervous system has been blocked by complete spinal anesthesia, normal blood pressure can be maintained by a continuous infusion of adrenaline at the rate of 0·45µg/kg/min; consequently, the total amount of adrenaline active in the body has been calculated as 0·71µg/kg (Guyton and Gillespie, 1951). According to Bülbring and Burn (1949), 20 to 80 per cent of the effect of adrenal blood collected during stimulation of the splanchnic (sympathetic) nerves is due to noradrenaline. And stimulation of the splanchnics provokes a discharge of as much as 100µg of adrenaline (Bülbring and associates, 1948); thus an infusion of 3 to 116µg, as in Freeman's experiment, may not be too far above the physiological limit.

line counteracts the effects of hemorrhage, as Cannon assumed, but seems to aggravate them.

Adrenaline and the heart rate. – Cannon also suggested that the increase in heart rate and blood pressure produced by adrenaline materially aids in preparing the organism for emergency action.

Whether increased blood pressure and heart rate is favorable for muscular activity depends on the amount of blood available, its distribution in the body, and the force of the heart beat. If the amount of blood discharged at each beat (the stroke volume) remains constant, a faster beat will increase the output of the heart and improve the blood flow. When the heart rate increases, the stroke volume will also increase if the blood returns to the heart through the veins in sufficient volume and at sufficient speed. But the volume of the venous blood decreases in fear because of seepage through the capillaries. Unlike exercise and physical work, where the active muscles help to speed the return of venous blood, emotion that stops short of action does not improve venous return.

According to Cannon's own findings (1932, p. 152), the excitement of a cat facing a barking dog accelerated the denervated heart from 120 to 160 beats per minute, as long as the adrenals could be stimulated through the sympathetic nervous system. When the connexion was interrupted by denervating the adrenals, emotional excitement only increased the heart rate from 118 to 120 beats per minute. But according to Cannon's graph, the recorded amplitude of the heart beat was doubled after the adrenals were denervated. In this case, the stroke volume apparently did not remain constant during excitement, and the output of the heart was probably reduced.

In man also, an increase in heart rate does not always mean an increase in blood flow. With a heart rate of more than 100 beats per minute, there is a decrease in stroke volume and the heart actually reduces its output. Such a rate is not unusual during fear. Duncan and others (1951) reported, for instance, that patients with anxiety neurosis had a decreased cardiac output during the fear and apprehension connected with their first visit to the clinic. In one case, the heart increased to 128 beats per minute, yet stroke volume and cardiac output decreased appreciably.

Characteristically, the gradual improvement in efficiency during athletic training is accompanied by a *decrease* in the heart rate both at rest and during exercise (Bogard, 1937). According to Bogard, strenuous exercise results in a simultaneous increase of heart rate, stroke volume, and oxygen utilization; but the heart rate of athletes increases much less than that of untrained men and the stroke volume increases far more. Indeed, some athletes show no increase in heart rate during moderate exercise, but a considerable increase in stroke volume which takes care of the increased oxygen requirement (Best and Taylor, 1951). Consequently, work capacity does not depend exclusively or even primarily on the increased heart rate. This is confirmed by the study of Duncan *et al.* which showed that blood pressure and heart rate decreased in patients with anxiety neurosis after successful psychotherapy while their exercise tolerance increased.

Adrenaline and blood sugar. – Cannon further suggested that adrenaline energizes because it provides the muscles with an abundance of fuel by releasing stored glycogen from the liver.

However, adrenaline releases glycogen not only from the liver but from the muscles as well. Major and Mann (1932) have shown that adrenaline infusions decrease the glycogen content of muscles even when the concentration is so low that there is no rise in blood pressure (0·00016 milligram per kilogram per minute). Larger doses cause a more marked decrease in muscle glycogen. Since fear increases the blood pressure markedly, we may assume that the adrenaline secreted during fear will significantly reduce muscle glycogen.

It seems generally accepted today that adrenaline acts on sugar metabolism by breaking down muscle glycogen to lactic acid (glycolysis) and releasing glycogen from the liver (glycogenolysis). It does not contribute to the assimilation of blood glucose by muscle or other tissues; on the contrary, adrenaline seems to inhibit glucose utilization by slowing down its transfer from body fluids to tissue cells (Somogyi, 1951). For the *formation* of glycogen in liver and muscle, the carbohydrate hormones of the adrenal cortex (glucocorticoids) and insulin are necessary, but adrenaline has no part in this action (Verzár, 1939; Britton and Corey, 1940).

From this evidence we are forced to conclude that the increased blood sugar released by adrenaline secretion is not immediately available to the muscles; in fact, the presence of adrenaline seems to prevent glucose utilization. But it may be objected that adrenaline at least helps to convert lactic acid into glycogen indirectly, by increasing the respiratory rate, thus supplying an abundance of necessary oxygen. Let us see whether that is the case.

Adrenaline and oxygen utilization. – When the muscle contracts, glycogen is converted to lactic acid. If enough oxygen is available, the acid is immediately reconverted to glycogen, and there is practically no accumulation of lactic acid in blood or tissues. When oxygen is lacking or its supply inadequate, lactic acid accumulates. Its resynthesis into glycogen is first slowed and then prevented until further muscular contractions become impossible. Since adrenaline increases the respiratory rate, Cannon suggested that this is accompanied by an increased supply of oxygen which helps the laboring muscles by reconverting lactic acid to glucose.

However, adrenaline increases lactic acid concentration even in the resting organism. The increased oxygen consumption after adrenaline injection (20 to 40 per cent, according to Best and Taylor, 1951) is needed for the resynthesis of lactic acid into muscle glycogen. During strenuous exercise, there is more demand for oxygen than can be provided, even when the respiratory rate increases maximally. As work continues, muscle glycogen is synthesized at a slower and slower rate until no more is available for muscular action, and man or animal is exhausted.

In fact, adrenaline alone and strenuous work alone will exhaust muscle glycogen and increased oxygen will be needed to convert lactic acid back to blood glucose and muscle glycogen. If these changes are in the same direction so that either adrenaline alone or exercise alone eventually exhausts muscle glycogen, how can adrenaline (or sympathetic stimulation) provide additional energy reserves? Far from so doing, adrenaline draws upon the same glycogen store that is needed for muscular contraction. Thus it becomes understandable why fear or an adrenaline injection gradually inhibits muscular contractions and sometimes results in complete prostration.

There are some studies that have examined the functioning of the bodily economy during strenuous work. These should either prove or disprove our interpretation.

Muscular efficiency. – Strenuous athletic training for six months has produced several changes in the bodily economy which seem to imply that sympathetic activity has been reduced. Men in training who found a run exhausting at the beginning of training found it well within their capacity at the end; at that time, such a run resulted in considerably lower blood sugar and blood lactate levels than at the beginning (Robinson and Harmon, 1941). Since the oxygen requirements for the run remained the same, the breakdown of glycogen to lactic acid and its resynthesis into glycogen must have been more efficient, probably because adrenaline secretion was reduced. Von Euler (1953) pointed out that running *per se* does not result in increased adrenaline secretion. Such an increase is noted only when exhaustion sets in.

Patients who suffer from anxiety neurosis (variously called effort syndrome, vasomotor neurosis, neurocirculatory asthenia) do not tolerate exercise well. They show early exhaustion, increased lactic acid concentration, and greatly augmented oxygen consumption even during mild exercise. There is no doubt that these are effects of increased sympathetic stimulation with increased adrenaline secretion during chronic anxiety. During fear and tension, normal people have a similarly lowered exercise tolerance with symptoms of sympathetic overactivity (Duncan *et al.*, 1951).

Cohen and White (1951) have summarized a number of studies that throw light on the mechanism by which fear and anxiety impair muscular activity. These studies show that normal people could perform an exhausting treadmill run for twice as long as could patients with acute anxiety. The latter patients in turn showed twice as much endurance as did patients with chronic anxiety states. Apparently, the harmful effects of anxiety become more pronounced as time goes on. This is not surprising if fear or anxiety are cumulative, as we maintain.

Even during moderate exercise, the oxygen uptake of the neurotic patients was lower than that of their normal fellows, despite the fact that their faster breathing supplied them with more air than did the lower respiratory rate of normals. Both lactic acid and blood sugar of neurotics were higher than was found in the normal group even during moderate exercise (treadmill walk). During exhausting exercise (treadmill run), neurotics had a much lower oxygen consumption than normals and their blood lactate was three times higher. This means that the increased sympathetic stimulation in anxiety raises the respiratory rate during exercise but does not increase oxygen consumption. Lactic acid accumulates quickly, and very soon there is no more glycogen for muscular contractions and fatigue sets in.

This long look at the physiology of adrenaline shows that the subjective experience of weakness during acute or chronic fear is supported and explained by objective evidence. Adrenaline and sympathetic stimulation do not improve muscular perform-ance. Rather, they reduce efficiency by increasing lactic acid formation and by interfering with glucose and oxygen utilization. Sudden fear may bring a sudden urge to flee and so provide a powerful spur to action. When this urge leads to successful escape and the danger is past, the effects of sympathetic stimulation quickly subside. But when escape is impossible and fear becomes chronic, the physical and psychological effects of fear soon in-capacitate a man for serious work. Mental work becomes im-possible because attention is centered on the threatening danger. The central effect of fear makes it difficult to remember, imagine, or decide on action. Physical work becomes increasingly laborious because the cumulative effect of sympathetic stimulation seriously reduces muscular efficiency.

Anger and emergency function

According to Cannon's emergency theory, anger as well as fear induces sympathetic excitation and adrenaline secretion. But psychologically speaking, anger is different from fear. It is based on a different appraisal, namely, that something harmful can be overcome, rather than the appraisal that this something is so overwhelming that it is difficult to escape. Also, anger is experi-enced differently, as a tendency to fight, strike, and tear, instead of an urge to cower or escape. There is a sensation of tension and fullness instead of the sensation of weakness and tremor so noticeable in fear. Considering that the appraisal and the psy-chological experience are different, that the proposed action is different, and that the bodily sensations differ as well, there must surely be differences in the pattern of central nervous excitation and therefore in the physiological state. [. . .] What remains is to review such evidence as we can find that will throw light on the physiological state.

Anger and gastric function. – Perhaps the most convincing evidence for a physiological difference between anger and fear is found in the admirable studies of Wolf and Wolff (1943) on human gastric function. These authors describe careful observations over a number of years on 'Tom', a man with a chronic stomach fistula, in whom the blood flow to the stomach lining as well as the activity of the stomach could be observed in many different situations.

Wolf and Wolff found that fear regularly reduced gastric activity and blood flow. The situations they described doubtlessly did arouse fear. On one occasion when Tom's fistula was examined, a doctor came into the room, very annoyed because he had been looking for a record that was unaccountably missing. Tom had mislaid it but did not say anything because he was afraid he would be dismissed if his negligence were discovered. On that occasion, his stomach was practically bloodless and completely flaccid.

Whenever Tom was annoyed, angry, or resentful, his stomach reddened, and at the same time, stomach contractions and acidity increased. Another patient with a fistula showed similar changes on occasions when he became angry and used profane language. After the stomach was denervated by cutting the vagus nerve, this patient still had a flushed face and used profane language when he became angry, but his stomach no longer showed any changes. Wolf and Wolff also reported lowering of blood pressure (a cholinergic sympton) in a patient with hypertension whenever he was outspoken in his resentment of his wife, but a rise when he was presented at a conference and felt apprehensive.

During the last few years, several vagotomies have been performed on patients with gastric ulcer who did not improve on diet and drugs. Before the operation, ulcer pain was caused or aggravated by various emotional upsets, by anger, hostility, resentment, and worry. After the vagus was cut, such emotions no longer had any effect on their well-being. Parasympathetic excitation induced by these emotions could now no longer increase gastric acidity or stomach contractions, and could not aggravate the ulcer pain.

These observations demonstrated beyond any doubt that anger

produces effects on the circulation that are different from those produced by fear. Wolff (1950) has listed an impressive number of similar changes seen in the lining of nose, colon, and vagina, all of which seem to indicate that anger and resentment result in cholinergic excitation, while fear and anxiety seem to excite adrenergic nerves.

Anger and excretory functions. – Emotional defecation is abundant during fear (Hall, 1941; Tseng, 1942; Fleetwood and Diethelm, 1951) and ceases during anger (Tseng, 1942). Fleetwood and Diethelm mention it as one of the symptoms of marked anxiety, but do not list it as a symptom of anger or resentment. When parasympathetic influence is excluded, as for instance in vagotomy, there is often persistent diarrhea.

Tears, abundant during temper tantrums, are completely inhibited during fear – and the secretion of tears is the effect of parasympathetic excitation (Lund, 1930). Frequency of urination, which occurs both in fear and anger (Tseng, 1942), may be caused by two different mechanisms: during fear, by the relaxation of the sympathetically innervated sphincter; during anger, as a result of bladder contraction (a cholinergic symptom), which induces a reflex relaxation of the sphincter.

Cholinergic hormones in anger and resentment. – Adrenaline injection has induced anxiety attacks in neurotic patients, but so has the cholinergic drug mecholyl (Lindemann and Finesinger, 1938; Funkenstein and associates, 1949). However, the attacks differed according to the drug that produced them. Adrenaline injection was followed by pallor, tremor, weakness, and great fear; but mecholyl induced an attack with flushing, sweating, an increased flow of saliva, and marked agitation. These surely are two different if not actually opposed patterns, the first best described as fear, the second as agitation; and agitation is akin to worry rather than simple fear. Worry implies not a withdrawal from danger, as does fear, but a desperate urge to *do* something which gives the danger. This includes ceaseless mental activity to cope with rise to the characteristic agitation and may account for the cholinergic effect.

It may well be that the cholinergic excitation in agitated worry is accompanied by a secretion of noradrenaline. Fleetwood and Diethelm (1951), for instance, found a substance in the blood of patients suffering from 'anxiety' which was tentatively identified as noradrenaline. Other investigators reported that an injection of noradrenaline does not produce anxiety while adrenaline does (Smith, 1951; and others). This discrepancy seems to hinge on the meaning of the term 'anxiety'. Fleetwood and Diethelm's patients may have suffered from agitated worry (mecholyl anxiety), while Smith's patients may have felt acute fear (adrenaline anxiety).

Fleetwood and Diethelm also found evidence for several kinds of cholinergic stimulation during states of tension and anger. For instance, they found a cholinergic substance in human blood during emotional tension states (characterized by irritability, muscular tension, insomnia, inability to concentrate). Another cholinergic substance was found during anger and resentment (characterized by desire for revenge, hostility, sarcasm, criticism of others). It is tempting to suggest that the emotional tension might be a chronic form of anger or resentment, particularly because the cholinergic activity of the 'tension' substance was found to be considerably stronger than that of the 'resentment' substance. Fleetwood and Diethelm insisted, however, that these substances are not identical, though they both have a cholinergic action. Apparently, both tension and resentment were relieved by alcohol, while anxiety was reduced but not abolished. According to Smith (1951), the anxiety, tremor, and nervousness produced by an adrenaline injection were abolished if a drink of whisky was given at the same time. His patients commented that the adrenaline effect felt like the 'shakes' they had during a hangover, which also were abolished by taking a drink. We would suggest that alcohol depresses both the 'anger' and the 'fear' pattern in the action circuit, but apparently affects acetylcholine transmission more than adrenergic transmission, and among adrenergic nerves, affects noradrenaline-sensitive nerves more than those that are stimulated by adrenaline.

Noradrenaline and anger. – Funkenstein *et al.* (1952) suggested that a profound fall of blood pressure after the injection of mecholyl indicates excessive secretion of an adrenaline-like substance, while a moderate fall indicates excessive secretion of a noradrenaline-like substance. They based this inference on the observation that people given adrenaline show a significant fall of blood pressure after mecholyl while those given noradrenaline show a moderate or slight fall.

In a frustration experiment, Funkenstein *et al.* (1953) asked young men to solve difficult problems without paper and pencil, blaming them for stupidity when their answers were incorrect. Some of the men showed outright anger at this treatment ('anger out') while others blamed themselves or apologized ('anger in'). Still others showed anxiety. Funkenstein and associates found that individuals who showed 'anger out' had a cardiovascular pattern similar to that found after noradrenaline injection, that those who showed 'anger in' had an adrenaline pattern, and that those who showed anxiety had an exaggerated adrenaline pattern. Psychologically speaking, self-blame ('anger in') is closer to fear than to anger because the person appraises the situation as difficult and himself as inadequate in dealing with it. He feels helpless though he recognizes that the situation is not really threatening, and becomes impatient with his own reaction. Another study (Ax, 1953) showed that anxiety or fear (the subjects were intensely afraid of a possible shock from defective electrical wiring) produces a cardiovascular pattern like that seen after adrenaline injection, while anger produces a pattern like that appearing after noradrenaline injection.

Vrij and associates (1956) reported that noradrenaline, like adrenaline, induces the release of glucose from the liver; but unlike adrenaline, it leaves muscle glycogen untouched. This would mean that noradrenaline secretion increases the blood sugar available to the muscles without breaking down muscle glycogen, and so promotes muscular strength. This would explain why anger gives us the feeling of being stronger than usual, in contrast to fear which makes us feel weak.

These findings justify the inference that anger is accompanied by noradrenaline secretion and consequent rise in blood pressure and by cholinergic vasodilatation. Accordingly, there should be a different pattern of sympathetic excitation. Folkow and Von Euler (1954) have shown that hypothalamic stimulation from some points induces adrenaline secretion and from other points, noradrenaline secretion. We have suggested that the 'fear' pattern activates the former, producing vasoconstriction and adrenaline secretion, while the 'anger' pattern activates the latter, inhibiting the vasoconstrictor fibers and inducing noradrenaline secretion.

That aggression (hence anger) and noradrenaline secretion go together is shown by the fact that animals that prey upon others, and attack and fight a great deal, have mostly noradrenaline in their adrenal medulla (the lion's medulla contains 60 per cent noradrenaline against 40 per cent adrenaline), while rodents and other plant eaters that need not attack other animals for food, but flee from predatory enemies, have more adrenaline than noradrenaline in their adrenal medulla (rabbit and guinea pig have 85 to 100 per cent adrenaline). The same ratio holds within a species: the more fearful dogs secrete predominantly adrenaline, the more aggressive dogs predominantly noradrenaline (Funkenstein *et al.* 1953).

Finally, anger affects the muscular system differently from fear. It has been found to raise the level of general activity markedly in rats (Tseng, 1942), while fear reduces it. Anger and fighting result in an enlargement of the adrenal cortex (Christian, 1956), which promotes muscular power. Indeed, the fact that anger or rage is accompanied by increased activity and increased strength is so well known that psychoanalysis makes aggression the prototype of all nonsexual activity.

However, extreme anger will lead to incoordination. The urge to violent attack does not favor finely coordinated action. Also, there is a point at which something inimical may be judged as so threatening that it will arouse desperation rather than anger. Or the expression of anger itself may produce fear: the other person may retaliate, or the attack may destroy something a man may not care to lose. If fear is aroused in addition to anger, it will intensify sympathetic excitation and may change the outward symptoms. Popular speech correctly has it that a man is 'red with anger' and 'hot under the collar', but also that he is 'white with anger' and 'trembling with rage'.

Anger, panic, and startle. – Anger seems to be related to other reactions that show heightened activity, such as startle, panic states and epileptic seizures, and also to the sound-produced seizures (sometimes called 'experimental neuroses') in rats.

Tseng (1942), for instance, found that violent anger could be aroused in rats if they were confined in a body-size cage and teased with straws. After two weeks of daily teasing, ten out of nineteen rats had running seizures on sound stimulation. Of a comparable group of sixteen rats, left in their living cages undisturbed during these two weeks, only one had such an attack when retested. Since none of the total group had been found to have seizures on the initial test, it would seem that the difference in susceptibility between the two groups can be ascribed to the teasing of the experimental group which aroused vicious anger.

In an earlier publication (Arnold, 1944) it was suggested that the sound-produced seizure is an analogue to human epileptoid seizures rather than to human neurosis. This seems the more likely as it is now recognized that sound-produced seizures occur because of an inflammation of the middle ear which makes the rats more sensitive to noise. In epilepsy, there is increased susceptibility to stimulation, and thus intense sound or light may induce attacks.

It is a well-known fact that epileptic patients are inclined to be irritable and to have temper tantrums, and that anger or excitement often ushers in an attack. There is a similar connexion between anger and epileptoid reactions (panic states) in traumatic war neuroses, as pointed out by Kardiner: 'Easily aroused to anger, these patients are very prone to motor expression. They either break or tear objects in these fits of temper or strike the people who happen to be around them. . . . If the outburst is accompanied by loss of consciousness, the patient is usually dangerous' (1941, p. 95). There is an obvious connexion between such fits of temper and the psychomotor attacks we have discussed before. (We would suggest that in all these cases there is a hyperexcitability of the hippocampus, either constitutional (idiopathic epilepsy) or the result of traumatic experience (traumatic war neuroses) or, finally, acquired by a habitual indulgence in anger. In the third case, it seems to require an additional factor (like middle ear inflammation in sound-produced seizures) to lead to an epileptoid seizure.

Rats that have seizures on sound stimulation also show increased startle, and so did Kardiner's patients. This seems merely an indication that the action circuit is hyperexcitable.

Other emotions

Cobb (1950) thinks that love is accompanied by cholinergic excitation. He lists these symptoms: relaxed muscles, soft voice, vasodilatation, wide pupils, relaxation of intestines, rapid respiration, rapid heart beat, secretion of sex hormones, moist conjunctiva, salivation, and a feeling of warmth. Cobb emphasizes that these symptoms are characteristic for love and affection, not for sexual passion. However, this excitation would have to be moderate.

Psychologically, affection and sexual love are easily distinguished by their object and their aim. While all love aims to be with the beloved, the way of being together may range from liking to talk together, drink together, play together, to the love that wants to be together in the most intimate way possible. What is aimed for will depend on the appraisal of the person loved; and the emotion aroused by this appraisal will be mediated over the action circuit but show a different pattern in each case. Only when there is a sexual attraction and a sexual aim will there be excitation of the sexual organs, and thus sexual passion. Only a nursing mother will have prolactin secretion when she sees her babe or even thinks of him; and only if she enjoys nursing will there be a 'let-down' of milk during nursing (see Selye, 1934). There is evidence for saying that sexual love is a particular kind of love with a characteristic action pattern. To say that all love is basically sexual love and so imply that every action pattern that deviates from this 'basic' one is aim-inhibited, smacks of theory without evidence. Some parts of the action pattern are similar in sexual love and in other kinds of love, but other links in the pattern are decidedly different. The physiological changes aroused will depend on the kind of love felt, and the emotional experience, in turn, will depend on the way in which this particular situation is appraised – as long as we remember that such an appraisal is both immediate and intuitive, but also reflective, at least in the human being.

Any emotion felt at a particular moment necessarily depends upon the appraisal of the specific situation. This appraisal may give rise to nuances and combinations of emotion that beggar description or classification. It is neither possible nor profitable to distinguish these emotions on the basis of their physiological pattern of autonomic changes or emotional expression. A careful analysis of the situation can give us a hint, however, of what type of emotion we are dealing with. Once we know the broad divisions, it will be possible to predict the probable effects of all emotions that are related to these broad types.

As a start, it is sufficient to know, for instance, that fear excites the sympathetic nervous system and induces adrenaline secretion which has undesirable effects on the body when long continued. Such knowledge will let us understand the effects of chronic fear in neurosis and will enable us to introduce effective counter-measures. We also know that the most favorable condition for activity seems to be produced by mild cholinergic excitation as aroused by affection and interest. Both fear and anger are a spur to action but lose this effect if action does not overcome the obstacle or does not take us out of danger. Continuing fear and anger reduce the efficiency of action and disturb the economy of the organism.

To consider excitement an emotion, as has been often done (Cobb, 1950; Arnold, 1945), does not seem feasible. Excitement is common to many emotions: worry, despair, joy, or anticipation. It may be pleasant or unpleasant. And it may or may not be present in any one emotion; joy may be excited or calm; disappointment, agitated or resigned. Thus excitement seems to be a factor in the action pattern that goes with emotion, and not an emotion in its own right.

There may be important connexions between a given set of physical symptoms and a particular complex emotion. But what little we know of such relations owes more to popular wisdom and the efforts of novelists and poets than it does to experimental investigation. Homesickness, for instance, or longing for a particular person or thing, has long been known to have physical effects, as the word 'home*sickness*' indicates. To guess at these effects, we must consider the kind of emotion to which homesickness might be related: sadness and grief at the absence of what we love; hope alternating with despair, depending on our confidence at a given moment that we may go back or the suspicion that we shall never do so. The investigation of such emotions would require both careful psychological analysis and ingenious methods, 'psychosomatic' research of a high order. At the present time, psychosomatic methods are mainly employed to test inferences from speculative hypotheses rather than to explore the connexion between emotional experience and physical effects.

References

ARNOLD, M. B. (1942), unpublished observation.

ARNOLD, M. B. (1944), 'Emotional factors in experimental neuroses', *J. exp. Psychol.*, vol. 34, pp. 257–81.

ARNOLD, M. B. (1945), 'Physiological differentiation of emotional states', *Psych. Rev.*, vol. 52, pp. 35–48.

AX, A. F. (1953), 'The physiological differentiation between fear and anger in humans', *Psychosom. Med.*, vol. 15, pp. 433–42.

BEST, C. H., and TAYLOR, N. B. (1951), *The Physiological Basis of Medical Practice*, 5th edn, Baltimore, Williams & Wilkins.

BOGARD, W. (1937), 'Herzfrequenz und Herzsteigerungsleistung', *Arbeitsphysiol.*, vol. 9, pp. 505–13.

BRITTON, S. W., and COREY, E. L. (1940), 'Pancreatic and cortico-adrenal involvement in carbohydrate regulation', *Am. J. Physiol.*, vol. 131, pp. 790–8.

BROUHA, L., CANNON, W. B., and DILL, D. B. (1936), 'Heart rate of sympathectomized dog in rest and exercise', *J. Physiol.*, vol. 87, pp. 345–59.

BÜLBRING, E., and BURN, J. H. (1940), 'The effect of sympathomimetic and other substances on the contraction of skeletal muscle', *J. Pharmacol. exp. Therap.*, vol. 68, pp. 150–72.

BÜLBRING, E., and BURN, J. H. (1949), 'Liberation of noradrenaline from adrenal medulla by splanchnic stimulation', *Nature*, vol. 163, p. 363.

BÜLBRING, E., BURN, J. H., and SKOGLUND, C. R. (1948), 'The action of acetylcholine and adrenaline on flexor and extensor movements evoked by stimulation of the descending motor tracts', *J. Physiol.*, vol. 107, pp. 289–98.

BURN, J. H. (1945), 'Relation of adrenaline to acetylcholine in the nervous system', *Physiol. Rev.*, vol. 25, pp. 377–94.

CAMERON, A. T. (1936), *Recent Advances in Endocrinology*, 3rd edn, London, Churchill.

CAMPOS, F. A., CANNON, W. B., LUNDIN, H., and WALKER, T. T. (1928), 'Some conditions affecting the capacity for prolonged muscular work', *Am. J. Physiol.*, vol. 85, pp. 680–701.

CANNON, W. B. (1915), *Bodily Changes in Pain, Hunger, Fear and Rage*, 2nd edn, 1929, New York, Appleton-Century.

CANNON, W. B. (1932), *The Wisdom of the Body*, 2nd edn, 1939, New York, Norton.

CELANDER, O. (1954), 'The range of control exercised by the sympathico-adrenal system: a quantitative study of blood vessels and other smooth muscle effectors in the cat', *Acta Physiol. Scand.*, Suppl. 116, vol. 32, pp. 1–132.

CHRISTIAN, J. J. (1956), 'Reserpine suppression of density-dependent adrenal hypertrophy and reproductive hypoendocrinism in populations of male mice', *Am. J. Physiol.*, vol. 187, pp. 353–6.

COBB, S. (1950), *Emotions and Clinical Medicine*, New York, Norton.

COHEN, M. E., and WHITE, P. D. (1951), 'Life situations, emotions and neurocirculatory asthenia (anxiety neurosis, neurasthenia, effort syndrome)', *Psychosom. Med.*, vol. 13, pp. 335–57.

DARROW, W., and GELLHORN, E. (1939), 'The effects of adrenalin on the reflex excitability of the autonomic nervous system', *Am. J. Physiol.*, vol. 127, pp. 243–51.

DUNCAN, C. H., STEVENSON, I. P., and WOLFF, H. G. (1951), 'Life situations, emotions and exercise tolerance', *Psychosom. Med.*, vol. 13, pp. 36–50.

EULER, U. S. VON (1953), 'Adrenalin and noradrenalin in various kinds of stress', in *Symposium on Stress*, Washington, D.C., Div. of Med. Sciences Nat. Res. Council and Army Med. Serv. Grad. School W. Reed Army Med. Center, Washington, D.C., GPO.

FLEETWOOD, M. F., and DIETHELM, O. (1951), 'Emotions and biochemical findings in alcoholism', *Am. J. Psychiat.*, vol. 108, pp. 433–8.

FOLKOW, B., and VON EULER, U. S. (1954), 'Selective activation of noradrenaline and adrenaline producing cells in the cat's adrenal gland by hypothalamic stimulation', *Circ. Res.*, vol. 2, pp. 191–5.

FREEMAN, N. E., FREEDMAN, H., and MILLER, C. C. (1941), 'The production of shock by the prolonged continuous injection of adrenalin in unanesthetized dogs', *Am. J. Physiol.*, vol. 131, pp. 545–53.

FREEMAN, N. E., SHAFFER, S. A., SCHECTER, A., and HOLLING, A. E. and H. E. (1938), 'The effect of total sympathectomy on the occurrence of shock from hemorrhage', *J. clin. Investig.*, vol. 17, pp. 359–68.

FUNKENSTEIN, D. H., GREENBLATT, M., and SOLOMON, H. C. (1949), 'Psychophysiological study of mentally ill patients. Part I. The status of the peripheral autonomic nervous system as determined by the reaction to epinephrine and mecholyl', *Am. J. Psychiat.*, vol. 106, pp. 16–28.

FUNKENSTEIN, D. H., GREENBLATT, M., and SOLOMON, H. C. (1952), 'Nor-epinephrine-like and epinephrine-like substances in psychotic and psychoneurotic patients', *Am. J. Psychiat.*, vol. 108, pp. 652–62.

FUNKENSTEIN, D. H., KING, S. H., and DROLETTE, M. (1953), 'The experimental evocation of stress', in *Symposium on Stress*, Washington, D.C., Div. Med. Sciences Nat. Res. Council and Army Med. Serv. Grad. School W. Reed Army Med. Center, Washington, D.C., GPO.

GELLHORN, E. (1943), *Autonomic Regulations*, New York, Interscience.

GELLHORN, E. (1953), *Physiological Foundations of Neurology and Psychiatry*, Minneapolis, University of Minnesota Press.

GELLHORN, E., DARROW, C. W., and YESINICK, L. (1939), 'Effect of epinephrine on convulsions', *Arch. Neurol. Psychiat.*, vol. 42, pp. 826–36.

Neurophysiological Aspects

GUYTON, A. C., and GILLESPIE, Jr, W. M. (1951), 'Constant infusion of epinephrine: rate of epinephrine secretion and destruction in the body', *Am. J. Physiol.*, vol. 165, pp. 319–27.

HALL, C. S. (1941), 'Temperament: a survey of animal studies', *Psychol. Bull.*, vol. 38, pp. 909–43.

HALL, G. E. (1938), 'Physiological studies in experimental insulin and metrazol shock', *Am. J. Psychiat.*, vol. 95, pp. 553–66.

HARPUDER, K., BYER, J., and STEIN, I. D. (1947), 'The effect of intra-arterial injection of adrenalin upon blood flow of the human forearm', *Am. J. Physiol.*, vol. 150, pp. 181–9.

HARRIS, R. E., and INGLE, D. J. (1940), 'The capacity for vigorous muscular activity of normal rats and of rats after the removal of the adrenal medulla', *Am. J. Physiol.*, vol. 130, pp. 151–4.

HESS, W. R. (1949), *Das Zwischenhirn: Syndrome, Lokalisationen, Funktionen*, Basel, Schwabe.

INGLE, D. J., and NEZAMIS, J. E. (1949), 'Effect of adrenal cortex extract with and without epinephrine upon work of adrenally insufficient rats', *Endocrinol.*, vol. 44, pp. 559–64.

JACOBSON, E. (1934), 'Electrical measurement of activities in nerve and muscle', in M. Bentley and E. V. Cowdry (eds.), *The Problem of Mental Disorder*, New York, McGraw-Hill.

KARDINER, A. (1941). *The Traumatic Neuroses of War*, New York, Hoeber.

KEITH, H. M., and STAVRAKY, G. W. (1935), 'Experimental convulsions induced by administration of thujone: pharmacologic study of influence of autonomic nervous system on these convulsions', *Arch. Neurol. Psychiat.*, vol. 34, pp. 1022–40.

LINDEMANN, E., and FINESINGER, J. E. (1938), 'The effect of adrenalin and mecholyl in states of anxiety in psychoneurotic patients', *Am. J. Psychiat*, vol. 95, pp. 353–70.

LUCO, L. V. (1939), 'The defatiguing effect of adrenaline', *Am. J. Physiol.*, vol. 125, pp. 197–203.

LUND, F. H. (1930), 'Why do we weep?' *J. soc. Psychol.*, vol. 1, pp. 136–57.

MAHL, G. F. (1949), 'Effect of chronic fear on the gastric secretion of HCl in dogs', *Psychosom. Med.*, vol. 11, pp. 30–44.

MAJOR, S. G., and MANN, F. C. (1932), 'Glycogenolytic effect of epinephrine on skeletal muscle', *Am. J. Physiol.*, vol. 101, pp. 462–8.

MILHORAT, A. T., and DIETHELM, O. (1947), 'Substances in blood of patients during emotional states: effect on the isolated rabbit intestine', *Fed. Proc.*, vol. 6, pp. 165–6.

MINZ, B., and DOMINO, E. F. (1953), 'Effects of epinephrine and nor-epinephrine on electrically induced seizures', *J. Pharmac. exp. Therap.*, vol. 107, pp. 204–18.

MOHME-LUNDHOLM, E. (1953), 'The mechanism of the relaxing effect of adrenaline on smooth muscle', *Acta Physiol. Scand.*, suppl. 108, vol. 29, pp. 1–63.

OLIVER, G., and SCHÄFER, E. A. (1894), 'On the physiological action of extract of the suprarenal capsules', *J. Physiol.*, vol. 1, pp. i–iv.

OLIVER, G., and SCHÄFER (1895), 'The physiological effects of extracts of the suprarenal capsules', *J. Physiol.*, vol. 3, pp. ix xiv.

PARKINS, W. M., SWINGLE, W. W., REMINGTON, J. W., and DRILL, V. A. (1941), 'Desoxycorticosterone as prophylactic foretreatment for prevention of circulatory failure following hemorrhage and surgical trauma in adrenalectomized dog', *Am. J. Physiol.*, vol. 134, pp. 426–35.

RAMEY, E. R., and GOLDSTEIN, M. S. (1957), 'The adrenal cortex and the sympathetic nervous system', *Physiol. Rev.*, vol. 37, pp. 155–95.

RICHTER, C. P. (1951), 'Psychotic behavior produced in wild Norway and Alexandrine rats apparently by the fear of food poisoning', in M. L. Reymert (ed.), *Feelings and Emotions*, New York, McGraw-Hill.

ROBINSON, G., and HARMON, P. M. (1941), 'The lactic acid mechanism and certain properties of the blood in relation to training', *Am. J. Physiol.*, vol. 132, pp. 757–69.

ROGOFF, J. M., and STEWART, G. N. (1926), 'Studies on adrenal insufficiency in dogs: blood studies in control of animals not subjected to treatment', *Am. J. Physiol.*, vol. 78, pp. 711–29.

SELYE, H. (1934), 'On nervous control of lactation', *Am. J. Physiol.*, vol. 107, pp. 535–8.

SELYE, H. (1950), *The Physiology and Pathology of Exposure to Stress*, Montreal, Acta.

SMITH, J. J. (1951), discussion on p. 438 to: M. F. Fleetwood and O. Diethelm, 'Emotions and biochemical findings in alcoholism', *Am. J. Psychiat.*, vol. 108, pp. 433–8.

SOMOGYI, M. (1951), 'Mechanism of epinephrine-hyperglycemia', *Endocrinol.*, vol. 49, pp. 774–81.

TSENG, F. (1942), 'Differentiation of anger and fear in the emotional behavior of the rat', unpublished M.A. thesis, University of Toronto.

VERZÁR, F. (1939), *Die Funktion der Nebennierenrinde*, Basel, Schwabe.

VOGT, M. (1954), 'The concentration of sympathin in different parts of the central nervous system under normal conditions and after administration of drugs', *J. Physiol*, vol. 123, pp. 451-81.

VRIJ, C. J., GHO, B. K., DEGROOT, C. A., and WEBER, J. F. (1956), 'The effect of isopropyl-nor-adrenaline and nor-adrenaline on the glycogen content of skeletal muscle and liver of the rat', *Acta Physiol. Pharm. Neerl.*, vol. 4, pp. 524–31.

WOLF, S., and WOLFF, H. G. (1943), *Human Gastric Function*, New York, Oxford University Press.

WOLFF, H. G. (1950), 'Life situations and bodily disease', in M. L. Reymert (ed.), *Feelings and Emotions*, New York, McGraw-Hill.

Further Reading

CANDLAND, D. K. (ed.), *Emotion: Bodily Changes, An Enduring Problem in Psychology: Selected Readings*, Van Nostrand, 1962.

CAPLAN, D. (ed.), *Emotional Problems of Early Childhood*, Basic Books, 1955.

DAVITZ, J. R., *The Communication of Emotional Meaning*, McGraw-Hill, 1964.

GARDINER, H. M., METCALF, R. C., and BEEBE-CENTER, J. G., *Feeling and Emotion*, American Book Co., 1937.

GELLHORN, E., *Emotions and Emotional Disorders: a Neurophysiological Study*, Hoeber, 1963.

GLASS, D. C. (ed.) *Neurophysiology and Emotion*, Rockefeller University Press and Russell Sage Foundation, 1967.

KNAPP, P. H. (ed.), *Expression of the Emotions in Man*, International Universities Press, 1963.

OLDS, J., 'Pleasure centers in the brain', *Scientific American*, vol. 195 (1956), pp. 105–16.

REYMERT, M. L. (ed.), *Feelings and Emotions. The Wittenberg Symposium*, Clark University Press, 1928.

REYMERT, M. L. (ed.), *Feelings and Emotions. The Mooseheart Symposium*, McGraw-Hill, 1950.

WEST, L. J., and GREENBLATT, M., *Explorations in the Physiology of Emotions*, Psychiat. Res. Report No. 12, American Psychiatric Association, 1960.

Acknowledgements

Permission to reproduce the material published in this volume is acknowledged from the following sources:

Reading 1   Macmillan & Co. Ltd.
Reading 3   American Journal of Psychology.
Reading 4   Macmillan & Co. Ltd.
Reading 5   Clark University Press.
Reading 6   Random House, Inc.
Reading 7   D. Rapaport and the International Universities Press, Inc.
Reading 8   Northwestern University Press.
Reading 9   Clark University Press.
Reading 10 Presses Universitaires de France.
Reading 11 H. Bouvier u. Co. Verlag.
Reading 12 Elizabeth Duffy and The Journal Press.
Reading 13 John Wiley & Sons, Inc.
Reading 14 Clark University Press.
Reading 15 Robert Leeper and the American Psychological Association
Reading 16 Presses Universitaires de France.
Reading 17 The Ronald Press Company.
Reading 18 John Wiley & Sons, Inc.
Reading 20 McGraw-Hill Book Company.
Reading 21 McGraw-Hill Book Company.
Reading 22 P. H. Knapp and the International Universities Press Inc.
Reading 23 American Journal of Psychology.
Reading 24 American Medical Association.
Reading 25 Dr J. M. R. Delgado and the American Psychiatric Association.
Reading 26 Columbia University Press.
Reading 27 Columbia University Press.

Author Index

Subject Index

Subject Index

Penguin Modern Psychology Readings

Titles available in this series are: